Pairing Food & Wine

FOR DUMMIES®

by John Szabo

WILEY

John Wiley & Sons Canada, Ltd.

Pairing Food & Wine For Dummies®
Published by
John Wiley & Sons Canada, Ltd.
6045 Freemont Blvd.
Mississauga, ON L5R 4J3
www.wiley.com

For general information on John Wiley & Sons Canada, Ltd., including all books published by John Wiley & Sons, Inc., please call our distribution centre at 1-800-567-4797. For reseller information, including discounts and premium sales, please call our sales department at 416-646-7992. For press review copies, author interviews, or other publicity information, please contact our publicity department, Tel. 416-646-4582, Fax 416-236-4448.

Wiley also publishes its books in a variety of electronic formats. Some content that appears in print may not be available in electronic books.

Library and Archives Canada Cataloguing in Publication

Szabo, John

     Pairing Food & Wine For Dummies / John Szabo.

Includes index.

Issued also in an electronic format.

ISBN 978-1-11839-9-57-6

     1. Food and wine pairing.

2. Wine and wine making. I. Title.

TP548.S98 2012   641.2'2   C2012-902743-X

ISBN 978-1-118-39957-6 (pbk); ISBN 978-1-118-41427-9 (ebk); ISBN 978-1-118-41428-6 (ebk); ISBN 978-1-118-41430-9 (ebk)

Printed in the United States

1 2 3 4 5 RRD 15 14 13 12 11 10

WILEY

About the Author

John Szabo is the original Canadian master sommelier, earning the credentials in 2004, and is one of only 200 worldwide today. When not eating and drinking (professionally), he writes and reviews wines for `WineAlign.com`, `NationalPost.com`, `TorontoStandard.com`, *Maclean's Canadian Wine Guide, Wine Access* Magazine, *Grapevine* Magazine, and is wine editor for Toronto's *CityBites* Magazine.

John keeps his sommelier skills sharp as consulting wine director for the Trump Tower Toronto and for Toronto's Pearson International Airport, among other projects. And just to make sure all angles are covered and his experience well rounded, he owns a vineyard in Eger, Hungary, the J&J Eger Wine Co., where he makes small quantities of food friendly Kékfrankos. As a holder of a third degree black belt in Goju-ryu karate, his grapes are well protected, too.

Dedication

For my wife, Alexandra, and my children Esmai and Julius, who supported long hours of writing, regular absence, and hundreds of bottles of wine on the table each week as I looked for that perfect match.

Author Acknowledgments

No book is ever the product of a single person (not the good ones, anyhow). To list all the people with whom I've shared great, and not so great, moments of food and wine over the last 20 years, and from whom I've learned pretty much everything I know would take a separate book to list. But let them all be acknowledged here; food and wine come together in company, and rarely when one's alone.

I owe many thanks to Anam Ahmed, Acquisitions Editor for Wiley, who had the confidence to engage me in the first place, as well as my editor Chad Sievers, who miraculously turned my twisted phrases and convoluted thoughts into readable text, and who pointed out many gaps, shortcomings, and incomplete ideas in the manuscript that I did my best to clarify. I would also have been buried in an avalanche of cookbooks (or lost in the surf on the Internet) were it not for chef, author, and repository of knowledge on world cuisine, Michael Pataran. Michael contributed the lion's share of research into the traditional dishes from around the world that make up Part IV of this book, and his experience, particularly with eating and drinking Asian food, was invaluable.

Heartfelt thanks to my technical editor, author, and master sommelier Evan Goldstein, who was ever on hand to question, comment, and guide my ideas with his extensive knowledge on the subject of food and wine. No food and wine lovers should do without his two books, *Perfect Pairings* and *Daring Pairings*.

When things got a little hazy on the physiological side of tasting in Chapter 2, I was blessed to have Gary Pickering, PhD, Professor of Biological Sciences and Psychology and Research Scientist at Brock University in St. Catharines, Ontario, to look to for answers. Dr. Pickering is one of the world's foremost experts on supertasters, and if you want to find out if you're among them, go to his site at www.supertasting.com to test yourself.

I also owe sincere thanks to Wojciech Bonkówski, editor of the *Polish Wine Guide* (www.polishwineguide.com), who kindly ensured that my pairing suggestions with Polish food would not get me into trouble in Warsaw, as well as Bill Zacharkiw, wine columnist for the *Montreal Gazette,* who kindly shared the results of many of his legendary sessions on food and wine compatibility. I'd also like to mention François Chartier, a Québec-based sommelier and author of *Taste Buds and Molecules: The Art and Science of Food with Wine,* who's innovative line of inquiry has revolutionized the business of food and wine pairing. It's to him I owe the inspiration for the explorations on flavor harmony in Chapter 4.

And finally, all these ideas would have remained bottled up if I had nowhere to write them down. Aside from countless cafés, restaurants, libraries, foreign and domestic, I'd like to thank Domaine Pearl-Morissette in Niagara for putting me up during long writing sessions, as well as Marco Petrucci of 99 Sudbury in Toronto, who graciously allowed me to use his event space as an office when needed.

Publisher's Acknowledgments

We're proud of this book; please send us your comments through our online registration form located at `http://dummies.custhelp.com`. For other comments, please contact our Customer Care Department within the U.S. at 877-762-2974, outside the U.S. at 317-572-3993, or fax 317-572-4002.

Some of the people who helped bring this book to market include the following:

Acquisitions and Editorial

Associate Acquisitions Editor: Anam Ahmed

Production Editor: Pauline Ricablanca

Project Editor: Chad R. Sievers

Copy Editor: Chad R. Sievers

Technical Editor: Evan Goldstein

Editorial Assistant: Kathy Deady

Cartoons: Rich Tennant (www.the5thwave.com)

Cover photo: © SE&A cover photo
© Christopher Wadsworth for the
author photo

Composition Services

Project Coordinator: Kristie Rees

Layout and Graphics: Jennifer, Creasey,
Joyce Haughey, Christin Swinford

Proofreaders: Lindsay Amones, Penny L. Stuart

Indexer: Potomac Indexing, LLC

John Wiley & Sons Canada, Ltd.

    Deborah Barton, Vice President and Director of Operations

    Jennifer Smith, Vice-President and Publisher, Professional & Trade Division

    Alison Maclean, Managing Editor

Publishing and Editorial for Consumer Dummies

    Kathleen Nebenhaus, Vice President and Executive Publisher

    David Palmer, Associate Publisher

    Kristin Ferguson-Wagstaffe, Product Development Director

Publishing for Technology Dummies

    Andy Cummings, Vice President and Publisher

Composition Services

    Debbie Stailey, Director of Composition Services

Contents at a Glance

Table of Contents

Introduction

· ·

*P*eople have been eating and drinking wine together for as long as wine has been around. You don't need any special knowledge to do it. In the very early days, people didn't have much choice either; they ate and drank whatever was at hand — wine wasn't easy to ship and spoiled quickly. Yet over time, as the availability of wine grew and people could make choices, certain combinations of wine and food were clearly more pleasing than others. Early epicureans sought to understand what made those combinations work (so they could be repeated), and the business of food and wine pairing was born.

In the meantime, the standard approach has moved from a handful of rigid rules to complete food and wine anarchy, and back again to a sensible middle ground, where curiosity and creativity have as much a place as any orthodoxy. *Pairing Food & Wine For Dummies* comes at a time when the understanding of how you sense things and experience enjoyment has never been deeper. The scientific and hedonistic sides of food and wine pairing coexist in harmony today and support one another. The way I look at it, you can have a lot more fun today than ever before.

What's more, you're living in a world where the choice of wine and diversity of cuisine has never been greater. There are the classic regional food and wine matches to follow, but they won't help you much when you venture into cuisines not traditionally associated with wine nor in selecting dishes to match wines from new growing regions or unfamiliar grapes.

That's why *Pairing Food & Wine For Dummies* is your handy reference that covers the subject from every possible angle that I could think of, drawing on science, experience, inspiration, and endless inquisitiveness.

About This Book

This book takes on a big challenge: how to relay practical information about a complex subject to as broad an audience as possible, from first-timers getting their feet wet to seasoned pros looking to fill in some knowledge gaps. Plenty of other books are out there on the subject of food and wine pairing, but what makes *Pairing Food & Wine For Dummies* unique and helpful is its adaptability to different readers. I don't dictate a single strategy for getting it right, but I offer the approaches I know for making food and wine magic. That is, you're free to engage on whatever level you're comfortable with.

If you have a deep cellar but little experience in the kitchen, or you're handy with a knife but shy away from the corkscrew, this book provides some tips to get you started. If you're already a pro and want to delve into the technical details of sensory exploration or the psychology of pleasure, you can find that information in these pages, de-jargoned as far as possible. Or, if all you need is a quick answer on what to drink tonight with your dinner (sometimes people are just hungry and thirsty), I include that information as well.

This book also differs from others in its greater emphasis on cuisines that were once thought unsuitable for wine. It's true that Asian, Middle Eastern, and Latin American foods, for example, didn't really grow up with wine, and whichever old world, traditional wines that may have been available at the time that such a conclusion was arrived at probably weren't great matches, but the world has changed, and more wines and wine styles are available than ever before. Every dish has its match somewhere in the vast world of modern wine. If your mind is open, you can find something.

Be forewarned that I'm not one of the *demystifyers*, those who think that the subject should be dumbed down to the point of triviality. As you know, *Dummies* readers are no dummies; they're clever people who want straight answers to important questions, presented in an easy-to-read, no-nonsense format. The wine and food world is mystical, and it should be celebrated, not simplified. That's what makes it so fascinating, so I dive headlong into the details and do my best to deliver the answers you want in as clear a manner as possible.

Regretfully, the scope of this book doesn't allow for investigations into beer, spirits, sake, cocktail, or any other beverage pairings. As a sommelier, I'm naturally inclined to be open to (and personally enjoy) any and all beverages. I know that there are brilliant pairings to be had with drinks other than wine, and sometimes wine is *not* the best match. But I'll leave that discussion for another time.

Conventions Used in This Book

For the sake of clarity, I use the following conventions in this book to help you:

✔ I use *italics* to point out new terms, but don't worry about not knowing what they mean because I provide basic definitions close by.

✔ I use **boldface** to highlight keywords in numbered lists.

✔ I use `monofont` to highlight websites. If you want to check out any of the web addresses from this book, just type exactly what you see. I didn't insert any extra characters (like hyphens) when an address went onto a second line.

✔ The names of grape varieties, appellations, and geographical names are capitalized.

✔ Strictly speaking, flavor and aroma are the same thing, and I use the two interchangeably, or together, throughout the text. The usual distinction is that *aroma* is used to refer to smells that are sensed directly through the nose, while *flavor* refers to what you can smell via the retronasal passage in your mouth. As for taste, when I refer to taste, I refer to the specific sensations of salty, sweet, bitter, sour, and savory (umami) that can be sensed by your taste buds. Taste doesn't refer to flavor.

What You're Not to Read

I know you are busy, juggling all the bottles of life. So feel free to skip the sidebars, which are the shaded boxes of text that contain information that's nonessential to understanding how to pair wine and food. The sidebars are optional, but I think you'll find them too fascinating to miss.

Foolish Assumptions

While writing this book (and conducting all the heavy-duty research and grueling experimentation), here's what I assumed about you, the reader:

✔ You care about what you consume.

✔ You enjoy food and wine, and engage in their consumption at least occasionally, maybe even frequently.

✔ You have an open mind and are keen to experiment with your senses.

✔ You enjoy discovering new flavors.

✔ You don't think that enjoying food and wine together is pretentious hogwash, or maybe you do, and whoever bought this book for you just wanted to prove to you that taking a little more pleasure in drinking and eating isn't really all that bad an idea — nobody gets hurt.

✔ You've heard of at least a few grape varieties like Chardonnay and Cabernet Sauvignon, and know that many places around the world make different wines in different styles.

✔ The really keen among you have a book dedicated to wine on your bookshelf, maybe even the excellent reference, the latest version of *Wine For Dummies* by Ed McCarthy and Mary Ewing Mulligan (John Wiley & Sons, Inc.).

How This Book Is Organized

This book is designed to be a reference text that I hope you'll keep somewhere in the kitchen and thumb through regularly, whenever you're wondering what to drink. Eventually, when the training wheels are off, you won't need to read it anymore. The parts are as follows.

Part I: Appreciating the Marriage of Food and Wine: The Nose Knows

Part I of this book starts with an overview of what you can find in the rest of it. It then delves into the senses, how they physically work, and how your mind grasps the concept of pleasure. You can also find some practical experiments that can change the way you think about food and wine, and get you started on the road to enjoying the two of them together more often.

Part II: The Nuts and Bolts: Developing Strategies for Food and Wine Pairing

This meaty part contains five chapters packed with basic information about how food and wine work, or don't work, together. It includes all the basic theories, handy guidelines, and best practices to get you started, including how to serve wine like a pro.

Part III: Sorting Out the World of Wine

This part slices up the world of wine into a few manageable style categories — the basic starting point when considering what to drink with any dish. I use these categories throughout the book in order to avoid endless repetition of multiple grapes and regions that all produce more or less the same style of wine. It's a top-down approach.

Part IV: Uncovering the Best Wine Bets with World Cuisine (and Cheese)

This is where you go to find the best, and alternative, wine style matches for a wide range of worldly familiar and traditional dishes, as well as a variety of cheeses. I provide classic local wine pairings with dishes from regions where wine is produced — what a local sommelier would likely propose. I also discuss some culinary influences, cooking techniques, and ingredients. I discuss areas from the Mediterranean, North America, northern and central Europe, southern Europe, Asia, Latin America, Middle Eastern, and Northern African cuisine. I also discuss pairing wine with cheese.

Part V: Party Time! Pairing with Friends . . . and Professionals

This part deals with some important practical matters, such as finding the best places to dine out, reading a wine list, dealing with a sommelier, and hosting a party. This part even includes a chapter on what a sommelier is and how to become one, just in case you're interested.

Part VI: The Part of Tens

The Part of Tens is popular in all *For Dummies* books. Here you can find two chapters: one with ten wine-friendly foods and one with ten food-friendly wines.

Icons Used in this Book

Throughout the text, you see icons in the book's margins that alert you to certain types of information. Here's a glossary of those terms and what they mean:

This icon points you to practical suggestions for implementing the recommendations offered on a given subject.

This icon reminds you of important things to think about or do when considering the material being discussed.

When you see this icon, pay attention because you need to avoid something or keep your eyes open for something that could dampen your pairing.

Where to Go from Here

Like all *For Dummies* books, this one is designed to be modular; each chapter stands on its own and doesn't require that you read any of the other chapters to grasp the information. I provide cross references if certain concepts are more deeply explored in another chapter.

If you're an absolute newcomer to food and wine pairing, you may want to start at the beginning. If you've cracked a few corks in your day and want to fine-tune the selection process, you can dive in at any point in the book: starting with the wine, starting with the food, examining some classic regional pairings, and understanding why they work, delving into the world of sensory perception, or perhaps simply looking up a match with an unfamiliar dish. If you're not sure, flip through the index or table of contents and find a topic that interests you.

This book also doesn't contain detailed information about wines and wine-making, nor foods, cooking techniques, or recipes. In order to clarify some aspects of how food and wine work together, I do cover some of the basics. Even if you've never cooked and your knowledge of wine ends at fermented grape juice, you can still find tons of useful information on how to get more enjoyment out of each. Jump in wherever you like; you can take your own journey, stopping at the places relevant to you along the way. You'll likely come back for repeat visits. That's the way it works in the world of food and wine.

Part I
Appreciating the Marriage of Food and Wine: The Nose Knows

The 5th Wave   By Rich Tennant

"I want something that will go well with a retired admiral, a best-selling author, and a media wonk."

In this part . . .

This part introduces you to the contents of this book. It gets you started on understanding how your senses work, and how to put those senses into action when it's time to eat and drink wine.

Chapter 1 is the gateway: It gives you a little taste of what you can find in each of the parts and chapters of the book. Chapter 2 is for the hedonist in you, who wants to understand how the senses actually work. Just how do people smell and taste, what tricks does the mind play on you, and how does previous experience sway your preferences? It's packed with lots of information, so you probably want a glass of wine close at hand.

And when you're ready to dive into the action, Chapter 3 formally introduces you to food and wine. You can embark on some practical experimentation that may change the way you think about eating and drinking.

Chapter 1

The Whole Is Greater Than the Sum of the Parts

*M*ost people eat and drink wine without much conscious reflection. It's nourishment, refreshment, and pleasure; the nuances of how food and wine affect one another don't enter mainstream thought. And eating food you enjoy with wine you like is just fine, that is, until you have that experience when both the wine and the food are transformed into something more. Even if you're not paying attention, the resulting combination is so good you can't help but marvel at what is happening, and how.

For me, I started to pay a little more attention to what I was eating and drinking, noting what worked and what didn't, and trying to understand. I wasn't obsessive, but curious. That's what pairing food and wine is all about — making the whole a little better than the sum of the parts. I'm still happy to eat and drink things I enjoy without much preoccupation, but I'm also after that magic whenever possible. I'm guessing that you are, too.

This chapter serves as your jumping-off point to the many different strategies of thinking about food and wine. Flipping through these pages can help entice you to read the sections of the book that are most interesting and relevant to you.

Why Pairing Wine with Food Really Matters

Even in the wine business, a lot of people I know don't get too fussed about finding the perfect wine for everything they eat all the time. Some even think pursuing the perfect wine pairing is pretentious — just eat food you like and drink wine you enjoy and get on with it. And it's true; the marriage of food and wine is hardly a matter of 'till death do us part.

But then again, what do you have to lose by gaining a better understanding of eating and drinking? People discover how to cook so they can eat better, or they discover about wine to appreciate what they taste a little more. Looking more deeply into anything to squeeze a little more pleasure from life is part of the pursuit of happiness. Figuring out which wines and foods create a bit of sensory magic together falls into the same category. If you're going to eat and drink together, you may as well do it right.

Besides, after you've grasped the basic concepts, making a more suitable wine choice takes no extra effort. The more you experiment, the more intuitive it will become.

Focusing on What Makes a Good Pairing

You needn't be a chef or a winemaker to get your food and wine pairings spot on (few sommeliers are either). Before getting started on the journey to perfect pairings, I have good news for you: There's no such thing as universally perfect in the first place. People are all a little different, both physically and psychologically. That's why you want to have a basic understanding of how your senses — mostly smell and taste — work, how they may vary from person to person, and why you can like a pairing that doesn't work for somebody else.

You also need to consider concrete components of food and wine and how they interact. With just a few basic principles under your belt, you can take any wine or dish apart and focus on the elements that can make or break the match. And that's really all pairing food and wine is; it's not effortless — anything worthwhile takes some effort — but neither is it Newtonian calculus (and the homework is more fun). The next sections map out some general principles and strategies for pairing food and wine.

Rules? What rules?

Some books outline rules for pairing food and wine. You may also have heard that pairing food and wine has no rules, and you should just drink whatever you like. Here's what I think: The old rules of food and wine pairing, such as "red wine with red meat" and "white wine with fish" are a bit like clichés. A cliché starts out as an idea of great insight, but then loses its force through overuse, and as times change, becomes less relevant.

And these food and wine pairing rules, like clichés, have become diluted through the proliferation of, well, food and wine. Chapter 6 does address the truth about these clichés, but what was once a simple matter regarding a handful of traditional wines and traditional dishes that generated these valid dictums in the first place, is now a wildly complex field. Dozens of red wines go well with fish, and just as many whites go with red meat. And what's more, people understand why.

Advanced technology and the expansion into new wine growing areas around the world have led to wine styles that didn't exist when the rules were made up. And food, too, is constantly evolving. Ingredients and techniques from one part of the world are appropriated by another, and new dishes are created everyday. With all this change, the clichéd rules start to fall apart. So don't forget them, but don't exclusively rely on them either. And the exceptions are the most fun to discover; if there's anything I've discovered about food and wine pairing, it's to have an open mind.

Relying on the senses

Enjoying food and wine isn't all about the physical senses. In fact, it has a strong psychological aspect as well, as I explore in Chapter 4, although the senses are still pretty important. Understanding what "like" really means in the world of food, wine, and sensory experience can help you focus on how to get there.

In Chapter 2, I go into some detail about how you smell and taste, and importantly, the difference between what can be smelled and what can be tasted, because people often confuse the two sensations. I also examine the tactile sense in order to understand the texture of both wine and food, which can go a long way to making pairings more or less pleasant. In fact, in my experience, texture is the starting point for any match; aroma and flavor synergy is the icing on the cake. As a result, I explore things like the burning sensation of chile peppers and the rough texture of wines, as well as strategies to lessen their effects.

Zooming in on some basic strategies

More wines and foods exist than you could ever count, with a frightful number of possible combinations. But after you strip away all the noise, you're left with only a small handful of things for your senses to measure up. Getting the most out of the interaction of food and wine can enhance your enjoyment, and there's actually a little trick to eating and drinking at the same time. Something dynamic goes on in your mouth when you're eating and drinking — taste and tactile sensations change depending on what you put together. Chapter 3 is your starting point for putting the senses into action. I include some experiments you can put yourself through to discover the possible outcomes when food and wine get together.

Eyeing some simple practices when pairing

There's no single right way to go about pairing food and wine. You may already have a bottle of wine that you want to showcase with the right dish, or you may have decided first what's for dinner and want to find the right wine to match; there are simple approaches you can take for each case. Some practices you can follow to find the right wine when you've selected your dish include

- ✔ Focusing on finding the best wine *style* for the dish and forgetting the grape
- ✔ Seeking a wine with similar flavor intensity and weight as the dish
- ✔ Figuring out what the dominant taste or texture element of the dish is and which wine style will best complement or contrast
- ✔ Selecting a wine in the same *flavor family* as the dish, which has a natural affinity based on complementary aromas and flavors

I offer details on how to approach the pairing in Chapter 5.

When you have your wine set up and want to select a dish to match it, you want to consider the following points:

- ✔ Recognize the wine's style profile and look for foods that complement and positively affect its taste and texture
- ✔ Consider the wine's principal aromas and flavors and seek complementary or contrasting flavors in the dish
- ✔ Choose ingredients and a cooking method (poaching, frying, grilling, for example) that match the wine's flavor intensity

✔ Select a dish with similar weight, such as heavy wines with rich, heavily sauced dishes, or light, crisp wines with fresh/raw/lowfat dishes

✔ Avoid dishes in which the main taste sensations and texture will diminish the wine's positive aspects

Chapter 4 can help you with your cooking and the combination of ingredients, and it can guide your food and wine matching from a flavor perspective.

Other useful tips to consider when pairing food and wine include

✔ Keeping the pairing local, which means you look for local foods and wines to pair together

✔ Matching the acidity in a dish with acidity in the wine

✔ Making sure the wine is at least as sweet as the dish

✔ Complementing or contrasting flavor and texture

Chapter 6 provides a complete list of pairing strategies you can immediately implement. There I also draw on the wisdom of the ages and outline several case studies in classic regional food and wine matches: how they arose and why they work. Understanding why they work is even more important than knowing that they do, because you can then apply the same successful principles to other combinations of food and wine. If you follow these basic principles, you'll never go far wrong when you bring food and wine together.

Aging wine

If you've ever wondered which wines you should be cellaring and which you should drink as young as possible, then you need to consider what I refer to as the *pillars of ageability* of a wine, which are the following:

✔ Acidity

✔ Tannin/extract

✔ Sugar

✔ Alcohol

The more of each, the more age-worthy the wine. And these elements also give you an idea of how long you can keep a wine after you've opened it before it spoils — rarely a problem in my house — but useful information to have in any case. And understanding how a wine changes as it ages, usually for the better but not always, can help in choosing the best types of foods to highlight those grand old bottles. Young and old wines like different foods, as I discuss in Chapter 7.

Serving like a sommelier

If one of the secrets of great food and wine matches is starting with great wine, it follows that anything you can do to make the wine more enjoyable is good for the cause. Sommeliers have several tricks up their sleeves for shifting your perception from good to great (they can't perform miracles like turn vinegar back into wine, but they can swing the odds in favor of appreciating the wine a little more).

You can use these tricks so you and your guests can appreciate the wine a bit more:

- ✔ Using the right glassware
- ✔ Serving at the best temperature for the wine style
- ✔ Knowing what wines to decant and how
- ✔ Serving multiple wines in the right order

Chapter 8 includes lots of practical information like these tricks to make you look like a pro who's been pairing food and wine and serving wine for years, and you may just end up enjoying that pairing a little bit more.

Understanding Wines: Just a Quick Overview

The key to understanding wine is knowing what it tastes like, at least from a food-and-wine-pairing perspective. And I mean the basic taste profile, not the nitty-gritty nuances of flavor, which is a secondary consideration. As a result, getting into the habit of forgetting the grape is a good idea (I know, I know, you've been trained to believe that knowing the grape will give you all the answers, but I'm suggesting you forget all that) and going on style when looking at the match from the wine side. In these days of globe-trotting grapes, you can quickly see how not all Chardonnays or Sauvignon Blancs or Cabernet Sauvignons are created equal — growing region and producer influence have a lot more to say. Light or full bodied, crisp and dry, soft and fruity, wood-aged or not are some of the considerations that trump grape variety when looking for the right match (although certain grapes do often lend themselves more readily to a particular style).

Part III is where I simplify the broad world of wine into style categories. Knowing what style category your wine falls into is critical to success. This means you either need to know the wine at hand or rely on the description of the merchant or the sommelier (if you're at home you can always crack open the bottle and have a taste ahead of the meal, and adjust accordingly).

There's no universal consensus on wine style categories, but here are the categories I find most useful. See all the details on white wine categories in Chapter 9, red wine in Chapter 10, sparkling wine in Chapter 11, and sweet wine and fortified wine in Chapter 12.

- ✔ **Lightweight, crisp, and lean whites:** These whites are lean and mouth-watering, like a squeeze of lemon or a bite of green apple. They're unoaked and hail from cool growing regions for the most part. Sommeliers often describe them as *"minerally,"* meaning they taste like chalk or wet stone, which is a high compliment in the wine world.

- ✔ **Aromatic, fruity, round whites:** Most of the aromatic white grapes fall into this category. Aromatic wines lean toward being medium-full bodied with balanced alcohol and acidity, sometimes a little fuller and more unctuous, with pronounced aromas and flavors of fruits and flowers. Think of Muscat/Moscato, Pinot Gris, or Gewürztraminer, and you're in the right category.

- ✔ **Medium-full bodied, creamy, wood-aged whites:** This category covers the world's barrel-fermented and/or aged whites. Chardonnay is the most common candidate for the barrel treatment, but a handful of other grapes or regional styles are also aged in wood. Because of this process, they're often round and creamy-textured, with aromas and flavors derived from wood, like sweet baking spices and caramel.

- ✔ **Light-bodied, bright, zesty, low tannin reds:** These are the most food-versatile reds of the wine world. They have juicy, flavor-enhancing acidity, light body, and low tannins (not too rough or astringent). Most reds made without any barrel-aging fall into this category, along with certain grapes like Gamay and Pinot Noir. They're usually best with a light chill.

- ✔ **Medium-full bodied, balanced, moderately tannic reds:** This category groups a wide range of red wines that have more body and flavor intensity than zesty reds, yet they're well balanced on their own without excessive acidity, alcohol, or tannin.

- ✔ **Full, deep and robust, turbocharged, with chewy texture reds:** These reds are the heavyweights of the wine world: big, bruising, intensely flavored, well-structured reds. They're usually complex (lots of different aromas and flavors), while their chewy texture (from tannins) makes them age-worthy, too. Examples from the new world (outside of Europe) can have very ripe, jammy fruit flavor. Old world wines are usually a little more earthy and herbal-spicy. They're invariably aged in wood.

- ✔ **Sparkling wine:** These wines have *effervescence* — dissolved carbon dioxide. They can be fully sparkling, like Champagne, or more lightly effervescent like Moscato d'Asti. Sparkling wines are among the most food-friendly and versatile. I briefly cover all the methods to make wine bubbly in Chapter 11.

- ✔ **Sweet, late harvest wines:** This category is further split into straight up *late harvest* (grapes picked late when they're slightly overripe),

> *botrytis-affected* (when grapes are affected by a type of beneficial fungus called *botrytis*, or *noble rot*), and Icewine, when grapes are picked when frozen solid. Each of these different categories has a different range of ideal food partners.
>
> ✔ **Dry and sweet fortified wines:** The addition of neutral alcohol to wine, raising the overall alcohol level to anywhere from about 15.5 percent to more than 20 percent, is what distinguishes this category. They can be either dry or sweet.

Each chapter in this part includes a list of grapes and regions that usually fall into each category, but the world of wine is made up of exceptions. In the areas of the old world where wines are named by their official appellation, that is, by a combination of grape(s) + place + production methods that results in a more or less consistent wine style, such as Chablis or Sancerre, you can have a pretty good idea of what wine style to expect from the label alone, as long as you've done your homework. Otherwise, the grape name alone on the label is only a starting point to figuring out what style of wine you're dealing with.

Occasionally I get stuck in a wine rut. I find a grape that I like and keep drinking it, finding as many different examples as possible. Of course, drinking the same wine type is okay. But then along comes something new, and I'm reminded just how amazingly vast the world of wine is and how much I have yet to discover. Finding a new grape made in the style that I like is as exciting for me as making a new friend: someone to share new experiences with, to learn from, and have fun with. Use the styles in this part like an Internet dating service, matching up personal profiles. If you recognize a few personal favorite wines in any of the categories, chances are that any of the others in the same category are at least worth a first date. And who knows, you may find a new lifelong friend.

I give some general pairing guidelines on what types of ingredients, cooking methods, and dishes work best with each wine style category, using a sort of free-flowing, stream-of-conscious, visual diagram that I devised for each. It's like a visual map of the thought process I go through — a kind of physical rendering of the intuitive process — if handed a bottle of category X wine and asked to match it with food. You can follow the web of thoughts and considerations and the possible directions I may go in for all the different styles. It's not intended to tell you exactly what to pair with each wine style (although specific dishes are included), but rather how to think about what to match. Hopefully these visual aids can spark the same kind of intuitive, creative thinking in your mind when you've got a bottle of wine in hand and are wondering what to eat.

Applying the Rules: Pairing Food and Wine around the World

Sometimes you just need an answer quickly, such as when you're planning a dinner for friends and you need a wine for the meal, and you don't have time or inclination to do the research for what pairs well. You can find a multitude of food and wine pairing tables in the chapters in Part IV.

These tables list traditional dishes from all parts of the world, along with the best wine style to match. There's a specific recommendation, too, though it needn't be followed slavishly — remember it's the style that matters most. And just to be sure you're covered, I offer an alternative style recommendation and specific pairing for each (there's often more than one wine style that works with a dish). This should cover a good number of the dishes you're likely to come across, whether you're going Italian, Indian, Mediterranean, or Mexican. This list shows which cuisines are covered in each of the chapters in these two parts:

- ✔ **The Mediterranean:** Chapter 13
- ✔ **North America:** Chapter 14
- ✔ **Northern Europe:** Chapter 15
- ✔ **Central Europe:** Chapter 16
- ✔ **Southeast Asia, Japan, India:** Chapter 17
- ✔ **Mexico and South America:** Chapter 18
- ✔ **The Middle East and North Africa:** Chapter 19
- ✔ **Cheese:** Chapter 20

Looking at Your World

You've just been charged with choosing a great restaurant for an avid food and wine lover. Or maybe you've been handed the thick phonebook of a wine list and are entreated to find the best value. Or maybe you've been designated to host the next family reunion, or organize the next office party, drinks and all. It's time to take a break from the theory of food and wine and consider some real-world situations.

Whether you're dining in or out, you can make sure you have an enjoyable experience with the wine(s) you choose. The following sections address eating out and eating in.

When you dine out

Dining out presents many opportunities for memorable food and wine experiences, as long as you're in the right place. When heading out to dine, these tips can help you find the restaurants that are most serious about wine, before you even sit down:

Look for visual cues that indicate a wine-savvy establishment, such as the following:

- ✔ The type of stemware on the table
- ✔ How wines are stored
- ✔ How the wine list is presented

I also provide some tips on figuring out what is on the sommelier's mind when he or she puts together the wine program, which can give you clues about what to order and where the values are most likely to be found.

After you pick a restaurant, you also need to know what to reveal to the sommelier — what he or she is hoping to get from you — and what questions to ask in order to get the best possible food and wine experience. Chapter 21 covers the dining-out scenario.

When you dine in

Being a good host is no mean feat. There's a real art to organizing an event, impressing guests, and making them feel welcome and well looked after. You don't want to run out of wine, but you don't want to over-buy either. And what exactly should you buy? It depends of course on the event; intimate family gatherings or large weddings require different strategies. Chapter 22 is all about hosting the party.

Chapter 2

How People Smell, Taste, and Touch Food and Wine

● ●

In This Chapter

▶ Grasping how you smell food and wine

▶ Comprehending how you taste and touch food and wine

▶ Getting used to sensations: adaptation

▶ Experiencing pleasure

● ●

*T*his chapter is all about the mundane yet miraculous ways in which people experience smell, taste, and touch. That's, after all, what eating and drinking are all about. And you couldn't be living at a better time: The understanding of how people interpret their environment has increased exponentially in recent years, providing greater insight into the hows and whys of people's preferences. Scientists are delving ever deeper into the senses and the brain that unravels their messages, illuminating the coding and the pathways that lead to pleasure.

You surely needn't be a scientist to enjoy food and wine, but knowing a little bit about how the machine works can tip the odds in your favor for getting the pairings right more often. At the very least, doing so can make you more curious and eager to pay attention to what you eat and drink, which tends to lead to more enjoyment already. In this chapter, I cover what you need to know about tasting and smelling, and the importance of the tactile sensations of wine and food. I look at why some folks are supertasters, and others are less sensitive, and how people can all smell far more things than they can taste.

You discover about adaptation, that is, how you get used to smells and tastes and stop noticing them. And finally, I examine how people are programmed to compulsively avoid or obsessively pursue certain smells and tastes — part of a person's instincts to seek pleasure and avoid harm. Until I figured this out myself, I thought my regular craving for a rare-grilled bone-in rib-eye with an aged bottle of red was pure hedonism (which I've indulged at least a thousand times). Now I know that enjoyment was also fulfilling a primal instinct for survival, so I feel better about it.

Getting a Quick Lowdown: The Basics of Smelling and Tasting

On the surface, the mechanics of how people taste and smell are relatively straightforward. Both are so-called *chemical* senses: They allow you to identify the molecular composition of your surroundings (senses that wine drinkers and gourmands are forever grateful for), which is different from, say, hearing and seeing, senses that are triggered by sound and light waves and not molecules. In addition to being sources of pleasure, taste and smell have evolved as defense mechanisms to alert you to potentially harmful substances before they get too far into the body. Here is a quick snapshot of these two important senses:

- ✔ *Smell* allows you to sense a substance from a distance via airborne molecules, just as you do each time you swirl a glass of wine and then put your nose over the opening and inhale the volatile aromas.

- ✔ *Taste* requires you to get a little more up close and personal — the substance has to be in your mouth — where your taste receptors are. Taste is of course activated before you swallow, offering a last chance to spit if the substance isn't pleasing.

But what you can smell and what you can taste are two very different things. I examine these two senses (along with touch) in this chapter so you can see what role they play when you eat food and drink wine, and also so that you can understand my meaning clearly when I refer specifically to taste, aroma, or flavor sensations.

An ancient view of taste

The ancient philosophers spent a fair bit of time trying to understand the nature of taste. In the fourth century B.C., Democritus, the laughing philosopher (he valued cheerfulness highly), attempted to show how different taste sensations are determined by the shapes of atoms. He believed for example that jagged atomic food particles irritate the tongue, causing a bitter sensation, while smooth atoms that roll easily over the tongue cause a sweet sensation.

Plato was of a mind with Democritus, furthering the theory in *Timaeus*, a dialogue on the nature of the physical world, and in turn influencing Aristotle. In his *De Anima*, Aristotle described the four primary tastes: sweet, sour, salty, and bitter. Little has changed in people's understanding of taste for two thousand years.

Understanding How You Smell

Although everyone has a nose of unique proportions, they all basically smell the same way. You sense aromas via the olfactory neurons on the little hair-like projections behind your nose called *cilia*. When aromatic molecules land on these smell receptors, they trigger a distinct electrical impulse based on their composition, which in turn sends an electrically charged message to the olfactory bulb in the brain. Your brain then decodes the signal, and the aroma, familiar or foreign, is experienced.

The following sections examine the ins and outs of smelling, or *olfaction* (a technical way to say smelling), including the different ways in which aromas reach your nose, how smelling differs from the other senses, and why smelling is your most important sense when it comes to eating and drinking.

Following the path of aromatic molecules

In order to experience a smell, aromatic molecules can reach your neurons by two different routes, or as is often the case when eating and drinking, both routes. The resulting aromatic sensation is similar regardless of the pathway (although new evidence suggests that quality or intensity of the sensation may differ slightly):

- ✔ **Directly via your nose:** The most obvious route is directly from the environment into your nose. As such, the sense of smell acts as a warning mechanism, identifying things that may be harmful to you, such as rotten food or bad wine, before they get too close. Smelling is also of course a source of pleasure, and in the case of food and wine, sets up the anticipation of further gustatory pleasure to come.

- ✔ **Indirectly via your mouth:** The body allows for a second aromatic check after a substance is already in your mouth. An opening at the back of the mouth, called the *retronasal passage,* connects the mouth to the nasal cavity where all those olfactory receptors are. Aromas that you experience after something is in your mouth are a very big part of the enjoyment of flavor, and are often confused with taste. Strictly speaking, flavor is aroma (and I refer to smells sensed directly through the nose as *aromas* and those sensed via the retronasal passage as *flavor* in this book). But taste, as you see, is a totally different sensation that is independent from aromas and smelling, even if researchers now believe that olfactory sensations can affect taste perception and vice-versa.

Paying attention to all the aromas

The sense of smell is the most primal of your senses. It differs from all other senses because the receptor neurons are directly connected to the brain — in this case, the olfactory bulb — which is to say that the signals largely aren't mediated by or processed through other neurological structures (you don't think about them), as is the case with other senses.

Although humans don't seem to rely on smell as much as animals, it's nonetheless one of a person's most remarkably acute and sensitive senses. Current scientific literature suggests that humans can differentiate between about 10,000 different aromas. Each person has approximately 1,000 different types of receptors which, when stimulated by odorants, combine together to define aromas in much the same way as the fixed number of letters in the alphabet combine to create an almost infinite variety of words, or the way in which musical notes can be arranged to create an almost limitless range of melodies.

The challenge most people have is to associate a name with so many aromas. But it's also clear that people who are trained to recognize odors, like wine or perfume experts, don't necessarily have a more sensitive nose — they're just better at distinguishing smells and retrieving their names from memory. The way that you can increase your ability to discriminate between different smells and to then remember them is by doing a lot of attentive smelling — it's all about the practice.

Connecting smells to memories: A bridge to the past

Ever wonder why a certain smell can transport you instantly to another place or time, causing deep emotional feelings to arise before you can even consider why? For Marcel Proust, it was a scallop-shaped madeleine cookie and a cup of tea that transported him back to his childhood in Combray, France, in his epic novel *In Search of Lost Time*. For me, the merest whiff of a glass of fino sherry takes me instantly back to my early twenties and the tapas bars of southern Spain, where I'm munching on a piece of tangy sheep's milk cheese and popping big, crunchy green olives into my mouth while watching the toreadors dance with the bulls. Which smells take you away? Smell is a very powerful and evocative sense, one that can make you feel deeply and take you back into the past. The aromas of food and wine are potentially the greatest sources of pleasure.

Linking aromas and wine

The constant exposure to the aromatic composition of consumables, coupled with the vast range of aromas that you're able to detect, make smelling the most important aspect of enjoying wine (and food). Wine tasters pay a great deal of attention to the way a wine smells — it's the most vital step in the tasting process and the most significant differentiating factor between types of wine. And neuroscientists seem to agree. They estimate that around 90 percent of what people perceive as taste is actually smell (flavor), giving top-notch wines and foods an incredible complexity that the sensation of taste alone can barely hint at. That's why eating and drinking when you have a head cold is a real drag: You're unable to detect aroma and flavor, limiting the experience to just the basic taste sensations.

If you still doubt the importance of aroma in the overall flavor profile of food or wine, try this simple experiment: Grab an apple, plug your nose, and take a bite. What do you experience? With access to your olfactory receptors blocked, you can't smell anything. But you can still taste and touch. You can sense the sweetness of the apple, the acidity (especially if it's a green apple), and some aspects of the texture. But you don't notice any aroma or flavor. In fact, it could be any sweet-sour, slightly mealy substance in your mouth — not easy to identify as an apple. Now unplug your nose, and you can sense the apple aroma/flavor flooding in as your olfactory neurons are returned to action. The familiar "taste," that is, the familiar aroma and flavor, of the apple suddenly appears.

Experiencing 10,000 different aromas may be a stretch, but wines, especially the best ones, are incredibly well endowed aromatically. What starts out as fairly simple, sweet grape juice transforms during fermentation into an amazingly complex beverage. In addition to alcohol and carbon dioxide, the yeasts that carry out fermentation also spit out different aromatic molecules that lead to hundreds of unique smells. To listen to a pro wine taster describe the aromas in a glass of wine may seem like fanciful poetic license, but there's truth in the poetry. The same molecules responsible for, say, the smell of a ripe peach or strawberry, vanilla, freshly roasted coffee beans, or green peppers can be found in wine — the descriptions aren't pulled out of thin air (well, maybe once in a while)!

Examining How You Taste

Tasting, like smelling, requires some physical contact. Your aptly named taste buds, distributed mostly on your tongue but also on the roof and sides of the mouth, are what detect the sensation of taste. You experience taste sensations when molecules come into contact with the taste buds, causing them to fire in a certain way and send electrical signals to the brain where they're interpreted as the various recognizable taste sensations. Like smell, your taste messages are also sent to the more primitive brain centers where they influence emotions and trigger memories. But they also head to more evolved brain regions, where they can influence conscious thought. But although a person's amazing nose can recognize upwards of 10,000 aromas, the taste buds are currently believed to tune in to five taste sensations (possibly six, see the nearby sidebar), making their emotional impact less vivid overall than that of smell.

These sections take a closer look at the five tastes, their main sources and how to recognize them, and what people taste when they drink wine.

Naming the five senses

Human taste buds can detect five tastes. Aristotle has already recognized and described the first four tastes. The fifth, savory, also called *umami,* wasn't recognized until a couple thousand years later. Having an awareness of these five sensations and the distinctions between them is crucial when pairing food and wine together. (Refer to the later section, "Linking taste and wine.")

The five tastes are as follows:

✔ **Sweet:** You're undoubtedly very familiar with the sensation of sweetness. Your body is biologically programmed to enjoy this taste, because sweet things signal calorie-rich foods to your body, which promote survival. Technically, several natural substances cause a sweet sensation, most of which end in *–ose* like glucose, sucrose, and fructose. The most ready sources of refined sugar are sugar cane and sugar beets. Aside from these, ripe fruit is the most obvious source of natural sugars. For the record, grapes contain mostly glucose and fructose, and are about the only type of fruit with enough natural sugar to ferment into a stable, pleasant beverage. Other fruit wines must have additional sugar added.

A sixth taste?

The existence of five taste sensations is well established, but increasing evidence and agreement amongst taste researchers suggests that a sixth taste exists: the ability to taste fat, or more accurately, free fatty acids. Researchers believe that the unique taste is independent of the tactile sensations elicited by fats — that slippery, greasy texture in your mouth. Could this be yet another reason why people are drawn to cream sauces, deep-fried foods, and well-marbled beef? A number of taste researchers also believe that they'll discover additional tastes in the future — there's so much more to taste!

✔ **Sour:** The sensation of sourness is caused by the presence of various kinds of acids in the mouth. If you start to salivate while eating or drinking, it's a telltale sign that the substance contains a high level of acidity — it's your body trying to neutralize the acid with your basic, non-acidic, saliva. Acids naturally occur everywhere. Citric fruits have citric acid, dairy products have lactic acid, and green apples have malic acid. Tartaric acid is the main acid in ripe grapes, and therefore wine.

✔ **Bitter:** Many natural compounds have a bitter taste, sort of a lingering unpleasant taste in your mouth. Just think of all the poetic uses of bitter: bitter truth, bitter struggle, bitter cold, and so on. Some people are extremely sensitive to bitterness, while others are less so. In any case, most experience bitter flavors as unpleasant, which isn't surprising from an evolutionary standpoint because many naturally occurring toxic substances have a bitter taste. In other words, you're programmed biologically to avoid bitterness. Nonetheless, bitterness at low levels adds to the complexity of both food and wine.

Common encounters with bitter tastes occur with coffee and tea, which contain bitter-tasting caffeine, so most people add sugar to these beverages to balance the bitter taste. Hoppy styles of beer like pilsner and IPA, leafy greens, unsweetened cacao (chocolate), olives, citrus zest, and marmalade are also sources of bitterness, while certain cooking methods, particularly grilling, can add a charred, bitter flavor to food.

✔ **Salty:** The presence of sodium causes the familiar salty taste. Salt has the magic capacity to enhance the sensation of other tastes; without it, most food tastes bland and uninteresting. Salt is also a key component in preserving perishable foods, and is found in high concentrations in foods like cured meats. In the realm of food and wine pairing, salt is an important ally. It acts as a buffer against very astringent wines, and when added to food in the right amount, salt can make mouth-puckering wines much softer and smoother.

✔ **Savory:** Also referred to as *umami,* this taste sensation is most commonly caused by glutamic acid, more commonly found as monosodium glutamate (MSG). Foods that are rich in umami include fish and shellfish; fermented and aged products, such as aged cheeses, soy sauce, fermented fish sauces; vegetables like ripe tomatoes and Chinese cabbage; various mushrooms; dried bonito flakes; and grilled beef. Umami-rich foods also have a synergistic effect, making the sum more savory than the individual parts. This explains why, for example, pasta with tomato sauce is tasty, but is even better with a little grated Parmiggiano cheese on top: tomato sauce + aged cheese = a double umami whammy. Check out the nearby sidebar, "Umami, the savory fifth taste" for how this taste became recognized.

See also Chapter 3 for a more comprehensive list of foods dominated by one of the five taste sensations.

Worth your salt

Salt was once considered as valuable as gold. In fact, the English word *salary* can trace its etymology back 2,000 years to *sal*, the Latin word for salt. Salt was so highly prized for its food preservation and flavor-enhancing properties that it became a form of currency. The Roman historian Pliny the Elder wrote that in Rome, soldiers were often paid in salt. Eventually, this *salarium* came to signify a regular stipend paid in any form. The echoes of this etymology linger on in such expressions as "worth your salt," meaning that you're working hard and earning your salary.

Taste buds are distributed throughout your mouth. Until recently, thanks to a misinterpreted scientific paper, people commonly believed that certain regions of the mouth were only sensitive to specific tastes, such as the tip of the tongue being sensitive only to sweet tastes, and the back of the mouth picking up bitterness. But this so-called *tongue map* didn't stand up to rigorous scientific study. All the taste buds in all regions of the mouth — all over the tongue but also on the roof and sides of the mouth and the back of the throat — are capable of recognizing and interpreting the five taste sensations, albeit with greater or lesser sensitivity to each. The tip of the tongue is indeed more sensitive to sweetness, for example, but not exclusively.

Knowing why you know what you like

Humans are programmed to enjoy sweet tastes (a sign that the substance contains precious calories). The taste of umami-rich foods, too, signals the presence of proteins and amino acids, elements that are essential to your survival. In fact, most people are naturally drawn to sweet and savory things. Sensitivity to and tolerance of sour and bitter tastes, on the other hand, vary considerably from person to person. But because most poisonous substances are bitter, and acid can be an indication of spoilage in food or unripe (low calorie/nutrient) fruit, people have a genetically programmed aversion to sour and bitter things. As every chef knows, acid and salt in moderate amounts are excellent flavor enhancers, though too much of either is unpleasant.

Everyone varies in his or her capacity to perceive taste, and the differences can be significant, as it turns out. People can basically be categorized into three *taster status* classifications based on how sensitive they are to taste sensations. Bitterness is most often used as the benchmark of sensitivity. Your taster status also strongly influences your personal preferences when it comes to food and wine.

Umami, the savory fifth taste

Umami is a Japanese word meaning literally "delicious taste," coined by Japanese scientist Kikunae Ikeda, who hit upon the fifth taste sensation in 1908. Ikeda was trying to figure out why the broth of Kombu seaweed was so tasty, having a quality that couldn't be explained by sweet, sour, bitter, or salty tastes. He discovered that the broth was rich in glutamates, that a person's tongue was sensitive to them, and that people like the experience.

✔ **Supertasters:** They don't need tights and a cape to perform feats of tasting; they just have the right stuff. You can't train yourself to become a supertaster, no matter how many comic books you read or how many pushups you do. Supertasters are genetically programmed to be more sensitive than others. It's not that their individual taste buds are more finely tuned or sensitive; it's just that they simply have more of them than the average person. Being a supertaster isn't necessarily a gift from nature, however. It means you're hypersensitive to bitterness, and that the range of foods that you enjoy is reduced. Statistically, about 25 percent of people are classified as supertasters.

✔ **Nontasters:** Another 25 percent or so of people are classified as *nontasters,* which according to the medical definition, means that they are unable to detect the bitter compound known as PROP, which is used for such research. In other words, their taste buds are tuned out, or less sensitive, to bitter compounds. Nontasters can of course still taste; they just have a higher threshold of perception (that is, they need more of a taste stimulus to detect the taste). Evidence also suggests that nontasters are less sensitive to the other taste sensations because PROP sensitivity is a good general indication of a person's general taste sensitivity. But don't panic; I know several very sharp wine tasters who are technically nontasters. Training and experience matter greatly.

✔ **Medium tasters:** Everyone else, about half the population, fall somewhere in the middle, and are classified as medium tasters or simply tasters. This means that their sensitivity to bitterness is less acute than supertasters, but that they're also still able to detect bitter sensations that nontasters can't.

Linking taste and wine

All the taste sensations — sour, sweet, bitter, salty, umami — are experienced in wine. Here I briefly cover how these five tastes show up in wine.

Are you a supertaster?

So how tolerant are you to bitter tastes? Do you take your coffee or tea black without sugar? Do you crave leafy (bitter) greens? Your sensitivity to bitter things determines your taster status (well, technically your taster status is measured by your ability to sense a bitter compound called 6-n-propylthiouracil). The more sensitive you are to this compound, the more taste buds you likely have. But supertasters are more sensitive not only to bitterness, but also to sweetness, the burning sensation of spicy foods, and aspects of texture like mouth-feel and creaminess.

As you may expect, a sampling of wine experts shows a higher percentage of supertasters than the general population (though curiously, "foodies" aren't statistically more likely to be supertasters) — though being a supertaster is by no means a prerequisite to enjoying food and wine. Nontasters have fun too; they just tend to like different flavor combinations or are less sensitive (and therefore more tolerant) of intense taste sensations. If you're curious about your taster status, you can test yourself at www.supertasting.com.

Pucker up: Sour

Sourness, caused by the presence of acidity, is a major component of wine. Without it, wine would taste soft and flabby and would spoil quickly. Acidity is likewise a key flavor enhancer, and wine's high acidity is what makes it one of the most compatible beverages to drink alongside food. Most winemakers also agree that acidity is the most important factor in determining the age-ability of a wine — the more acid, the more age-worthy a wine will likely be.

Tartaric acid is the principal type of acid found in wine, though smaller quantities of several other acids are also usually present. Grapes grown in cool regions (imagine pine trees, not palm trees, growing around the vineyards) have naturally high levels of acidity, while warm-climate wines are usually lower acid. One way a wine can spoil is by the action of certain bacteria that produce high levels of *acetic acid,* which is essentially vinegar. Ironically, a high level of other acids in wine is what prevents acetic bacteria from spoiling it in the first place. Whatever the type, the levels of acidity in food and wine are a key consideration for making the most pleasant tasting match.

Refer to Part III for some specific examples of high acid and low acid wines and the different foods they pair well with.

A fairly direct correlation exists between sugar and acid levels in grapes. As they ripen, the sugar content rises and the acidity falls. The trick is picking them at the right moment when both are in balance. Adjusting acidity level in wine, both up and down, is common practice around the world. In certain warm grape-growing regions, it's necessary to artificially raise the acidity level by adding acid in order to render the wine stable. The easiest and most natural way to reduce the sour taste of wine is a process known as *malolactic*

fermentation. Winemakers allow naturally occurring bacteria to transform the harsh green malic acid (think green apples) found in unripe wine into softer lactic acid (think yogurt). The result is a rounder, smoother taste, as well as less fruity and more buttery aromas and flavor. The vast majority of red wines and most barrel-fermented white wines undergo malolactic fermentation.

A spoonful of sugar: Sweetness

A sweet taste in wine is due mainly to leftover, unfermented sugars (called *residual sugar* in wine parlance) that the yeasts didn't convert into alcohol. The most common category of sweet wine includes late harvest wines, in which the grapes are so ripe that yeasts are unable to ferment all the sugar, resulting in a wine with residual sugars. Typically, the amounts of residual sugar range from almost imperceptible at 3 to 4 grams per liter, up to as much as about 400 grams in the sweetest of sweet wines (that's a 40 percent sugar solution!).

There are also artificial ways to make wines sweet: Many wineries (even if they'd never admit to it) have been known to sweeten their so-called dry wine with fresh or concentrated grape must to broaden its appeal. In any case, the amount of sugar in a wine plays an important role in figuring out which foods it will match best with. Refer to Chapter 12 for some specific sweet wines and the different foods they pair well with.

Rare but strong: Bitterness

Extreme bitterness in wine is rare, thankfully, but you can perceive it in low levels now and then. Bitterness is a minor but important component in wine flavor, derived mainly from *polyphenols*, a group of naturally occurring compounds that includes tannins (also the source of the astringent, mouth-puckering texture) and color pigments. Also, dry wines made from very aromatic grapes like Muscat or Gewürztraminer, have a mildly bitter but pleasant taste, especially if the winemaker leaves the grape skins in contact with the juice to extract more of these aromatic flavors. Downplaying the bitter taste of wine is one of the strategies for successful food and wine pairing. Check Part III for some examples of bitter wines.

No shaker needed: Salty

Salt, too, can be found in trace amounts in wine. Few wines can be considered truly salty, but vines grown in areas with salty groundwater inevitably absorb some of the salt via the roots or the leaves (where overhead sprinklers are used) and deposit it in the grapes. Measurable salts then find their way into wines, which can have a vaguely salty taste.

For example, the mighty Murray River, Australia's longest river, contains considerable amounts of salt thanks to rising water tables, in turn caused by clear cutting forests and excessive crop irrigation. Vineyards irrigated with water from the Murray can often have a markedly salty taste. Wines that have been artificially de-acidified (common in cold growing regions), and wines with a high pH (often from warm regions) can also have traces of perceptible salt. Overall, salty taste in wine plays a very minor role in the food and wine pairing experience.

Delicious-tasting wines

Research is on-going, but researchers believe that glutamates and amino acids are found in appreciable amounts in certain wines and are the source of their umami taste. It's speculated that wines made from grapes fully ripened over a long, even growing season, and those aged for prolonged periods before and after bottling (especially when aged on the spent yeast cells after fermentation, like Champagne) tend to have the greatest concentration of savory umami taste.

Touching Plays an Important Role When Pairing Food and Wine

The sensations of aroma and taste are a big part of the eating and drinking experience, but there's more to it than that. The sense of touch, known as the *tactile sensation*, also comes into play. When wine tasters refer to the mouth feel, viscosity, or the texture of a wine, they're really talking about its tactile sensation, the impact that the wine has on sensory receptors tuned in to the sense of touch. Matching the textures of food and wine, or more commonly using food to alter the texture of wine, is one of the secrets of successful pairings. The following sections take a closer look at how touching is necessary when pairing food and wine.

Tapping into your tactile sensations

Tactile sensations are most often described by analogy. Words like velvety, silky, creamy, and plush frequently appear in wine descriptions, as do other descriptive terms like smooth, round, and soft, or conversely, hard, rough, chewy, and astringent. These terms convey the type of tactile sensation that is experienced by you, the drinker. Texture is, of course, a big part of the food experience, too. Where would roast chicken or pork be without that crispy skin, or cream of mushroom soup without the creamy mouth-feel?

Sensations of temperature and the spicy burn or cooling sensation of certain herbs and spices like chile peppers or mint are also part of touch. The serving temperature of both food and wine has an impact on texture, and even on the perception of aromas and flavors, and are thus also important considerations in food and wine pairing.

Helping you detect texture: Your trigeminal nerve

The *trigeminal nerve* is largely responsible for the sensation of texture and the perception of irritation in the nose and mouth. Trigeminal fibers are found in the nose and are part of the structure of taste buds, leading to some confusion between taste and texture. Often the two sensations interlink and overlap, like the perception of tannin, which causes both a bitter taste and an astringent texture.

Tannin in wine comes from the grape skins and stems. Because most white wines are made without any skin contact, they have much lower levels of tannins than reds, which must be soaked along with the skins in order to extract the red color. Tannin makes the mouth feel rough and dry, and causes a drawing, puckering, or tightening sensation often called *astringency*. Tannins do this by binding to salivary proteins, thus robbing saliva of its ability to lubricate the mouth. You notice this roughness more when you move your tongue around, which is something you do when eating and drinking wine.

Aside from tannin, the trigeminal nerves are called into action by a wide variety of stimulants: the fizzy tingle of carbon dioxide in sparkling wine, the nose-tingling and mouth-burning sensation from hot peppers of all kinds, black pepper, ginger, mustard, horseradish, wasabi, and even onions and garlic, to name a few. Alcohol also causes a mildly burning sensation, and high proof spirits can really burn.

Dealing with the burn of chiles and other spicy foods

Capsaicin, the potent chemical that gives hot chile peppers their burn, has a profound immediate and long-term desensitizing effect on your palate. It usually takes a few seconds, but as soon as the burn heats up, people's taste buds become less sensitive to other taste sensations like sweet and bitter. The desensitizing fades with the burning, though studies show that people who regularly eat a lot of chiles are chronically desensitized.

Addiction to spicy food is fact, not fiction: Spice causes the release of *endorphins,* a compound that causes a feeling of exhilaration and well-being that's similar (albeit perhaps less intense), to the feeling when making love! People accustomed to spicy food are also less sensitive to the burning irritation, and are able to focus their attention back to flavors, whereas occasional spice eaters tend to be too distracted by the pain to enjoy much flavor or taste.

How the world cools the burn

Every culture where spice is a big part of the cuisine has hit upon its own remedies to cool the burn. For example, starchy corn is a good antidote in Central and South America, and invariably accompanies spicy foods in one form or another. In Hungary, the starch comes in the form of bread, dumplings, rice or potatoes, which are never far away from a spicy *paprikás*. Fatty *ghee* (clarified butter) is used for cooking in Indian dishes to counterbalance hot spice, while *raita*, a fatty, sour, salty mixture of yogurt, cucumber, and other spices, is served alongside hot curries (capsaicin is fat soluble, so fatty substances like ghee and raita are effective at diluting and cooling). Pineapple (sweet) is used in the Philippines, and sugar is added the world over from Asian dipping sauces to southern-style barbeque sauce to balance spicy heat.

This phenomenon of desensitized taste buds explains why the best wines are usually left in the cellar when really spicy food is served. Your taste buds are too numb to enjoy all the flavor nuances found in great wines. What's more, high alcohol accentuates the burning sensation of spice, making a mild burn even more severe.

To cool the burn, try

- Starch (potatoes, bread, corn, plain rice, beans)
- Fat (whole milk, cream, yogurt, olive oil, butter/clarified butter, cheese

Cold liquids provide significant but temporary relief — that's why reaching for a cold beer is an automatic reaction. But carbon dioxide also exacerbates the burning sensation, so the physical cooling effect doesn't last long. Forget water. Because capsaicin doesn't dissolve in water, the pain goes away only temporarily and can return worse than before because you've now distributed the burn throughout the mouth.

Sweetness on its own is by all accounts the most effective fire-quenching technique. It's even more effective when combined with acidity (which causes salivation and thus rinses the mouth) and served cold. Knowing this, the most effective antiburn wines are thus those that are off-dry or sweet, moderate alcohol, high acid, and served cold. Think of an off-dry or sweet Riesling from Germany, or a fruit-packed new world with a sweet impression like Viognier or Zinfandel wine, served chilled, and you're in the right space.

Measuring the heat

That clue that sweetness is a good antidote for the burn of capsaicin comes from the most commonly used scale to measure the intensity of the stinging sensation: the Scoville scale. Wilbur Scoville was an American chemist who hit upon the idea of classifying the relative heat of various substances by using an alcohol-based extract of capsaicin, which is then added incrementally into a sugar-water solution until a panel of tasters can just detect their trigeminals tingling. The hottest known chiles, such as habaneros or scotch bonnets, have a rating up to 350,000 Scoville units, which means that their extract must be diluted more than 350,000 times before the capsaicin sting is no longer sensed.

Seeing How Repeated Exposure Can Dull Your Awareness of Flavors: Adaptation

Humans experience *sensory adaptation*, a gradual reduction in the awareness of aromas, flavors, and tastes due to repeated exposure. *Adaptation* accounts for the fact that people don't smell their own perfume after a short while and smokers are unaware that they smell like smoke. Your house, too, probably has a particular smell that you can no longer identify because you're constantly exposed to it. Try cooking an intense curry in your house: After a few hours you'll no longer smell it, but then step outside for a few minutes to clear your nose and return inside. You'll be greeted by a powerful smell of curry that you didn't notice on the way out. That's adaptation.

The phenomenon of adaptation occurs when eating and drinking. After the first sip or two of coffee, for example, you're no longer really tasting the coffee. It's for this reason that wine tasters, at least when tasting for professional reasons, spit. Consumption of alcohol obviously clouds judgment, but the unnatural act of spitting liquid is a signal to the brain to pay attention. Thus tasters are able to focus their senses and still distinguish between flavor and taste nuances in dozens of wines in a session.

Adaptation also means that the very first mouthful of food and sip of wine is the most revealing and informative, highlighting the success or failure of the pairing. The good news is that if the pairing isn't outstanding, after a couple of bites, nobody will likely be paying attention anymore.

Understanding Pleasure: Loving Your Dopamine

Have you ever wondered what makes you feel good? It has to do a lot with dopamine. *Dopamine* is a neurotransmitter; in other words, it's what your brain cells use to communicate with one another. Pleasurable sensations cause a release of dopamine in the part of the brain that generates pleasurable feelings, literally flooding your mind with that *feel good* feeling. It's what scientists call the *reward effect*. The taste of excellent wine or food, seeing an old cherished friend, or listening to your favorite song all trigger dopamine release.

But it's not just the moment of taste or the act of listening to music that gives you pleasure. The expectation of good things to come plays an important role, too. The next sections look at the timing of dopamine release and the importance of acquiring a taste for something before pleasure can be had.

Expecting pleasure is almost as good as the real thing

The expectation of pleasure is highly motivational; it's what drives you to do many things. Some dopamine is actually released *in anticipation of* pleasurable events. It's your brain telling you (or you telling your brain) that something good is about to happen. That's why the mere thought of a juicy steak or a delicious wine can make you feel good before you've done any eating or drinking. Some scientists go so far as to say that anticipation, *the wanting*, of something is even more powerful than the actual moment of consummation, the actual *liking* of whatever it is. It can be hard for things to meet your expectations.

Giving taste a chance

The trick is, in order for dopamine to be released, it has to be a predictable reward, something you know will bring you pleasure. That's why enjoying unfamiliar aromas and tastes is difficult the first time you encounter them. You won't, or can't, get any anticipatory pleasure for something you've never had. On the contrary, you're more likely to be wary of the unknown. People have a natural aversion to unfamiliarity and strangeness, and the system works in reverse: You tend to anticipate something unpleasant. And given the powerful influence of people's perceptions, actually liking something you were expecting not to is hard. You set up an expectation to dislike, so you probably will.

Your dopamine transmitters at work: Sit back and enjoy

Imagine you're on a terrace in the south of France, gazing over the azure Mediterranean. You're already having a pretty nice time, and your dopamines are flowing. Then you consider the menu and the wine list. You order a cool, crisp glass of rosé and a *tarte niçoise*, a puff pastry tart with cherry tomatoes, black olives, caramelized onions, and anchovies. It's a classic southern France pairing, and you're expecting perfections. More dopamine release means more pleasure.

The waiter brings over the wine, the glass already dripping with perspiration. You swirl the glass to awaken as many aromatic molecules as possible out of their chilly slumber. You place your nose over the opening and inhale deeply. A symphony of escaping molecules enters your nose and assails your odor receptors. Without conscious thought, each molecule affixes itself to one or more of your 1,000 receptors, immediately triggering an electrical signal that flashes across various pathways at unfathomable speeds to the *limbic system*, the emotional and memory center of the brain. Some of those messages give you the "aahhh" feeling, and the involuntarily urge to smile tugs at the corners of your mouth as you feel helplessly happy. The familiar smells evoke pleasant memories of your last trip to the Côte d'Azure, or maybe of a previous good glass of rosé, or an afternoon seaside moment. These thoughts flash across the screen of your mind, at first almost subliminally, and then more and more clearly focused as the messages reach the frontal cortex and the origin of conscious thought. Now you say "wow".

Then you take a sip. The cool, crisp-tart liquid enters your mouth; acid molecules activate your taste receptors, signaling the body to start secreting saliva. The moderate alcohol causes a gently warming sensation, thanks to its interaction with the trigeminal nerve, while you also detect the cool temperature and its refreshing sensation thanks to those same nerves. Only milliseconds behind, aromatic molecules, now warmed up by your body and even more active, are making their way up the retronasal passage to latch on to your odor receptors. Yet more of the wine's flavor is detected as it warms in your mouth: strawberries, raspberries, wild herbs, and more. Emotional feelings are sparked again, and the memory reel starts to roll, activating specific memories, feelings, and thoughts. You're having a nice afternoon. More pleasure awaits as the tart arrives and the food and wine come together.

Acquiring a taste

Enter what people call an *acquired taste:* Caviar, olives, or anchovies, for example, alongside hundreds of other things, don't give most people much pleasure on the first encounter because their flavor is both unfamiliar and strong. But after you and your dopamines get used to what to expect — the flavor becomes familiar — then you can start to enjoy, and even crave things that you would never have dreamed of eating before. I remember the first time I tried an olive, when I was about seven years old. I thought it was about the most disgusting thing I had ever put in my mouth. But I persevered over the years, trying another olive here and there just to make sure I wasn't missing out on something, and today, I could eat barrels full of olives. I acquired the taste.

That's not to say that you'll come to like every type of strange food and every combination of food and wine, but give it a chance, especially if either the wine or the food is totally unfamiliar. Who knows; in time, it may come to be your favorite combination. I've learned to keep an open mind when thinking about pairing wines with food. It's happened often enough that the least expected combinations yield the best results. If I weren't open to trying new variations and flavor combinations, I'd have missed out on a lot of unexpected pleasure.

Considering the importance of familiarity and expectation in the experience of pleasure, and that experience is highly personal, the most critical piece of this puzzle is you. Outside of inviting smells and pleasant tastes, all your previous personal experience comes to bear on the moment — the past haunts you! You are the one interpreting the experience after all, and you have the greatest influence on the success (or failure) of a food and wine moment.

Take the sweet test

If you're keen to test your perception of sweetness, try this little exercise:

1. **Take four standard 8-ounce glasses of lukewarm water.**

2. **Add a teaspoon of sugar to the first, two to the second, three to the third, and four to the fourth, marking each glass with a sticker on the bottom indicating how many spoonfuls of sugar were added.**

3. **Stir to dissolve, and refrigerate.**

4. **When cool, ask someone to mix them up, and then taste and see if you can put them back in order of sweetness.**

5. **After you master that, try adding the same number of teaspoons of lemon juice to each glass of sweetened water and repeating the experiment.**

Notice how the increasing acid counterbalances the increasing sweetness. Then play some more. You may notice that a glass with two teaspoons of sugar and no lemon juice tastes sweeter than a glass with four teaspoons each of sugar and lemon juice — it's all about the balance. Now you're starting to think like a winemaker.

Chapter 3

Introducing Food and Wine: A Classic Couple with Ups and Downs

In This Chapter

▶ Maximizing the taste of food and wine together

▶ Getting a handle on how wine changes with food

▶ Classifying the outcomes of mixing food and wine

*F*ood is enjoyed alongside many different drinks. In fact, you can find many great matches with juices, mineral water, soda, beer, spirits, sake, and cocktails, among others, and wine certainly isn't always the best match. However, something about the combination of food and wine is unique and works more often than other beverages. Wine is the most complex of them all (judging by the sheer range of aromas, flavors, and tastes), and the alcohol level is generally moderate enough to enjoy a glass or two without adverse affects. Perhaps most importantly, wine has high natural acidity — a critical factor that makes it the most compatible drink around. Chances are pretty good that you can find a suitable choice for just about every dish imaginable.

Most people eat and drink, but few are actually fully experiencing the match. This helpful chapter gives you some practical how-tos along with the basic building blocks of food and wine pairing. I start off by outlining the best way to get the full effect of food and wine together — a little refresher on how to eat and drink wine to the max.

In order to tune up your taste buds and clearly illustrate the effects of food taste and texture on wine, I outline a simple experiment that you can do at home with some common ingredients likely on hand, or easily acquired. And finally, I describe the basic possible outcomes, from the sublime to the ridiculous, when food and wine get together.

Tasting Food and Wine Together: The How-To

Believe it or not, there's an art not only to food and wine pairing, but also to eating and drinking at the same time and getting the most out of a match, that is, if you care to pay attention to the harmony or discord going on in your mouth. Most people don't think about it consciously, and aren't solely focused on finding a food and wine epiphany at the table every time, which is just fine. But you care, because you're reading this book (hopefully with a glass in hand and a little nibble on the side), and you want to experience the full effect of the tragedies and triumphs that await you.

When drinking wine while eating food, wine at the table can

- ✔ Rinse and refresh between bites
- ✔ Complement and enhance the food
- ✔ Improve in taste and texture thanks to the food
- ✔ Chill out, and neither affect, nor be affected, by the food

These sections examine this relationship a bit closer to see how you can taste your food and wine together.

Rinsing and refreshing between bites

Most people use wine, or any beverage for that matter, as a *rinsing agent,* a liquid to clear away what's in your mouth between bites of food. Some interaction still happens between the residual molecules of food and the sip of wine you take after you've finished swallowing, but for the most part, one partner in the food and wine dance has already left the floor. Saliva has diluted any remaining taste components, and *adaptation* (getting used to a smell so you don't notice it anymore; see Chapter 2 for more) has desensitized your nose to nuances of aroma and flavor. So by the time you sip the wine, not much dancing is going on.

Rinsing and refreshing can be good if the wine and food aren't really well-suited to each other. Rinsing and refreshing also explains in part why some people are perfectly happy drinking whatever wine they like with whatever food they're having. I know some of my colleagues may look on in horror if a guest orders a big, tannic red wine with a plate of raw oysters (which the majority of tasters, trained or not, will agree isn't a good match). But just maybe, the pause between bivalve and Barolo is long enough that the metallic flavor caused by the combination of salty iodine-rich oysters and abundant tannins in Barolo is mostly avoided, and nobody gets hurt.

On the other hand, this bite-pause-rinse-refresh approach also draws the curtain on a beautiful duet. All the wonderful synergy between two perfectly matched partners is missed if they're not experienced together. So if you want to give the dance a chance, read the next section.

Tasting and drinking at the same time

The best way to get the most out of a food-and-wine-pairing experience is to get both the wine and the food in your mouth at the same time. Doing so can be a challenging feat with certain foods, especially soups (try not dribbling on yourself when you open your mouth, full of soup, to take a sip of wine). With a little practice you can master it in no time.

To try this experiment, stick to my suggested steps, the way I taste food and wine at the same time:

1. **Taste the wine and pay attention to the experience.**

   Do it first before the food interferes with its flavor and texture.

2. **Pause and do the same with the food.**

   Try to get a handle on the dish without any distraction.

3. **Try them together.**

   Take another bite and chew until the food is more or less broken down, your saliva has had a chance to bring tastes into contact with your taste buds, and aromas/flavors have made their way back up to your nose. In other words, it's the point at which you're getting the full flavor experience of the dish. This is the perfect moment to take a sip of wine and pay attention as everything co-mingles and intimately gets to know one another, and the beautiful dance unfolds.

   At this time, you can experience the synergy of aromas and flavors, and the harmony of tastes. After that, you can just get on with enjoying the moment.

Grabbing a Bottle and Experimenting

Because every food and wine pairing, even the simplest combinations, involves more than one element of aroma and taste, even the pros can find the process complicated to decode and understand the positive or negative interactions with so much going on.

To make matters simpler for you, I've outlined a simple little experiment in which you can experience more or less on their own all the basic taste sensations — sweet, sour, bitter, salty, and savory. By doing this exercise in the next sections, you can see clearly how each basic taste on its own changes the taste and/or texture of wine. You can experience, for example, exactly how acidity or how sweetness in food affects the taste of a wine without interference from other taste sensations.

For this experiment in taste sensations, you need the following items:

- One bottle of wine (or more if you like; any type will do)
- Lemon or lime wedge (sour)
- A slice of red apple or dried fruit (apricots, raisins, prunes) (sweet)
- A pile of salt (salty)
- A few shelled walnuts (bitter/astringent)
- Unseasoned, rare-cooked beef (no salt or pepper) (umami)
- Tabasco or other hot sauce, cracked black pepper, or raw chile peppers (spice)

Working the experiment

Before you begin this simple taste experiment, remember that you're only focusing on the pure taste sensation. You're not interested in the aroma or flavor of anything. Because you're only focused on taste sensation, it doesn't matter whether you use a lemon or lime, a slice of fruit, or black pepper. Likewise, you can use any type of wine. You're not looking at how it tastes, but rather seeing how it *changes* for you when paired with the various taste sensations. All wines are affected in the same way, though the intensity of the change may differ depending on how much of a key taste a wine has — higher or lower acid, drier or sweeter, bitter (tannic) or less so, for example.

Stick to these steps for this simple experiment:

1. **Taste the wine first on its own, before you've had any food, and take note of its basic structure.**

   Focus on these three questions:

   - Is it dry or sweet?

   - Is it high acid (mouthwatering) or low acid (soft)?

   - Is it smooth textured (low, ripe tannin) or rough and astringent (high tannin)?

2. **Taste one food item, and have a sip of wine while the food is still in your mouth.**

   Observe how the food affects the taste and texture of the wine. Refer to the earlier section, "Tasting and drinking at the same time" for how to let the two co-mingle in your mouth.

   Some people find it easier to focus just on taste sensations without the distraction of any aromas or flavors by plugging their nose as they sample the food and have a sip of wine. Plugging your nose blocks your olfactory neurons and eliminates the aroma and flavor, leaving you only able to taste sweet, sour, bitter, salty, and savory sensations (refer to Chapter 2 for more on these sensations). Now you're looking for the changes in the way the wine tastes, caused by each food item.

3. **Work your way through each type of food by taking a sip of wine with it and observing the changing taste sensations.**

   Be sure to pause for a few moments between each combination to allow your palate to readjust, and sip some water.

   As you do this experiment, you should notice that food impacts the taste of wine much more than wine impacts the taste of food. A lemon doesn't become more acidic nor salt saltier by drinking wine, for example. But notice how each of these tastes dramatically affects the wine's taste. You're beginning to grasp the food and wine dance.

Recognizing what you experience

Knowing how each taste modifies wine gives you some amazingly useful insight into what taste combinations work. You can make an average wine that much better by enhancing its good side, or reducing its bad side, with the right food. You may likely experience the following during this experiment as you go through each taste and wine combination:

- **Wine with acidic foods (lemon):** The high acid makes wine taste sweeter and less acidic, creating a milder, softer texture. This change isn't surprising, because pretty much anything you put into your mouth after biting into a lemon seems sweeter and lower in acidity by comparison. Most people like this change. The exception may be a wine that is already very sweet on its own — it might become too sweet or cloying after high acid foods.

- **Wine with sweet foods (apple/dried fruit):** This taste gives you the reverse effect of acidity — sweet foods make wines taste more sour (higher acid) and bitter, intensifying the wine's texture and making it harder. If your sample wine is slightly sweet to begin with, the sweet food makes the wine taste drier. If you have a tannic red wine, the sweet food makes the wine taste even more astringent, sour, and bitter. Have you ever seen dry reds paired with dessert? Most people dislike this change, though a small percentage of the population enjoys the heightened sour-bitter sensation, especially those individuals used to bitter things, like black coffee, tea, or cruciferous vegetables.

✔ **Wine with salty foods:** Salt, like acidity, softens the texture of wine. It makes fruity flavors more pronounced and sweeter in all wines, and takes the bite out of tannins in reds (makes the wine seem smoother). Judicious salt addition to the right foods is the best way to soften the texture of young, robust red wines, which is a good change. Salt can also exaggerate the burning sensation of alcohol, a factor to consider when serving high alcohol wines with salty foods.

✔ **Bitter/astringent foods:** The slightly bitter and astringent walnut makes wine taste even more bitter and astringent. If there is already bitterness in the wine (from tannins, barrel-aging, and/or skin contact during production), you notice a cumulative, additive affect. Bitter and astringent foods don't affect white wines as much as reds (because they don't usually contain tannins and are therefore less bitter and astringent), and are thus generally good matches with bitter/astringent foods. High-acid white wines can also make food less bitter — think of squeezing lemon on your broccoli rabe or other bitter greens — so it's a win-win match.

✔ **Wines with umami-rich foods (cooked beef):** Like sweet and bitter/astringent foods, umami intensifies the taste of wine. Bitterness, astringency, and acidity are more pronounced. If the wine has been aged in oak, the umami-rich food makes the wine seem even oakier, maybe too oaky with savory foods. Umami also has an additive effect in both food and wine — umami+ umami= more umami flavor (a good thing because people like savory tastes), which is why umami-rich dishes work well with fully mature, savory wines, whose tannins have softened over time and texture has turned silky smooth, with no hard edges to intensify.

✔ **Wines with spicy foods:** Although spiciness isn't one of the five main tastes (it's a tactile sensation — see Chapter 2 for more on spice), it's nonetheless an important consideration in many dishes. The burn of spicy foods actually causes a minor, temporary inflammation of the mucus membranes and taste buds in your mouth. This effect initially heightens the sensation of other irritants, such as astringent tannins or high acidity. Oak seems more pronounced and fruit is diminished. But in time, as your palate becomes de-sensitized, this effect is reversed, reducing the impact of taste sensations on the taste buds to the point where the wine seems to have very little taste or flavor. In other words, spicy foods are a killer for wine. When spicy food hits the table, save your best wines for another time.

Putting Food and Wine Together: Four Outcomes

For all the apparent complexities of matching wine and food, all the results can be summed up into four main outcomes. These results are hardly official. They're just my take on how I classify my experiences.

 If you're really dedicated to understanding how food and wine work together, and want to remember the experiences, I suggest that you write down your observations. Writing them down can help you keep track of what you've discovered, particularly because alcohol is invariably involved, along with sometimes pleasant but distracting company. I keep a little notebook in my pocket to jot down my experiences, which I refer to now and then when looking for new combinations or inspirations for pairings. I usually sort each experience into one of the following four categories. **Remember:** The worst experiences are often the most educational (and memorable).

The Switzerland: Staying neutral

The reality about pairing food and wine is that it's rarely a total disaster. Most pairings result in shades of gray on the pleasure scale: various degrees of decent, good, better, or best. A lot of pairings, I'd say even the majority of food and wine combinations, fall into what I call the *Switzerland:* Neither the food nor the wine is dramatically changed.

All parties carry on with their business, maintaining neutrality and refusing to be engaged. The wine is fine, the food is fine, and the combination of the two is neither better nor worse than either on its own. There's no real synergy or antagonism. As such, Switzerland pairings are neither memorably good nor bad, and probably you'll just carry on with the meal and conversation without paying too much attention to food and drink. No harm done.

Not a pretty picture — the natural disaster

Every once in a while food and wine meet and the result is highly unpleasant. This result is what I call the *natural disaster* — when both the food and the wine were in the wrong place at the wrong time and combine to taste worse than either did on its own. Because of people's varying sensitivities to taste sensations and personal preferences, universal natural disasters are few and far between.

Shades of green: Enemies of wine

A little chemistry reveals why certain foods are enemies of wine and why you should probably steer clear of them with a glass of wine in hand. If you're planning on having a gathering or party with the wine flowing, avoid these three veggies. (Of course, I'm not anti-veggie. If you're not drinking wine, eat up!)

✔ **Asparagus** (the green variety) gets its bad rap from *methionine,* a sulfur-containing amino acid that when cooked turns into a compound that smells like rotten cabbage. Mix that with most wines, especially red, oak-aged and tannic, and you get a metallic, unpleasantly green taste. But cooking method matters; steamed or boiled asparagus is the worst form, while grilled asparagus is considerably less troublesome. Temper the bite of boiled asparagus with a rich hollandaise sauce, for example, and serve with a crisp, high-acid white.

I find Grüner Veltliner or Sauvignon Blanc work particularly well, even with steamed or boiled asparagus.

✔ **Brussels sprouts** are also problematic; their pronounced bitter taste (thanks to *phenylthiocarbamide*) makes most wines unpleasantly bitter. Again, high-acid, crisp, and dry whites are your best bet, because the acid tempers the sprouts' bitterness.

✔ **Artichokes** are the third veggie. They're everybody's textbook bad boy. With artichokes, the culprit compound is *cynarin,* a curious little acid that makes everything you taste afterwards seems objectionably sweet and flabby. But knowing this, you can save that unbearably acidic wine from the drain: Serve it up with artichokes and presto, your tart little wine is suddenly soft, sweet, and fruity!

In my experience, the pairings that most often end in predictable tragedy (albeit a first world–type of tragedy) seem to include seafood and shellfish. The oils in fatty fish like mackerel or black cod, or the sweet, umami-rich taste of scallops, for example, are disastrous with big, tannic red wines by most people's accounts. Together they taste like you're licking a can of tomatoes: metallic, bitter, and sour — I think you'll agree that that doesn't sound terribly nice. Other notoriously challenging foods with a high probability of causing natural disasters are really strong, runny cheeses (see Chapter 20 on pairing wine and cheese), along with things that come in shades of green. Check out the nearby sidebar for a discussion of these unfriendly vegetables paired with wine. Otherwise, dishes that are badly unbalanced on their own — maybe overly acidic or sweet or bitter — can also wreak havoc with wines.

One outshines the other: The solo spotlight

In this pairing, things start to get more interesting with a good solo in the spotlight. Here either the wine or the food shines supreme for its marvelous balance, depth, and complexity, without the need for a supporting actor. It's a monologue or soliloquy, in which the performer who's been written out of the script exits quietly to stage left, unharmed and content not to be interfering with the performance. This pairing can happen when a chef — especially one not known for his or her modesty, and feared for an unwillingness to work in partnership with the sommelier — creates a dish that is absolutely perfect on its own, a faultless balance and harmony of flavors achieved in the kitchen before the dish reaches the dominion of the sommelier. At this point, all that's required is a soft-spoken wine that won't get in the way of the food's shining spotlight. Light, fresh, crisp whites, sparkling wine, and low tannin red wines are the most versatile in this scenario.

Sometimes the wine shines. The dish becomes the backdrop, the frame, the canvas on which the wine paints its beauty. Whenever I have a special bottle that I want to enjoy to the fullest, I choose simple, sparse staging so that there's no confusion regarding who's in the spotlight. A classic rare roast of beef au jus with a first-rate mature Pinot Noir is a prime example: The roast makes a complementary but subdued partner and allows the complex Pinot to shine.

Pure heaven: The magical duet

Sometimes everything comes together: the magical duet. These sought-after moments are rare; even the pros can't reliably hit them, or even re-create them from a known script. You can't even think about all the variables — an extra dash of spice here, a more or less fresh piece of fish there, a minute or two less time on the grill, not to mention the constantly evolving wine, the changing company, your mood — a thousand and one things conspire to create the moment, and no two are ever the same. So don't sweat it; nobody gets it right all the time. But reading this book can help your batting average to improve. When you get it just right, it's a home run, a triumph, like endless hours of panning for gold to finally find that one nugget.

When the magical duet happens, the chef and the sommelier work together to get all the senses involved in the action and harmonize in the expression of pleasure. Neither the dish nor the wine has to be perfect on its own; the chef considers which textural and taste elements will fill in the blanks on the wine's canvas, while the sommelier selects the right finishing "condiment" for the food: the appropriate wine. Then the aromas and flavors of both the food and the wine meld together to become greater than the parts, like the perfumer's myriad essential oils blended just so to create the perfect fragrance, the ultimate expression of the parts. The food sculpts and polishes the texture of the wine, bonding seamlessly with it, while the wine unlocks hidden pockets of taste and textural sensations in the food. Very likely, too, the company is pleasant, the setting spectacular, and your mood better than fair. That's magic.

Experiment with more obscure wines

You may drink Pinot Gris or Chardonnay a lot. Sometimes you want to try more obscure wines with your favorite foods. If so, check out these wines. These whites are all generally crisp, dry, low or no-oak, while the reds are soft and zesty. They're worth tracking down, especially if you're traveling in these regions and find yourself surrounded by foreign grapes and don't know where to start.

Some reds include

- Zweigelt (Austria)
- Kadarka (Hungary)
- Trousseau/Bastardo (Jura, France, and Portugal)
- Mondeuse (Savoy, France)
- Sangiovese, pelaverga, grignolino, nerello mascalese, frappato (Italy)
- Agiorgitiko (Nemea, Greece)
- Blauer portugieser/kékoporto (Germany, Hungary)
- Tempranillo, mencía (Spain)

- Merlot (international; new world style)

Some whites include

- Grüner veltliner, rotgipfler (Austria)
- Assyrtiko, moscophilero, roditis (Greece)
- Garganega, verdicchio, arneis, cortese, pecorino, friulano (Italy)
- Rkatsiteli (Georgia, Russia)
- Vermentino/rolle (Sardinia, Tuscany, Provence, California, Australia)
- Verdejo and godello (Spain)
- Encruzado, arinto, verdelho (Portugal)
- Furmint, hárslevelü (Tokaj, Hungary)
- Welschriesling/olaszrizling (Eastern Europe)
- Pinot blanc (Alsace, international)
- Silvaner/sylvaner (Alsace, Germany)
- Chasselas, petite arvine (Switzerland)

Part II

The Nuts and Bolts: Developing Strategies for Food and Wine Pairing

The 5th Wave   By Rich Tennant

"Brother Dom Perignon, everyone really enjoys your sparkling mayonnaise and blanc de turnip soup, but could there not be something else you could make with these grapes?"

In this part . . .

Welcome to the nitty gritty of the book. If you're particularly serious about eating and drinking, and you want to absorb all the ground rules about what should and shouldn't work (at least as I see it), then this is the part for you.

In these chapters I reveal why the sommelier's job is so challenging (just to set you at ease), before diving into a bottom-up look at how tastes and aromas and flavors interact. I look at common ingredients and grape varieties that share aromas and flavors, which in turn make them naturally complementary — a sort of shopping list of things that go well together most of the time. I give you options and strategies for starting the match by considering the food first, or by starting with the wine first, depending on what you like best, what mood you're in, or what the situation demands.

Here you can also find pretty much everything I know about the theory of food and wine matching. I cover topics, such as determining the dominant component of a dish, considering the cooking method, looking to complement or contrast flavors and textures, and taking a regional approach to pairing.

I also reveal some sommelier's secrets on how to serve wine — the right glassware, temperature, decanting (or not) — as well as some tips on aging wines and pairing mature wines with food. Better grab a generous glass and settle in.

Chapter 4

Food and Wine Pairing 101: Getting It Right (Most of the Time)

*T*his chapter gets you started on the basics of thinking about food and wine together. After reading this chapter, you can recognize that, just as not everyone likes the same music or art or movies, the same wine and food combinations don't work for everyone — you bring a lot to the table. Some people are diehard foodies with an interest in wine, while others are wine fanatics who also like to eat. And with this in mind, I examine two basic approaches to pairing: one that starts with the food and one that starts with the wine. I also go deeply into the consideration of complementing or contrasting aromas and flavors, tastes, and textures. How you approach it is entirely up to you, and of course, you can go both ways, depending on your mood.

And what do you do if the table has multiple dishes at the same time? From tapas bars in Spain to tavernas in Greece, and all throughout Asia, multi-course dining is the rule, not the exception. I look at some strategies to handle the wide spectrum of flavors. Conversely, when the meal comes out course after course, what's the best way to order things so that excitement grows and your palate doesn't fall asleep and miss the main event? Read on to find out. And for the impatient (or the really hungry and thirsty), I suggest you skip to the last section where I lay out some handy guidelines for quick perusal that can set you on the right track without too much fuss.

Recognizing That Pairing Is Personal

Set yourself at ease and strike from your mind that universally perfect pairings exist. Here's why: Your mother was right. You're special; no one is quite like you, which means that what works for you when matching wines and foods doesn't necessarily work for everyone else, and vice versa. Because no two people are identical, two people sitting side by side, enjoying the same food with the same wine at the same time, are living two different experiences, perhaps similar, but maybe also quite different.

You can easily get caught in the trap of believing that something is wrong with your palate because you're not enjoying the wine, or the food, or the food and wine together, like your neighbor is. But some people are *supertasters,* blessed (or cursed) with an abundance of taste receptors; others are blissfully tolerant of strong taste sensations. Many of the differences are genetic (see Chapter 2 for a discussion of supertasters versus nontasters), but tasting also has to do with the nurture side: What you've experienced in the past determines what you like now. Solid evidence suggests that you shouldn't, or even can't, always go with the flow.

In the following sections, I look at how your preferences for certain tastes are determined in part by what you have grown up eating, and how your enjoyment of food and drink is also altered by what you think about them (as opposed to what you actually experience with your senses).

Realizing your taste preferences: What was in your lunchbox?

Did you grow up eating salads and vegetables or cookies and cakes? And now, do you put cream and sugar in your coffee, or do you take it black and unsweetened? In the world of taste and preference, familiarity breeds appreciation, not contempt. The familiar tastes of childhood are the ones that you tend to enjoy most, precisely because they're familiar and therefore comforting.

Taste preference has a strong cultural aspect. North Americans, for example, have high sugar diets: Everything from soft drinks to crackers contains some form of sugar (just check the list of ingredients in almost all processed foods next time you're in the supermarket). Many foods also have a heavy reliance on milk, butter, cream, and vanilla, which show up in thousands of recipes. As a result of the constant exposure to sweet tastes and creamy textures, North Americans on average have a statistical dislike of their less familiar opposites: bitterness and astringency. These taste preferences also translate to the wine world. Big, creamy, jammy wines? Bring 'em on.

On the other hand, consider southern Europeans. The dominant fat in this part of the world isn't butter but olive oil, not butter, which is markedly more bitter. And bitter greens — rapini, arugula, chard, chicory, and so on, make frequent appearances at the table. As a result, food and wine preferences in this part of the world lean toward more tolerance of, even preference for, bitter over sweet tastes, while astringency and acidity are also welcome familiar friends. Pick up a bottle of traditional Italian Chianti, and you can see what I mean by a preference for firm, tart, astringent, savory, and bitter.

Look at Southeast Asia and you'll notice that the natives seem to be able to consume mass quantities of chile peppers with oral (and intestinal tract) impunity, and that they also drink a lot of tannic and bitter teas. So, would you expect North Americans, southern European, and Asians to all like the same food and wine pairings?

Recognizing that meddling rational side

Genetics, culture, and thought all distinguish individuals. People are full of odd whims, erratic moods, and sentimental attachments. So what does that have to do with matching food and wine? Well, the reality is, growing evidence shows that all your human foibles deeply affect your world of perception.

The conflicting emotional and rational sides of the brain barge in, full of their preconceived notions about the world, trying to influence the way you interpret your sensory experiences. A tomato plucked straight from the garden tastes better than the identical tomato wrapped in cellophane and bought at the supermarket, because that's what you think should be the case — just as plenty of wine tastings have shown that a famous label or huge price tag cause a sudden gush of superlatives, even if it's bad wine poured secretly into a big-name branded bottle.

You likely aren't aware of it, but evidence also shows that eating with friends makes food taste better, that traditional foods are tastier if you're told they're traditional, and that battered, deep-fried crickets are perfectly enjoyable, provided you taste them before you know what's on the plate. The human sensory system — how you perceive the outside world by seeing, hearing, smelling, tasting, touching — isn't passive like a camera opening its shutter and capturing an image. It turns out that the camera — that you in fact — are fundamentally involved in creating and shaping that image; you see what you want to see and fill in a lot of blanks. All your experience, your context, deeply affects how you interpret your sensations.

This information is just to let you know that the sommelier's job of matching food and wine is harder than you think. So you shouldn't get too stressed, either.

Starting with what you like

Choosing foods and wines you enjoy is the most logical starting place when looking for successful pairings, and more importantly, for enjoyment, which is what you're after. Chicken curry and Vin Jaune from the Jura may well be a brilliant match, but if you hate curries and have never tasted Vin Jaune, it's less likely that you'll really enjoy the experience.

I don't mean you should never try new things. On the contrary, always keeping an open mind is important. But rather than jumping into unknown territory with both feet, you may want to try a new wine with your favorite food, or your favorite wine with a new dish as a start. If the match doesn't work out, then you can always switch to the rinsing-between-bites strategy (see Chapter 3), and at least you'll be enjoying one half of the equation.

Choosing Which Comes First: The Wine or Food?

So, are you a foodie or a wino? *Foodies* are people who enjoy eating a lot, and are keen to experiment and try new foods. They may enjoy drinking wine, too, but for them, food is the main event. At a restaurant, they always choose their dish before even picking up the wine list. They're flexible about what they drink, but they have strong opinions on what they eat.

Winos are the opposite. When a wino dines out, he or she immediately pores over the wine list after sitting down, chooses the wine first, and then looks at the menu to select a dish that will work with the wine. They're flexible about what they eat, but they're very clear on what they want to drink. (Naturally, people can be both foodies and winos depending on the occasion.) So, where are you most flexible — with the wine or with the food?

Knowing whether you're more flexible about what you eat or what you drink is the first step in setting up the match. In the following sections I look at both scenarios, with some strategies for getting it right no matter which direction you come from. And remember, you don't have to be exclusively either a foodie or a wino; I have a split personality and switch back and forth. Most people do however generally fall more often on one side than the other. Moonlighting as your alter ego is okay, too.

Matching Food to Wine: The Wino

I taste a lot of wine and am pretty clear about what I like and don't like. I'm far more flexible when it comes to food — I'll happily eat just about anything as long as it's not still alive (with some exceptions). So I'm a wino; I get the less flexible choice — the wine — out of the way first and go from there. The way I see it, no matter how magical the synergy between a wine and a dish may be, if it's a type of wine that doesn't set my dopamines aflutter, then the pairing will never be a ten-out-of-ten moment for me.

So when dining out, I choose the bottle first before considering the food (and when paying restaurant mark-ups for wine, I make sure it's something I like). I've no problem backtracking then to find a dish on the menu that will complement, or at least not kill, the wine. If I'm cooking at home, then I create a menu that showcases the wine in the best way, especially if it's a special bottle I've been saving for the right moment (see Chapter 25 for some suggested dishes to serve).

This approach has another advantage: The food can be altered right up until the moment it's served. I open and taste the wine before the food is served so that I can tweak the dish if necessary — a little adjustment to the acid or salt levels can take the pairing to a new level. But the wine, on the other hand, can't be materially changed (other than playing with temperature or decanting — see Chapter 8 for tips on serving wine). It is what it is at the moment it's served.

These sections cover some strategies on pairing foods to wines. I discuss how the style of the wine is a more important consideration than what grape(s) the wine is made from, and give some clues as to how you might know what style the wine will likely be from just reading the label.

Forgetting the grape and going with style

Food harmonizes with wine texture, taste, and flavor, not the name of the grape on the wine label. I've discovered along the way that the grape variety alone is often of very little help when looking for the right pairing. The trouble is that the wine style can vary so much. For instance, Chardonnay from Chablis in northern France has little to do with Chardonnay from Napa Valley in California, even if the grape is exactly the same. The one is lean, steely, and full of nerve, while the other is round, generously proportioned, and buttery. Ceviche may be a perfect match for the first, and butter chicken may be right for the second. But switch them around, and you'll have fewer smiling faces sitting at your dining table.

People often focus so much on the grape and not the style, especially with the most popular, widely grown international grapes — household names like Chardonnay, Sauvignon Blanc, Cabernet Sauvignon, Merlot, Pinot Gris/Grigio, Pinot Noir, and others. They grow in so many different places, climates, and soils, and they're interpreted by so many different winemakers with so many different tools in their winemaking kit, that any consistency related to genetics is all but gone.

I find pairing to wine style is more useful. In the chapters in Part III, I set out a manageable handful of wine styles into which pretty much the entire world of wine can be slotted, regardless of the thousands of different varieties currently grown. Although it's a starting point, remember that nothing beats first-hand experience. Taste before you buy whenever possible. If you can't taste, ask the merchant or server which of the main style categories the wine falls into (and Part III gives you the vocabulary).

Knowing what to expect from a bottle you've never tried

If you're completely in the dark about a bottle, ask for help from the merchant/sommelier/gift giver. If that person isn't much help, the wine's label can still give you some help. Look for the few clues you can find about the wine's geographic origin, price, and even the label style, to pry open the mystery and shed some light on what to expect. In this age of the smartphone, you can also instantly check out details on virtually every wine via the Internet, too.

Going on a virtual tour of the region

Wine is one of the few consumer goods in the world that is intimately tied to its place of origin, so read the label to discover where the wine was made. The wine may be as general as southeastern Australia or as specific as a single vineyard, but in either case, you can visibly read the wine's country/region or origin. Dust off your geography knowledge and take yourself on a virtual tour of the region. What does the place look like? Do you visualize palm trees or pine trees growing around the vineyards? Clear blue ocean waters or snow-covered peaks in the background? Can you ski there in winter?

Climate affects wine style as much as any other factor. The cooler the region — pine trees and/or mountains and skiing — the lighter, crisper, and more tart fruit-flavored (lower alcohol, higher acidity) the wine is likely to be. Conversely, swaying palms and subtropical temperatures translate into robust, full-bodied, ripe orchard, tropical, or even dried/baked fruit-flavored wines. Are there exceptions? You bet. But you have to start somewhere.

Pricing: The (imperfect) guide

Price is also a useful though imperfect guide to wine style. As with any consumer good, price is skewed by things such as brand recognition, scarcity, and celebrity endorsements. But all things being equal, the more expensive the wine, the more stuff that people expect in high-priced wines, such as flavor intensity, depth, ripeness, complexity, structure, tannins, oak flavor, and the like, it will have. An expensive wine often needs time in the cellar for all these pieces to fit together, so it may not be the best choice for drinking tonight. If you insist, and especially if it's red, you want to match it to a dish that softens texture — something with high protein, fat, and salt content, such as a hard, tangy piece of cheese or well-marbled steak (see Chapter 3 for more on how food changes the texture of wine).

On the other hand, inexpensive wines are generally lighter, fresher, and fruitier, with little or no oak and ready to enjoy straight off the shelf. Cheap wines are perfect when you want some easygoing, versatile refreshment, such as when the table has multiple dishes at the same time, or when serving really spicy food that would clobber all the benefits worth paying more for in expensive wine.

Interpreting the label

If the region, grape/appellation, or producer means nothing to you, the next most useful bit of information on the label is the alcohol level, which the law requires. Wines range from about 5.5 percent at the very lowest end (for sweet, fizzy Moscato d'Asti) up to 22 percent for some *fortified* wines, to which neutral grape spirit has been added, so the range is huge. But sticking to dry table wines, the range shrinks to around 11 to 16 percent. The alcohol level can give you three useful clues:

- **Body:** The higher the alcohol, the more full-bodied the wine. Alcohol contributes to *viscosity,* the sensation of richness and roundness in the mouth.

- **Flavor range:** Because alcohol depends on ripeness, the riper the grapes at harvest, the more alcohol you'll end up with. At the upper end of the scale, above 14 percent, wines taste more like ultra ripe, sweet tropical fruit, or even baked/cooked/dried fruit.

- **Texture:** High-alcohol wines are generally softer and creamier with lower acidity. These factors combine to give a vaguely sweet impression even in the absence of sugar (alcohol on its own has a slightly sweet taste).

Label design

The design of the label itself is another potential clue to wine style. In fact, most consumers base their wine-purchasing decisions on the label alone. What is it about a label that attracts attention? Producers know that the right packaging is key to success, and labels are intended to convey the product's image, and in turn attract consumers who view themselves in the same way (remember, people like familiar things).

Colorful, whimsical labels with cute animals transmit the message of fun, unpretentious wine, full of lively fruit and soft, widely appealing texture. A stately château or gothic script straight out of the 18th century, on the other hand, delivers an unambiguous message of traditionalism. In wine terms, this image means a solid, age-worthy wine, firm and austere, the way your grandfather would have liked it. Likewise, a stylish, fashionably modern design denotes stylish, modern wine: highly polished, generously fruity and oaky, and probably ready to enjoy now.

Matching Wine to Food: The Foodie

Foodies, those individuals for whom the food comes first, are more flexible than winos about which wine is served. The dish is the most important element of the pairing; it's the main source of dopamine stimulation and pleasure. The wine, too, can be great, but needn't be. Its role is to support the lead actor, without boldly bulldozing the affair. If you're a foodie, you select the most tantalizing dish on the menu or create your own perfect at-home meal, and then you set about figuring out which wine will work best with it.

In the following sections, I show you how to look at a dish like a sommelier, focusing on the parts and cooking methods that determine the best wine match. I examine two opposing strategies: complementing or contrasting texture and flavor. Many sommeliers have contributed to establishing these principles over decades of *serious* research (for an excellent discussion, look also to technical editor Evan Goldstein's first book, *Perfect Pairings: A Master Sommelier's Practical Advice for Partnering Wine with Food* (University of California Press)).

Determining the primary or dominant component of the dish

As a foodie, you take your cue from the most intense taste component of a dish to make the match. A wise sommelier once said: "You can't match wine to chicken." What? Well of course you can. What is meant is that chicken rarely comes unadorned — it's just the vehicle to deliver other flavors and tastes (and if it does, it's so neutral in flavor that any wine will pair well with it). Roasted with lemon and herbs, *coq au vin*, Cajun-style, in Thai green curry, whatever the case, the preparation — the dominant taste — is key.

You have to know what comes on the chicken and how it's prepared to figure out the best match.

The same is true for all dishes. I start by looking for the main taste: Is the dish very salty, bitter, spicy, sweet, sour, or particularly savory? I then narrow the wine choice down to the style that will improve next to the dominant taste, like a tart wine with a high acid dish, or a slightly sweet wine with sweet foods. See Chapter 3 for more details on how taste affects wine.

Remembering the sauces, condiments, or side dishes

Don't forget that the main ingredient listed on the menu often isn't the dominant element in a dish — it's the sauce or condiment that matters, and which can drive the pairing. Most forms of protein, whether fish, poultry, red meat, or tofu, carry the chef's intended tastes, texture, and flavors, like canvas holding paint. Barbeque sauces, curries, braising liquids, chutneys, salsas, chimichurries, moles — just about every imaginable sauce carries the taste sensations and aroma/flavor compounds that can determine the best match.

In the case of strongly sauced dishes, focus your matching on the sauce's dominant taste. For spicy curries, for example, the primary consideration is the burn of chiles. I'd select a wine with a degree of sweetness to counter the spice and little or no oak that would be exaggerated by it. Braising liquids are usually umami-rich, making them great foils for mature, umami-rich wines. High acid sauces, such as vinegar or lime-based chimichurris, need a high acid wine to balance, or a high acid, sweet (or fruity) wine if the condiment is especially spicy. Matching the particular flavors of the sauce with similar flavors in wine is a secondary consideration, but part of a magical duet to be sure.

Cooking up different methods

If the sauce or condiment isn't the prime driving factor, consider the cooking method, which has a huge impact on flavor intensity. For example, imagine poached versus pan-seared versus oven-roasted versus wood-oven roasted versus charcoal barbequed. Each of these cooking methods kicks up the flavor intensity a notch no matter what you're cooking. And the more intense the flavor of the dish, the more intensity it can handle in the wine without getting lost. With poached rainbow trout for example, you may serve a light, crisp, delicate unoaked white. When pan-seared or barbequed, a more full-bodied, even lightly oaked white, dry rosé, or lighter style red wine is a better match.

Touching on texture: Making wines softer and smoother

Texture is an important part of both food and wine enjoyment. Remember that food changes the texture of wine, but wine doesn't really change the texture of food. A wine can do little to save a soggy, mushy, rubbery, chewy, or leathery dish, and cooks try to avoid these textures. But food can do much to improve the texture of wine, or at least highlight the more appealing sides. Most people (with exceptions) prefer softer, rounder, and smoother as opposed to harder, leaner, and more austere, and with the right dish, you can serve wines that otherwise may be unpleasantly chewy, tannic, or acidic on their own, but absolutely perfect with a dish that works to soften the wine. See Chapter 3 for a discussion on the textural interaction between wine and food, and the later section on matching or contrasting texture.

Finding flavor harmony

When pairing food and wine, considering the flavor match (or contrast) comes after looking at taste and texture harmony, which is where most pairings are made or broken. Although it may seem a good idea to serve a Mediterranean herb-flavored dish with a wine of similar flavors, if the wine becomes unpleasantly astringent or tart or sweet because of mismatched tastes and textures, you'll quickly forget about any synergy of flavors.

People adapt to flavors (and start to ignore them; see Chapter 2 for additional insight) much more readily than they adapt to textures. For me, after I figure out the most appropriate wine style for the dish, be it light, zesty, low tannin red, or rich, bold, and fruity new world–style red, only then do I set about looking for complementary aromas and flavors to perfect the pairing. See the later section, "Matching versus contrasting flavors" for all the details.

Identifying the Contrast or Complement: Well, Thank You Very Much

The following sections contain two basic, but opposite approaches to making the match, whether starting with the food or the wine. Finding the right partnership is all about the contrast or the complement, that is, looking for the same flavors and textures in both food and wine, or looking for their opposite. Often both approaches work in various situations, so it's up to you which way you feel like going tonight.

Matching versus contrasting textures

The texture of food also can be either matched or contrasted by your wine selection. A soft, unctuous, ripe California Chardonnay with a silky-smooth corn chowder, sumptuous white Burgundy with poached halibut, or crisp, dry sparkling wine with crunchy deep-fried calamari are examples of matching food and wine textures.

Contrasting texture, like contrasting flavor, is a little less intuitive and more challenging, at least in my experience. Remember that most people prefer softer, smoother textures to harder, more astringent textures. Big, voluptuously textured foods like buttery mashed potatoes or cream-based sauces tend to also have big flavors, which can easily overwhelm a light, thin, delicate wine. It's not a disaster, but the wine gets steamrolled, so I hope you didn't pull a cherished special bottle you've been waiting years to drink. Likewise, light, crunchy-textured foods, usually in the form of raw ingredients on the plate, such as salad greens or very lightly cooked vegetables, are usually accompanied by acidity of some form (vinaigrette or a squeeze of lemon) and often have an inherent bitterness, both of which can make soft, smooth-textured wines seems overly flabby. So I find in most cases that mirroring textures is the most successful approach, but never be afraid to experiment.

Whether contrasting on complementing, consider the texture of the dish. It could be crisp, such as deep-fried calamari or southern-style fried chicken, or crunchy like delicately steamed vegetables or certain raw foods. Fat and oil in food (animal, dairy, vegetable, nut, and so forth) contribute to a softer, creamy texture, as in cream of mushroom soup or beef Stroganoff, while cooking methods also determine not only flavor intensity but also texture to a large degree, such as the soft, melt-in-your-mouth texture of slow-braised beef cheeks of short ribs, or the chewy texture of a rare-cooked steak.

Mirroring texture

Select a wine with a texture that mirrors what's on the plate. For example, a firm, chewy, tannic old world–style red works nicely with similarly chewy, rare-grilled beef, while much softer-textured braised beef dishes are delicious with round, soft, new world–style reds or mature wines without any hard, astringent edges. Creamy mushroom soup or beef Stroganoff would be enjoyable with an equally smooth and creamy-textured white wine, but would make a light, crisp wine seem even lighter and leaner, generally not a desirable change. Crispy-crunchy foods work with crunchy, high acid wines, ones that are like biting into a crisp green apple.

Contrasting texture

Some of the more successful contrasts involve pitting high acid wine against rich, fatty food. Take a zesty Italian Sangiovese with mouth-watering acid and drink alongside a rich pasta Bolognese, or a crisp, unoaked Chardonnay-like Chablis with a Burgundian classic dish, snails in garlic butter: In both cases it's lean, tart, and crunchy versus creamy, fatty, and chewy. The crunch of acid and carbon dioxide in dry Champagne or sparkling wine is also a refreshing contrast to the velvety-smooth texture of an oyster. The one slides effortlessly down the throat while the other perks up the taste buds.

At the very least, if a true synergy between food and wine isn't there, then your mouth will get a good scouring between bites, and maybe even keep your arteries running a little clearer.

Matching versus contrasting flavors

Flavor families focus on the concept that certain ingredients pair well together because they share flavor compounds. For example, sweet corn and lobster, onions and garlic, basil and tomato, are successfully brought together because they have overlapping, complementary flavors.

Wines also share many aromatic compounds with food, such as the peachy flavor of both Riesling and cooked pork, or the matching flavor of crème caramel and sweet, barrel-aged late harvest wines. No wonder they match well together — they have such a similar flavor profile. As with anything involving food and wine, complementing flavors isn't foolproof, but it's a good start.

Harmonizing flavors

Take classic whitefish ceviche. The key element in the dish isn't the fish, which is just a simple protein vehicle (it could be bay scallops, grouper, halibut, tuna or whatever); it's the acid (lime or lemon juice) used to "cook" the raw fish that matters, along with its toothsome texture. Because acid intensifies the astringency and bitterness of tannins, you want to avoid most reds. Acid also makes soft wines taste sweet and flabby and oak oakier — equally unpleasant directions. So the answer? A dry, high acid, unoaked white is your starting point. This type also matches the firm texture of the fish, while salt focuses its fruit flavors.

Crisp, unoaked whites are made in dozens of places around the world, and all work just fine. But to take the match to the next level, you can look to flavor: The main flavors here are cilantro and other fresh sweet herbs in the parsley family, and green pepper is also included in most ceviche recipes. You get a nice synergy of aroma and flavor by choosing a crisp dry white that also has flavor in the same family, like Sauvignon Blanc. For one last expert's touch, look for regional harmony: Ceviche is typically Latin American, so go to a place in that part of the world where crisp, dry, unoaked Sauvignon Blanc is made. Chile's Casablanca or Leyda Valleys come to mind. Bingo — taste, texture, flavor, and regional harmony — the magical duet. (Refer to Chapter 6 for more on regional pairings.)

Diverging flavors

Looking for contrasting flavors is another option. A fresh, fruity, red berry-scented rosé and a curried chicken salad, for example, or a full-throttle, super ripe, jammy Zinfandel with southern-style, smoky barbeque back ribs share few flavor similarities, but the pairing works because of the stark contrast between food and wine. These two different sets of flavors work to set one another off to better effect — think of it like the *Odd Couple* pairing. Sometimes too much of the same is boring, whereas opposites attract, and double the pleasure.

Dealing With Multiple Dishes on the Table versus Successive Courses

All's well and fine when you're dealing with one course and one wine; you can work your magic one pairing at a time. But what do you do when the table has multiple dishes at the same time? Most Chinese, Indian, Latin American, and Mediterranean meals involve lots of different flavors on the table all at once. The simple answer is to forget about perfect harmony across the board (which is impossible anyway), and work with versatile wines.

Tannins and oak are the likely culprits when a pairing goes awry (bitter taste, astringent texture); they're the most reactive elements in wine. In the wrong partnership, they're intensified to the point of unpleasantness. With everything else, no real natural disasters occur. Thus the most versatile wines have low/no oak or tannins.

Balanced, crisp, dry white, red, and sparkling wines are more or less foolproof. Although they occasionally get railroaded by big flavor and sweet or spicy foods, nobody will get hurt. Think of such wines as the wedge of lemon or lime that accompanies everything from oysters to tacos to pad Thai to grilled lamb chops. Zesty wines enhance flavor, and at the very least, rinse out your mouth between bites. When serving multi-dish meals, I like to throw two, three, or even more different types of wine on the table and let guests have at it, discovering their own Switzerlands or solo spotlights (see Chapter 3 for more information).

The next sections deal with how your palate can get tired and de-sensitized after an onslaught of flavors and textures, and how to order the wines in a multicourse with the goal of minimizing this palate fatigue.

Being aware of palate fatigue

Like your muscles at the gym, overuse wears out your olfactory neurons and taste buds over a period of eating and especially drinking wine. It's called *palate fatigue,* a fancy way of saying that you can't taste and distinguish between flavors anymore, and that your brain doesn't really care. I don't mean simple intoxication, though that's also a consideration, but rather basic physical exhaustion.

Pro tasters claim that they can taste dozens of wines in a session (spitting, of course) and still make sense of them, but most normal individuals lose their faculties after far fewer glasses. In my experience, a dinner with any more than five or six different wines is stretching it, so make sure you're aware of palate fatigue when serving long, multicourse meals. If you've gone overboard, then very likely toward the end, nobody will pay much attention to the wine and food pairings that you've worked so hard to get right.

Ordering the wines for a dinner

For a multicourse meal, you can order the wines in such a way as to not knock out your taste buds off the top. By moving from lower to higher intensity, your guests can enjoy each wine in a fitting progression such that the preceding doesn't overpower the following, and each can be appreciated to the fullest. Refer to Chapter 8 for more information about what order to serve wines in a multicourse meal.

Referencing Some Handy Guidelines for Your Quick Perusal

The next sections contain your quick reference for basic combinations to avoid or seek out with food and wine. Stick these suggestions in your back pocket, follow as many of them as possible, and things should work out well enough most of the time. They may even lead to a little food and wine magic.

Fight in your weight category

One of the most effective strategies is to pair wines and foods of equal flavor intensity, relative weight, and texture. Match equal weights — light with light, heavy with heavy, and so on. In wine, alcohol and sugar are the great body boosters. The more of either (or both), the more full-bodied the wine is. In food, fat is the main contributor of body and comes in many forms. Dairy fat (butter, milk, cream, yogurt, crème fraîche, cheese, and so forth), animal fat, vegetable oils (corn, canola, olive, palm, avocado, and so on) and nut oils (coconut, peanut, walnut, sesame, and such) all contribute body to a dish — a greater sense of weight, richness, and mouth-coating flavor.

The richer the dish, the more substantial the wine needs to be in order to stand its ground and not be overwhelmed by the food. Lobster in a citrus beurre blanc with new world, warm climate Chardonnay is a prime example of full-bodied with full, fatty flavor, as is an Indian *nalli korma,* (braised lamb shank with cashew, saffron, green chile, masala, yogurt, and cardamom) with a big and bold, generously alcoholic Shiraz-Viognier from the Barossa Valley.

Contrarily, light, crisp-textured, low-fat dishes, such as fresh salads with vinaigrette, cruciferous vegetables (without butter), raw or lightly cooked seafood and shellfish (such as sushi and sashimi), or seafood paella often pair marvelously with equally light, crisp, high acid wines (red, white, or rosé). Acidity in the wine enhances the flavors of such foods, while high sugar and/or alcohol would just get in the way and steamroll the food.

Acidity needs acidity

You want to match high acid foods with high acid wines. The effect high acid foods have on wine is quite dramatic. Acidic foods make wines taste softer and fruitier, even sweeter. Unlike the synergistic effect of, say, umami + umami creating even greater savory tastes, acidity matched with acidity cancels each other out, allowing more fruit flavor in the wine and ingredient flavor in the dish to emerge. (Refer to Chapter 3 for more details.) In some instances, wines that seem overly shrill and acidic when sipped on their own become milder and softer, and more enjoyable, when served with a salad dressed with tart vinaigrette, or sauerkraut, for example.

Fish oils love acidity but hate tannins

You want to avoid highly tannic wines with fatty fish to save yourself from that fishy aftertaste. Fish contains fish oil, which has an abundance of omega-3 fatty acids. Omega-3s offers several health benefits according to most studies, but also cause difficulties for the sommelier in finding the right wine match. Tannic acid, found in astringent red wines, seems to clash with omega-3 acids, with the net result being an unpleasantly metallic aftertaste in the mouth.

For this reason, stay away from tannic, astringent wines with fatty fish (low-tannin, zesty reds can work). Fish with particularly high levels of omega-3s include tuna, salmon, halibut, shark, swordfish, tilefish, anchovies, and mackerel. Scallops, too, are one of the most troublesome foodstuffs to pair with wine.

High acidity, on the other hand, is perfect for cutting through the fatty acids of fish and coaxing more flavor out of the flesh — hence the reason why most fish is served with a lemon, lime, or other source of acid alongside, or built into the accompanying sauce.

Red wine and fish don't mix

The dictum of avoiding red wine with fish is as old as fish and red wine, but the actual cause of the unpleasantly fishy-metallic taste provoked by certain fish and wine combinations has remained somewhat elusive. The most recent research into the underlying chemistry of the mismatch has uncovered the possible culprit: iron. Research showed that the formation of the compounds responsible for the disagreeable fishy aftertaste (in this study, scallops were used) depended directly on the iron content of the sample wine — the more iron in the wine, the more pronounced the fishy aftertaste — as confirmed by a panel of sensory experts as well as by *gas chromatograph,* a fancy machine that measures the relative concentration of volatile compounds. When scallops were soaked in wine, the high-iron samples created more of the compounds responsible for the bad flavor, and at higher intensities, than the low-iron samples.

This research is at once interesting and frustrating, because you can't easily know how much iron is in a wine, short of chemical analysis; it depends on the iron content in the soil where the grapes were grown and a myriad of processing and storing decisions mostly unknown to the consumer. But because iron most likely comes from grape skins, and all red wines are made with skin contact (but only some whites), it follows logically that red wine generally contains more iron than white. It also seems likely that thicker-skinned red varieties would result in higher iron content on average (more room to store iron), while these same thick-skinned grapes result in more tannic wines (thicker skins equal more tannin to extract). Thus big, tannic wines most likely have higher iron content. So the tactic of avoiding tannic reds with fish is a sound start. But until you actually taste the combination, you'll never really know. I've been surprised before by a few tannic wine and fish combinations that work nicely.

Tannins love fat and salt

Serve tannic wines with fatty, salty food. *Tannins* are the natural compounds that give reds (and very occasionally, whites and rosés) their astringent, mouth-puckering texture, and vaguely bitter taste. Most people find astringency and bitterness disagreeable, so try and lessen their sensory impact when selecting food to match. Salt and fat, especially animal fat, buffer tannins. The fat coats and protects your mouth against the rough astringency of tannins. On the other hand, high acid foods make tannins seem even more astringent and hard.

Tannins and spice, not so nice

Avoid tannic wines with spicy (hot) food. Chiles and other ingredients contain *capsaicin,* the compound that gives them their burn and causes irritation in the mouth, sometimes even significant pain. Tannins, too, with their astringent texture, are oral irritants. If you want to avoid the double irritation of burning astringency, avoid tannic wines with spicy foods.

Acidity cuts saltiness

Serve salty foods with high acid wines. Acidity causes you to salivate — it's your body attempting to neutralize the acid with your (basic) saliva. A sip of crisp wine, which induces saliva, can dilute the high salt concentration of certain foods. The saliva in turn diminishes the salty taste.

On the flip side, because salt is also an unmatched flavor enhancer, high salt foods can make otherwise lean and modestly flavored wines into soft and fruity delights. Think of that pinch of salt added to cantaloupe or other fruits to enhance the sweet taste and boost the fruit flavor: Your wine could also benefit from a wee dash of salt from food.

Sweets need sweets

Serve a wine that's at least as sweet, if not sweeter, than the food accompanying it. This strategy follows from the logical sweet-sour continuum. Anything you taste directly after eating something sour will seem relatively sweeter, and anything you eat after something sweet will seem relatively more sour — it's a basic theory of relativity.

Because most likely you don't want your wine to appear leaner and more sour than it is after a bite of food (most people naturally prefer softer, fruitier, and sweeter things), make sure it can hold its own. If it's as sweet or sweeter than the dish, it'll be just fine. This concept holds true not just for very sweet dessert courses, but also for any savory dishes that have a noticeably sweet profile from the inclusion of such inherently sweet ingredients as fruit, beets, sweet potatoes, or honey, if not straight sugar or syrup of some kind.

Beware the oak tree

Really oaky wines tend to railroad most foods, so avoid them with anything but the most intensely flavored dishes. All high flavor-impact cooking methods, such as charring, grilling, and roasting, can generate enough smoky, charred-bitter flavors to match up to oakier styles of white or red wine. All things considered, low or unoaked wines are far more versatile at the table.

High alcohol + spicy = fire

Avoid really high-alcohol wines with really spicy foods. Capsaicin is soluble in alcohol, meaning that the burn of chiles and other hot spices is dissolved and therefore actually lessened by moderately high-alcohol wines, but up to a point. By moderately high-alcohol, I mean up to about 14 percent; much beyond that, and especially when you're into the fortified wine category at 15.5 percent alcohol and more, you reach the point of diminishing returns and actually increase the burn.

At low concentrations, alcohol has a vaguely sweet taste. At high concentrations, it has a burn of its own — think of a shot of grappa or tequila or scotch at 40 percent and more. Remember that burn? High-alcohol wines thus contribute to the burning sensation of spicy foods, adding fuel to the fire, literally. Already hot dishes can become unbearable, though it must be noted that some cultures, and some people, enjoy the burn of comestibles.

Spicy + sugar = no (or minimal) fire

Lessen the burn of spicy foods by serving an off-dry or sweet wine. Different cultures around the world have developed different strategies for mitigating the burn of spicy foods — dairy fat, starch, acidity, and others — but by all accounts, the most effective anti-spice measure is sugar. Whether it's the sweet chutney served with an Indian curry, the fresh mango served with Thai curries, or the actual sugar used in hot Szechuan dishes to balance the heat, sugar calms the burn. The appropriate wine pairing can do the same (but don't expect the burn to disappear altogether, which is fine, because you probably ordered the dish for a little heat in the first place).

Chapter 5

Focusing on the Food: Flavor, Aroma, and Taste Harmony

*W*hen pairing food and wine, one of the first things to consider is the dominant taste sensation of the dish, which in turn affects the taste and texture of the wine. Though most of the common things you eat are wonderfully complex combinations of multiple aromas and different tastes, some food items are dominated by a single, dominant taste, such as sweet, sour, bitter, salty, or savory, or the tactile sensation of spiciness, or at least one that determines the best wine pairing. The bitterness of certain leafy greens, the umami taste of mushrooms, or the saltiness of soy sauce, for example, are what guide your wine pick when these ingredients dominate a dish. In this chapter, I provide a quick roundup of some foods with their dominant taste profiles, so if you come across them on the plate, you know they need to be considered when picking your best match.

After you consider the taste harmony, you can move on to fine-tuning the match: considering the aromas and flavors of the main ingredient(s). Despite a seemingly limitless array of flavorings, ingredients can be broken down into general associations based on similar aromas and flavors. I call them *flavor families*, which are groupings of common things used to flavor foods like herbs and spices, but also some fruits, vegetables, dairy products, and even proteins, which share aroma and flavor compounds. I focus on three families: parsley, terpenes, and sotolone; think of them as food relatives, sharing more or less DNA depending how distant they are.

These families help you better identify a food's main flavoring and allow you to understand the interconnectedness of common combinations such as dark chocolate and coconut, cucumber and dill, or vanilla and cream, for example. These timeless pairings have an affinity for one another, and they appear jointly again and again in recipes from all over the world because they're just naturally complementary — and that's because they share a significant number of flavor molecules.

In this chapter, I also highlight some grape varieties that make wines with similar or complementary aromas and flavors, the naturally synergistic combinations from an aromatic perspective, which almost always pair well.

This chapter can spark your culinary creativity in the kitchen. You can use the information provided as building blocks for your own flavor explorations to arrive at new, unusual combinations. And with some familiarity with the main flavor families and the grapes related to each, the ultimate step of matching wine and food can also come more naturally.

Considering Taste First: Picking Out the Main Sensations

Taste is often the main driver of successful pairings. After the main sensation is sorted out with a suitable match, the quest for aroma and flavor synergy begins. Foods have complex tastes, rarely identified by a lone sensation. All successful food creations are a balancing act, like the bitter-sweet duo of dark chocolate, or sweet-sour-salty-spicy combination of a typical Asian dipping sauce. But in many cases, dishes are sufficiently dominated by one of the five tastes (or by hot spice — a tactile sensation but included along with taste) to make that the defining element in a wine pairing. The pronounced bitterness of certain leafy greens, the high acid of a vinaigrette-dressed salad, or the burning spice of a vindaloo, for example, are the main considerations that drive your wine choice over considerations of flavor. The following sections include lists of foods that fit under each main taste category.

To utilize the following sections, look at the main ingredients in a dish and see if any of them turn up in one of the following lists under the five taste sensations or pungent spice. Chances are if any of these listed ingredients figure in the dish, they'll be an important consideration when picking your wine match.

The presence of hot chile peppers in just about any recipe (or one of the other ingredients listed under "Piquant performers"), on the other hand, is your key ingredient. Your pairing in this case will be governed by the burn of spice.

Salty stuff

Saltiness is one of the five main taste categories. Although sodium chloride, or salt, doesn't occur naturally in significant levels in raw foods, it's near ubiquitous in processed and preserved foods, which are the major source of salt in your diet aside from what you add from the shaker. Because salt is both a flavor enhancer and a preservative, just about everything that comes in a package, jar, or can contains salt. Here are some common preserved or processed ingredients that can raise the salty taste of any dish:

- Anchovies
- Bacon
- Capers
- Fish sauce
- Hard cheese

- Miso
- Olives
- Pickles
- Soy sauce
- Store-bought broth

When choosing wines with salty foods, keep the following in mind for successful matches:

- Choose wines with some residual sugar, or an impression of sweetness from ripe grapes and fruity flavors, red or white. Salty and sweet make a nice couple.
- Choose young reds with a firm texture that could use a little softening, because salt renders wines milder and less astringent.
- Avoid high-alcohol or very oaky wines — both these elements will be exaggerated.

Sweet things

Sugar, like salt, is added to foods in refined forms to sweeten and preserve them. But unlike salt, sugars also occur naturally in a healthier, unrefined form in unprocessed foods. The following naturally sweet foods can increase the sweet taste in dishes:

- Beets
- Butternut squash
- Birch syrup
- Corn
- Cream/whole milk
- Dried fruit of all kinds

- Fruit (especially when cooked or dried)
- Honey
- Maple syrup
- Sweet potatoes
- Yams

For successful matches with sweet foods, you want to choose a wine that is at least as sweet as the food being served.

Bitter bites

Many bitter compounds occur naturally in the food you eat. Scientists often use *quinine* — what gives tonic water a bitter taste — as a benchmark for bitterness, but there are dozens of other common bitter substances. The following foods have a pronounced bitter profile:

- Arugula
- Asian bitter gourd
- Broccoli
- Cabbage
- Caffeine
- Cauliflower
- Chicory, escarole
- Citrus peel

- Cress
- Dandelion greens
- Olives
- Rapini
- Turnip
- Unsweetened cacao (bitter chocolate)
- Watercress

For successful matches with bitter foods:

- Avoid bitter and tannic wines.
- Choose crisp, high-acid whites.
- Choose soft, fruit-forward reds.

Sour and tart sources

Acid, which gives food a sour or tart taste in varying degrees, naturally comes in many forms. Like salt, acid is a preservative (bacteria don't like to swim in acidic waters), and is a key component in pickled and brined foods. Every balanced dish, from vinaigrette-laced salads to stews, needs acid to bring flavor alive. Here are some food-based sources that can raise the tartness:

- Apples (especially green apples)
- Cheese (especially goat's cheese)
- Citrus fruit
- Kimchi

- Pickled vegetables
- Sauerkraut
- Sour cream/crème fraîche
- Vinegar of all types
- Yogurt

For successful matches with sour foods:

- ✔ Choose high acid wines.
- ✔ Avoid sweet or low acid wines, which will taste flabby and cloying.
- ✔ Avoid tannic and bitter (red) wines.

Savory (umami) substances

Glutamic (amino) acids trigger the savory taste. *Umami* means "delicious taste" in Japanese; see Chapter 2 for more details on umami. It occurs naturally in many foods and is also added widely in the form of monosodium glutamate (MSG). Here's a list of amino acid-rich foods:

- ✔ Anchovies and anchovy sauce
- ✔ Caviar
- ✔ Chinese cabbage
- ✔ Cooked onions, spinach
- ✔ Crab meat
- ✔ Cured ham, dried sausages
- ✔ Dried bonito
- ✔ Grilled, aged beef
- ✔ Hard, well-aged cheese, such as Parmigiano or Manchego
- ✔ Ketchup
- ✔ Konbu
- ✔ Miso
- ✔ Fish sauce (nam pla)
- ✔ Mushrooms
- ✔ Nori (seaweed)
- ✔ Ripe/sundried/cooked tomatoes
- ✔ Scallops
- ✔ Soy sauce

For successful matches with savory foods:

- ✔ Avoid very oaky wines.
- ✔ Avoid very tannic/astringent wines.
- ✔ Select equally savory wines (see later section, "Considering wines that go with sotolone.")

Piquant performers

Although the heat from spice isn't technically a taste sensation (it's a tactile, or touching sensation), it's such an important factor in food and wine pairing that I include it here among the key taste sensations. Usually if the burning presence of spice is felt, it overrides all other tastes and becomes the dominant element in a dish. And people like spicy things. Hot sauce now outsells ketchup in the United States, underscoring the popularity of *piquant*. Here's a list of ingredients that will give your food a nice burn.

- ✔ Black pepper
- ✔ Chiles (all types)
- ✔ Cinnamon
- ✔ Clove
- ✔ Ginger

- ✔ Horseradish
- ✔ Mustard seed
- ✔ Turmeric
- ✔ Wasabi

For successful matches with spicy foods, keep these tips in mind:

- ✔ Choose off-dry or medium-dry wines.
- ✔ Choose full-bodied wines with moderate, but not excessive, alcohol. *Capsaicin* — what gives spice its burn — is soluble in alcohol (up to about 14 percent; more than that and the alcohol will start to burn, too).
- ✔ Avoid oaky wines, bitter wines.

Considering Aroma and Flavor: Identifying Everyone in the Family

Food and wine together are also sources of incredible aroma and flavor diversity. Hundreds, even thousands of different flavors, occur naturally, many of which you come across every day as you eat and drink. Since the beginning of time, people have been searching for the best combinations that enhance one another and that make for a more pleasurable ensemble than any one ingredient on its own. This section looks at the potential for aroma and flavor harmony between food and wine.

Instinctively, and even cross culturally, certain flavor combinations have emerged again and again as more successful than others, such as onions and garlic, tomato and basil, or lemon and fresh oysters. Other combinations are more specific to certain regions and cultures, like ginger and beef in China, bacon and cheese (burger) in North America, or prosciutto and melon in Italy.

Having a basic understanding of how these flavor combinations came to be and which families they belong to is useful as you're trying to find a memorable pairing. The following sections explain how some recipes were developed by people like you and me who ran into them, liked them a lot, and continued to use them again and again. Other food pairings were developed in the lab as scientists experimented and discovered tasty combinations.

I explain the main flavor families that you come across all the time and list the common ingredients that belong to each, so you have a starting point for making the match with no matter what you find on the plate.

Playing food and wine by ear, the old fashioned way

Many of the universally successful flavor combinations were arrived at through trial and error. In fact, for the last 7,000 or so years, the art of finding food combinations (and of pairing food and wine) was based, like recipe making, on pure experimental trial and error. Chefs and home cooks, like musicians playing by ear, relied on their senses to find harmony. Until recently, people had no idea about the number of shared flavor compounds, and therefore possible synergy, between vastly different ingredients; they simply liked combinations because they tasted good together.

The composition of wine, too, was rather mysterious until lately. Grape varieties and classic regional blends of course had their individual flavor profiles — a common range of aromas and taste characteristics that made them distinct and recognizable. Wine experts relied on their sense of smell and taste alone to arrive at these profiles, using familiar analogies of fruits, vegetables, herbs, and spices to describe them.

Even though science has made pairing food and wine a lot easier (refer to the next section), pairing food and wine is still mostly about using nothing but your own olfactory neurons and taste buds to see what works. You just have another means now to set you on the right path to success and to spark ideas. If you want to experiment, try different combinations of the ingredients within the same flavor families listed in the following sections. Each of these ingredients shares at least a few flavor molecules, and some share up to 50 or even 100 compounds. In theory, they should taste great together, and you can discover a new favorite flavor combination of your own. In practice, however, it doesn't always work out — science can only take you so far and the sense of smell and taste rule over any lab reports.

Going from trial and error to science

Today scientists can identify the specific aromatic compounds that contribute most significantly to each food ingredient's or wine's flavor profile. In fact, a whole branch of science is dedicated to revealing the molecular similarity between things you find in your kitchen or garden. And the number of shared compounds between wine and food is startling. As a wine taster, I feel vindicated, knowing that I wasn't just making up a bunch of stuff when describing the raspberry or peach or herbal flavor of a wine. The same flavor molecules are found in both food and wine!

Although people did amazingly well without well-equipped scientific laboratories, the recent revelations of aroma and flavor composition arrived at through high-tech scientific investigation have largely confirmed what people already knew. Lamb, for example, flavored with savory herbs like thyme and rosemary, is a standard classic, and now people understand why: Lamb meat itself contains measurable amounts of *thymol* — exactly the same substance that makes thyme smell like thyme. Likewise, pork, believe it or not, shares flavor molecules with apricots, another successful combination on the plate. Wine tasters also knew that Sauvignon Blanc reminded them of green peppers, and now the same aromatic molecules have been found in both.

This newfound knowledge isn't just reassuring; it has also opened the door to explore new, potentially tasty combinations of different foods and wine that don't readily come to mind. Who would have guessed, for example, that caviar and white chocolate share 73 flavor compounds?

Simply because food and wines share flavors doesn't guarantee that they'll taste good together — it's often about taste and texture first — but nonetheless it's a solid starting point. The good news: Scientists in lab coats with fancy machines may have made the process easier, but they haven't eliminated the fun of conducting your own food and wine matching experiments.

Livening It Up with the Parsley Family: Fresh Fine Herbs

The so-called *fine herbs* used in the kitchen belong mainly to the *parsley family,* also sometimes called the *carrot family* (or more technically *Apiaceae* or *umbelliferae*). This large group comprises about 3,700 species of aromatic plants and shrubs with a high concentration of essential oils, which makes them very aromatic. Think light, fresh salads, raw vegetables, and sweet herbs and you're in the family category. If the parsley family were a color, it would be light blue; if it were a dance, it would be classical ballet (without the tragedy).

The main aromatic theme in the parsley family is anise/licorice/mint. Many members of this family are also "cool," that is, they give a pleasant cooling sensation in the mouth — just imagine the refreshing taste of mint.

The essential oil anethole is the main element of flavor linking the parsley family. It's the principal flavor in anise and fennel, star anise, and licorice, and is closely related to estragole, found in tarragon and basil. Menthol (mint) and eugenol (clove and basil) are also important components.

The following sections break down the parsley family into herbs, spices, vegetables, greens, and even some fruits that belong to it. For some experimental fun, you can take traditional recipes and exchange some of the ingredients for others in the same family. For example, take a classic tomato-basil pasta sauce and use tarragon instead — it'll be a variation on the classic theme, or make your next ceviche with grapefruit juice instead of lime, and lemon grass instead of coriander. And then when you add in the wine, the fun of experimenting really begins.

Focusing on parsley family herbs

Head to the fresh herb section of the grocery store to find the aromatic herbs in this family, which include the following:

- Angelica
- Basil (all types)
- Chervril
- Cicely
- Coriander/cilantro
- Dill
- Hyssop
- Lemon grass
- Lovage
- Mint (all types)
- Parsley
- Shiso — red and green
- Tarragon

Examining spices in the parsley family

Head to the dried spice section of the grocery store to find the fragrant spices in this family, which include the following:

- Anise
- Ajowan
- Asafoetida
- Caraway
- Clove
- Cumin
- Fennel seed
- Ginger
- Nutmeg
- Star anise
- Turmeric

Going for the veggies, greens, and fruits in the parsley family

The vegetables, greens, and fruits in the parsley family are located in the fresh produce section of the grocery store (you may have to head to a specialty grocer to get some of the more obscure items). They include the following:

- Artichoke
- Black radish
- Carrots
- Celery
- Chicory
- Daikon radish
- Dandelion
- Eggplant
- Endive
- Escarole
- Fennel
- Gala apple
- Lamb's lettuce
- Parsnips
- Jerusalem artichoke
- Salsify
- Savoy cabbage
- Tomatillo
- Yellow beets

Singing with the parsley family: White and red wines

Certain white and red grapes are more naturally suited than others to pair with the parsley family. For white wines, your best bets are lively, aromatic, unoaked wines from cooler grape growing regions. Many of the white grapes in the following list have a fresh, herbal flavor profile, and so are natural partners. No two of these grapes are of course identical, but given their partial flavor overlap and family resemblance, the door is open for you to experiment and expand your horizons. You were thinking Sauvignon Blanc tonight? Why not try a Verdejo or a Friulano instead for something different? When these alternative wines are made in a similar style (as in dry, fresh, unoaked), whatever pairing you planned for the Sauvignon Blanc should still work, or at least not be a total disaster.

The white grapes and wines that work best with the parsley family (especially when made in a fresh, unoaked style), include the following:

- Albariño/Alvarinho
- Aligoté
- Arneis
- Catarratto
- Chardonnay (unoaked)
- Chasselas
- Cortese
- Encruzado
- Friulano
- Garganega
- Greco di Tufo
- Grüner Veltliner
- Malvasia
- Pinot Blanc
- Riesling
- Sauvignon Blanc (un-oaked)
- Verdejo
- Vermentino

When it comes to reds, avoid heavy, very tannic (bitter) wines with pronounced barrel-aging aromas when matching dishes dominated by the parsley family, and opt for crisper, fresher styles instead. Some red grapes and wines that pair well with the parsley family are as follows:

- Barbera
- Cabernet Franc
- Dolcetto
- Grenache
- Mencía
- Nebbiolo
- Pinot Noir (especially lighter styles)
- Syrah/Shiraz (lighter, cool climate styles)
- Valpolicella (a blend of grapes)

Rockin' with the Terpene Family: Resinous Herbs and More

The other main family of aromatic herbs and spice (though there is some overlap) are those whose aromatic profiles derived from the family of organic compounds called *terpenes*. Terpenes are the major aromatic components of tree resins — like pine trees — and are found in many herbs and spices, flowers, and fruits, including grapes. In fact, *terpenic* is a term sometimes used in (highbrow) wine-tasting circles to describe the particularly resinous, spicy, floral scent common in certain grapes. If terpenes were a color, they'd be dark green; if they were a musical genre they'd be rock 'n' roll — loud and obvious.

Hundreds of possibilities for synergy exist in this family, from a classic rosemary-rubbed leg of lamb with a eucalyptus-scented Australian Cabernet Sauvignon, to a more unusual pairing of resinous herb-infused lamb stew with a rich Alsatian Riesling.

The main aromatic compounds in the terpene family are linalool (orange, rose, rosewood, coriander), geraniol (rose, citronella, geraniums), nerol (orange blossom), terpineol (pine oil, lapsang souchong tea) and hotrienol (fresh green flowers, citrus).

The following sections break down the terpene family into its component herbs, spices, edible flowers, vegetables, fruits, and proteins. Like the other flavor families, there's room to play around with new combinations by switching out one ingredient for another, or finding new complimentary combinations within the family.

Naming terpene herbs, spices, and flowers

You should have no trouble finding the herbs, spices, and flowers in the terpene family; they're intensely aromatic, the sorts of things that you can smell immediately when you walk into a room. Many of them are also used for aromatherapy. They include the following:

- Bay
- Bergamot
- Coriander/Cilantro
- Eucalyptus
- Lemongrass
- Marjoram
- Nutmeg
- Oregano
- Rosemary
- Sage
- Thyme
- Verbena

Naming terpene spices and edible flowers

The herbs, spices, and flowers in the terpene family are often used in perfumery. They'd be what the perfumer would call *base notes,* the low notes like the double base makes, which set the foundation for the higher, lighter notes made by the smaller string instruments. You can recognize some exotic spices and familiar flowers in the following list:

- Cardamom
- Cedar
- Cinnamon
- Clove
- Ginger
- Juniper
- Lavender
- Pepper
- Rose

Identifying terpene fruits, veggies, and proteins

There are some surprising fruits, vegetables, and especially proteins, that belong in the terpene family, things you'd likely never suspect to share any similarities. They include the following:

- Avocado
- Bell pepper
- Carrot
- Celery root
- Chickpea
- Citrus zest and blossoms
- Cured ham
- Lamb
- Litchi
- Parsnip
- Pineapple
- Pork loin
- Rabbit
- Roast chicken
- Strawberry
- Tomato

Focusing on grapes and wines that complement the terpene family

Terpenic is a term thrown around in certain wine circles. That's because many grapes, mostly white, contain measurable amounts of terpenes. Take the incredibly fragrant Muscat grape, for example. Those wild floral aromas, like a blast of spring or (high quality) bathroom freshener, are courtesy of the presence of terpenes. And because Muscat is one of the oldest grape varieties known, and it's the mother of hundreds of other varieties, its terpenic DNA has made its way around the world. Such intensely floral aromas are rarer in red grapes, aside of course from the black-skinned version of Muscat, but nonetheless, several red grapes and blends have their own subtler flowery smells, and more frequently, resinous herb notes like rosemary and bay.

In the next sections, I list a few of the white and red grapes from which you can expect some of these lovely smells. Again, although complementary aromas are only one part of a perfect match, they're a good starting point. So pull out those herbal-scented Mediterranean reds with your next rosemary and thyme-scented leg of lamb, or that pungent Gewürztraminer with a Thai coconut curry scented with bergamot, lemongrass, and cilantro, and enjoy the aromatic synergy.

White grapes and wines in the terpene family include the following:

- Albariño
- Auxerrois
- Chasselas
- Gewürztraminer
- Maria Gomes/Fernão Pires
- Moschophilero
- Muscat
- Müller-Thürgau
- Optima
- Pinot Gris
- Riesling
- Roussanne
- Scheurebe
- Sylvaner
- Torrontés
- Viura

Refer to Part III for more information about these different types of white wines. As for red grapes and wines, the following can synergize with the terpene family:

- Black Muscat
- Cabernet Sauvignon
- Douro blends (Portugal)
- Grenache
- Lacrima di Morro d'Alba (Le Marche, Italy)
- Malbec
- Southern French blends/Grenache-syrah-mourvèdre (GSM)
- Syrah/shiraz

Refer to Part III for more information about these different types of red wines.

Groovin' with the Sotolone Family, the Aromatic Equivalent of Umami

Sotolone is the very potent aromatic compound chiefly responsible for the distinctive pungent, earthy-sweet flavor of curries, fenugreek, lovage, caramel, and maple syrup, among others. I think of it as the aromatic equivalent of the umami taste: sapid and savory, even when sweet (refer to Chapter 2 for more information about this taste). If sotolone were a color, it would be dark brown, like roasted tobacco or molasses (both of which contain sotolone). If it were a musical genre, then it would be R&B. Sotolone and its relatives are powerful flavor enhancers.

The following sections list the most sotolone-rich foods and the wine styles equally endowed with these R&B aromas and flavors. The synergy of sotolone on the plate and in the glass is amazing.

Eyeing sotolone-rich and complementary foods

Notice that all the foods I list in this section are treated in some way: roasting, grilling, drying, smoking, reducing/concentrating, curing, or aging. Whether or not they actually contain sotolone, these methods of processing create the characteristic burnt, nutty, sweet-caramelized, and curry-like aromas and flavors that make them part of the family. You can use them to complement one another, as in grilled striploin with a sauce made from dried wild mushrooms, or as a striking contrast to bright, fresh flavors, such as the Italian classic of prosciutto and fresh cantaloupe.

Sotolone-rich and complementary foods include the following:

- Aged/cured ham
- Aged vinegars (such as balsamic)
- Brown sugar
- Caramel
- Cooked rhubarb
- Curries (varying combos of curry leaf, cumin, cardamom, cinnamon, bay leaf, and chile peppers, among others)
- Dried fruit (prunes, figs, dates)
- Dried mushrooms
- Freshly roasted coffee beans

✔ Grilled aged meats

✔ Grilled vegetables

✔ Maple syrup

✔ Molasses

✔ Smoked peppers (chipotle)

✔ Soy sauce

✔ Sweet potatoes/yams

✔ Toasted coconut

✔ Toasted hazelnut, pistachio

✔ Vanilla

Considering wines that go with sotolone

The following list looks at wine styles rather than specific grape varieties. Like with sotolone-rich foods, it's the processing techniques rather than the raw materials that create the flavors in the sotolone family.

So what makes for a good wine alongside a sotolone-rich food? Three main factors:

✔ **Maturity:** The older a wine is, the more burnt, dried fruit, sweet-caramelized flavors it will have.

✔ **Barrel aging:** The longer in barrel the better. In fact, many of the aromatic attributes of barrel-aged wines mirror those in sotolone-rich foods: caramel, brown sugar, toasted coconut, coffee, vanilla, maple syrup.

✔ **Ripeness:** Wines made from very ripe grapes tend to give the impression of sweetness, even when no sugar is present in the wine. This vague sweet sensation — what wine tasters might call *jammy* fruit — work well with the savory-sweet character of foods in the sotolone family.

Look for wines that spend prolonged periods in wood before bottling, such as Sherry and Tawny Port. Many sweet wines (especially those made from grapes affected by *noble rot*, which is a benevolent fungus that affects grapes under specific conditions and causes a miraculous transformation), like Sauternes, and Hungarian Tokaji Aszú are rich in sotolone aromas. Old dry white wines also develop similar aromas, as do aged spirits, especially dark rum, and sake (especially *koshu* style, or aged sake).

But if really old or sweet wines aren't your thing, then look for wines made in warm climates resulting in super-ripe grapes, and fermented and/or aged in barrel, especially using a high percentage of new wood barrels. California, Australia, Argentina, Chile, and South Africa, for example, have plenty of options to offer that would groove with the sotolone family, as do the warmer corners of Southern Europe. Think rich, ripe Chardonnay or Fumé Blanc, Southern Rhône whites, barrel-aged Viognier, and generous new world–Cabernet Sauvignon and Merlot, Argentine Malbec, Australian Shiraz, Southern French blends, and the big guns from Italy like Brunello di Montalcino, Barolo and Amarone, for example.

The following is a list of wines that pair well with sotolone-rich foods, being themselves in the same aromatic family. In fact, they're often the same wines that match well with umami-rich foods.

Dry wines include

- ✔ Amarone
- ✔ Barolo
- ✔ Barossa Valley or McLaren Vale Shiraz (Australia)
- ✔ Brunello di Montalcino
- ✔ Cabernet Sauvignon (ripe, new world style)
- ✔ Champagne (vintage)
- ✔ Malbec (Argentina)
- ✔ Merlot (ripe, new world–style)
- ✔ Traditional method sparkling wine (five+ years)
- ✔ Vin Jaune (Jura, France)

Some sweet wines include

- ✔ Aged *vins doux naturels* (sweet, fortified wines)
- ✔ Amontillado Sherry (can be dry)
- ✔ Beerenauslese
- ✔ Madeira (can be dry)
- ✔ Oloroso Sherry (can be dry)
- ✔ Sauternes
- ✔ Tawny Port

- Tokaji Aszú
- Trockenbeerenauslese
- Vin Santo
- Vintage Port (10+ years)

The original Champagne and oysters match

When oysters are on the table and champagne is called for, the order today means only one thing: champagne brut or extra brut — the dry stuff. But that classic pairing is fairly recent. Up until about 1880, *all* Champagne was sweet; no producer made dry champagne. Records show that some special cuvees contained up to 30 percent sugar, which is very, very sweet.

Jean François du Troy's famous painting *Le Déjeuner des Huitres* (The Oyster Lunch) dates from 1735. In it, he depicts a rowdy group of gentlemen courtiers relishing platter after platter of freshly shucked oysters. The floor and table are strewn with empty shells, and empty straw-filled baskets used to transport oysters lie prone on the ground. They're also clearly drinking copious amounts of white wine out of cut crystal flutes. The wine bottles are the short, rounded flagon type that was common for champagne at the time (and some houses like Gosset still use the shape). Two gentlemen can be seen pouring the wine from an impressive height above the glass, also common practice in those days to release as much carbon dioxide as possible, which may otherwise interfere with comfort and digestion. The champagne was certainly sweet, the oysters clearly fresh, and the merriment of the moment unambiguous: that's the original champagne and oyster match.

Chapter 6

Considering Regional and Historical Angles for Pairing Food and Wine

There you are, menu or bottle in hand, hungry and thirsty, wondering where to start. What wine goes best with that filet mignon and blue cheese? Or what food goes best with that oak-aged Chardonnay you've been dying to open? Chapter 5 discusses the basic strategies for matching from the food angle (also look to Chapter 3 for more on starting from the wine's perspective). This chapter adds to your arsenal of strategies with some alternative angles based on geography and history. One of the easiest concepts to grasp in the world of wine and food is "what grows together goes together." So I consider pairing from a regional view, looking at some of the tried-and-true combinations of local food and local wines that have been around for centuries. With a basic grasp of geography, this can work for you.

Beyond geography, I offer some textbook pairings with explanations, ones that have been around for centuries. These are the sorts of matches that virtually everyone can agree work well together.

Focusing on Regions: Where the Wine Was Grown

When you're stuck about which food and wine to pair together, think region-ally and act immediately. Not coincidentally, all the world's classic wine regions have well-developed local cuisines with their own identities, as strong as the wines' regional profiles. It's a simple truth: People who make wine also generally like to eat. And if you're ever in wine country looking for a restaurant recommendation, just ask a good winemaker, because he or she always knows the best local dining options.

Over the course of centuries of eating and drinking, locals have learned to take the foods available and transform them into something that's pleasant when washed down with their wine. Local recipes had to make do with what was available locally and seasonally, and the people cooking devised techniques to prepare foods in such a way as to work well with the local wines. And very likely, too, wines were shaped, as far as local grapes, climate, and soil would allow, to harmonize at the table with what was available. A cynic may argue that devising dishes that showed off local wines was all perhaps a highly complicated effort to sell more wine — the winegrowers had to find a way to present their wares in the best light to travelers. And serving a wine with just the right dish never fails to make it seem delicious.

It's interesting to observe how many of the world's emerging wine regions, those still experimenting with various grapes and wine styles and searching for a regional wine identity, often have a less well defined, or at least less easily defined local culinary tradition, too. Individual chefs in the new world are more likely to have signature dishes than the region as a whole. And now, with cultural influences felt from all corners of the planet, gastronomy will likely stay in constant flux, encouraging endless creativity, and so much the better for you and me and everyone else. Globalization is continually eroding the orthodoxy of food and wine in the old world (also good news), leading to new possibilities and openness to experimentation. You can still garner a few lessons from the classics. In fact, knowing the classics is a great jump-off point for you to discover your own new matches, a sort of personal globalization of food and wine.

The next sections look at three case studies of classic regional food and wine pairings, exploring how the wine style and the local cuisine have come together in harmony. Then I list a few more perfect pairings from some of the world's iconic regions to help you on your journey.

What grows together goes together

Although looking at the region isn't always a slam-dunk strategy, identifying where the dish you're about to eat originated and matching it to a wine from the same place is definitely a good start. But don't be blinded by this concept to the exclusion of every other possibility. If the regional match doesn't work — and it surely doesn't all the time — then look to the rest of this book for the reasons why, as well as for a more suitable pairing.

The following three case studies of classic regional matches look more closely at *why* they work so well together, whether by coincidence or design. Remember that you can apply the same successful pairing principles to many other combinations of food and wine, substituting either side of the equation for something similar.

Case study No. 1: Southwestern France

Southwestern France is the heartland of rich, hearty, swashbuckling Gascon cuisine. Here, the duck is king. The key elements of a classic confit of duck are fat (skin and residual duck fat), salt (from the curing), and protein (the meat). Salt softens the texture of wine, and fat and protein are also excellent tannin buffers (see Chapter 3). This dish can handle pretty big wines.

And Southwestern France is the land of bold and tannic, firm and tart, rough-and-tumble sort of country wines, like Cahors, one of the leading appellations in the region with its reds based on the notoriously chewy Malbec variety. The three main elements in duck confit work to soften the tannins and allow fruit to emerge, while the wine's acidity cuts through the richness of the fat-poached duck and contrasts with its crispy skin. *Wah lah*, the regional pairing of Cahors and confit of duck is born. Which came first, the duck or the wine? I'd say it doesn't really matter. It just works.

Case study No. 2: Loire Valley

Crottin de Chavignol from the Loire Valley is one of France's most famous cheeses, with its own controlled appellation of origin. Crottin (said to be named after the *crotte* of local goats, the French word for dung) is a small, cylindrical goat's cheese with a particularly tangy taste — goat's milk is higher in acid than cow's — and chalky texture. Although Sancerre comes in pink and red, the classic pairing is with the white version, a Sauvignon Blanc that's bone dry and very crisp, like a blast of green apple and lemon on the palate with some green grassy notes thrown in for good measure.

The pairing works because the cheese's twang of acid finds its equal in the wine — acid food needs acid wine, each cancelling the other out — while the salt teases out a little more green apple and citrus fruit than you would have noticed on the first sip. The slightly chalky taste and texture of the cheese is echoed in the chalky-stony minerality of the wine, which, after all, is grown on some of France's chalkiest limestone soils on the hills around Chavignol. The lean wine is softened and enriched; the cheese is enlivened and enhanced, making a perfect regional harmony.

Case study No. 3: Piedmont

The northwest corner of Italy is famous for the *tuber magnatum*, better known as the white truffle, which grows in the Langhe and Monferratto hills. Fresh truffle is usually simply shaved at the last minute over some neutral canvas such as fresh egg *tagliolini* pasta tossed in a nugget of fresh butter, or lightly scrambled eggs. The delectable perfume of the truffle does the rest. Barolo is the most majestic wine of the Langhe hills south of Alba. The grape is *Nebbiolo*, a fickle, late-ripening variety that makes firm and tannic wine that demands patience.

But as you're waiting for the hard tannins to soften, so too are aromas developed, born of simple fruit and matured into an unforgettable display of faded roses, dried tobacco, tar, and, you guessed it, truffle. Barolo and white truffles is a pairing of aromatics and flavor more than texture and taste. It's enough sometimes just to sit and allow the smell of the white truffles over steaming pasta to fill your nostrils, and then swirl and sniff a generous glassful of Barolo, allowing both sensations to meet at the olfactory bulb. And as your brain decodes the mysterious beauty, you'll wonder how on earth the fruit of the vine can come to resemble the smell of a subterranean tuber that grows quite literally among its roots.

Counting on the wisdom of the ages, guided by experience

Other parts of the world have their own classic regional food and wine pairings. These pairings aren't groundbreaking or new. In fact, you'd likely find the same list in a 19th-century treatise on the same subject. What makes these classic pairings is the wisdom of the ages from years of trial-and-error experimentation already done for you. But this isn't an endpoint. The advantage you have is that you live in a time where the farthest point on the planet is little more than a day's travel, and products from every corner can find their way to your kitchen and cellar.

Whereas once the only thing around to drink with your crottin was Sancerre, now the choice is near limitless. As you see in Part III, the world's countless wines can be distilled into a few basic style categories. So use this wisdom of the ages as a starting point: If, for example, Sancerre goes well with crottin, then very likely so will many other whites in the lightweight, lean, and crisp category.

In the kitchen, you can tweak these classic recipes by exchanging some of the key flavorings for others in the same family of ingredients listed in Chapter 5. Why not, say, add a lavender rub to your rack of lamb to shift the match from Bordeaux to a eucalyptus-scented Coonawarra Cabernet from Australia? Or substitute fennel seed on the same lamb to echo the licorice nuances of a robust Malbec from Mendoza? The world is, quite literally, at your disposal. Here are some other classic regional pairings to help you get started:

- Muscadet and oysters where the Loire meets the Atlantic
- Vinho Verde and grilled sardines on the Portuguese coast
- Red Burgundy and boeuf Bourguignon on the Côte d'Or
- Riesling and sauerkraut/choucroute garnie in Alsace and Germany
- Bordeaux and lamb raised on the nearby salt marshes of Aquitaine
- Fiano di Avellino and fresh buffalo's milk mozzarella from the Bay of Naples

> ✔ Tempranillo and wood oven-roasted suckling pig in Castilla y Léon
>
> ✔ Provençal rosé and saffron-infused seafood bouillabaisse
>
> ✔ Tokaji aszú and Hungarian foie gras in the land of sweet wine and goose liver
>
> ✔ Sweet, botrytis-affected wines of the Burgenland and the legendary pastries of nearby Vienna

Identifying Some Classic Pairings to Help You Start

These sections lay out a few classic pairings with more detailed explanations of why they work so well together. These pairings represent a minute fraction of time-tested combinations, but the logic and reasoning behind each match can get you thinking along the right lines to arrive at hundreds of other successful combinations: You want to identify the key elements to consider in both food and wine and understand why they work together.

Bubbles and oysters

Champagne and oysters are considered luxury goods, status symbols of sorts, and are likely to be socializing in the same circles anyway. But then again, the combination works, even when the lower classes are out to dine (and don't forget that oysters were a staple in the diet of the working class in 19th-century New York).

Oysters grow in cold, salty seawater and are harvested traditionally in months without an "r" (best to avoid them during their reproductive season when they become milky). Depending on the species and the region, oysters have an original, salt-brine tang tempered by implicit sweetness. Metallic, tinny notes (oysters are higher in zinc than any other food) make them troublesome with tannic red wines: The combination increases the metallic taste to the point of unpleasantness. Herbal, grassy, or even cucumber flavors are also common, so you can invite white wines to play. The majority of dry crisp, unoaked whites are solid matches for oysters. And considering that a wedge of lemon is the most common accompaniment (or some other form of acid), this makes perfect sense.

But sparkling wine takes the match to the next level. Champagne especially is itself chockfull of minerally, seashell flavors, again unsurprising because the vineyards of Champagne are planted essentially on old oyster beds, the accumulation of billions of shelled sea creatures in what was once an inland sea. Champagne has naturally high acid — the squeeze of lemon on the oyster —

plus an almost imperceptible amount of sugar (in brut Champagne) to mirror the vaguely sweet finish of oysters. So far, so complementary. The bubbles bring it home. The lively effervescence of carbon dioxide is the perfect contrast to the velvety smooth texture of the oysters. Just as the bi-valve slides effortlessly down the throat with a gentle caress, the Champagne arrives to liven back up the party and ready the mouth for more.

Sweets and blues

As most wine lovers know, when cheese and wine meet, it's frequently a natural disaster. I don't mean the processed supermarket kind of cheese — that's as harmless as it's tasteless. I mean the cheese-lover's types of cheese, well-aged, oozing, and stinky, that wreak havoc, especially on red wines. Of course exceptions, such as the Sauvignon Blanc and goat's cheese, do exist. Another classic match includes sweet wine and blue cheese. (See Chapter 20 for more on wine and cheese pairing.)

Blue cheeses are the flavor heavyweights of the cheese world, almost certainly discovered by accident. You'd have to think that the first soul to taste a moldy, stinky, blue-veined piece of cheese did so out of sheer desperation. Whereas once the healthy molds found in cheese aging caves did the job naturally (such as those in Roquefort, France), today, cheeses have cultures of *penicillium* added to them in order to form those curiously tasty marbled veins of furry blue-green mold.

The pungency imparted by bacterial activity, coupled with the generous salt content of blue cheeses, makes their flavor and aroma profile intense to say the least. Few wines stand a chance, except for wines of equal flavor intensity. As if by natural design, grapes attacked by their very own mold, *botrytis cinerea* (also known as noble rot; see Chapter 12 for more info), yield wines with serious depth of flavor, just like the sweet chutney that often accompanies a cheese board. And importantly, noble rot results most often in intensely sweet wines, which is a perfect contrast to the cheese's saltiness. The wine is sweet and flavorful; the cheese is pungent and salty. The two make a perfect match.

Another classic sweet-blue matchup is the noble English Stilton blue and Portugal's most famous wine, Port. The long aging process in cask delivers the Port's flavor. Tawny Ports can spend up to 40 years in wood, during which time they develop beguilingly complex dried fruit and nut aromas, another traditional accompaniment to the cheese board. And the sweetness comes from *fortification*, stopping the fermentation with the addition of alcohol before all the grape sugar has been converted (see Chapter 12 for more info), resulting in a wine that's both sweet and strong, strong enough to equalize the salty intensity of Stilton.

Cabs and slabs

The phrase "cabs and slabs" must have first been muttered in an American steakhouse. This phrase refers, of course, to (young) Cabernet Sauvignon and steak, perhaps the most classic American food and wine pairing around. But the concept of matching rare-grilled beef with big, bold red wine is as old as the dictum "red wine with red meat" itself.

So why does this pairing work? Cabernet Sauvignon is a deep colored and equally deep flavored red grape; its skins are thicker than most, which is where the color comes from, and it also has firm tannins. Its big structure makes it a prime candidate for the softening effects of barrel-aging as most are, at the same time adding another dimension of smoky, toasty, baking spice flavors to dark berry and black currant fruit. In all but the hottest climates, it also has a characteristic fresh herbal note. Many people are happy to drink bold Cabernets on their own, but they're even better when served up alongside a rare T-bone or New York strip.

This pairing works on three levels:

- **Flavor:** Steak is most often cooked on the grill, a cooking method with high flavor impact. A little charring is inevitable, giving meat a bitter flavor, along with the smoke imparted by the grill. Cabernet answers with its own toasty-smoky nuances from the barrel.

- **Taste:** The mildly bitter taste of the wine's tannins meets the pleasant bitterness of charred protein.

- **Texture:** The salt applied to the meat, along with its fat and protein, serve to soften Cabernet's texture. The once big, bold red becomes softer and fruitier; the steak retains it delicious savory-ness, and everybody's happy.

Zesty reds and pizza

The principle taste components of a classic red-sauced pizza like the *Margherita* (tomato sauce, buffalo's milk mozzarella, and a few fresh basil leaves) are sour, savory, and vaguely sweet from the tomato sauce, along with an herbal lift from the basil. The cheese lends some body and creaminess, but it has a very mild flavor and is a minor consideration overall in the match.

A tailor-made wine for such a dish brings its own acidity to balance the acidity of the tomato sauce (and not seem overly sweet in comparison), yet sufficient sweet fruit flavor to rival that of ripe tomatoes (and not come across as overly tart) — it's a fine sweet-sour balance. Tomatoes are also high on the desirable umami (savory) scale, a taste that works synergistically with other sources of umami. So a savory wine becomes even more savory with tomato sauce, and vice versa — a good thing. Italy is full of grapes and regions that produce savory, zesty wines. One of the most famous is *Chianti Classico*, made from Sangiovese grown in the Tuscan hills between Florence and Siena. Chianti is known for its particularly savory, dusty, tart red fruit and resinous herb flavors, with firm texture and juicy acid. When paired with the Margherita, zesty meets zesty, savory enhances savory, and herbal flavors co-mingle. Chianti Classico and pizza Margherita is about as good a match as it gets.

Pinot and duck

No one knows exactly when this classic meeting of wine and bird first occurred, but it must have been a felicitous moment. The specific classic pairing is duck breast, or *magret de canard,* simply pan-seared or roasted, served with a glaze of some kind, and a firm, juicy, savory old world–style Pinot Noir like Burgundy.

Most duck magret recipes call for a tart, acid-based sauce made from such things as red berries (cherry, pomegranate, raspberry, cranberry), oranges, tamarind, or balsamic vinegar, or alternatively, exotic spicing such as Chinese 5-spice or hoisin glaze. Such sauces/glazes naturally enhance the flavors of duck meat itself; chefs over the world have learned through extensive trial and error. Another bit of investigative work reveals that duck shares some overlapping flavor compounds with many of these ingredients, confirming that things that share flavors often, if not always, work well together.

Enter the Pinot. The typical, textbook flavor profile of Pinot Noir reads like an ingredient list for a duck recipe. The wine is full of its own tart red berry flavors and exotic spicing like cinnamon, clove, Sichuan peppercorn, and ginger (especially wood-aged versions of the variety). Is it any wonder then that Pinot and duck go so well together, especially when the sauce/glaze used on the plate serves to increase the overlap of shared flavors? And even beyond undeniable flavor synergy, there's taste and textural compatibility as well. Pinot is a relatively low-tannin variety thanks to its thin skins, meaning that excessive astringency is rarely a bother — the texture is often downright silky smooth.

Duck meat is lean (aside from the skin, which is usually rendered until crisp), free from the marbling fat found in cuts of red meat, for example, which plays such an important role in taming the tannins of grapes like Cabernet Sauvignon. Pinot Noir is perfectly comfortable alongside lean meat; its texture is not in need of softening. And if you hit a piece of fatty skin, Pinot's relatively high acidity is there to cleanse the palate between bites. Its acidity also plays the same flavor-enhancing role of tart sauces and glazes most often served with duck. The more exotic the sauce, the older your Pinot Noir should be, having had time to develop its own exotic aromas and flavors. Just try Peking duck with a ten-year-old top-notch Burgundy for a magical duet.

Chapter 7

Age Isn't Just a Number: Age and Pairing Rules

A lurking, uneasy feeling creeps up as you grab that special bottle for a gastronomic celebration: Is this the right time? Am I opening this bottle too soon? How will the wine have changed, and what should I serve to create a magical match that will highlight the wine?

How long to age wine is one of the most frequently asked questions, which isn't surprising, given the amount of reverence paid in wine circles to dusty old bottles buried in subterranean cellars. You also have the question of whether you'll even like what happens to wine over time — wine changes — and exactly what happens, and especially how quickly, remains shrouded in some mystery. As with all things wine, some personal preference is involved in the answer. In this chapter I examine these questions and more. I look at the wines that just get old, as well as those that not only stand the test of time, but also improve with age. I even share some tips on how to know which is which.

Related to aging wine is the practical consideration of how long you can keep that unfinished bottle kicking around, before putting it on the shelf with the rest of the vinegars. Wine is perishable. For the hopefully rare moments when you do have leftovers, I provide some tips on keeping them fresh until you get around to polishing them off.

And what about the relationship to food? Just as your affinities change with time, the connection between wine and food also changes. As wine matures and its flavor and texture change, the magical match also shifts. I explore some of the ways to give grand old bottles the respect they've earned.

Understanding How Wine Matures

The fact that wine changes, and occasionally even gets better over time, is one of the things that makes wine such a unique consumer product. On the flipside, this change makes wine vexing, because the rate of this mysterious metamorphosis can't be precisely known. Ambient temperature and fluctuations, humidity, size of the bottle, the type of closure, (such as cork, screw cap, plastic stopper or glass stopper, and the quality of each), and most importantly what's inside (and all the processes used to make the wine in the first place) all affect the rate at which wine matures. Much research has been conducted, and people do know more or less what is happening, just not how quickly it happens.

Not nearly as many wines need aging as you may think. A combination of factors such as changing market demands, expansion of vineyards into warmer regions, and technological advances in winemaking have conspired to leave fewer and fewer wines that require time before they reach that magical mix of maturity and drinkability. Most — I'd say upwards of 90 percent of reds and 95 percent of whites — are pretty much at peak on release, or at least delicious and ready to enjoy. Most wines just get old and tired — they *oxidize,* subject to the ravaging and inexorable effects of oxygen and time. I've had many bottles that were hanging in there, but made me wish I had enjoyed the wine several years earlier.

The following sections explain specifically what happens to wines as they age and how you can determine at what degree of maturity you like your wine.

Aging wine: What happens

All wines travel along a similar evolutionary continuum over time, with changes in color, texture, aromas and flavors, and even the level of sweetness. Innumerable chemical reactions are going on between wine's essential components — alcohol and acids (and sugars, if present), plus the molecules responsible for aroma, flavor, texture, and color — all aided and abetted by oxygen. Chemists use terms like *esterification* and *polymerization* to describe these reactions. Good thing this book is *Pairing Food and Wine For Dummies* and not *Chemistry II For Dummies,* so I won't get too technical for you. No wine is immortal (though some can live for a couple hundred years or more), and eventually all end up turning to vinegar, the inescapable conclusion to a wine's life.

Here are the general changes that are all going on at the same time as wine ages:

> ✔ **Color evolves:** In red wines, the pigments responsible for color begin to stick together with other molecules, eventually becoming so large that they *precipitate,* that is, they drop out of the wine and form the sediment

found in the bottom of bottles of old red wines. At the same time, the effects of oxygen turn them from bluish red to brownish red. In white wines, color pigments are similarly oxidized and turn from pale yellow to dark brown. A deep amber or topaz-colored white wine or a very pale garnet-brown red wine is a sure sign of advanced maturity.

✔ **Texture softens:** Important textural changes happen over time, especially in red wines. *Tannins,* the compounds that give young reds their astringent, furry texture, also combine like pigments and fall out of the wine. (Check out Chapter 10 for the complete lowdown on tannins.) This combining and softening of tannins result in a gentler, smoother mouth feel, like losing the rough wool sweater and slipping into a delicate silk nightgown. The perception of acidity also reduces over time, even if the pH doesn't change, because acids and alcohols link to make other aromatic compounds. (The *pH* is a measure of how acidic a wine is, which is an important component of its age-ability, not to mention food compatibility.) The change in white wines isn't as significant, though they also grow silkier and softer over time. The changing texture is a significant factor when considering what to pair with old wines. (Refer to the "Serving Mature Wines with Food" section later in this chapter for more information.)

✔ **Aromas and flavors develop:** You've probably heard the term *bouquet,* a poetic way of describing the smell of mature wine, which can only be acquired after a little patience in the cellar. *Bouquet* means that aromas change from fresh and fruity — like a bowl of fresh berries — to dried, cooked, or candied fruit aromas, like berry compote or pie. Other aromas emerge seemingly out of nowhere, such as nutty, caramelized, honeyed, earthy, medicinal, and potpourri notes. These aromas add another dimension of complexity to the wine, broadening the spectrum of enjoyment.

✔ **Wood-aged wines lose their obviously oaky taste:** This change means that the aroma and flavor of wood, once like the icing on a cake — a separate layer of flavor — meshes in with everything else and becomes another dimension of flavor. However, some wines, especially those with excessive new oak and only modest fruit concentration, may taste even oakier over time as the fruit dissipates.

✔ **Perception of sweetness decreases:** Although the measurable sugar content of wines doesn't change over time, the perception of the sweet taste decreases thanks to the development of ever-more complex flavors. This means that wines that tasted quite sweet when young will seem relatively drier after a few years in the cellar or wine rack. Very old dessert wines may even taste dry, an important consideration when serving at the table.

✔ **Wine becomes vinegar:** The natural end of all wines is vinegar. If maturity is pushed too far, in other words, the wine is too old, it will have oxidized to the point at which it smells like vinegar and nail polish remover — clear signs of decrepitude. At this point, you can't turn back. You've unfortunately waited too long, and your wine is dead. (And I wouldn't pour it on my salad, either.)

Determining whether you like them old or young

Considering the things that happen to wines as they age that I discuss in the previous section, you have to ask yourself whether this change is positive or not. There's no correct answer, of course. Picking the best moment to drink a wine is largely a matter of personal preference and the types of flavors you prefer. Do you like your fruit fresh or dried? Do you like the smell of dried flowers, damp earth, mushrooms, forest floor, and caramel? Or the freshly roasted coffee, dark chocolate and vanilla smell of a youthful, oak-aged wine?

So what do old and young wines look and taste like?

Madeira, the granddaddy of them all

Once one of the most sought-after wines in the world, held in such high esteem that it was used to toast the US Declaration of Independence in 1776, Madeira is the world's most indestructible wine. That's because Madeira is already cooked and oxidized by the time it reaches the bottle. Like Port, Madeira is a fortified wine, with about 18 to 20 percent alcohol. The type known as *malmsey* is also very sweet, while the unique volcanic soils of the island of Madeira ensure that even ripe grapes are rich in searing, life-preserving acidity. But here's where it gets a little medieval: The wine is left to age for years, sometimes decades, in old wooden barrels in the attic of Madeira lodges on the island. There it sits, slowly oxidizing and baking in the sub-tropical heat under the roof, undergoing a series of amazing changes that give Madeira its inimitable nutty, caramelized, barley sugar flavor. What's more, once in the bottle, Madeira is virtually indestructible — it can't oxidize further or get any more cooked. Many bottles from the late 1700s are still around today to amply prove the point.

This unusual transformative process was hit upon by accident. Portuguese sailors on their way to Brazil stopped in Madeira to reload supplies before the Atlantic crossing, and wine was naturally part of the cargo, fortified to survive the long voyage. Quite by surprise, they realized that the wine became rather delicious after several months in the hold of a sailing vessel, rocking on the sea in the tropical conditions of an equator crossing. Such was the fancy for the results that by the 1700s, Madeira wines were priced in part on the number of equator crossings they had completed, the more the better. When it became impractical to ship wines across the ocean, a way was sought on the island to re-create the unique if unusual conditions of a 17th century sailing vessel on its way to the colonies. Ironically, the term *maderized*, applied to any other wine except Madeira, is a derogatory description meaning cooked and/or oxidized.

- **An old wine:** One of the greatest pleasures of a more *mature* wine is the texture — that silky, smooth mouth-feel that can only be achieved with patience. The gadget has yet to be invented that can speed up the evolution of texture that happens naturally over time. Some wines do demand a little cellar time, including those mostly red wines that are closed, rough-textured, and astringent when first released. You can also expect the color to be more brownish red, and the range of aromas and flavors to reflect what you'd expect to happen to fruit or flowers over time: Fresh turns dried, and complexity develops.

- **A young wine:** It's full of freshness — fresh fruit, fresh flowers, fresh spices, what wine tasters would call primary flavors. They can be delicious, because fresh fruit is delicious, but the range of flavors is less developed, that is, there's less complexity. The texture of red wines built to age can be downright unpleasant: chewy, astringent, mouth-puckering — these need time — but are in the minority. Fresh whites are generally sharp and crisp, aspects that will also mellow over time.

For me, knowing how long to keep a young wine before it gets too old is a question of balance. Fine wines gain complexity with time. The brazen fruit and chocolaty oak of young wines may be pleasant but aren't transcendental, but then again, neither is a mixture of dead leaves, beef bouillon, and soy sauce. I hope to hit wines at the point when the bouquet has started to form and the wine has gained in complexity, but before all the fruit has flown south for the permanent winter. That's my personal definition of mature. Everything else is just young or old wine.

The Pillars of Age-ability: Figuring Out Whether to Keep or Drink Now

Knowing whether a wine is likely to have held up or even gotten a little better over time is useful information to have at-hand before you serve that wine at your dinner party. So how can you determine whether a wine has a long shelf life or whether you need to drink it within a year or so? The wines with the greatest shelf life are those with an abundance of at least two or more of the major natural preservatives in wine, namely:

- Acidity

- Alcohol

- Sugar

- Tannin/extract

All four of these elements are natural protectors that extend the shelf life of wine. Both acid and alcohol make wine less hospitable to bacteria and other spoilage organisms that could degrade it. And sugar, too, although a favorite food of yeasts, makes life tough for other unwanted organisms. As any home jam maker knows, the sweeter the jam, the longer it will last. And finally, tannins and other compounds that make up what's called extract in wine (technically *polyphenols*) are natural antioxidants, protecting wine from the ravaging effects of oxygen.

Vintage Port is an extreme example of age-worthy wine. It has high alcohol (it's fortified up to about 20 percent), it's very tannic when young, and it contains a lot of residual sugar. It's not really acidic, but nor is it flabby. Port can improve over the course of a century or longer. In fact, when young, it's not very much fun to drink.

At the other end of the scale, inexpensive, dry, fruity whites are the least likely candidates for the cellar with a long shelf life. You want to consume these wines within one to two years after harvest, and the sooner the better. They have little protection: no tannin, no sugar, and only modest alcohol; acidity is the only thing potentially holding them together. Their fresh fruit flavors quickly fade and die in the bottle without any protection, leaving a tired, oxidized, bruised apple-flavored wine. Likewise, commercial-style soft, supple reds (low tannin and acid) are enjoyable when young and fruity, but offer little after the fruit has dried out and faded away. Don't waste long-term space in the cellar or in your wine rack with these wines (keep them close by the door with easy access, and don't forget about them for more than a year or so).

One basic guideline that indicates a wine's potential shelf life is price. Getting the extra stuffing into a wine to make it age-worthy means higher production costs. And by extra stuffing I mean more concentration of all, or at least some of the elements previously mentioned, as well as the flavor concentration that comes from low yielding grapevines (less fruit produced per plant reliably translates to more flavor concentration, but also less wine). The majority of wines under $20, red, white, or sparkling, fall into the drink-now category.

Beyond price, here are some guidelines on which wines to cellar and which to drink now:

- **Sweets:** Sugar is an effective preservative. Anything in the sweet wine section is generally age-worthy, especially sweet white wines with high acid — think late harvest Riesling, Chenin Blanc, Sauternes, and other noble rot wines like Tokaji, and similar ones. The best sweet wines can live to see their 100th birthday.

- **Dry whites:** Most dry whites and rosés are best enjoyed young and fruity. The exceptions are those with high acidity such as Riesling, Chardonnay, and Chenin Blanc grown in a cool climate, because acidity is an excellent stabilizer and preservative. Barrel-fermented/aged white wines are also generally more age-worthy than wines matured in an oxygen-free environment like stainless steel or concrete vats, because slow exposure to air stabilizes them. Expect the very top examples of white wine to last (and even improve) for five to ten years from the vintage date, and occasionally, a little bit longer still.

✔ **Dry reds:** Dry red wines are by and large more age-worthy than dry whites, thanks to their tannin content. To produce red wine, grape skins are left to soak in the juice/wine for anywhere from a few days to a few months (white grapes are usually pressed and immediately separated from the skins before fermentation). This maceration process not only extracts the red color pigments from the skins, but also a full range of compounds called *phenols* (including tannins), which act as a natural buffer against the damaging effects of oxygen. (Check out Chapter 10 for more on tannins.) Red wines made from thick, phenol-rich-skinned grapes, like Cabernet Sauvignon, Syrah, Nebbiolo, Malbec, and Mourvèdre, are thus naturally protected against the air that seeps inescapably in through corks and even screw caps, making them more age-worthy. The small amount of air that does seep in works instead beneficially to soften the astringent edge of tannins while creating even more complex aromas and flavors.

Not all red wines are created equally. Some have a shelf life equivalent to dry white wines: very short. Dry, low tannins reds like Gamay, Grenache, Barbera, Dolcetto, lighter style Pinot Noir, and similar ones should also be consumed young to capture the fruit.

✔ **Sparkling:** Traditional method sparkling wines are the most age-worthy of the bubbly types (see Chapter 11). In addition to carbon dioxide, which effectively keeps oxygen away, they also have high acidity and often a pinch of residual sugar to protect them. And because the main interest in the flavor profile of traditional method sparklers isn't fresh fruit but rather the toasty, yeasty-biscuity aromas that arise from aging on the spent yeast cells after fermentation, there's no fear of losing freshness — they've already lost it. Top-level vintage Champagne can live for decades. Most Charmatt method sparkling wines for which freshness is critical, like Moscato d'Asti and Prosecco, are in the drink-as-young-as-possible category.

Sulphur dioxide: The magic preservative

In addition to the naturally occurring preservatives in wine (acidity, tannins/extract, alcohol, and sugar), winemakers can also add preservatives to extend the shelf life of their wines. *Sulphur dioxide* is the oldest and most common — it's been around in winemaking for at least a couple of thousand years. SO_2, as it's known, is both an antimicrobial and an antioxidant, two useful properties that stabilize wine. It keeps harmful bacteria at bay, prevents rogue yeasts from re-fermenting any residual sugars, slows down the inevitable browning of wine color, and distracts oxygen molecules from their business of bruising fresh fruit flavors. Virtually all wines have some SO_2 added; without it, the world would be full of dull, oxidized wines. Too much, however, and a wine can smell like a sulphur hot spring, not to mention cause an adverse allergic reaction in some people. The indication *contains sulfites,* is a legal label requirement in most countries.

Knowing How Long Wines Can Be Kept after They're Opened

After you pull the cork (or unscrew the cap), the clock is ticking. It's only a matter of time before your wine turns to vinegar, the inescapable end for fermented grape juice exposed to air (that hasn't been filtered by your liver). But like maturing wine in the cellar, how quickly it turns depends on several factors. Frustratingly, there's no easy-to-remember, straightforward relationship between wine region or grape variety and stability. Like all things related to wine, this question is complicated. You have an advantage though: You've opened and tasted the wine, so you know what type of wine you're dealing with, rather than guessing at an unopened bottle.

In the next sections, I share what I've learned about which wines stubbornly hang on and which check out quickly. I also give some tips on how and where to store open bottles to prolong the inevitable.

Observing open bottles

I often have many bottles of wine open at the same time, more than I could possibly drink in a day (a hazard of the occupation). These usually end up on the counter or in the fridge (with a cork in them), to be revisited later. Retasting these wines from time to time is fascinating to see how they've changed and whether they're still alive or dead. It can reveal much about the wine's integrity and composition, and whether the wine is ultimately cellar-worthy (that's if I have another unopened bottle). As a result, I have considerable experience in the matter.

As a rough guideline, wines that are candidates for long aging in the cellar are the ones that will also last the longest once opened. Old wines of any color, however, fare badly in my experience; they are too delicate and oxidize after even a day.

The following list walks you through what I've observed in my experiments with open bottles. You can refer to this list again and again to determine whether your favorite bottle of white or red will taste okay after being open for a few days. You ultimately make the final choice whether it's drinkable or not:

   ✔ **Barrel-aged wines fare better.** Perhaps counter intuitively, wines that are exposed to more oxygen during the winemaking process (such as wines aged in wooden barrels) tend to be more stable later on. This oxidative character is part of the intended wine style. In essence, because they're already slightly oxidized when they reach the bottle, they're more stable and better able to withstand exposure to air after they're uncorked. I once tortured a decidedly oxidative white wine for more than a month. By the end of my experiment, it was just starting to *open up,* which is to say it was just beginning to reveal its fruity and floral aromas!

✔ **Fresh, fruity wines die fast.** Contrary to wood-aged or oxidative wines, those that have been zealously protected from oxygen since birth and bottled very young, fresh, and fruity, die fastest. It's like what happens to my (lily-white) skin when I take a holiday down south over the winter. Within 30 seconds under a tropical sun I start to look like a lobster — I need either serious sunblock or slow and gentle exposure to UV rays at the tanning salon before fully exposing myself to the sun. Wine, like skin, needs gentle exposure to the elements to toughen it up, or it dies from the shock. If the wine is fresh, delicate, and fruity, drink up.

Don't panic: Most wines last longer than expected. Even light, un-oaked, fruity white and red wines last two or three days or more without sacrificing much. They're still drinkable even after a week, just a little less aromatic and fruity. It would probably take at least a month at high temperatures to turn the lightest wines to vinegar. Big robust reds can chill out for a week or longer, and some actually improve, as they would in the cellar. Oxidative-style wines like Sherry, Madeira, Tawny Port, Vin Jaune, and the like change little over a month or even longer. Crazy Georgian wines aged in clay amphorae for years before bottling *need* a month to open up.

Keeping those open bottles

The refrigerator, or any cool environment, is the best place to keep open bottles. Lower temperature means slower chemical reactions (oxidation), which will in turn extend the shelf life of an open bottle. Even better is to keep an empty half bottle around for those (hopefully rare) occasions when you don't finish the bottle.

Pour the leftovers out of the 750ml into a clean 375ml (assuming you have less than half a bottle leftover), and store the half bottle in the fridge with a stopper. The smaller container means less exposure to oxygen, which is what kills wine after all, and you can likely double or triple the life span.

Many other gadgets and preservation systems are available, such as vacuum pumps, floating disks, and nitrogen sprays. Although these gadgets can also extend the shelf life of open wines, nothing is more effective than finishing the bottle.

Serving Mature Wines with Food

Wines undergo changes in aroma, flavor, and texture as they age. As you'd expect, what you might pair with a young, robust red isn't necessarily the ideal match for the same wine after ten years in the cellar. Here are some points to consider:

- **Texture softens:** Aged red wines are less tannic and astringent, more like silk than wool. This means that they're more versatile than their tannic, youthful iterations, and less weary of the enemies of tannins — bitter and acidic elements in food. They don't require high salt, fat, and protein content to round out the rough edges. For example, you can move from charcoal grilled, well-marbled beef — great with young reds — to braised dishes; it's a match of similar textures.

- **Aromas and flavors develop:** With changes from fruity to caramelized, medicinal and savory, mature wines gain their own umami tastes. I like to mirror this savory flavor in the dishes I serve with old reds: Mushrooms, dried herbs, hard cheese, sundried tomatoes, aged beef or lamb, and so on, are all superb foils. Nutty and dried fruit flavors work well with aged whites.

- **Wines become more delicate:** Mature wines are more fragile and can easily be overwhelmed by pungent or intensely spiced foods. They're best served with subtle dishes that won't overwhelm. Simplicity is the way to go here: A classic roast of beef au jus (easy on the horseradish), wild mushroom risotto, or an unadorned piece of aged, hard cheese (nothing runny, stinky, or blue) like Manchego or Parmigiano, for example, is a perfect way to highlight a bottle of great old red wine.

Chapter 8

Serving Wine: Essential Strategies to Follow

*Y*ou've fretted, researched, consulted, and emptied your pockets to ensure that you have just the right wine for the occasion, and then, disappointment. But before you blame the winemaker or merchant or critic or friend, consider this question: Was the wine given a fair chance? The way you serve wine does make a difference. The temperature, whether or not it's decanted, even the type of glassware affects your perception of a wine. I know, I know, yet more bloody things to consider in the already over complicated world of wine. But you may as well do everything you can to maximize your pleasure with a few tricks of the trade.

In this chapter you get a grip on how temperature changes what you smell, taste, and touch in wine, and which wines show best at which temperatures — important considerations for food pairing. I look at how different types and shapes of glassware can change you enjoyment of wine, if not the actual chemical composition, by changing your state of mind, and suggest the basic types you should have in your cupboard.

Decanting, too, is part of the ritual of wine service for some wines. I share the lowdown on why, which, how, and how long. By the end of this chapter you should be serving wine like a pro.

Knowing When: Serving Wine in the Appropriate Order

A well-designed dinner, like a well-written play, has a flow that keeps you engaged and looking forward to the next scene. When serving multiple wines throughout a meal, the way to keep your guests in a state of expectation is to serve the wines in increasing order of intensity and complexity. Serve wine in this order:

- ✓ **The first wine:** You should start with a wine that gets the appetite flowing and builds anticipation for what's to come. The best choices to start with include high-acid wines, such as Champagne or other dry sparkling wines, for example, which get the gastric juices flowing in anticipation of food. Crisp dry, still white wines can also serve the same purpose.

- ✓ **The next wine:** Wines should progressively notch up the flavor magnitude and complexity, so that you're not left wishing you were still drinking the previous wine. Serving a really complex, top-notch wine upfront takes the sizzle out of everything else that follows. Build up to your highlight wine of the night, when the meal reaches its climax.

- ✓ **The last wine:** You should finish by gently letting down the diner. A drop of sweet wine is usually appreciated.

Aside from the artistic aspect of wine service order, you also have some practical taste considerations. For instance, serving a really light wine after a full-blown, robust wine makes the light wine seem virtually like water. Or serving a dry wine after a sweet wine makes the dry wine seem even drier, astringent, and more sour, just like serving a dry red wine with a sweet dish usually ends in disaster.

Here are the general rules to follow regarding the order of wine service (though like all rules related to wine, don't be afraid to break them once in a while, for artistic reasons):

- ✓ Light before full-bodied

- ✓ Delicate before bold

- ✓ Dry before sweet

- ✓ Lower alcohol before higher alcohol

- ✓ Sparkling before still (except sweet sparkling)

- ✓ Younger before older (The older is more complex. *Note:* serving a young, really robust red before a delicate old red wine can knock the stuffing out of your palate and reduce enjoyment of the older bottle.)

Note that I didn't say, "White before red." Although that practice is common, and on the whole, red wines are usually better placed after white wines, it's not always the case. On plenty of occasions, serving a serious white after a light red makes more sense, for instance when you have a great bottle of barrel-fermented Chardonnay with a little bottle age for added complexity. It would be a letdown to follow that with a simple, easy-quaffing red like basic Gamay, Merlot, or Sangiovese.

Serving Wine at Its Intended Temperature

When it comes to eating and drinking, temperature matters. You wouldn't serve cold porridge or hot gazpacho, would you? Cold cheese straight from the fridge offers only a shadow of its aroma and flavor potential, while warm soft drinks are mostly sugary, aggressively carbonated, and hard to swallow.

Chefs also know through experience that any dish served cold, such as terrines, patés, or soups, need to be slightly more salted than the same dish served hot, because people's perception of salt decreases at lower temperatures; that's to say things taste less salty. The interplay between temperature and sensory perception likely occurs by many mechanisms, including the direct action of temperature on sensory receptors, but in any case, scientists have shown that people's taste receptors are modulated by temperature change. Basically, the same foods and wines taste different at different temperatures.

So when you're serving wine, you want to consider the effects, both positive and negative, of the wine's service temperature. Table 8-1 lists different wine types and their optimal serving temperatures in both Fahrenheit and Celsius.

Table 8-1	Recommended Serving Temperatures for Wine
Wine Style	*Temperature in Fahrenheit (°C)*
Full-bodied red wines, Vintage Port	64° (18°C)
Tawny Port	63° (17°C)
Medium-bodied red wines	59°–61° (15°–16°C)
Amontillado Sherry	57°–59° (14°–15°C)
Light-bodied (unoaked) red wines	55°–59° (13°–15°C)
Full-bodied, barrel-fermented white wines	54° (12°C)

(continued)

Table 8-1 *(continued)*

Wine Style	Temperature in Fahrenheit (°C)
Medium-bodied white wines	46°–50° (8°–10°C)
Dry rosé, light-bodied, unoaked white wines, off-dry and sweet wines	44°–48° (7°–9°C)
Vintage sparkling (Champagne), extra-brut (no sugar added)	48° (9°C)
Fino sherry	43°–46° (6°–8°C)
Non-vintage sparkling wine, Charmat method, sweeter styles of sparkling	43°–45° (6°–7°C)

The following sections spell out the details of how serving wine at different temperatures alters the wine's character, including important changes to its aromatics and texture.

Maximizing the wine's aromatics: The smell

Temperature affects the volatility of *aromatic compounds,* that is, their capacity to become airborne and thus reach your nose, where you can then smell them. Most of the time, the more volatile a wine's aromatic compounds are, the more enjoyment you can get out of smelling the wine.

Temperature dramatically affects aromatic compounds. At a chemical level, when a substance is warm, its molecules vibrate fast. When cold, they slow down. In other words, the colder a wine is, the slower and less volatile its aromatic compounds are, and thus the less aromatic a wine will be. At the other end, when a wine is too warm, many of the enjoyable aromatic molecules are so active they're gone before you can smell them, leaving little but the light burn of alcohol vapors.

No matter the color (red, white, pink, orange), temperature affects the aromatics of all wine types in the same way. Here are a couple simple guidelines you can use:

 ✔ **The more aromatically interesting a wine is, the warmer you should serve it.** By *aromatically interesting* I refer to how complex the wine is. In order to maximize your smelling pleasure for complex, top-flight wines, you want to serve:

- Top whites at around 53°–57°F (12°–14°C). This is incidentally the recommended storage temperature for all wines, or what a sommelier would call *cellar temperature.*

- Top reds at around 64°–68°F (18°–20°C). This is slightly warmer than cellar temperature, but cooler than the average ambient temperature in your home or in a restaurant.

Much above 64°–68°F (18°–20°C), and it's back to alcohol vapors.

✔ **The simpler the wine (or the poorer the quality), the cooler you should serve it.** Doing so allows you to maximize the refreshment angle, because there isn't much to smell in any case. In order to maximize your enjoyment for simpler wines, you want to serve:

- Whites between 39°–43°F (4°–6°C). This is probably the temperature that your fridge is set to. Twenty to thirty minutes in a bucket with ice and water will also get you there.

- Reds at around 57°–61°F (14°–16°C). Reds are trickier because of tannins and texture, which are also affected by temperature (see the next section), but most cheap red wines are fresher, livelier, and more drinkable, not to mention less ho-hum, when served with a light chill. Thirty minutes in the fridge or a few minutes in ice water can achieve this temperature.

Serving wines cooler is a great way for disposing of those second-rate, cheap wines you receive as gifts over the holidays.

Focusing on texture and taste

Beyond aromatics, temperature also affects wine texture and taste. Wine served cold seems

✔ More acidic (which makes it more refreshing)

✔ More tannic (which makes it more astringent and bitter)

Serving wines cooler increases their crispness, fruitiness, and astringency, while serving wines warmer gives them more of an alcohol taste. They're also flabbier, less fruity, and less astringent.

This is why red wines are generally served warmer than whites: They contain *tannin* (the substance in wine that causes the astringent, drying, mouth-puckering sensation), while whites rarely have any tannin at all. The curious thing about tannin is that you perceive its drying effect more at lower temperatures. That means if you take the same tannic wine and serve it at both 50°F (10°C) and 64°F (18°C), the cooler sample will appear more astringent and more bitter, perhaps unpleasantly so. At 64°F the wine will still be tannic, but much more tolerable. Then when decanted and served with a little salty protein, the tannins may no longer be a significant factor at all.

Because most whites and rosés don't contain tannin, you can serve them chilled without the fear of increasing that astringent sensation, while emphasizing the refreshment factor and favoring fruity over alcoholic aromatics. Barrel-aged whites, on the other hand, are not only likely to be more aromatically complex, but also likely to contain some tannin derived from the wood. Therefore, they're best served slightly warmer than unoaked whites.

When wines are served too warm, such as at the ambient temperature in most homes and restaurants (around 70°–75°F, 22°–23°C), they lose their impression of freshness. Like with aromatics where the vapors of alcohol come to dominate, the perception of acidity is lessened, making the wine taste flabby and alcoholic.

Many reds grapes have naturally low tannin levels (mostly grapes with thin skins), such as Gamay, Pinot Noir, Grenache, Tempranillo, and Barbera. These wines are more enjoyable when served with a chill, as are most unoaked reds of any variety (but remember those exceptions!). You can increase the fresh, fruity aspect without danger of making them too astringent. And because the majority of wines produced today are intended for immediate consumption, that is, with little tannin that would otherwise harden and turn astringent at cool temperatures, you can serve just about every white, rosé, and red at least slightly chilled, especially in the summer and with spicy foods.

I have my own anecdotal evidence from restaurant experience that customers served wine cooler drink more, and more quickly. I chalk it up to greater refreshment. Proper serving temperature is an often-overlooked trick of the trade to increase sales.

Serving sweet and sparkling wines

Temperature also affects the perception of sugar and carbon dioxide. Keep these two factors in mind when serving sweet and sparkling wines:

> ✔ **When served cooler, a sweet wine tastes less sweet.** The sweet sensation caused by residual sugar in wine is reduced at lower temperatures (while the freshness is increased), just as the perception of salt in food is lowered when it's served cold. Hence, off-dry and sweet wines are served chilled, emphasizing fruit and decreasing the sweet-cloying aspect. However, don't serve all sweet wines, especially complex, high quality wines ice cold because you'll miss out on the aromas and flavors that make them interesting (and expensive) in the first place. It's a fine balance.

> ✔ **Sparkling wines taste less aggressively effervescent and the bubbles last longer at lower temperatures.** Sparkling wines are likewise served chilled to slow down those CO_2 molecules. At higher temperatures they're more agitated and thus more aggressive on your receptors (like warm, fizzy pop), not to mention they escape more quickly, leaving a flat glass of former bubbly behind. Cooler temps also help to lessen the sweetness that virtually all sparkling wines have and improve the crisp, vibrant aspect. But still keep the basic rule in mind: The better the wine, even sparkling, the warmer you should serve it, up to about 50°F (10°C) for top flight vintage Champagne, for example.

When in doubt, serve cooler rather than warmer. The wine will eventually warm up. Wine served too warm from the start is doomed, unless, of course, you live in an igloo.

Getting temperature right if you don't live in a castle

The dictum of serving wines at cellar or room temperature (what the French would call *chambré*) probably dates from the days when folks lived in castles in some northern European principality. No doubt that even in summer, the temperature inside those thick stone walls rarely rose above 60°–64°F (16°–18°C), which happens to be an ideal temperature for most red wines. Similarly, the deep subterranean cellars in those castles hover somewhere around 49°–53°F (10°–12°C) most of the year, a fine temperature to serve your serious whites.

Because I don't live in a castle, my chambré isn't so ideal. Like me, most people keep their homes at around 70°–75°F (22°–24°C), which is a little warmer than ideal for even the biggest reds. And in the summer, especially without air conditioning, or on the patio under the sun, it can get downright hot. Some intervention is required.

Whites at room temperature need a couple of hours in the fridge to chill down to serving temperature. Most reds require about 20 to 30 minutes in the fridge before serving. Just remember to maintain that temperature, either with a simple ceramic, stainless steel, or acrylic cooler, the kind that requires no ice or water, or by dipping in and out of a bucket of ice and water (don't leave the wine in the bucket for more than 30 to 40 minutes or it will get way too cold). Otherwise pour and return to the fridge in between refills.

If you didn't get organized ahead of time, the fastest way to cool a bottle is in a bucket of water and ice, about half and half. Ice alone, with all those air pockets in between the cubes, is far less effective at chilling; water is a much more efficient conductor (and good luck getting the bottle back in the ice-packed bucket). Two minutes in a bucket will drop the temperature by about a degree

Celsius. So if your wine is at room temperature, count on about 12 minutes to bring it down to the right temperature for a light-medium-bodied red, or about 25 minutes for a basic white. You can use the freezer too, but I've frozen countless bottles in mine, so if you have a memory like I do, set a timer — 10 minutes for reds, 20 to 25 minutes for whites.

Don't forget to store unfinished bottles of wine, red or white, in the fridge. They won't spoil as rapidly; all reactions, including oxidation, occur more quickly at higher temperatures. (See Chapter 7 for more information.) And remember to bring your red out of the fridge 20 minutes or so before serving to bring it back to the best serving temperature.

Using the Right Glassware

Depending on whom you ask, the question of how important the drinking vessel is in the overall enjoyment of wine can yield widely varying opinions. From "any old tumbler will do" to "only the finest hand-blown crystal stems will do justice," the spectrum is wide. Here's what I think: Glassware matters. But not only for the reasons you may think. In the next sections I look at both the effects of the imagination, as well as the effects of physics brought about by different glasses.

Is it all in the mind? Perception is powerful

What you think of the glass that the wine is served in has an impact on your enjoyment of it. I've done some sneaky experiments of my own, serving great wine in a Styrofoam cup or plonk in my finest crystal, just to test reactions. And the results? For most people, even the most humble wine tastes pretty good in a hand-blown crystal glass, while it's tough for anything to shine in Styrofoam. Pouring a cheap wine into a bottle with a famous label and big price tag isn't much different; the mediocre is suddenly transcendental.

The actual wine obviously doesn't change, but your perception does. And as scientists understand more and more, perception is a bigger part of enjoyment than any hard-working wine grower would care to admit (although the marketing companies have figured it out). They know that innumerable variables are capable of distorting your perceptions, so that you imagine differences that don't actually exist. Just as any smart sommelier knows, an engaging story, theatrical decanting, fine stemware, and an outward approval of your wine choice all serve to predispose you to enjoy a wine. And the trick almost always works; it's not only about the wine, but also what you believe (or are led to believe) about it.

Impressing your guests with glassware: Just a status symbol

You only need visit one of the countless museums around the world with an impressive collection of wine vessels from antiquity to the present to illustrate their importance in society and the wine-drinking ritual. They were, and still are, status symbols — an outward sign of respect toward guests, those who are worthy of the household's finest cups, as well as what is served in them, a wine worthy of an elaborate, decorative, carefully selected vessel.

But heavy lead crystal, hand-blown Venetian glass, inlaid designs, intricate patterns, vibrant colors, precious jewels, silver, and gold don't do anything to improve the aromas and flavors of wine. Indeed, they may detract from them. All these design elements have but one purpose: to impress the user, like a work of visual art that serves no purpose other than to set your dopamines firing. The particulars of design are merely a question of fashion.

In ancient Greece, the terracotta or ceramic *kylix* (chalice), with titillating scenes painted on the inside and revealed only when emptied, was the wine cup of the upper class. In George Ravenscroft's days (1632–1683), it was the brilliant purity of lead crystal glasses, a novelty of the time, which most impressed. Today, it's George Riedel's creations: thin, sleek, generously proportioned, hand-blown crystal stems said to be designed in such a way as to enhance the characteristics of specific wine grapes and styles.

The only thing these vessels have in common is that they're designed for maximum positive impact on the user. In the end, you usually end up enjoying the wine more than you would drinking from a humble cup.

You can use this trick to your own advantage and maximize your and your guests' enjoyment. Just as if you believe your host has pulled out his or her finest glassware to honor you and the wine served, or that the glass chosen is the ultimate vessel to exalt the qualities of the Pinot Noir, scientists know you'll like it more. Considering the significant cost of even basic wine relative to other nonessential consumer products, investing in a decent set of wineglasses makes sense. Otherwise, it's kind of like getting a top-of-the-line home entertainment system, but not bothering to take the last step and getting the right speaker stands to project the sound just so — you're not maximizing your investment. The glassware doesn't need to be $100 hand-blown crystal stems, but for the cost of a few decent bottles of wine upfront, get yourself a set of glasses that can enhance your enjoyment for every other bottle you buy afterwards. I'd say that's worthwhile mileage.

Eyeing your three basic stemware needs

Most people have neither the budget nor the space to store sets of three dozen different wine glass shapes. Although serving Riesling in a specially designed Riesling glass and Sangiovese in its tailor-made stem may be fun, it's not practical or necessary. In fact, you can get away with a single, versatile shape for *all* types of wine. At my house, when nobody's looking, I use the same medium-sized, 17-ounce glass for *everything*. Although the manufacturer describes it as being suited for full-bodied whites and young reds, it's also great for fine sparkling wines, dessert wines, and even full-bodied reds. (Admittedly, tasting out of the same type of glass helps to level the playing field for each wine and takes one more variable out of the equation when I'm reviewing wines for publication.)

But because pure enjoyment is what you're after, and presentation is part of the art of enjoyment, you want to understand that psychological perceptions aside, practical physical differences between the main types of wine glasses also make some more appropriate for certain types of wines than others. The following sections discuss the minimum three basic types of stemware you want to have on hand:

The slender, shapely flute: Sparkling wine

The tall, slender flute traditionally used for sparkling wine has both a practical and an aesthetic advantage. The shape allows you to watch those tiny little bubbles on their journey up to the surface, a mesmerizing display on its own. But more practically, the narrow width of the glass translates to a smaller surface area/volume of wine ratio, which is to say that you have a lot of wine in the glass relative to how much of it is in contact with the air. And because carbon dioxide can only escape at the surface, the smaller the surface area, the longer the bubbles stay in the wine. Your sparkling wine stays sparkling longer.

The flute should contain between at least 8 to 12 ounces. This way, even with a standard-sized pour (about 5 ounces), the glass still has some headspace above the wine for the aromas to gather.

The downside to a shapely flute is that you lose some of the aromatics of the wine because a smaller surface area also means less runway for aromatic molecules to take off and fly up to your nose. That's why flutes designed for high-end Champagne have wider bodies to make sure you can enjoy the smell, too.

Why white wine glasses are smaller, but needn't be

You probably know that white wine glasses are usually smaller than red wine glasses. Why? The simple answer is that whites are traditionally served chilled, while reds aren't. Thus you can fill a large glass of red wine without worrying about having to guzzle it down before it warms up to the ambient temperature. But a large, full glass of white wine would likely be warm and flabby by the time you get to the last couple of sips. So some genius from a bygone era determined that serving white wines in smaller glasses would be better, so they would need refilling with chilled wine, more often. As such you'd be prevented from perpetrating such an egregious vinous impropriety as drinking warm white.

The glass size has nothing to do with whites being less complex or less aromatic or otherwise less worthy than reds. In fact, white wine glasses don't have a standard size, but you want to look for one with a capacity of between 10 to 18 ounces. Any smaller and it's easy to overfill. You can serve dry or sweet white wine, rosés, light reds (served chilled), and fortified wine in this size glass. When pouring the wine, don't fill the glass up more than two-thirds full. Otherwise, swirling is a real challenge and there's no space for the aromas to gather.

Practically speaking, the more aromatic and complex the wine, whether white, red, pink, or whatever, the larger the glass should be. The large surface area of a big glass maximizes take-off points for fragrant molecules. If you can remember not to overfill your large glass with white, there's no reason not to use a full-sized wine glass for your complex whites, too.

Fat bowl, narrower, sheer rim, stem

Regardless of the size of the glass, in terms of the basic shape, look for a glass that has a wider bowl than rim. This way you can safely engage in the wine drinker's favorite sport: swirling. The wide bowl allows you to vigorously swirl your glass, exposing ever-more aromatic molecules to the air and setting them free, while the tapered shape up to a narrower rim keeps the wine *inside* the glass where it belongs. The narrower opening also concentrates all those inviting aromatics so that your nose can capture them before they disappear into the ether. The rim should be sheer rather than rolled, putting less glass between your lips and the wine. Rolled rims are like sitting in the bleachers: You're too far from the action.

Look for a glass with a capacity of 18 to 28 ounces. The larger the glass, the more you'll maximize the aromatics. (But you don't want a fish bowl either; if the glass is too big, you lose the aromatics in too much headspace, or you need to empty a full bottle into the glass, which I don't recommend.)

I also prefer glasses with stems. Many manufacturers make high-end stemless glasses, and while they're easier to store and less breakable (most glasses snap where the stem meets the bowl), I find that fingerprints on the bowl, especially when eating greasy finger foods, looks uninviting and detracts from enjoyment, and having to hold the bowl with your hand warms wine up too quickly.

Fending off bubbles with the *coupe* and the *swizzle stick*

In the heady days of the tight corset dress and rigid etiquette in the courts of Europe, the effects of drinking effervescent wine could be, well, embarrassing. Imagine sipping on a carbonated beverage with your entire upper torso constricted in a tightly-drawn, high-class equivalent of the straight jacket. You guessed it; the carbon dioxide enters and is expelled rather quickly, or you suffer from the pain and pressure. Yet Champagne was then, as it still is today, *de rigueur* for social gatherings of the upper classes, putting society ladies, as well as gentlemen with less rigorous body control, in an awkward place. Enter the *coupe*. The Champagne coupe is a very wide, flat-bottomed stemmed glass. Contrary to the flute, it offers the maximum surface area

possible to dissipate the annoying carbon dioxide (that champagne producers worked so hard to get into the wine in the first place). Within minutes the wine is flat, making the drinking of it far less potentially embarrassing. Today the coupe is best used for building Champagne towers or for serving daiquiris.

Likewise, the now-rare Champagne swizzle stick, a long stick with a flayed end made of ivory, crystal, or silver, depending on your station, was used to beat the bubbles out of sparkling wine. Much like a whisk, the carbon dioxide would be all but gone after some vigorous stirring, and drinking could proceed with greater peace of mind.

Decanting or Not Decanting

To decant or not decant — that is the question that causes anxiety and occasionally arguments even amongst the pros. Because *decanting* (pouring a wine out of its bottle into some other container, also called *carafing*) can improve, or detract, from the enjoyment of a wine, and showing a wine at its best is part of the success of food and wine pairing, just as serving food at the right temperature is, decanting is worth a little look, which I do in these sections.

Understanding what decanting does

Ask any sommelier why wines are decanted and you'll get the same answer:

- To separate from sediment that deposits in some wines over time
- To quickly warm up a wine served straight from the cellar
- To impress your guests with your skill and care
- To aerate big, robust, young red wines, or tightly wound earthy-mineral white wines

The first three reasons are pretty straightforward and cause little discussion. Old wines, especially reds, contain sediment that, while harmless, looks alarmingly murky and tastes like a spoonful of sand. So carefully pouring off the clear wine into a decanter or carafe (or any container large enough to hold the contents of the bottle) and leaving the solid stuff behind makes sense.

Likewise, a big red served straight from the cellar at 54°F (12°C) would likely be more interesting at 64°F (18°C). By pouring it into a decanter and then into a glass, both at room temperature, you gain several degrees almost immediately as the containers gently warm the liquid. After a couple more minutes, your wine is at the perfect temperature (no microwave required). And lastly, although you may argue the showbiz aspect of decanting, the truth is that lots of drinkers still dig the extra attention paid both to them and the wine. Decanting their wine makes them feel special.

The real contention surrounds the fourth point: Do young wines actually improve when they are allowed to breathe? Does a good dose of air really enhance aromatics and soften texture, as the textbooks contend? Will an hour or more of air hasten development, replacing a few years in the cellar?

In a word, yes, at least most of the time. I've done plenty of experimentation with young, robust wines and find that although nothing replaces the transformation you get from a few years, or decades, in a cellar, a little air does open up the aromatics, and even softens the texture, if only marginally. You can get air into wine several ways, but nothing beats a good ol' fashioned decanting a few minutes or up to several hours before you serve the wine. (I've even tried using a blender, which, for the record, is *not* recommended!)

Decanting like a pro: What you need

If you decide to decant your wine, especially old wine with sediment, you need the following:

- ✔ **A container larger than the bottle you're decanting:** Technically any container, from a milk jug to a cut lead crystal decanter can do the job. Just make sure it's clean, and remember that, like fancy glassware, a beautiful decanter can make a better impression than an over-sized Dixie cup.

- ✔ **A clean napkin to wipe the crud off the bottle neck:** Wipe once before you pull the cork (after you've removed the capsule) and once again after you've removed the cork. (The inside neck of the bottle on really old wines often has some built-up sediment that you don't want to pour into the decanter.)

- ✔ **A source of light:** You need to be able to see when the sediment reaches the neck of the bottle so you know when to stop pouring: Traditionally it was a candle; today, a flashlight, a bright overhead light, or even sunlight streaming in through a window are effective if you position the bottle correctly.

✔ **A steady hand when decanting for sediment:** It requires a slow, even pour to avoid disturbing the sediment. (When decanting wines for aeration, the more vigorous, the better.)

All you need is the container if you're decanting young red or white wines for air, rather than sediment. In this scenario, I usually just tip the bottle upright and let the wine gurgle violently into the decanter to maximize aeration. (Horror! You're bruising my wine!)

Knowing what to decant

Here is my simple rule: Open the wine ahead of time and pour yourself a small taste. If it doesn't seem that interesting (closed, astringent, dull), then you won't lose much by decanting and giving it some air. If the wine seems perfectly enjoyable, just put the cork back on (or screw cap) and set aside until you're ready for it. The tiny amount of air it gets from just opening it won't affect the wine. Otherwise, consider these sections:

What to decant for aeration

If you're thinking of decanting, you want to decant the following wines for aeration:

✔ Most medium-full bodied, balanced, moderately tannic reds (1 to 5 years old)

✔ All full, deep and robust, turbocharged reds, with chewy texture (1 to 5 years old)

✔ Certain lightweight, crisp and lean, and medium-full bodied, creamy, wood-aged whites (1 to 3 years old, to know which could benefit from the treatment)

You also can check out Chapters 9 (whites) and 10 (reds) for a description and list of common wines in these categories. Larger containers like the traditional, wide, flat-bottomed captain's decanter (so called as it was the decanter of choice for sea captains; its large base made it stable enough to stay upright even when the sea was pitching and rolling) work well for wines being decanted for aeration because they maximize surface area of the wine in contact with the air.

How long to decant young wines

You want to decant younger wines about an hour or more ahead of serving. This amount of time is usually sufficient, although I know of some producers of Amarone in the Veneto, Italy, for example, who recommend decanting their wines a day ahead of time. Just remember that if the wine still isn't all that aromatically interesting by the time it hits the table, it will still continue to open in the glass. But if all the aromas have already escaped, there's no getting them back.

Err on the side of shorter rather than longer decanting times. Wines will continue to open and develop in the glass, while excessive time in the decanter will oxidize the wine.

What to decant for sediment

When considering which wines to decant to eliminate sediment, focus your attention on any reds in the medium-full bodied and full, turbocharged categories, older than about 6 years of age.

When planning to decant an old red wine, stand the bottle upright for at least 12 hours (the night before is even better) so the sediment has time to settle at the bottom of the bottle. Handle the bottle with minimum movement to avoid disturbing the sediment afterwards, and during the decanting process. Old, delicate red wines decanted for sediment fare better in thinner, narrower decanters with less air contact, preserving the delicate aromatics that you've waited so patiently for.

A growing number of unrefined, unfiltered red wines are on the market that can throw sediment even when young. Sediment in young wines is almost always a good sign; it means that nothing has been stripped out of the wine by excessive filtering. Treat these like older reds and decant to remove the sediment. Many of these wines will vaunt their minimal handling on the back label, warning that a light deposit will form, so at least you know what to expect.

How long to decant old wines

Decant really old red wines immediately before serving, so you can enjoy sniffing the delicate aromas as they develop in the glass. The perfume of old wine is often fleeting, too, so decanting too far ahead may mean missing out on the aromatic symphony, like a fatal pause between pulling the soufflé out of the oven and serving — wait too long and it collapses.

What not to decant

Certain wines don't benefit from carafing. Such wines include

- Most light-bodied, bright, zesty, low-tannin reds
- Rosés
- Most aromatic, fruity, whites
- Most lightweight, lean, crisp whites
- Sparkling wine, Fino Sherry, Tawny Port, most dessert wines

The majority of wines in these categories have little to gain (and lots to lose) by decanting. The sudden rush of air is likely to send aromatics scurrying, which is what makes up a large part of their enjoyment.

Part III
Sorting Out the World of Wine

The 5th Wave   By Rich Tennant

"What do you mean you forgot the white wine?! You know darn well I can't serve fish without white wine!"

In this part . . .

This part gets you started on sorting out the world of wine into manageable bits — ground zero for finding the right match. On the surface, the wine world appears vast and infinitely complex with thousands of places, producers, and grapes, and hundreds of thousands of different wines. Here I distill this overwhelming world into a handful of basic style categories into which every wine produced can be slotted.

The specific grape or region doesn't matter as much as the general style of wine — whether light or full-bodied, dry or sweet, smooth or astringent, and so on, at the top level of food and wine pairing. The style distinction is more critical than nuances of aromas and flavors (those considerations come at the next level). In these chapters, I define each category and pull together the list of grapes and regional wines that generally fall into each, along with the production factors that lead them there.

These chapters also provide general pairing guidelines for each wine style — what to look for and avoid for each, as well as pairing trees, linking each style to both general ingredients and cooking techniques, as well as specific dishes from around the world that pair well.

Chapter 9

Going with Dry Whites and Rosés

In This Chapter

▶ Sizing up white and rosé wine styles

▶ Shopping for whites and rosés

▶ Pairing whites and rosés with food

1 love white wine. It's given less respect than red wine, but I wager that the more you taste, the more you will gravitate to whites. They can be amazingly transparent reflections of their growing region (which is exciting for wine folks), and they're extremely versatile at the table (which is exciting for sommeliers). And it's a myth that they aren't as complex as red wines.

I also group rosés along with whites in this chapter because although rosé starts out on the road to becoming red wine, it finishes the process as you'd do for whites, and more resembles a white than a red wine. Rosés and whites also pair well with similar foods, and are generally served at the same temperature and in the same type of glassware. It's a myth that all rosés are sweet.

This chapter covers the main styles of dry whites and rosé, including the common grapes and places that most often make each style. I also provide a *pairing tree* for each category that is a visual representation of the general tastes, aromas, and flavors, and cooking methods that point you toward the general types of foods for which they're best suited, with a few specific dishes to get your creative juices flowing.

Understanding the Different Styles of White Wine

White wine is wine with little or no red or pink color. It ranges from almost colorless to deep amber gold, depending on many factors, such as the grape variety, the growing region, and especially how old the wine is. Grapes with green-gold or pale pink skins when ripe make white wine exclusively; you can also make white wine from red grapes, because virtually all grape juice is colorless, even the juice of grapes with black skins. Think of white Champagne made from black-skinned Pinot Noir (to make red wine you have to soak the pigment-rich skins with the juice; see Chapter 10 for more on red wine production). Keep in mind that I also consider wines with a very pale pink (or a Gris tinge as the French would say), or even an orange-amber tinge, in this section — white wine comes in many shades!

You can make basically three styles of white wine:

- Lightweight, crisp, and lean
- Aromatic, fruity, round
- Medium-full bodied, creamy, wood-aged

Virtually all the world's white wines can be put into one of these categories. In the following sections I give a brief explanation of each, followed by the common grapes and places that make them.

You may notice some overlap between categories — naturally you didn't think categorizing would be that simple, did you? For example, the same grape can play in different categories — it changes style when it's grown in different climates and treated in different ways. So when you're not sure, go beyond the grape and look to clues, such as the region/appellation, price, alcohol level, and other details often on the back label, such as whether or not the wine was fermented and/or aged in oak to figure out which style category it properly belongs to.

Eyeing the lightweights: Crisp and lean

Dry, lightweight whites usually come, though not always, from cool climates (think of coniferous or deciduous trees surrounding the vineyards instead of palm trees or eucalyptus). They're made in stainless steel tanks or some other neutral container that doesn't impart any flavor. They have fresh but subtle citrus fruit or herbal flavors, mouth-watering acidity, moderate alcohol (11 to 13 percent), and light body. The vast majority are best drunk young, within the first one to three years. These wines are highly versatile, like a squeeze of lemon on your favorite dish, meaning that you can drink them with just about any food without fear of causing a *natural disaster* (a bad food and wine experience).

If you're shopping for lightweight, crisp and lean whites, head to a respectable purveyor and ask for one of the following grapes that commonly produce lightweight wines:

- Chardonnay (unoaked)
- Chenin Blanc (dry, unoaked)
- Pinot Grigio

✔ Riesling (light, dry styles)

✔ Sauvignon Blanc

Some other typically lightweight white wine grapes by specific country and region include the following:

✔ **Australia:** Hunter Valley Semillon

✔ **Austria:** Inexpensive Grüner Veltliner (*klassic, steinfeder,* and *federspiel* styles)

✔ **France:** Sancerre and Pouilly-Fumé (made from Sauvignon Blanc), dry Chenin Blanc, Gros Plant, Muscadet (also known as Melon de Bourgogne) and other basic white from the Loire, basic Chablis, Aligoté and basic Mâcon blanc from Burgundy, Pinot Blanc, and Auxerrois from Alsace, Savoie whites, Picpoul de Pinet from the Midi, and Gaillac blanc and Jurançon sec from the southwest

✔ **Greece:** Moscophilero from Mantinia, and Roditis

✔ **Hungary:** Dry Furmint (no oak), Szürkebarát (Pinot Gris), and Olaszrizling

✔ **Italy:** Northeastern Pinot Grigio, Friulano (from Friuli), Frascati, basic Soave, Gavi, Grechetto, Grillo and most Sicilian whites, Trebbiano d'Abruzzo, and Vermentino (especially from Sardinia)

✔ **Portugal:** Most Vinho Verde (made from several grapes including Loureiro, Avesso, Alvarinho and Arinto), basic whites from Estremadura, and Bucelas

✔ **Spain:** Basic Rias Baixas and other northwestern whites made from Albariño and other related grapes (Loureiro, Trajadura) the Txacoli wines of Basque Country made from Hondarrabi Zuri, simple unoaked, and dry wines of the Penedès

✔ **Switzerland:** Chasselas

Aromatic, fruity, or more assertive

The second category of white wines includes those that are aromatic, fruity, or more *assertive* (which means more aromatically intense or concentrated, with distinct flavor profile). Wines in this category are a step up in body and weight from the lightweight and lean whites, but they are still refreshing and unoaked. They have a soft, more *rounded* texture (no sharp edges), lower acidity, and more generous alcohol. Aromas and flavors are moderate to intense, fruity, and/or floral. Some not particularly aromatic grapes are also in this category, included because of their rich, assertive flavors that increase the intensity factor without perfume.

If you're shopping for aromatic, assertive whites, look for wines made in moderate or warm climates, from one of the following popular grapes:

- Gewürztraminer
- Marsanne/Roussanne blends (no oak)
- Muscat (all types)
- Pinot Gris (also known as Pinot Grigio)
- Riesling (riper styles)
- Sauvignon Blanc (riper styles)
- Viognier

The following lesser known white grapes and regions also often produce aromatic or assertive whites:

- **Argentina:** Torrontés
- **Austria:** Top-level Grüner Veltliner (especially from the Wachau, Kamptal, and Kremstal) and Gelber Muskateller (Muscat)
- **Croatia:** Posip
- **France:** Alsatian whites (especially Riesling, plus Gewürztraminer, Muscat, and Pinot Gris), top level Chablis, Midi blends (no oak), and top level Chenin Blanc from the Loire
- **Greece:** Assyrtiko from Santorini and Macedonia, Robola from Cephalonia, and Malagouzia from Attica and Epanomi
- **Hungary:** Hárslevelú, Irsai Olivér, and Muskotály (Muscat)
- **Italy:** Arneis and Timorasso from Piedmont, Falanghina, Coda di Volpe, Greco di Tufo and Fiano di Avellino from Campania, top Pinot Grigio, Friulano and Ribolla Gialla from Friuli, Verdicchio from Le Marche, and top Garganega from Soave
- **Portugal:** Maria Gomes and Antão Vaz
- **Spain:** Albariño from Rias Baixas, Verdejo from Rueda, and Godello from Valdeorras/northwestern Spain
- **Switzerland:** Petit Arvine from the Valais

Full-bodied, wood-aged

The third general style of white wines is full-bodied, wood-aged whites. These wines share the characteristic of being fermented and aged in barrel. The use of oak creates an additional layer of flavor and occasionally textural changes (such as a light *astringency* from the tannins present in wood) that aren't usually found in unoaked whites. The sheen of roasted, toasty oak, full of vanilla, caramel, coffee, nuts, clove, and other sweet baking spice aromas and flavors (what wine pros call *torrefaction* aromas) makes this a crossover category into the realm of reds. (Check out Chapter 10 for more information on red wines.)

Barrel-aged whites also usually undergo the secondary fermentation process called *malolactic fermentation,* in which harder malic acid is transformed into softer lactic acid, creating a rounder, smoother texture and buttery flavor (see Chapter 2 for more information on linking taste and wine).

You prefer white wine but want to eat a steak? Choose from this category. If you're shopping for full-bodied, wood-aged whites, look for some of these grapes, which are often (but certainly not always) aged in wood (if in doubt, inquire with your merchant or sommelier):

- ✔ Chardonnay

- ✔ Fumé Blanc (another name for Sauvignon Blanc when it's wood-aged)

- ✔ Rhône style blends (Marsanne, Roussanne, and so on)

- ✔ Sauvignon Blanc-Semillon blends

- ✔ Viognier

Some other typically full-bodied, wood-aged white wine grapes/appellations include the following:

- ✔ **France:** Top white Burgundy from all appellations, Condrieu and Hermitage blanc from the Northern Rhône, Châteauneuf-du-Pape blanc and other wood-aged southern Rhône and Midi whites, top white Bordeaux, top Jura whites, and dry Chenin Blanc from the Loire Valley (especially Savennières and certain Vouvray)

- ✔ **Italy:** Top white blends from Friuli

- ✔ **Portugal:** White blends from the Douro Valley, Alentejo, Dão, and Encruzado (mostly from Dão)

- ✔ **Spain:** White Rioja

- ✔ **South Africa:** Top Chenin Blanc from the Coastal Region and Rhône style white blends from Swartland

Getting a Lowdown on Versatile Dry Rosés

Many people have a general impression (which is somewhat justified) that all rosé wine is sweet and cheap, which is because many of them are. But it's not always the case. The category in this section encompasses truly dry rosé wines. Despite the obvious difference of color, dry rosé plays a similar role at the table as do white wines, which is why rosé is included in this chapter.

Specifically, treat dry rosés for pairings like you would treat either lightweight, crisp whites, or medium-full bodied, unoaked whites. I deal with sweeter styles of rosés along with the rest of the sweet wines in Chapter 12, because that's the category they belong to when it comes to thinking about which food to serve alongside.

Dry rosé is the sommelier's best friend. It's the go-to wine whenever you're in doubt as to which wine to serve (and Champagne isn't in the budget). It's usually a little fuller and more flavorful than most light whites, yet it's not as tannic and astringent as reds can be. It's as happy with fish as it is with red meat, and performs like a gracious host catering to everyone's needs when the table is filled with different dishes. Although it may not always be the perfect match, it's rarely ever bad. In fact, it's really no surprise that as the world grows fonder of eating and drinking wine, rosé consumption around the world is growing in leaps and bounds. As a result, production is being stepped up to meet demand; rosé is now made virtually everywhere you find red wine, and from virtually every black-skinned grape.

There are no official categories for rosé, but variations in production methods lead to differing styles and quality levels. These sections highlight the two main methods to make rosé wine.

The bloody type

More elegantly known by the French as a *rosé de saignée*, this type of rosé is made literally by bleeding a bit of juice out of a tank of red wine (no first-aid kit required to drink it), before the juice has absorbed much color. Rosé de saignée is a byproduct of the red winemaking process, almost like an afterthought. In order to make more concentrated red wine, winemakers drain a bit of the liquid (after crushing the grapes and adding the skins and juice into a tank), in order to increase the ratio of skins-to-juice left in tank. More skins and less juice equals more extracted red wine.

The part that's drained off is what becomes the rosé. The short contact with red grape skins turns the juice pink, which is then treated like white wine: fermented and bottled early to capture the fresh, fruity side. Making this extra juice into wine is more economic than pouring it down the drain.

The serious type

A few places around the world, most notably Provence in the South of France, have a tradition of *bonafide* rosé making. And when you set out to make rosé in the first place, rather than as a byproduct of red winemaking, the results are usually a bit more serious (and expensive!).

In this type of rosé, the harvest is timed so that the balance of sugar, acid, and flavor in the grapes is appropriate for rosé wine, and not red wine. Grapes are crushed and added to a vat for red winemaking, but then all the grape juice is drained from the skins after a short period (usually about 12 to 24 hours, depending on the desired color), and fermentation occurs in a separate tank.

Shopping for dry rosé

Be sure to inquire with the merchant or sommelier whether the bottle you're considering is a dry or off-dry style of rosé, because there's no ready way to tell from the label alone. An imperfect guideline is price: Good-quality dry rosé wines tend to cost a little more than generic, commercial off-dry rosés. Some of the common grapes made into dry rosé include

- ✔ Cabernet Franc
- ✔ Cabernet Sauvignon
- ✔ Cinsault
- ✔ Gamay
- ✔ Grenache/garnacha
- ✔ Malbec
- ✔ Merlot
- ✔ Pinot Noir
- ✔ Sangiovese
- ✔ Syrah

Some traditional countries/regions where you can find the good stuff:

- ✔ **France:** southern Rhône Valley, Provence, and Corsica
- ✔ **Italy:** Tuscany, Bardolino Chiaretto (Veneto)
- ✔ **Spain:** Navarra, Penedès, Cigales, and Rioja

Bringing Food and White/ Dry Rosé Wine Together

When you consider food and wine pairing from the perspective of style categories first, rather than grape varieties or regions, each style can be matched with a range of complementary foods, such as fresh oysters with dry, lightweight stony whites, or spicy green curries with aromatic, fruity, round whites — regardless of the particular grape the wine is made from. This method is far from perfect. Of course, styles have variations and therefore better pairings within each category, but it's a great starting point.

Think of this pairing strategy like the classic 80-20 rule. These basic styles provide 80 percent of the answers to the general question, "Which type of wine should I choose with this dish?" (and 80 percent is a pretty good grade to get on any pairing). You can even stop there or go on to fine-tuning the pairing in pursuit of the magic duet, the last 20 percent.

Figures 9-1, 9-2, and 9-3 are what I call pairing trees. They're visual representations of possible complementary pairings, beginning with the wine style in the center, and branching out to link to the various principal ingredients and cooking methods, and finally to some specific ingredients and dishes, which pair well with the wine style in question.

Use these pairing trees to find a specific food match for the wine that you've already selected (assuming you know what style category it falls under), or to inspire you to think up new complementary dishes by following the logic that branches out from the general matching principals for each style.

Figure 9-1: A pairing tree for full-bodied, soft, wood-aged white wines.

Illustration by Wiley, Composition Services Graphics

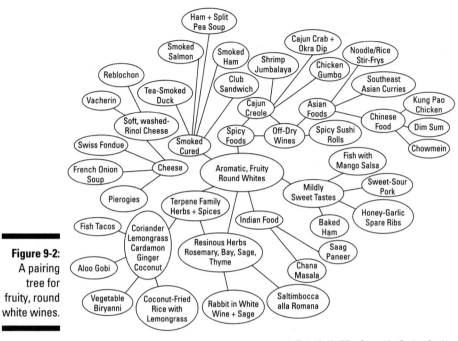

Figure 9-2:
A pairing tree for fruity, round white wines.

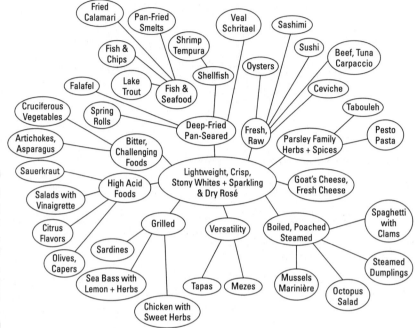

Illustration by Wiley, Composition Services Graphics

Figure 9-3:
A pairing tree for lightweight, crisp, stony white wines, sparkling wines, and dry rosés.

Chapter 10

Turning toward Dry Reds

· ·

· ·

*R*ed wines are considered the serious wines of the wine world in part because they age better than dry whites thanks to their tannin content. The variety of red wine styles available today is amazing. From light and fruity to robust and turbocharged, you can find a red wine to match just about any dish.

This chapter covers the main styles of dry red wines, including a large sampling of the grapes and places that deliver each style. You can utilize this information to make your wine shopping more fruitful (pun intended) and lead you straight to the wines that you're looking for to match with that special dish. I also break out the pairing tree, giving you a visual wine and food pairing tool for each wine style category for quick-and-easy success at the table with corkscrew in hand.

Sizing Up Red Wine: What Makes Red Wine Different from White Wine

Red wines are obviously different from white wines in one important aspect: texture. Anybody can realize that by tasting red wine next to white wine. Red wines all have more or less of a mouth-puckering, astringent sensation that white wines usually don't have, and they also generally have lower acidity, which is why red wines usually pair differently than white wines with food. And the differences start with the grapes and how they're treated in the winery.

Red wine grapes aren't really red. The skins are red (actually, more like deep purple), but the juice inside is clear, just like the juice of white (or rather golden-tinged) grapes. You've probably drank plenty of white wine made from red-skinned grapes: Champagne anyone? In fact, about two-thirds of the grapes planted in Champagne are red, yet 95 percent of Champagne production is white. How do they do that? They simply crush the red grapes and immediately separate the juice from the skins, before the color pigments in the skins paint the juice red.

The logical flipside is that in order to make red wine, winemakers must intentionally leave the juice in contact with the grapes' colorful skins. Winemakers call this the *cuvaison* or *maceration.* They're literally macerating (soaking) the pigment rich skins with the juice/fermenting wine in order to extract color. But color pigments aren't the only useful little compounds in grape skins. The other big protagonist in the red wine story is tannin.

Tannins are part of the larger group of compounds called *polyphenols.* They occur naturally in many plants, trees, and in certain fruits. The word derives from *tanna,* an old German word for oak or fir tree (think *tannenbaum*). Oak barrels in which certain wines are aged are a source of tannin in wine, but grape seeds and skins, and occasionally stems when included in the winemaking process, are the principal sources. Tannin is an antioxidant that increases the longevity of wine, adds structure, and when present in large amounts, gives wine an astringent, sometimes even chewy texture.

White wines are rarely made with any maceration of the skins (or for only very short periods) and thus contain very little tannin. This is the main difference between red and white wine, especially when considering food pairings. Tannins, with their bitter taste and astringent texture, are a major consideration for the match.

Comprehending the Styles of Red Wines

Red wines come in all shapes, sizes, and flavors, but they can basically be categorized under one of the following three styles:

- ✔ Light-bodied, bright, zesty, low tannin
- ✔ Medium-full bodied, balanced, moderately tannic
- ✔ Full, deep and robust, turbocharged, with chewy texture

Like all wines, the flavor profile depends on what type of grape(s) are used, the growing region, and winemaking techniques. Other aspects, such as how deep the color is and how tannic the wine is depend largely on grape genetics. Some grapes, like Cabernet Sauvignon, Shiraz, or Malbec, have naturally thick skins that contain ample tannins and color pigments. You have to work pretty hard to make a pale, soft wine out of these grapes; they're naturally dark and chewy. Other grapes like Pinot Noir, Gamay, or Grenache are thin-skinned, with far fewer color pigments and tannins. You'd have to work very hard to make a deep, highly extracted Pinot Noir, for example, because most are naturally pale and delicate.

In these sections, I look closer at the three types of red wines and the different expressions you can find when you're shopping. These guidelines are general; remember exceptions exist for everything. After all, this is the world of wine.

Light-bodied, bright, zesty, low tannins

The light-bodied, bright, and zesty wines have low tannins. They're kept fresh and lively by brisk acidity and unencumbered by too much tannin or wood. Light reds rarely score big with the critics, decried for their simplicity, but they're some of the most fun and pleasant wines to actually drink. I like to serve these wines with a slight chill to enhance the freshness factor and fruit flavors. They taste like a bowl of fresh ripe berries, and they're generally best when young, within one to five years of the harvest. Their food-friendly acidity and low tannin make these juicy reds very versatile, able to dance with a wide range of tastes, textures, aromas, and flavors.

The category is broad: Most inexpensive, entry-level, cool climate reds fall into it. Exceptions abound with finicky, hard-to-grow grapes like Pinot Noir that are rarely cheap, no matter what the style. But when in doubt, let (lower) price be your guide.

When shopping for lightweight, juicy reds, look for the following types, based on the variety of grape. Start your search in the sections that stock wines from cooler regions — think northern Europe and the deep southern hemisphere like Tasmania, and avoid places where it doesn't snow in the winter. The alcohol level will also guide you; lightweight reds rarely have more than 13 to 13.5 percent alcohol.

- Barbera
- Cabernet Franc
- Gamay
- Pinot Noir
- Sangiovese
- Tempranillo

Some lightweight red wine grapes by specific country and region include the following:

- **Argentina**: Wines from Patagonia (Pinot Noir, Malbec)

- **Australia:** Tasmanian Pinot Noir

- **Austria:** Zweigelt, basic Blaufränkisch, and St. Laurent

- **Canada:** Most inexpensive to moderately priced reds from the Niagara Peninsula, Prince Edward County, and reds from Nova Scotia and British Columbia's northern Okanagan Valley and Vancouver Island

- **France:** Beaujolais (except top crus like Morgon or Moulin-à-Vent), basic Cabernet Franc–based reds from Anjou-Touraine, Pinot Noir from Alsace and the Loire Valley, basic Burgundy, entry-level Bordeaux and Bergerac, Trousseau, and Poulsard from the Jura

- **Germany:** Blauer Portugieser, basic Pinot Noir

- **Hungary**: Kadarka, basic Kékfrankos, Pinot Noir from northern Hungary

- **Italy:** Basic Barbera and lighter Dolcetto from the northwest, Valpolicella and Bardolino from the Veneto, the mountain reds of Alto-Adige and the Val d'Aosta, basic Chianti and other Sangiovese-based wines, elegant Frappato and basic Etna Rosso from Sicily, Ligurian reds

- **New Zealand**: Lighter styles of Marlborough Pinot Noir

- **Portugal:** Inexpensive wines from Dão, Bairrada, and Lisboa

- **Spain:** Joven (no wood aging) Rioja and Ribera del Duero, lighter Bierzo, Valdepeñas, basic reds from Navarra and the Penedès

- **Switzerland:** Dôle du Valais

Medium-full bodied, balanced, moderately tannic

These wines are the middleweights of the wine world: a little more substantial and structured than the juicy lightweights, yet not as powerful and chewy as the heavyweights. The wine is all about balance, with neither excess nor deficiency of any components like acid, alcohol, or tannins. Many of the world's best and most age-worthy wines fall into this category. They usually need a few years after harvest for all their stuffing to smooth out, like a pebble sculpted by a stream, and for their full aroma and flavor potential to be realized.

Use price as your starting guideline, because just about any grape in any region, taken seriously enough, can make middleweight wines. Only the coolest reaches of the wine world are forever constrained to make lightweight reds, that is, until an exceptionally warm vintage comes along. The additional expense of lowering yields and aging for longer before release, often in (expensive) wood, means that the average bottle price has to be higher than the entry level unless you uncover an exceptional bargain.

When shopping for medium-full bodied reds, look for wines from the following countries, regions, and/or grape varieties. Beyond finding the following types, it's also always a good idea to ask the merchant or sommelier about the particulars of the wine, for example exactly how tannic or astringent the wine is, and whether it is closer to medium or full bodied. Remember that producer influence and vintage variation can result in widely varying styles even within a given region and/or grape variety. The alcohol level also guides you; medium-full bodied reds usually fall between 13 to 14.5 percent alcohol.

- **Argentina:** Malbec from Patagonia and Salta, lighter styles from Mendoza, especially the Uco Valley subregion, Bonarda from Mendoza

- **Australia:** Shiraz from the Clare, Eden, and Hunter Valleys, Pinot Noir from Mornington Peninsula and Adelaide Hills, Shiraz and Cabernet (and blends) from Coonawarra and Margaret River

- **Austria:** Reserve-level Blaufränkisch and red blends from the Burgenland

- **Canada:** Reds from central and northern Okanagan Valley and the Similkameen Valley in British Columbia; warm vintage, red blends from the Niagara Peninsula in Ontario

- **Chile:** Traditional style Bordeaux blends and Carmenere from the Maipo and Colchagua valleys, old vine Carignan from the Maule Valley, Bío-Bío, Limarì and Elquì Valley reds

- **France:** Classic Bordeaux and Burgundy, Syrah from the northern Rhône, all but the biggest blends from the southern Rhône and the Languedoc-Roussillon

- **Hungary:** Egri bikavér; Szakszárdi Bikavér; Kékfrankos, Pinot Noir, and Bordeaux blends from Villány, Szekszard, and Eger, as well as the southern shores of Lake Balaton

- **Italy**: Ripasso-style Valpolicella, Nero d'Avola from Sicily, barrel-aged Barbera from Asti and Alba, Rosso Conero, Montepulciano d'Abruzzo, classically styled Chianti Classico, Vino Nobile di Montepulciano, Carmignano, Morellino di Scansano, Sangiovese di Romagna, the Nebbiolos of the Valtellina, Cannonau di Sardegna, Teroldego Rotaliano, reds blends of Friuli

- **New Zealand:** Pinot Noirs from Marlborough, Martinborough, and Central Otago; Bordeaux blends and Syrah from Hawkes Bay and Waiheke Island

- **Portugal:** Blends from the Alentejo, Lisboa, Setubal Peninsula, and Dão, and the balanced reds of the Douro Valley

- **Spain:** Traditional Rioja, Ribera del Duero, and Bierzo

- **South Africa:** Classic Cabernet blends and Pinotage from Stellenbosch, Paarl, and Franschhoek; Pinot Noir from Overberg (Walker Bay) and Constantia

- **United States:** Voluptuous Pinot Noirs from Sonoma and the Central Coast and Santa Cruz Mountains, Merlot, Cabernet Franc, lighter style Zinfandel, Oregon Pinot Noir, and lighter Merlot from Washington State

Full, deep and robust, turbocharged, with chewy texture

The heavyweights of the wine world, these robust reds are full bodied, generously proportioned, and highly age-worthy. They're mostly at the upper end of the price scale, though many warm, new world regions can make these bruising reds in the medium price range as well. These wines need lots of sunshine and warmth to bring grapes to the degree of ripeness at which alcohol levels will be high, usually 14 percent or more, while skins thickened by the penetrating rays of the sun deliver high measures of polyphenols — color and tannin. The top wines in this category can improve over a couple of decades in the cellar, and some exceptional bottles are still tasty after half a century.

If you're in the market for one of these fuller red wines, look for the following types, based on the country, region, or variety of grape. You'll find these wines in the sections stocking bottles from mostly popular and famous wine regions (places you may have heard of). The alcohol level on the label is around 14 percent or higher, and the price is in the premium range.

- **Australia:** Barossa Valley and McLaren Vale, especially Shiraz, Cabernet Sauvignon, and GSM blends

- **Canada:** The Cabernet blends and Shiraz/Syrah from the southern Okanagan in British Columbia

- ✔ **France:** Châteauneuf-du-Pape and the most serious southern Rhône blends, Hermitage and Côte-Rôtie in the northern Rhône, Bandol in Provence, expensive versions from the Languedoc-Roussillon, warm vintage, modern-style Bordeaux (especially Pomerol, St. Emilion, Margaux, Pauillac, St. Estèphe, and St. Julien)

- ✔ **Italy:** Barolo, Barbaresco, Amarone della Valpolicella, Brunello di Montalcino, super-Tuscan blends, Primitivo from Puglia, Montepulciano d'Abruzzo, Aglianico from Campania (Taurasi) and Basilicata, Sagrantino di Montefalco in Umbria, and Sforzato della Valtellina in Lombardy

- ✔ **Portugal:** The top wines of the Alentejo, the tannic, Baga-based reds of Bairrada, and top-level Douro and Dão blends

- ✔ **Spain:** Toro, Priorat, new wave Rioja (*Reserva* and *Gran Reserva*), and Ribera del Duero

- ✔ **South Africa:** Rhône-style blends from Swartland, Paarl, top-level Cabernet Blends, and Syrah from Stellenbosch

- ✔ **United States:** Cabernet Sauvignon from the Napa Valley as well as Alexander and Knights Valleys in Sonoma, Bordeaux and Rhône-style blends from Paso Robles, Zinfandel from Amador County and the Sierra Foothills, and Washington State Syrah and Cabernet Blends

Knowing What Foods Work Well with Red Wines

If you're ready to pair foods with red wine, you've come to the right place. Here I provide three figures, that I call pairing trees, to give you a visual representation of possible complementary pairings. I place the wine style in the center and branch out to link to the various principal ingredients and cooking methods, and finally to some specific ingredients and dishes that pair well with the wine style in question.

Use Figures 10-1, 10-2, and 10-3 to find a specific food match for the wine that you've already selected (assuming you know what style category it falls under), or to inspire you to think up new complementary dishes by following the logic that branches out from the general matching principals for each style.

Figure 10-1:
A pairing tree for full-bodied, robust, turbocharged red wines.

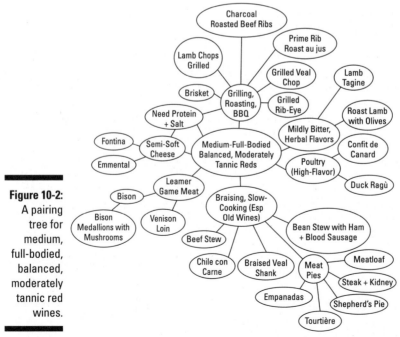

Figure 10-2:
A pairing tree for medium, full-bodied, balanced, moderately tannic red wines.

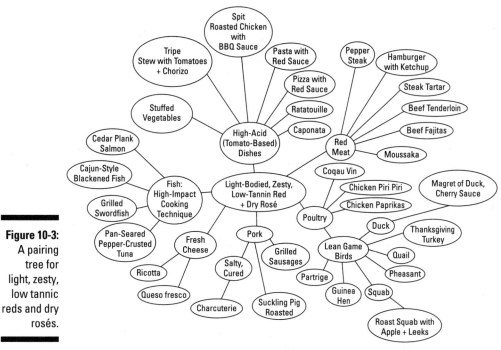

Figure 10-3:
A pairing tree for light, zesty, low tannic reds and dry rosés.

Illustration by Wiley, Composition Services Graphics

Chapter 11

Scoping Out the Sparkling with Bubbles

. . . .

In This Chapter

▶ Knowing the grapes and places to look for bubbly

▶ Making the bubbles — how they do it

▶ Finding the right foods for sparkling

. . . .

Sparkling wine comes in many styles and from just about every wine-growing region in the world. Theoretically, you can make *sparkling wine* (wine with bubbles from carbon dioxide) out of any grape variety, but in practice, only a few grapes lend themselves to the really good bubbly. Winemakers can use several different ways to get the bubbles in the wine. Each method of sparkling wine production yields a slightly different style, and thus the perfect pairing depends not only on the region and the grape, but the method, too.

In this chapter I look at which grapes and places excel in making sparkling wine, as well as the essential info on production technique. And of course, I also give a few windows into a world of possible pairings with sparkling wine.

Picking the Grapes and Places that Make the Best Sparkling Wine

The best sparkling wines in the world come from cool climates, such as northern France, northern Italy, the coolest part of California, Canada, and so on. Wherever the growing season is relatively long and cool, grapes can reach the right level of flavor development before too much sugar is accumulated and acidity lost. Overripe grapes make coarse, alcoholic, flabby sparkling wine, which is the precise opposite of what most producers aim for. Although any grape can be turned into sparkling wine, the grapes that are best suited to the task include the following:

- ✔ **Chardonnay:** The main white grape used in Champagne and other traditional method sparkling wines from around the world. One hundred percent Chardonnay sparkling wines are sometimes labeled *Blanc de Blancs* (meaning "white from whites").

- ✔ **Chenin Blanc:** A white grape from the Loire Valley, used to make dry or semi-dry sparkling wine under several appellation designations.

- ✔ **Muscat/Moscato:** A very aromatic grape, whose most famous bubbly expression is the sweet, frothy Moscato d'Asti of Piedmont in northern Italy.

- ✔ **Pinot Blanc:** This is a member of the large Pinot family of grapes, which makes soft, modestly aromatic sparkling wine. It's often part of a blend.

- ✔ **Pinot Meunier:** Considered the second-string red grape of Champagne, included in blends for its fruity aromatics. Pinot Meunier–based sparkling wines don't usually age as well as those made from Chardonnay or Pinot Noir.

- ✔ **Pinot Noir:** This is the headlining red grape of Champagne, prized for its structure and complexity. Champagnes and sparkling wines made from 100 percent Pinot Noir, or from a blend of Pinot Noir with other red grapes like Pinot Meunier, are usually labeled as *Blanc de Noirs* (meaning "white from black").

- ✔ **Prosecco (glera):** Northeastern Italy's pleasantly aromatic, pear and green apple–scented white grape is used most frequently to make fresh, off-dry, or medium-dry sparkling wine.

The method used to make sparkling wine has a greater impact on the flavor profile than the particular grapes that are used. If you prefer fruitier flavors, look for sparkling wines made using the Charmat or ancestral methods (I describe them in this chapter). If your preferences lean more toward toasty, fresh pastry, and brioche-like flavors, opt for wines made using the traditional (Champagne) method. Traditional method sparkling wines are expensive to produce and therefore sell for relatively high prices, but offer the most complexity. If you like sweeter styles of wine, look for the *sec, demi-sec, demi-doux, or doux* on the label (refer to the "Reading the Label: What the Names Really Mean" section). Sparkling Muscats are also usually made sweet, as in *Moscato d'Asti* or *Asti Spumante*.

Comparing Champagne versus sparkling wine

All Champagne is sparkling wine, but not all sparkling wine is Champagne. Champagne is a geographical region in northern France. The term *Champagne* is also a protected appellation of origin for sparkling wine made in the region. A bottle labeled as Champagne guarantees that the wine inside is made exclusively from authorized grape varieties grown within the demarcated region of Champagne, and using only permitted grape-growing/winemaking techniques. The appellation thus guarantees that all wines labeled as Champagne meet basic minimum quality levels and match an accepted wine style.

The authorities who oversee the production and marketing of Champagne have spent a great deal of time and money to protect the Champagne name. They prevent wineries outside the region from labeling their wines as Champagne, which was common in the past (many less-scrupulous producers were looking to bank on the success and reputation of the real, original Champagne). Nevertheless some regions around the world, most notably California and South America, where companies have been making and selling "Champagne" for many years, have been grandfathered in and are able to use the term, much to the dismay of true Champagne producers.

Most Champagne is *non-vintage*, which is to say that it's a wine blended from more than one growing season, or *vintage*, in wine parlance. One Champagne producer — Krug — prefers to use the term *multi-vintage* rather than non-vintage, which is in fact more accurate and less confusing. A *vintage* Champagne is a sparkling wine made entirely from grapes grown in a single growing season. The year in which the grapes were harvested appears on the label. Vintage Champagne also requires longer ageing by law than non-vintage before it can be released for sale.

Understanding How Bubbles Get In

Although you probably aren't going to start producing your own sparkling wine, having a grasp of how sparkling wines are made is important. This information can help you understand how sparkling wines differ from one another, and which style is best suited to which foods (as well as why there's such a dramatic price difference between different styles). All sparkling wines start off as normal still wines (called *base wines*). It's the magic of how the bubbles get in that differs. Sparkling wine is made in four principal ways, which I discuss in the following sections.

Touting the traditional method

The *traditional method,* sometimes referred to as *champenoise, classico,* or *cap classique,* is the most expensive, labor intensive, and highly regarded method for making sparkling wine. Champagne and most of the world's top bubbles are made this way. Traditional method sparkling wines have a toasty-yeasty aroma and flavor, very fine bubbles, can improve with age, and can stand up to more intensely flavored foods.

The key to this method is a secondary fermentation in the bottle. A still (non-effervescent) base wine is put in bottle along with a little yeast and some sugar, and then sealed. The yeasts go to work, fermenting the sugar and creating a little more alcohol and carbon dioxide. Because the bottle is sealed, the gas can't escape and remains dissolved in the wine.

A crucial aspect to the flavor of traditional method sparkling wines is how long the yeast cells are in contact with the wine. After the bottle is sealed, the wine spends a long time in contact with the spent yeast cells (a minimum of 15 months for non-vintage Champagne, and up to three years minimum and often much longer, for vintage-dated Champagne). During this ageing period, the wine looses fruitiness; picks up toasty, yeasty, brioche-like notes; and develops a rounder, creamier texture. The longer the ageing, the more pronounced the flavor transformation. Before shipping out for sale, the yeast cells are removed and the bottle re-corked and a little sugar (called the *dosage*) is added, which determines the level of sweetness in the finished wine. Refer to the later section, "Reading the Label: What the Names Really Mean" for information on how to read bubbly labels.

If you're shopping for traditional method sparkling wines, be prepared to spend some money. They're the most expensive sparkling wines in any market. Look for a bottle from one of the better traditional method sparkling wines by country and region listed here

- **Australia:** Tasmania, Adelaide Hills
- **Canada:** Niagara Peninsula, Prince Edward County, the Okanagan Valley, and Nova Scotia
- **France:** Champagne, anything labeled *crémant* (d'Alsace, de Bourgogne, du Loire, de Bordeaux, de Jura, and so on), Vouvray, and Saumur
- **Italy:** Franciacorta DOCG in Lombardy, Trento DOC in Trentino, anything labeled *metodo tradizionale*
- **Portugal:** Bairrada Espumante DOC
- **Spain:** Cava (mostly from the Penedès), anything labeled *metodo tradicional*
- **South Africa:** Anything labeled *methode cap classique*
- **United States:** California: Mendocino, Napa Valley (especially Carneros), Anderson Valley, Sonoma (Russian River Valley and especially Green Valley); Oregon, New York State, Washington, and New Mexico

Charmat

The most widely used method of making sparkling wine is called the *Charmat method*, named after Frenchman Eugene Charmat who hit upon the process at the turn of the 20th century. This method is sometimes referred to as *Martinotti*, *Italian method*, *tank method*, or *cuve close*. Charmat method wines are fruity/floral, with moderate bubbles and are best consumed young. They can be paired with the same foods as lightweight, dry whites or off-dry whites (if they're slightly sweet, such as extra-dry prosecco).

Rather than re-ferment in bottles as per the traditional method, the base wine is kept in tank. Yeasts and sugar are added, the tank is sealed, and the secondary fermentation takes place. Because the volume of wine relative to yeast is so much larger in a tank than a bottle, the wine picks up very little toasty-yeasty flavor. In fact, this type of wine is bottled generally as soon as the second fermentation is finished, without any ageing, to preserve the fruity, floral fragrance of the grape varieties that this method is best suited to. The most emblematic examples of this style are Italy's sweet Moscato d'Asti and dry/off-dry Prosecco.

Charmat method wines are less expensive to produce than traditional method wines because no labor-intensive manipulation of individual bottles is necessary, and the ageing time is also considerably shorter. They're also less complex and age-worthy, and are meant to be enjoyed as young as possible to capture the freshness of youth.

When shopping for Charmat method sparkling wines, expect to pay less than you would for traditional method sparkling wines. You can find this type of wine from just about every country. Quality varies widely, so follow the advice of someone you trust or let price guide you; the best examples are invariably a little more expensive than the average. Northern Italy's Prosecco is the world's most popular type of Charmat method sparkling; when in doubt go for this.

Charmat method sparkling wines can be identified by the following label terms in various countries

- ✔ **France:** Wines labeled as *vin mousseux*
- ✔ **Germany:** Wines labeled as *sekt* or *Deutscher sekt* (these terms can also occasionally apply to traditional method wines, but they're rare in Germany)
- ✔ **Italy:** Wines labeled as *spumante* (fully sparkling), such as Prosecco di Valddobbiadene e Conegliano; frizzante (lightly sparkling), such as Moscato d'Asti/ Asti Spumante, and Lambrusco

> ✔ **Portugal:** Wines labeled as *espumoso*; the term *espumante* is reserved for traditional method wines
>
> ✔ **Spain:** Wines labeled as *espumante* or *espumoso*; the Charmat method is also known as *granvás*
>
> ✔ **Elsewhere:** Labeled as either Charmat or *cuve close*

Heading back in time: The ancestral method

The *ancestral method* (also known as the *methode ancestrale*) is the most ancient way of making sparkling. In a word, ancestral method wines are lightly effervescent, dry to medium-dry, fruity, and occasionally a little cloudy. These wines can be paired with the same foods as dry or off-dry still whites and rosés.

Taking a closer look at the ancestral method

The *ancestral method* is the most ancient way of making sparkling wine, pre-dating Champagne by perhaps a century or more. Records at the Abbey of St. Hilaire near Limoux in the Languedoc, France, show that sparkling wine was made there as early as 1531.

Ancestral sparkling wine wasn't so much of an invention as an accident, made possible after the development and widespread use of glass bottles. Winemakers had already discovered that in springtime, certain wines would "come to life" again. What was occurring was that as temperatures warmed, yeast woke up and continued fermenting any residual sugars in the wine. But before bottles, wines were largely stored and shipped in *cask* (wooden barrels of varying sizes). Because casks are porous, the carbon dioxide produced by any re-fermentation during storage or shipping naturally dissipated. But if the wine had already been bottled before it came back to life (kind of like burying someone alive), the gas would remain trapped inside with nowhere to escape. The result was a miraculously lively wine, which some attributed to the work of the devil, not least because quite often bottles would spontaneously explode from the pressure inside, causing serious injury to cellar workers. The now-famous monk Dom Pérignon, often mistakenly credited with the invention of Champagne, actually spent most of his life trying to figure out how to stop bottles from exploding.

Today, the sparkling wines of Limoux (Blanquette de Limoux), Bugey-Cerdon, and Clairette de Die in France are still made according to the ancestral method. A few producers around the world (including in Canada) have also revived this ancient method, though it is a rarity.

With this method, you take wine that's still undergoing fermentation and bottle it. The yeasts continue their work of converting sugar into alcohol in the closed bottle, and because carbon dioxide is a byproduct of fermentation, the gas remains trapped in the bottle. *Voilà,* sparkling wine is the result. Ancestral method wines can sometimes be cloudy if the dead yeast cells remain in the bottle (much like the various types of bottled fermented beers), are the least effervescent of the sparkling types, and are occasionally a little sweet if the yeast cells pack it in before their job is done.

Injecting carbon dioxide

The cheapest and easiest way to make sparkling wine is the carbon dioxide injection. This method is the "soda pop" of the wine world — cheap and uncomplicated bubbly that serious drinkers give no respect to. You simply take a closed tank of still wine, inject it with CO_2, and then bottle it under pressure. This method is used for the most modest quality wine; the bubbles are coarse, and the wine quickly goes flat. And by law, at least in the United States, such wine must be labeled as *carbonated wine.* If you see this on a label, then flee; it's usually terrible stuff.

Reading the Label: What the Names Really Mean

Sparkling wines come in different degrees of sweetness. The overwhelming majority, even those considered dry, still have some residual sugar (literally dissolved sugar in the wine, an often welcome addition to balance out the fierce acids that are a natural consequence of the cool climates in which top bubbly is most often made). But the label can be confusing and misleading, considering that the label term *extra-dry,* for example, actually means quite sweet.

If you're standing in the wine section of your grocery store or in a wine shop and wondering whether a bottle of bubbly will taste dry or sweet, refer to Table 11-1, which is a quick reference list that orders common sparkling wine label terms from truly bone dry to very sweet:

Table 11-1	Deciphering a Sparkling Wine's Label
Label Term	*Permitted residual sugar (E.U. Standards)*
Brut zero (also: brut non-dosé, pas dose, pas opéré, brut sauvage, brut nature, extra brut)	0 to.5%
Brut	.5 to 1.5%
Extra-dry	1.2 to 2.0%
Sec	1.7 to 3.5%
Demi-sec	3.3 to 5.0%
Doux	Above 5.0%

Wine labeled as brut zero (or any one of the other common terms listed in the table) have less than .5 percent of sugar, which means less than 5 grams of sugar per liter of wine. These wines taste very, very dry. Brut styles also taste dry even though they contain up to 15 grams of sugar per liter, thanks to high acidity. It's only when you get to extra-dry levels and up that you can start to taste the sweetness in the wine. Any wine labeled *doux* tastes sweet to very sweet. Know what style you're looking for and look for the appropriate term on the label.

Why dry isn't so dry

The seemingly confusing nomenclature to indicate sweetness levels in Champagne/ sparkling wine evolved from the days when all Champagne was made sweet, very sweet in fact. Louis Roderer's famous prestige cuvee called Cristal, which was made initially for Russian Tzar Alexander II in 1876, for example, originally contained a whopping 30 percent sugar, or 300 grams of sugar per liter — that's sweet bubbly. When drier styles of Champagne eventually came into fashion in the late 1800s, they were indeed *relatively* dry in comparison even though they still contained quite a lot of sugar, and thus were labeled as *sec*, or dry to distinguish them from the really sweet stuff. By today's standards, what was considered pretty dry back in the late 1800s is actually quite sweet. As even drier wines emerged on the market, terms had to be retrofitted to indicate that these wines were drier than dry (extra-dry), and eventually brut and brut zero, with virtually no sugar added.

Pairing Sparkling Wines with Food

Sparkling wine is a sommelier's best friend. Most people are in a festive mood when they drink bubbly because of its intimate link with celebration. And happy people tend to enjoy everything, including eating and drinking together, a little bit more and the experience is usually positive. Thus serving sparkling wine means that the sommelier's job of creating memorable experiences is already half done.

Dry sparkling wine also happens to be very versatile with food, able to pair with a very wide range of dishes. In fact, finding truly bad pairings with dry sparkling made using the Charmat or traditional method is nearly impossible. And though the carbon dioxide that gives sparkling wine its prickle is a major feature of the wine's overall profile, in terms of pairing dry sparkling wines with food, they behave very much like lightweight, crisp, still white wines. So for this reason I include dry sparkling wine on the pairing tree for lightweight whites in Chapter 9.

And because sweet sparkling wines behave similarly to other sweet still wines with food, I include sweet sparkling wines on the pairing tree for sweet wine styles in Chapter 12. Refer to this pairing tree for complementary food pairings for sweet sparkling wines.

Chapter 12

Perusing Off-Dry, Sweet, and Fortified Wines

Sweet and fortified wines were once the most sought-after wines on earth. A quick perusal of wine references in literature from antiquity up to the 20th century, and even glimpses at old auction catalogues and the very first restaurant and merchant wine lists, attest to their immense popularity and handsome value. In fact, until railways and steamships hastened transport, sweet and fortified wines were just about the only wines regularly traded around the world because they were the only wines stable enough to withstand endless bumpy cart rides and long river and sea voyages. And in the days before readily available sugar, naturally sweet substances like honey and sweet wine were revered with quasi-religious fervor.

Today the ubiquity of the sweet granular stuff has made the taste of sweet wine less rare and treasured. Everywhere you turn in the supermarket sugar has been added, while naturally sweet wines have been marginalized to the outer edges of dinner and the infrequent celebratory occasion. Sommeliers lament this fact, because sweet wines can make some of the most memorable matches. *Fortified wines,* too — those to which extra alcohol has been added — are likewise less popular than they once were. But insiders know that these great worldly classics, the Ports, Madeiras, Marsalas, and Sherries of the world, offer some of the most extraordinarily complex wines for your money. One of the most indelibly etched food and wine moments of my life arose from the unexpected beauty of a dry Palo Cortado Sherry and a savory old piece of Manchego cheese — it was like *foie gras* without the foie — a revelation.

Should you choose to venture into the realm of sweet and fortified wines, you can find their secrets in this chapter, along with tips on which foods they work best with.

Identifying the Sensation of Sweetness

The taste of sweetness is probably your most familiar taste sensation; it's certainly the one people are most genetically programmed to love. Although the presence or absence of sugar is pretty obvious, say, in your bitter coffee or tea, the sweet impression of some wines can be caused by more than just sugar. In the next sections I clarify what is meant exactly by sweet wine and what else causes a sweet sensation. Degrees of sweetness exist, ranging from just perceptible to ultra-cloyingly sweet like caramel syrup.

Distinguishing between real sweetness and impression of sweetness

So what exactly is the difference between sweet wines and those that just seem a little sweet? Allow me to clarify so that you and I are speaking the same language.

- ✔ **Sweet wine:** This wine contains measurable amounts of residual sugar (also known as RS in wine lingo).

- ✔ **Wine with a sweet impression:** This wine tastes vaguely sweet, with little or no sugar involved, because of factors I outline here.

Making this distinction is important because many wines taste implicitly sweet in the absence of any sugar due to the interaction of these other components in wine:

- ✔ **Acidity:** *Acidity* is the great equalizer, affecting the perception of sweetness to a large degree. With too little acid, just about any wine, even dry wine, tastes vaguely sweet (because of alcohol), and when excessive, it can make even truly sweet wine taste virtually dry.

- ✔ **Alcohol:** *Alcohol* on its own has an inherent, vaguely sweet taste, in addition to its contribution to body, texture, and the impression of weight on the palate.

- ✔ **The flavor of ripe fruit:** The *flavor* you get from ripe grapes grown in warm places can also be confused with an actual sweet taste.

- ✔ **The influence of oak barrels:** The flavor imparted to wine when it's aged in oak barrels, especially small (225 liter), new oak barrels, reminiscent of caramel, toffee, chocolate, and maple syrup, among other things, can give dry wines an impression of sweetness on the palate.

Put those four together (and they very often are together — ripe fruit, low acid, high alcohol, and barrel-aging), and the result is a distinctly sweet taste impression in a technically dry wine.

Just think of a super ripe, jammy Aussie Shiraz, a fig-, prune-, and raisin-flavored Malbec from Argentina, or a soft, tropical-fruit and caramel-oak-flavored Chardonnay from California. Although all three are technically dry, they sure can taste pretty sweet, and more importantly, play the role of off-dry wines at the table. That's to say that when a dish calls for a wine with some sweetness, you don't necessarily have to pick a wine with sugar in it. Sometimes the illusion of sweetness is good enough to make the match. This should be good news for those who don't like sweet wine; they can still find a suitable partner for all but the sweetest and spiciest foods.

Knowing how sweet is sweet

When tasting wine, you want to be able to determine whether a wine is dry, off-dry, medium-dry, medium sweet, or *really* sweet. Sometimes labels can give you an indication, and sometimes you're left guessing. Unfortunately, I don't have an easy answer for you, other than tasting the wine or trusting the person who sells it to you.

In any case, the relative amount of sweetness, or the sweet impression, in wine versus food matters most when making the match. If you remember only one thing from this chapter, it should be this: Make sure that the wine is at least as sweet, or sweeter, than the food it's served with. Otherwise, the wine will seem thinner, lighter, and drier than on its own, which is generally a bad thing.

Making a Wine Sweet

Winemakers use numerous ways to make sweet wines, all with the aim of creating a wine with residual sugar. In these sections, I explore the various production methods with an eye on taste, flavor, and sweetness profiles, which are your keys to finding the best matches for these wines.

Stopping the fermentation

Fermentation is the conversion of sugar into alcohol, so if you can stop the process before it's fully completed, then you end up with a sweet wine. To stop wine fermenting, winemakers have one of two options:

- ✔ They add alcohol. Refer to the "Adding alcohol: Fortification" section later in this chapter for more information.

- ✔ They chill down the wine to the point at which yeasts stop working, add some sulfur dioxide to fully knock them out, and then filter. This technique is used all over the world.

If you start with only just-ripe, as opposed to overripe or otherwise concentrated grapes, the resulting wine with stopped fermentation will be relatively low in alcohol and not much more than off-dry or medium-dry. German Riesling (labeled *kabinett* or *spätlese*) is a prime example, especially those from the Mosel, where the acid levels are generally so high that a little residual sugar is welcome. The fermentation is stopped when about 8 to 9 percent alcohol is reached, leaving a pinch of sugar to balance out the taste. These wines are fresh and fruity for the most part with little or no aging before bottling (though they can age well once they're in bottle). They're rarely sweet enough to pair well with desserts, but they can work well with mildly sweet-tangy and/or lightly spicy foods.

Another high-profile example of the stopped fermentation technique is sweet, frothy *Moscato d'Asti* from Piedmont in Italy (and its less well-known but delicious red cousin *Brachetto d'Acqui*). Here the fermentation is stopped at around 5.5 percent alcohol, yielding a medium-sweet, lightly effervescent, very fruity and grapey wine that can be delicious with fresh fruit-based desserts, or all on its own.

Late harvesting

As the category name implies, a *late harvest* wine is made from grapes that are picked later in the season than they normally would be to make a dry wine. I discuss the three main categories of late harvest wine in the following sections.

Late-harvest wines

Straight-up, late-harvest wines (such as *vendanges tardives* in French and *vendemmia tardiva* in Italian) are made most often from white grapes that are left to overripen on the vine. Late into the season, sugars accumulate, acidity falls, and the grapes start to shrivel. The evaporation of water further concentrates sugars. By the time the grapes reach the winery, they contain more sugar than yeasts are able to convert into alcohol. The yeasts die before the job is done, resulting in a wine that contains residual (unfermented) natural sugars. Depending on the timing of the harvest and thus the degree of overripeness, late harvest wines range in sweetness from just off-dry to fully sweet, although most in this category are at least medium-dry, up to medium- sweet. Flavors usually run in the ripe orchard fruit spectrum (pear, peach, apricot), adding some dried fruit and honeyed nuances with even later harvest; barrels aren't generally used for aging, though of course there are plenty of exceptions.

Late-harvest wines are the most common type of sweet wines made all over the world, but they're usually best from cool growing regions where there's also natural acidity to balance, such as northern France (Loire Valley, Alsace), Germany, Austria, Canada, and New York State.

Noble rot wines

Noble rot wines, also known as botrytis-affected wines, (*pourriture noble* in French, *Edelfaüle* in German, *muffa nobile* in Italian, and *aszú* in Hungarian), are, like late-harvest wines, made from grapes that are left hanging on the vine until late in the growing season. But rather than simply reach a state of overripeness, a naturally occurring fungus called *botrytis cinerea* attacks the grapes. Under the right conditions, botrytis sets in on the grapes and punctures the skins (like the mold that attacks the fruit in the bowl you left out on the counter too long), allowing water to evaporate. The resulting berries become shriveled and highly concentrated (and look highly unappetizing), but when fermented, yield some of the most marvelously complex sweet wines on the planet.

Botrytis thrives under very specific conditions, namely periods of humidity and moisture followed by periods of warm, dry weather. Continually humid conditions result simply in rotten grapes; it's the noble kind of botrytis that winemakers are after, and only a few places around the world have the right conditions for this process to happen naturally and regularly. As a result, noble rot wines are quite rare and usually expensive.

Noble rot wines share some common traits, regardless of the region or grape variety involved (almost always white grape varieties). They're medium to deep gold in color, and on the palate they're soft and rich, usually very sweet, with a thick, viscous mouth-feel that's like heavy cream. The best also have high underlying acidity to prevent them from being too syrupy (and botrytis also concentrates acidity along with sugar). Typical flavors include dried peach and apricot, quince, marmalade, honey, and honeysuckle. These wines are also frequently aged in barrel, adding a range of caramel, toffee, butterscotch, tea, tobacco, exotic spice, and sweet baking spice flavors.

Noble rot wines are best served with desserts of similar sweetness and texture for a complementary match, such as sauternes and crème brulée. Richly textured savory dishes such as foie gras (pan-seared, mousse, or paté) is a regional classic pairing in several places famous for their noble rot wines, while blue cheese (Roquefort, gorgonzola) is another classic. Refer to the "Selecting Foods to Go with Sweet Wines" section later in this chapter for more suggestions.)

Some of the world's best-known noble rot wines (and their grapes) include:

- **Austria:** Beerenauslese (BA), ausbruch, trockenbeerenauslese (TBA), various grapes, various regions, especially in the Burgenland near the Neusiedlersee

- **France:** Sauternes, also Barsac, Monbazillac, Cerons, Cadillac, (Bordeaux, Semillon-Sauvignon Blanc-Muscadelle blends); Sélection de Grains Nobles (SGN) from Alsace, made from Riesling, Pinot Gris, Gewürztraminer, and Muscat; Chaumes, Quarts de Chaumes, Côteaux du Layon, and Vouvray Moelleux (Loire Valley, Chenin Blanc)

✔ **Germany:** Beerenauslese (BA), trockenbeerenauslese (TBA), different grapes though most often Riesling, especially from the Mosel and Rheingau

✔ **Hungary:** Tokaji Aszú (near the town of Tokaj in northeastern Hungary, made usually from a blend of grapes including Furmint, Hárslevelú, and Muskotály [Muscat], labeled in increasing order of sweetness as 3,4,5, or 6 Puttonyos Tokaji Aszú, or the sweetest of them all, *aszúesszencia* and the pure *natúr esszencia*)

Icewine

Icewine (also known as *Eiswein* in German) is an extreme form of late-harvest wine and the exclusive product of a small handful of regions. Winegrowers wait patiently late into the autumn or early winter (occasionally even midwinter or early spring) for temperatures to drop to at least 19° F(–7°C) or –8° C in Canada, and often even lower. At this temperature the grapes are nearly frozen solid. They're picked and crushed immediately while still frozen so that water, in the form of ice crystals, is left behind in the press. Only the extremely sugar-rich, unfrozen portion of the grape juice is extracted. The concentrated juice is then fermented, but the yeasts die off well before all the sugar is converted to alcohol. Most Icewines are very sweet and rarely aged in wood, so that they retain their pure, concentrated orchard fruit flavors.

Although Germany is the birthplace of Icewine, Canada produces more of it than any other country by a good margin. You may occasionally hear of other places producing it, but there are precious few regions where it is consistently cold enough during the winter to make Icewine production commercially viable (and warm enough in the summer to grow grapes in the first place). Icewine is made from at least a dozen different grapes, including red grapes like Cabernet Franc and Cabernet Sauvignon, but I find Riesling gives the best results, thanks to its balancing natural acidity. The most widely used variety is Vidal, however, and the majority of it comes from Ontario, Canada.

Drying: passito style

Picking normally ripe, healthy grapes and then drying them is another way to concentrate sugars and produce sweet wines. This method may be the original method of sweet winemaking, practiced by the ancient Greeks, among others. Today it's the same method used to make commercial raisins. Grapes can either be left to dry in the sun on mats, as is done in Greece and Spain, or in well-ventilated rooms, as is done more frequently in places like the Veneto or Tuscany in Italy (where the process is called *appassimento* to produce *passito* or *recioto* style wines). The drying treatment is applied to both red and white grapes, and the resulting wines are almost always very sweet, thick, and full of dried fruit flavors like raisins, dried figs, prunes, and caramelized citrus fruits. When aged for long periods in barrels, as dried grape wines often are, they develop plenty of intriguing flavors, such as toffee, caramel, burnt sugar, maple syrup, molasses, and roasted nuts.

Examples of sweet dried grape, passito wines include

- **Cyprus:** Commandaria
- **France:** The Rhône Valley and the Jura's *vin de paille*, and Jurançon in southwest France
- **Greece:** The Muscats of Patras, Rio Patras, and Samos (nectar), Mavrodaphne of Patras, and the Vinsanto of Santorini
- **Italy:** Vin Santo (from various regions, especially Tuscany), the Veneto's Recioto di Soave and Recioto della Valpolicella, and Friuli's Picolit

Adding alcohol: Fortification

It's unclear when the idea of adding alcohol (a grape-based distillate) to grape must, partially fermented or fully fermented wine was hit upon, but it's a technique that's been around for at least a few centuries. Originally it was probably a simple means of ensuring that your wine didn't turn into vinegar when shipped to distant lands. As people know, spirits are infinitely more stable than wine, which is highly perishable, and wine with added alcohol likewise has a longer shelf life. No doubt winemakers quickly discovered that the resulting beverage could be quite tasty, too, and be made in a variety of styles. The process of adding alcohol is called *fortification* and results in a *fortified* wine, which can be dry or sweet, depending on when the alcohol is added.

Big and bitter

In addition to sweet wines, a short period of drying can also be used to make big and rich dry wines as well, most famously the Amarone della Valpolicella in the Veneto, and Sforzato della Valtellina in Lombardy, Italy. A couple of months of drying evaporates only about a third of the grapes' water content, so that when crushed and fermented, yeasts are still able to convert all the sugars into alcohol. The result is a full-bodied, high 15 to 17 percent alcohol wine that's dry. In fact, *amarone* means literally "big and bitter," from the Italian amaro or "bitter," in reference to the wine's lack of sweetness compared to other recioto-style wines. But because of their generous alcohol and sweet-raisin fruit flavors, they often give an impression of sweetness on the palate, making then appropriate matches for such things as dark chocolate, usually reserved for truly sweet wine pairings.

Dry fortified

Dry fortified wine is made by first fully fermenting grape juice until no sugar is left and then adding alcohol. Dry fortified wines have between about 15.5 percent and 22 percent alcohol and no residual sugar. The best known examples are dry Sherries like *Fino* and *Manzanilla*, and *Sercial Madeira*. Some dry fortified wines are later sweetened before bottling by adding either sweet wine, fresh grape juice, or concentrated grape must. Refer to the "Adding something sweet" section later in this chapter for more info.

Sweet fortified

Sweet fortified wines are far more common than dry, and they can be made from any grape variety. To make them, winemakers add alcohol to fresh grape juice or partially fermented wine. By suddenly boosting the alcohol to about 18 percent or above, which is a toxic level by yeasts' standards, the yeasts are killed. The remaining unfermented sugars are left in the wine. These wines all fall under the general category of *vins doux naturels* (VDN) or naturally sweet wines. They are said to be naturally sweet because the residual sugar is natural grape sugar, with nothing added.

The timing of the fortification determines the level of sweetness. The sooner the winemaker adds alcohol to stop the fermentation, the sweeter the wine will be. When spirit is added to totally unfermented grape juice, the resulting beverage (technically called a *mistelle* because it's not really wine, just grape juice and alcohol) is very sweet — it retains the full amount of sugar contained in the ripe grapes. Their flavors are relatively straightforward and grapey because they're made without fermentation, which is why they're often aged in barrel to add another dimension of nutty, dried fruit notes. Examples of classic mistelles include *Pineau des Charentes* from the Cognac region, *Floc de Gascogne* from Armagnac, *Ratafia* from Champagne, and *Macvin du Jura*, all from France.

Aside from mistelles, sweet fortified wines are partially fermented and then fortified. In Port, for example, the typical house style of each producer determines the timing of the alcohol addition. The Port house of Graham's style is on the sweeter side (earlier fortification), for example, while Taylor Fladgate, Cockburn, and Dow's are relatively drier styles. Port by and large is less sweet than Icewine, noble rot, and the syrupy sweet versions of dried grape wines.

Portugal's Douro Valley and the island of Madeira, France's Midi, and Marsala in Sicily are the original centers of VDN production, but the style has since spread around the world. In the early part of the last century, for example, Australia's entire wine industry depended on sweet fortified wines. The legacy lives on in some areas such as Rutherglen in Victoria, whose marvelous Muscats accounted for an astonishing one-quarter of Australia's total wine production by the turn of the 19th century.

I mention sweet styles of Sherry because they fall under the category of sweet fortified wines, though they aren't technically VDNs. Cream Sherries, sweet Olorosos, and the like are fortified after fermentation and thus start out fully dry. They're later blended with various sweeteners (sweet dried grape wine, or cooked or fresh grape must) to the desired level of sweetness.

The length of aging in cask before bottling is a key factor to consider when pairing these wines with food. Sweet fortified wines can be bottled very young with little or no aging, such as many types of Muscat VDNs, which keeps all those wonderfully fresh, grapey, floral flavors intact. Other styles, like Tawny Port, Banyuls, and Madeira can spend years in barrel, even decades, before being bottled. There's even a special term for wines that are put through extreme aging called *rancio.* Wine made in the rancio style are aged in barrel, often under direct sunlight, where they become both *maderized* — literally cooked as for Madeira wine — and oxidized, taking on a peculiar but inviting flavor of rancid nuts and totally caramelized, dried fruit. This technique is typical of southern France and Spain.

In any case, as with any wine, the longer in barrel, the less fresh and the more nutty, dried/cooked/baked fruit, spice, and caramel flavor you'll have. Color is your best clue as to how long the wine spent in barrel. Wines made from white grapes turn amber-brown after long aging, while red wines lighten in color and turn a tawny-brownish red over time.

Common sweet fortified wines include the following:

- **Australia:** Victoria (Rutherglen Liqueur Muscat and Tokay)
- **France:** Banyuls, Rivesaltes, Maury, Muscat Saint-Jean de Minervois, Muscat de Frontignan, Muscat de Beaumes de Venise, and Rasteau
- **Italy:** Marsala (Fine, Superiore, Vergine, and Stravecchio)
- **Portugal:** Port (vintage and tawny styles), Madeira (Bual and Malmsey), and Moscatel de Setúbal
- **Spain:** Sherry (sweet Oloroso, PX, Moscatel, and cream Sherries)

Adding something sweet

The simplest way to make sweet wine is to sweeten dry wine with sugar, grape juice, or concentrated grape juice, or another sweet wine. This process is limited for the most part to inexpensive, basic commercial wines. The Germans call the sweetening agent *süssreserve* ("sweet reserve"). Fresh grape juice is added to (generally lower quality) wines to round them out. Aside from sweet styles of Sherry that I previously note, wines that are sweetened are rarely much more than off-dry to medium-dry and aren't aged before bottling, making them simply fresh and fruity.

Selecting Foods to Go with Sweet Wines

When people think of matching sweet wines with food, the dessert course is the first thought. Certainly many brilliant sweet wine and dessert pairings exist, but remember that sweet wines aren't just for dessert. In fact, I don't like calling sweet wines "dessert" wines for that very reason. People tend to forget that sweet wines can be great matches for savory dishes, too. Although drinking sweet wines before dessert isn't terribly popular these days, and having a multicourse meal paired with all sweet wines can get a little heavy, exploring the occasional sweet-savory match to get you out of the box is well worth it. You may be surprised at just how delicious sweet-savory combinations can be.

In the following sections you can find some tips on pairing the various types of sweet wines with food, as well as a pairing tree for easy visual reference.

Not just for dessert

One of the most memorable food and wine pairing dinners I've hosted involved a five course meal, each served with a different style of Tokaji Aszú. But the most celebrated match of the night was not a classic foie gras and tokaji pairing (indeed classic everywhere foie gras and sweet wine production coincide, like Alsace and southwest France), but rather a 5 Puttonyos Tokaji Aszú (quite sweet but balanced) with a slow-braised bison short rib, enlivened with exotic Asian five-spice (recipes vary, but fennel, cinnamon, star anise, clove, and Szechuan pepper are the standard five). It was one of those magical duets — a perfect synergy of aroma and taste. Sweet wine balanced salty and spicy food, its acidity sliced through the fatty richness of the braised meat and its liquid, and umami met umami head-on. Barrel-aging aromas of cinnamon, clove, and nutmeg in the wine were echoed in the dish while the licorice-like flavor of fennel and star anise set off dried orchard fruit flavor.

That's an extreme example, but off-dry or medium sweet wines are more versatile then you may think. Try late-harvest Pinot Gris with roast or grilled pork, off-dry Riesling with an implicitly sweet-tasting crab salad, or a *sec-tendre* (off-dry) Vouvray with rabbit rilletes. Game meat, too, can be a perfect foil for moderately sweet wines; their intense flavor is in need of an equally intense wine. Why do you see so many game meat recipes that include fruit, like sauces based on wild blueberries or currants or lingonberries, or wild boar or venison terrines with apricots or prunes? The strong flavor of game meat works well with sweet tastes, a strategy you can mirror in your match-making. If there's a sweet element in the dish, then chances are very good that a sweet wine with synergistic flavors will make the cut.

But also for dessert

Of course, sweet wines most often make their appearance after the main course has been served, when it's time for cheese or dessert. See Chapter 20 for tips on classic wine and cheese pairings. This section also includes some classic dessert pairings.

Most successful dessert pairings work best on complementary aromas and fla-vors. Think fresh fruit with fresh fruit and dried with dried. The flavor synergy you get from drinking a fresh, lemon-scented modestly sweet late-harvest wine with a sweet-sour lemon tart or fruit flan, for example, is highly appealing. But a rancio-style, nutty, dried fruit-flavored Tawny Port or sweet Oloroso Sherry usually works better with a dessert that contains similar dried fruit flavors, like plum pudding or Christmas cake. Custards and crème brulées are marvel-ous with barrel-aged, noble rot sweet wines that share similar sweet spice (vanilla) flavor and creamy, unctuous texture.

Think of selecting a sweet wine pairing as the pasty chef thinks about com-posing a dessert plate: What goes well together? A medley of berries, peach and apricot flan, chocolate and raspberries, chocolate and caramel, custard and vanilla, or honey and nuts — pick up on one of the major themes of the dessert and find its echo in the wine. Consider the ripe berry compote flavors of Vintage Port or Banyuls with a flourless chocolate cake, the sweet caramel and vanilla flavor of a wood-aged Sauterne with custard or crème brulée, or the intensely nutty notes of a Vin Santo with a sultry pecan pie. These complementary matches are foolproof, as long as you keep in mind rule No. 1: The wine needs to be as sweet or sweeter then the dessert.

Check out Figure 12-1.This figure is what I call a pairing tree. It's a visual representation of possible complementary pairings, beginning with the wine style in the center of the figure, in this case sweet wines, and branching out from there to the various styles of sweet wine. Each style is then linked to the principal ingredients and cooking methods, and finally to some specific ingre-dients and dishes, that are best suited to each wine style.

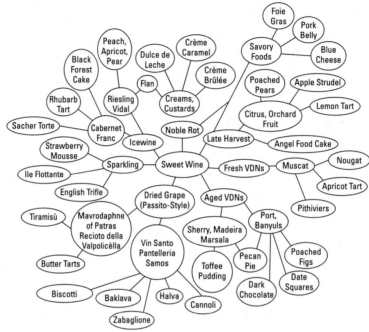

Figure 12-1:
Pairing
with sweet
wines.

Here are a couple of guidelines for pairing with sweet wines:

- **Late harvest:** Citrus and orchard fruit-based desserts, fresh or baked, light mousses, angel food cake, almond cake.

- **Noble rot:** Custards, creams, baking spice (cinnamon, vanilla, nutmeg)-scented desserts (especially with barrel-aged BA wines), carrot cake.

- **Fresh VDNs (no/short barrel aging), sweet sparkling wine:** These wines usually pair best with fresher, fruit based desserts.

- **Aged VDNs and sweetened fortified wines:** These types of sweet fortified wines work magic with desserts that share these flavors, such as dishes based on dried figs, prunes, dates, anything containing nuts, or caramel, chocolate or coffee-flavored.

Part IV

Uncovering the Best Wine Bets with World Cuisine (and Cheese)

In this part . . .

This part is your quick reference resource for looking up wines to drink with specific dishes from around the world. There's no theory or explanation to bog you down, just straight-up recommendations. Wondering what might work with roast turkey, double cheeseburger, or spaghetti with clams? Look it up here.

Although this part covers a huge swath of the planet, from Asia to northern Europe and the Mediterranean, North and South America, and a few other places in between, it's not a comprehensive encyclopedia of regional cuisines. But each chapter does cover many of the classic dishes that you'd come across in local restaurants or regional cookbooks. You can find a brief intro on common ingredients and cooking techniques, as well as some general guidance on pairing wines to certain types of regional cuisine where appropriate.

For each dish, I list the best wine style, along with a specific grape/appellation (without producer or vintage year) that I've found works well. In countries/regions that also produce wines, I suggest a typical regional pairing — what a local sommelier would most likely pull out for you if you were having the dish there. As a backup, I provide an alternative wine style and wine recommendation for each dish, as there's usually more than one possibility.

Oh, and I didn't forget the cheese course — every type of cheese and its best wine style match, along with tips on hosting a wine and cheese party, are in Chapter 20.

Chapter 13

Heading to the Mediterranean: Land of Olive Oil

*E*ver since people recognized the healthiness of the Mediterranean diet several decades ago, many other parts of the world have embraced the traditional foods and recipes of these countries. The diet is distinguished by its reliance on fresh vegetables and fruit, herbs, grains, beans, rice and pasta, seafood, poultry, and of course olive oil. If northern Europe is the land of butter, in southern Europe and the Mediterranean, olive oil is the principal cooking fat as well as condiment to be used in, and on, virtually everything, including some sweets.

Wine, too, is an essential staple in this part of the world. The Romans, who were largely responsible for the spread of viticulture throughout the Mediterranean Basin and into northern Europe, considered wine a nutritious beverage to be taken at every meal. Each country and even distinct regions within these countries have developed their own particular style of Mediterranean cooking based on similar ingredients. Each, too, has its own regional wine specialties that more often than not make for a perfect match with these local foods.

This chapter explores some of the most emblematic traditional regional preparations, many of which are already familiar to you. I suggest a classic regional wine pairing for each, for both the style and a specific recommendation. In the rare instances where nothing suitable is locally made, I give the next best style option with an example. As with all other sections in this part, the recommendations are intended to be a starting point for further discovery rather than an end.

Heading to Southern Italy and the Islands

All regions south of Rome, including Campania, Basilicata, Abruzzi, Molise, Apulia, Calabria, and Sicily (and its beautiful Lipari and Pantelleria Islands, source of brilliant dessert wines), are considered part of southern Italy. The large island of Sardinia, too, falls under the spell of the south, if born of a very different history.

Historically, aside from the small percentage of wealthy landowners, southern Italy was a very poor region. Most people made do with a mainly vegetarian diet, relying on garden vegetables and greens, breads and pastas, and fruits, to build up enough energy to go back to work in the fields. Yet out of this poverty emerged a cuisine of remarkable imagination, turning what little was on hand into a veritable feast for the senses. Everything is based on the quality and freshness of basic ingredients. Here is where you can find Italy's best figs, lemons, blood oranges, peppers, eggplant, capers, and the Rolls Royce of tomatoes — the San Marzano — grown on the volcanic slopes of Vesuvius.

Seafood is naturally in abundance, from calamari to swordfish to sea bass and tuna. On feast days, lamb and kid, poultry, and game birds are the roasts of choice; this isn't the land of cows or dairy products. Most cheeses are firm and aged, with the exception of the wonderfully soft and fresh buffalo's milk cheese *mozzarella di buffala* from Campania and *burrata* from Apulia.

The food here is all about freshness and simplicity, featuring vibrant flavors; lively herbs; the acidic twang of tomatoes, lemons, and capers; the salty crunch of anchovies, and the like. High acid white wines and savory, but not oaky reds work best here. Not surprisingly, the majority of southern Italian wines fall into these style categories (save for the ultra-modern versions aiming more at the new world style than the old). Getting it wrong is difficult if you stick to the styles that the locals have been drinking for generations. These sections point out some common southern Italian dishes and my wine pairing choices.

Salads and starters

No Italian meal is complete without a salad of some kind. But the salads that are served at the beginning of the meal are more complex preparations, usually involving some kind of protein (seafood, meat, cheese). Simple green salads with vinaigrette are always served after the main course as a digestive aid, without any wine accompaniment.

Antipasti (singular: antipasto) means literally "before the meal." The composition and variety of antipasti served varies greatly from region to region, but they often include seafood, cured meats, olives, pickled or grilled vegetables, and cheese. Antipasti are served at the table as the first course in a traditional meal, and as such differ from the French hors d'oeuvres, which are passed around before sitting down to the table.

Considering that a typical antipasto platter contains a variety of ingredients, and that vinegar is often featured somewhere, the best wine option is generally a bright, crisp, unoaked dry white, rosé, or even red, served with a slight chill. Table 13-1 suggests a few popular dishes and my wine suggestions. Don't bother looking for the perfect match, but rather think of the wine as a condiment for the antipasti, like a versatile squeeze of lemon.

Table 13-1	Pairing Wine with Southern Italian Starters	
Local Dish Name (English)	**Best Wine Style (Example)**	**Alternative Wine Style (Example)**
Buttariga/bottarga (Sardinian smoked mullet caviar and olive oil)	White: Lightweight, crisp, and stony (Vermentino di Gallura)	White: Lightweight, crisp, and stony (Santorini Assyrtiko)
Insalata caprese (tomato, mozzarella di bufala, basil)	White: Lightweight, crisp, and stony (Costa d'Amalfi Bianco)	White: Lightweight, crisp, and stony (Rias Baixas Albariño)
Insalata di polipo (boiled octopus with lemon and olive oil)	White: Lightweight, crisp, and stony (Campania Falanghina)	White: Aromatic, fruity, round (Greco di Tufo)
Calamari fritti alla Siciliana (fried squid with cumin)	White: Lightweight, crisp, and stony (Etna Bianco)	White: Lightweight, crisp, and stony, sparkling (Franciacorta)
Arancini (deep fried rice balls filled with mozzarella)	White: Lightweight, crisp, and stony (Frascati)	White: Lightweight, crisp, and stony, sparkling (Prosecco)
Insalata Siciliana (cherry tomatoes, capers, anchovies, basil)	White: Lightweight, crisp, and stony (Etna Bianco)	White: Lightweight, crisp, and stony (Vermentino di Gallura)
Caponata (fried eggplant, tomatoes, capers, green olives)	Red: Light-bodied, bright, and zesty (Sicily Frappato)	Red: Light-bodied, bright, and zesty (Loire Valley Cabernet Franc)
Carciofi alla romana (braised artichokes roman-style, stuffed with mint, garlic, breadcrumbs)	White: Lightweight, crisp, and stony (Frascati)	White: Lightweight, crisp, and stony (Sancerre Sauvignon Blanc)

Primi: The first course

The first serious course (*primi*) in a southern Italian meal is often some kind of *pasta secca*, dried pasta made without egg (egg-based pasta is a northern Italian specialty), soup, or rice dish. Portions are small, because the primi follows the antipasti, and the main course, salad, and dessert are yet to come. Table 13-2 lays out my suggestions for wine with the primi.

Table 13-2	Pairing Wine with Southern Italian Primi	
Local Dish Name (English)	*Best Wine Style (Example)*	*Alternative Wine Style (Example)*
Pepata di cozze (mussel and clam soup with tomato)	White: Lightweight, crisp, and stony (Falerno del Massico Bianco)	Rosé: Dry (Côtes de Provence)
Spaghetti con piselli e menta (spaghetti with mint, peas, garlic)	White: Lightweight, crisp, and stony (Campania Falanghina)	White: Lightweight, crisp, and stony (Loire Valley Sauvignon Blanc)
Pasta con le sarde (pasta with sardines)	White: Lightweight, crisp, and stony (Sicily Inzolia)	White: Lightweight, crisp, and stony (Rias Baixas Albariño)
Pasta al nero di seppia (pasta with cuttlefish ink sauce)	White: Aromatic, fruity, round (Fiano di Avellino)	White: Aromatic, fruity, round (Colli Orientali del Friuli Friulano)
Spaghetti alle vongole (pasta with clams in white sauce with garlic, olive oil, pepper)	White: Lightweight, crisp, and stony (Greco di Tufo)	White: Lightweight, crisp, and stony (Gavi di Gavi)
Pasta putanesca (pasta with anchovies, black olives, capers, chilies)	Red: Light-bodied, bright, and zesty (Lacryma Christi Rosso)	Red: Light-bodied, bright, and zesty (Chianti Sangiovese)
Bucatini all'amatriciana (long tubular pasta with tomato and guanciale [salt pork])	Red: Light-bodied, bright, and zesty (Cesanese del Piglio)	Red: Light-bodied, bright, and zesty (Rosso di Montalcino)
Spaghetti alla carbonara (spaghetti with egg yolks, guanciale, pecorino)	White: Lightweight, crisp, and stony (Castelli Romani Bianco)	White: Lightweight, crisp, and stony (Chablis)

Local Dish Name (English)	Best Wine Style (Example)	Alternative Wine Style (Example)
Orecchiette alle cime di rapa (ear-shaped pasta with rapini)	White: Lightweight, crisp, and stony (Locorotondo Bianco)	White: Lightweight, crisp, and stony (Muscadet)
Malloreddus (semolina gnocchi with saffron sauce)	White: Lightweight, crisp, and stony (Vermentino di Gallura)	Rosé: Dry (Côtes du Rhône)
Spaghetti all' aglio olio e peperoncino (pasta with olive oil, garlic, hot peppers)	White: Lightweight, crisp, and stony (Campania Coda di Volpe)	White: Aromatic, fruity, round (Alto Adige Pinot Grigio)

Pizza: An infinite variety

Southern Italy gave the world the pizza (*pizze* in Italian), in all its glorious diversity. The pizzas from Rome have a particularly thin and crisp crust, while those from Naples have slightly thicker, softer crust. The pizza is usually a meal unto itself, occasionally served after a light antipasto and followed by a simple green salad. I list in Table 13-3 some of the most traditional types of pizza; obviously the possibilities are near infinite.

When considering which wine to pair, start from the bottom up. All pizzas are either red (tomato-based), or the so-called *pizza bianca,* white pizza without tomato. Zesty, savory, high acid reds (such as Chianti or other Sangiovese-based reds) are the classic match with red pizza, meeting the acidic, umami-rich tomato sauce head-on. Beyond that, the nuances of more or less spice (spicy sausage, chile peppers), saltiness (anchovies, olives, cured meats) or bitter elements (artichokes) can tweak the match slightly. White pizzas can shift either toward whites, reds, or rosés depending on the particular ingredients, but all in all, you should treat the pairings as formally as you treat the pizza itself. I find it generally best to avoid big, jammy, tannic, oaky reds and oaky, creamy whites (though the latter work nicely with the ham and pineapple variation), which tend not to jive well with the rustic flavor of traditional pizza.

Table 13-3	Pairing Wine with Pizza	
Local Dish Name (English)	*Best Wine Style (Example)*	*Alternative Wine Style (Example)*
Pizza marinara (tomato, garlic, oregano)	Red: Light-bodied, bright, and zesty (Campania Piedirosso/Aglianico)	Red: Light-bodied, bright, and zesty (Chianti Sangiovese)
Pizza Napoletana (tomato, anchovies, capers, oregano)	Red: Light-bodied, bright, and zesty (Aglianico del Taburno)	Red: Light-bodied, bright, and zesty (Valpolicella)
Pizza margherita (tomato, basil, mozzarella)	Red: Light-bodied, bright, and zesty (Penisola Sorrentina Rosso)	Rosé: Dry (Bandol rosé)
Pizza bianca (sliced potatoes, olive oil, salt, rosemary)	White: Aromatic, fruity, round (Fiano di Avellino)	Rosé: Dry (Sangiovese rosato)

Secondi: Main courses

Secondi, or main courses in southern Italy are typically fish, poultry, or meat-based, though you can also find several traditional vegetarian dishes. A traditional Italian restaurant separately sells the *contorni*, side vegetable dishes. Focus on the main course itself when considering the wine match (refer to Table 13-4), and remember that the sauce more frequently drives the pairing than the particular protein involved.

Table 13-4	Pairing Wine with Southern Italian Secondi	
Local Dish Name (English)	*Best Wine Style (Example)*	*Alternative Wine Style (Example)*
Pollo al mattone (herb-marinated chicken cooked under a brick)	White: Aromatic, fruity, round (Fiano di Avellino)	Red: Light-bodied, bright, and zesty (Cerasuolo di Vittoria)
Pollo al marsala (chicken in marsala sauce)	White: Full-bodied, soft, wood-aged (Contessa Entellina Bianco)	White: Aromatic, fruity, round (Chateauneuf-du-Pape blanc)
Calamari ripieni alla Siciliana (calamari stuffed with raisins, anchovies)	White: Aromatic, fruity, round (Sicily Grillo)	White: Lightweight, crisp, and stony (Alsace Riesling)

Local Dish Name (English)	Best Wine Style (Example)	Alternative Wine Style (Example)
Pesce spada alla ghiotta (swordfish rolls in tomato sauce)	Red: Light-bodied, bright, and zesty (Cerasuolo di Vittoria)	Rosé: Dry (Cabernet rosé)
Tonno alla Palermitana (tuna Palermo-style marinated in white wine, lemon, garlic, rosemary, broiled, served with pan-seared sardines)	White: Aromatic, fruity, round (Greco di Tufo)	Rosé: Dry (Sicily Nero d'Avola rosato)
Porcetto (suckling pig with myrtle)	White: Lightweight, crisp, and stony (Vermentino di Gallura)	Red: Light-bodied, bright, and zesty (Chianti Sangiovese)
Tiella di verdure (casserole of baked vegetable with mozzarella and basil)	White: Lightweight, crisp, and stony (Locorontondo Bianco)	Red: Light-bodied, bright, and zesty (Niagara Peninsula Cabernet Franc)
Saltimbocca alla romana (veal cutlet roman-style with raw ham and sage, simmered in white wine and butter)	White: Aromatic, fruity, round (Soave Classico)	White: Lightweight, crisp, and stony (Verdicchio dei Castelli di Jesi)
Agnello con le olive (roast lamb with olives)	Red: Medium-full bodied, balanced, moderately tannic (Montepulciano d'Abruzzo)	Red: Medium-full bodied, balanced, moderately tannic (Salice Salentino)
Braciole di Maiale (pork loin with tomato sauce, garlic, capers, pine nuts)	Red: Light-bodied, bright, and zesty (Aglianico del Vulture)	White: Aromatic, fruity, round (Fiano di Avellino)

Dolci: Desserts

Dessert in southern Italy is more often than not a bowl of seasonal fresh fruit. A small glass of a traditional sweet passito-style wine, such as *Moscato* or *Passito di Pantelleria,* is a great accompaniment, as is a sweet, sparkling Moscato d'Asti. More elaborate desserts were usually reserved for festival days and holidays, though even these have made their way into current mainstream culture and are served at all times in restaurants both in Italy and abroad. In Table 13-5, you can find some of the more traditional sweets of the south, which frequently involve fresh or dried fruits, nuts, honey, and fresh cheese, along with some pairing suggestions.

Table 13-5	Pairing Wine with Southern Italian Desserts	
Local Dish Name (English)	**Best Wine Style (Example)**	**Alternative Wine Style (Example)**
Torta ai pistacchi (pistachio tart)	Sweet: Passito (Passito di Pantelleria)	Sweet: Passito (Muscat of Samos)
Torta caprese (flourless chocolate cake)	Red: Sweet fortified (Aleatico di Puglia Liquoroso)	Sweet: Fortified red (Douro Valley Late Bottled Vintage Port)
Torta ricotta e pera (tart with ricottta cream, poached pears, biscotti)	Sweet: Passito (Moscato di Pantelleria)	Sweet: Sparkling white (Moscato d'Asti)
Cannoli (fried dough stuffed with ricotta cheese, raisins, cinnamon)	Sweet: Fortified amber (Marsala Superiore Riserva)	Sweet: Late harvest, noble rot (Ruster Ausbruch)
Brucellato (shortbread cake stuffed with dried fig, raisins, almond)	Red: Sweet fortified (Aleatico di Lazio, Puglia)	Sweet: Passito red (Recioto della Valpolicella)
Struffoli (fried dough with honey)	Sweet: Passito white (Passito di Pantelleria)	Sweet: Sparkling white (Moscato D'Asti)

Pairing Wine with Southern French Food

Much like the landscape, the cuisine of Provence and the Midi in southern France can be best described as nuanced. As the gentle pastel colors drew artists from all over the world to settle and paint landscapes here, the food draws inspiration from a riot of colorful ingredients, fresh and vital, offering a rich array of shapes, textures, and flavors with no hard or aggressive edges. Rolling hills of lavender, bay, thyme, rosemary, basil, and jasmine perfume the air as they do the food.

Southern France is a region where food and wine have evolved together over millennia. There exists a beautiful synergy between traditional dishes and regional wine styles. The best known wines of the coastal area, the pale, delicate rosés of the Provencal hillsides, are marvelously versatile. They seem tailor-made, with their gentle sweet and resinous herbal aromatics (called *garrigue* in this part of the world), for the subtle, aromatic, herb-inflected cuisine dominated by fruits of the sea. And then as the fare gets a little more hearty and robust inland, the wines too, gain in depth and structure. From the substantial red blends of the southern Rhône and the Languedoc, to the finely etched, smoky and spicy Syrahs of the northern Rhône, passing through richly textured whites and sweet fortified reds and whites, you can find a local wine for every preparation.

These sections take you on a brief culinary tour of this magical land and inspire you to eat and drink in the southern French way.

Salads and starters

Considering the variety of fresh produce available for most of the year, vegetables are taken seriously in Provence. They're served both raw and cooked and are featured in virtually every meal. Table 13-6 points out my wine suggestions for salads.

Table 13-6	Pairing Wine with Southern French Starters	
Local Dish Name (English)	*Best Wine Style (Example)*	*Alternative Wine Style (Example)*
Salade Niçoise (mixed salad with tuna, green beans, boiled egg, anchovies)	Rosé: Dry (Côtes de Provence)	White: Lightweight, crisp, and stony (Marlborough Sauvignon Blanc)
Pissaladière (onion, anchovy, black olive tart)	Rosé: Dry (Tavel)	Red: Medium-full bodied, balanced, moderately tannic (Ribera del Duero jóven)
Légumes farcies (stuffed vegetables: red bell pepper, eggplant, or tomato stuffed with rice, salt pork, cheese)	Rosé: Dry (Côtes de Provence)	Red: Light-bodied, bright, and zesty, low tannins (Côtes du Rhône, basic)
Brandade de morue (thick purée of cod, olive oil, garlic, milk)	White: Aromatic, fruity, round (Cassis)	Rosé: Dry (Côtes de Provence)
Soupe au pistou (potato, leek, and mixed bean soup with pistou sauce)	White: Aromatic, fruity, round (Côtes du Rhône blanc)	White: Aromatic, fruity, round (Alsace Pinot Gris)
Escargots à la Provençale (snails with garlic, olive oil, white wine)	Rosé: Dry (Côtes de Provence)	White: Aromatic, fruity, round (Crozes-Hermitage blanc)
Tapenade (chopped black olives, garlic, capers, oil)	Rosé: Dry (Coteaux d'Aix en Provence)	White: Aromatic, fruity, round (Coteaux Varois blanc)

Main courses

Like other Mediterranean regions, proximity to the sea makes seafood a principal staple, though as you travel farther inland up the Rhône Valley, meat, especially lamb and sheep, gain more prominence.

You won't find bold spices here; classic Provençal cuisine is all about delicate aromatics. Chefs rely on condiments such as *aioli* (garlic mayonnaise), *pistou* (basil pesto), and *rouille* (olive oil, garlic, breadcrumbs, saffron, and red pimentos) to enhance all manner of fresh fish, vegetables, soups, stews, and meats. Table 13-7 highlights some of my wine suggestions for these main courses.

Table 13-7   Pairing Wine with Southern French Main Courses

Local Dish Name (English)	Best Wine Style (Example)	Alternative Wine Style (Example)
Moules marinière (mussels with wine and herbs)	White: Lightweight, crisp, and stony (Picpoul de Pinet)	White: Aromatic, fruity, round (Alto Adige Pinot Grigio)
Bouillabaisse (seafood stew with small fish, saffron, herbs)	Rosé: Dry (Côtes de Provence)	White: Aromatic, fruity, round (Cassis)
Ratatouille (vegetable stew with eggplant, zucchini, bell pepper, tomato)	Red: Light-bodied, bright, and zesty, low tannins (Côtes du Rhône, basic)	Rosé: Dry (Bandol rosé)
Daube Provençale (beef braised in red wine, vegetables, garlic, provençal herbs)	Red: Full, deep, and robust, turbocharged, chewy texture (Bandol Mourvèdre)	Red: Full, deep, and robust, turbocharged, chewy texture (Chateauneuf-du-Pape)
Carré d'agneau aux herbes de Provence (rack of lamb with provençal herbs)	Red: Full, deep, and robust, turbocharged, chewy texture (Bandol Mourvèdre)	Red: Full, deep, and robust, turbocharged, chewy texture (Chateauneuf-du-Pape)
Souris d'agneau braisé (braised lamb with thyme and rosemary)	Red: Full, deep, and robust, turbocharged, chewy texture (Gigondas)	Red: Full, deep, and robust, turbocharged, chewy texture (Barossa Valley Shiraz)

Desserts

Dessert in Provence is rarely a complicated affair. It's often as simple as fresh or dried fruit, nuts and honey, or a light fruit tart or pastry. Muscat de Beaumes de Venise is the classic southern Rhône fortified white wine, usually served young to capture the marvelous perfume of the Muscat grape. It's the wine of choice with most Provençal sweets, though of course not the only option. Table 13-8 offers a few alternatives for these desserts as well.

Table 13-8	Pairing Wine with Southern French Desserts	
Local Dish Name (English)	*Best Wine Style (Example)*	*Alternative Wine Style (Example)*
Pithivier (puff pastry pie with almond paste)	White: Sweet fortified (Muscat du Cap Corse)	Sweet: Late harvest noble rot (Vouvray Moelleux)
Calissons d'Aix (petal shaped almond cookies with orange)	White: Sweet fortified (Muscat de Beaumes de Venise)	Sweet: Passito (Moscato di Pantelleria)
Tarte aux abricots (apricot tart with honey)	White: Sweet fortified (Muscat de Beaumes de Venise)	Sweet: Icewine (Niagara Peninsula vidal)
Nougat (almonds, honey, caster sugar)	White: Sweet fortified (Muscat de Beaumes de Venise)	Sweet: Late harvest noble rot (German Riesling beerenauslese)
Tarte Tropézienne (large brioche filled with pastry cream, kirsch)	White: Sweet fortified (Muscat de Beaumes de Venise)	Sweet: Fortified amber (Rivesaltes Ambré)

Dabbling in Spain and Spanish Cuisine

At the mention of Spain, most people conjure up the images of beaches, bull-fights, and relentless sun. These images are classic Andalucía, Spain's southern-most region with its emblematic towns of Granada and Sevilla, and of course where Sherry is produced. But Spain is far more diverse. No fewer than five languages are spoken in Spain: Catalan, Valencian, Galician, and Basque, along with standard Spanish. And the culinary landscape reflects this linguistic diversity. The northern shores of what I call "green" Spain are home to plenty of seafood and crisp whites. Basque cuisine is as unique as the language, and is one of the most developed in all Europe. Southern Spain is Europe's vegetable garden and orchard, supplying most of the other EU members. Nevertheless, Spain is still the land of olive oil — it's among the world's most prolific producers.

The following sections try to characterize Spanish foods and wine in a few pages and offer you some classic food and wine pairings.

Tapas/pintxos and appetizers

Tapas, or *pintxos,* as they're known in Basque country, are bite-sized morsels served in bars as snacks, usually at lunchtime or late afternoon/early evening before heading out for a full meal. The name derives from the Spanish word *tapa* meaning "lid."

Tapas are more a way of life (eating) than a style of cooking, encouraging plenty of social interaction. Going out for tapas is usually done in groups, with friends gathering after work or on weekend afternoons for a few drinks and snacks, always standing and chatting around the bar. Barhopping from one place to the next is customary; rarely do you stay in one place for more than a drink or two. This way you can experience the specialties of several bars — tapas is all about diversity.

Traditional tapas include hard cheeses, various cured sausages (*embutidos*) and hams *(jamón)*, preserved vegetables (peppers, olives, artichokes, white asparagus), or seafood. Tapas culture has evolved significantly with ever-more elaborate preparations. Listing them all is impossible, so Table 13-9 lists some of the most commonly encountered tapas, grouped together where the best wine style is the same. Put together a varied platter of tapas, chill some bottles, and invite your friends over.

Table 13-9	Pairing Wine with Spanish Tapas	
Local Dish Name (English)	*Best Wine Style (Example)*	*Alternative Wine Style (Example)*
Tortilla Española (thick omelet with potatoes poached in olive oil)	White: Lightweight, crisp, and stony, sparkling (Cava)	White: Aromatic, fruity, round (Valdeorras Godello)
Jamón serrano/Ibérico/Jabugo (Spanish acorn-fed, cured ham)	White: Fortified dry (Fino/Manzanilla Sherry)	White: Lightweight, crisp, and stony (Rioja Reserva blanco, aged)
Embutidos (various types of sausages like chorizo, morcilla [blood sausage], salami)	Red: Light-bodied, bright, and zesty, low tannins (Rioja Jovén Tempranillo)	Rosé: Dry (Navarra Rosado blend)
Pulpo a la Gallega (Galician-style boiled octopus salad with olive oil, paprika)	White: Lightweight, crisp, and stony (Rias Baixas Albariño)	White: Lightweight, crisp, and stony (Santorini Assyrtiko)
Boquerones al vinaigre (anchovies in vinegar)	White: Lightweight, crisp, and stony (Txacoli de Vizcaya)	White: Lightweight, crisp, and stony, sparkling (Muscadet)

Local Dish Name (English)	Best Wine Style (Example)	Alternative Wine Style (Example)
Boquerones fritos (fried anchovies)	White: Lightweight, crisp, and stony (Txacoli de Vizcaya)	White: Lightweight, crisp, and stony, sparkling (Cava)
Calamares fritos (fried squid)		
Gambas al ajillo (garlic prawns)		
Gambas pil-pil (chile and garlic prawns)		
Buñuelos de bacalao (salt cod fritters)		
Berenjenas fritas (deep-fried eggplant)		
Almejas con vino blanco (clams in white wine)		
Pesacaíto frito (small fish deep-fried in olive oil)		
Ensalada de atún y huevos (tuna and egg)	Rosé: Dry (Cigales Tempranillo Rosado)	Red: Light-bodied, bright, and zesty, low tannins (Cru Beaujolais Gamay)
Pimiento asado y atún (tuna and red pepper salad)		
Atún y aceitunas con pan (tuna and olive tapenade crostini)		
Croquetas (potato croquettes)	White: Full-bodied, soft, wood-aged (Rioja Blanco crianza or reserva)	White: Full-bodied, soft, wood-aged (Côtes du Roussillon Villages blanc)
Champiñones al ajillo (garlic mushrooms)		
champiñones al pimienta (mushrooms and peppers)		
Patatas bravas (crispy potatoes in spicy tomato sauce)	Red: Light-bodied, bright, and zesty, low tannins (Ribero del Duero Jovén Tempranillo)	White: Aromatic, fruity, round (Rueda Verdejo)

Soups and stews

Spain has a great tradition of soups and stews. Legumes, such as lentils, chick-peas and various kinds of beans, are used in abundance to create hearty one-dish meals to provide energy and sustenance through the cold winter months. Most regions have their own variations, such as the *fabada Austuriana*, a substantial dish from Asturias made from large white beans, pork shoulder, chorizo, and blood sausage, or the *Cocido Madrileño*, Madrid's famous chickpea, cabbage, pork belly, chorizo, and blood sausage stew. In the northwest corner of the country in Galicia where fishing is the main industry, seafood-based stews are common, usually including octopus, cod, and gooseneck barnacles *(percebes)*. Such heavy dishes are always eaten at lunchtime, the main meal of the day in Spain.

In southern Spain, where temperatures during the summer months regularly hover around 40°C, people favor lighter soups and even chilled soups. The most famous example is gazpacho, a purée of raw tomatoes, cucumbers, bell peppers, garlic, olive oil, and vinegar, served cold with crusty bread and a cool glass of Fino Sherry or other light, crisp dry white or rosé wine. Table 13-10 shows some of my wine suggestions for these dishes.

Table 13-10	Pairing Wine with Spanish Soups	
Local Dish Name (English)	**Best Wine Style (Example)**	**Alternative Wine Style (Example)**
Gazpacho (tomato-based vegetable soup served chilled)	Rosé: Dry (Navarra Rosado Garnacha or Tempranillo)	White: Lightweight, crisp, and stony (Loire Valley Sauvignon Blanc)
Salmorejo (chilled tomato, bread, oil, garlic, and vinegar soup served with serrano ham)	White: Fortified dry (Fino or Manzanilla Sherry)	White: Lightweight, crisp, and stony (Valdeorras Godello)
Cocido Madrileño (chick-pea-based stew with cab-bage, pork belly, chorizo, blood sausage)	Red: Medium-full bodied, balanced, moderately tannic (Valdepeñas Tempranillo)	Red: Light-bodied, bright, and zesty, low tannins (Cariñena Garnacha)
Callos a la Madrileña (tripe stew from madrid with tomato, blood sau-sage, chorizo)	Red: Light-bodied, bright, and zesty, low tannins (Rioja Jóven Tempranillo)	Red: Medium-full bodied, balanced, mod-erately tannic (Napa Valley Merlot)
Fabada Asturiana (Asturian bean stew with ham hock, chorizo, blood sausage)	Red: Medium-full bodied, balanced, moderately tannic (Bierzo Mencía)	Red: Medium-full bodied, balanced, mod-erately tannic (Ribera del Duero Tempranillo)

Main dishes

Spain is equally rich in seafood, poultry, game, and meat dishes. Preparations are usually simple, relying on the quality of ingredients rather than elaborate recipes and complex sauces. As such, most common main courses are highly wine friendly. Table 13-11 includes some of my favorite dishes along with the classic local wine matches and recommended wine style for each.

Table 13-11	Pairing Wine with Spanish Main Dishes	
Local Dish Name (English)	*Best Wine Style (Example)*	*Alternative Wine Style (Example)*
Chuletillas al sarmiento (milk-fed lamb chops grilled over vine clippings)	Red: Medium-full bodied, balanced, moderately tannic (Rioja Reserva)	Red: Full, deep, and robust, turbocharged, chewy texture (Toro Tempranillo)
Cochinillo asado (roast suckling pig)	Red: Light-bodied, bright, and zesty, low tannins (Ribera del Duero Jovén)	White: Aromatic, fruity, round (Rueda Verdejo)
Cordero (lechazo) asado (wood oven-roasted milk-fed lamb)	Red: Full, deep, and robust, turbocharged, chewy texture (Jumilla Monastrell)	Red: Full, deep, and robust, turbocharged, chewy texture (Bordeaux Haut-Médoc)
Bacalao a la Vizcaína (stewed salt cod with garlic, red peppers)	White: Lightweight, crisp, and stony (Txacolì de Vizcaya)	Red: Light-bodied, bright, and zesty, low tannins (Piedmont Barbera)
Conejo a la cazadora (hunter-style braised rabbit with mushrooms, tomatoes, brandy, white wine)	White: Full-bodied, soft, wood-aged (Priorat Blanco white blend)	Red: Light-bodied, bright, and zesty, low tannins (Burgundy Pinot Noir)
Pato al jerez (duck in Sherry sauce)	Dry fortified: Amber (Amontillado Sherry)	Red: Medium-full bodied, balanced, moderately tannic (Rioja Reserva)
Rabo de toro (braised oxtails in red wine)	Red: Full, deep, and robust, turbocharged, chewy texture (Ribera del Duero Reserva)	Red: Full, deep, and robust, turbocharged, chewy texture (Maipo Valley Cabernet Sauvignon)
Trucha a la navarra (fried trout stuffed with serrano ham)	White: Lightweight, crisp, and stony (Valdeorras Godello)	White: Lightweight, crisp, and stony (Chablis)

(continued)

Table 13-11 *(continued)*

Local Dish Name (English)	Best Wine Style (Example)	Alternative Wine Style (Example)
Paella Valenciana (saffron rice with chicken, rabbit, duck, snails, beans)	White: Lightweight, crisp, and stony (Rioja Blanco Reserva)	Red: Light-bodied, bright, and zesty, low tannins (Bierzo Mencía)
Paella de mariscos (seafood paella)	White: Lightweight, crisp, and stony (Rias Baixas Albariño)	White: Lightweight, crisp, and stony (Austria Grüner Veltliner)

Desserts

The Spanish love custards and other milk or cream-based desserts. *Flan*, a custard served with caramel sauce, is one of the most popular desserts in Spain. Almonds and hazelnuts are used frequently for various cakes, as well as *turrón*, Spain's famous nougat. *Churros*, fried dough sprinkled with sugar and sometimes dipped in chocolate sauce, is a popular late night or early morning snack, especially after the bars have finally closed.

Andalusia is best known for its fortified sweet wines, most notably from Sherry and Malaga. These are what you'd be drinking alongside most desserts in Spain. In Table 13-12, I offer some of the more common desserts with recommended wines styles and typical regional pairings.

Table 13-12   Pairing Wine with Spanish Desserts

Local Dish Name (English)	Best Wine Style (Example)	Alternative Wine Style (Example)
Turrón (almond and honey nougat)	Sweet: Fortified amber (Oloroso Dulce Sherry)	Sweet: Passito (Muscat of Rio Patras)
Torta de Santiago (almond cake)	Sweet: Fortified white (Pale Cream Sherry)	Sweet: Late harvest (Mosel Riesling auslese)
Flan (custard with caramel sauce)	Sweet: Fortified amber (Oloroso Dulce Sherry)	Sweet: Late harvest noble rot (Barsac)
Arroz con leche (rice pudding)	Sweet: Fortified amber (Moscatel)	Sweet: Late Harvest (Niagara Peninsula Icewine Vidal)
Churros con chocolate (deep-fried dough with chocolate sauce)	Sweet: Fortified amber (PX Sherry)	Sweet: Passito (Mavrodaphne of Patras)

Passing through Portugal: Portuguese Food

Despite the geographical proximity, Portugal's food reveals different influences from Spain's. The fiery *piri piri* chile pepper from former colonial possession Mozambique, for example, is now ubiquitous in the Portuguese kitchen. Piri piri is the base of the spicy sauce that accompanies the highly popular grilled or rotisserie chicken served in *churasqueiras*.

But piri piri aside, most traditional Portuguese dishes are relatively mild and thus easy to pair with wine. Plenty of local selection is available; approximately 200 different indigenous grape varieties grow in Portugal, offering a dramatic range of wines from cool coastal areas like Vinho Verde, sturdy mountain wines from the Douro and Dão, and the soft, ripe wines of the southern plains in the Alentejo region. These sections explain some of my picks for a few traditional Portuguese dishes with the wine pairing that the locals would most likely be drinking alongside each.

Fish and seafood

Portugal is a seafaring nation, and seafood is interwoven with culinary culture. Among the many varied species of fish consumed in Portugal, none is more important than *bacalhau* (cod), a symbol of Portuguese cuisine. Cod is more often than not salted and dried, as the North Atlantic cod fishing tradition pre-dates refrigeration and thus the more ancient preservation method became the tradition that is still followed today.

Among cooking methods, the *cataplana* is a uniquely Portuguese cooking vessel used frequently for seafood preparations. It's traditionally made of copper and shaped like a clamshell; ingredients are put inside and it's closed and sealed with a latch. The seafood then boils/steams inside, keeping all its flavors in the finished dish. Table 13-13 lists some of my wine suggestions for Portuguese seafood.

Table 13-13	Pairing Wine with Portuguese Seafood	
Local Dish Name (English)	*Best Wine Style (Example)*	*Alternative Wine Style (Example)*
Shrimp piri piri (shrimp with piri piri pepper sauce)	White: Lightweight, crisp, and stony (Vinho Verde)	White: Lightweight, crisp, and stony (Alsace Riesling)

(continued)

Table 13-13 *(continued)*

Local Dish Name (English)	Best Wine Style (Example)	Alternative Wine Style (Example)
Cataplana de mariscos (seafood stew with tomato and potato cooked in a traditional copper vessel called a catapalana)	White: Lightweight, crisp, and stony (Bucelas Arinto)	White: Lightweight, crisp, and stony (Sancerre Sauvignon Blanc)
Açorda de mariscos (seafood with mashed bread, garlic, coriander, olive oil, water, salt, eggs)	White: Full-bodied, soft, wood-aged (Dão Encruzado blend)	White: Lightweight, crisp, and stony (Vinho Verde Alvarinho)
Sardinhas grelhadas (grilled sardines)	White: Lightweight, crisp, and stony (Vinho Verde)	White: Lightweight, crisp, and stony (Muscadet)

Main dishes

Portuguese main courses are hearty and satisfying. Boiling, stewing, and grilling are the most common methods of preparation, though *leitão*, the wood oven-roasted suckling pig specialty of the Bairrada region is an exception to the rule. One of the more unusual dishes is *carne de porco a alentejana*, a typical dish of the Alentejo region that combines sautéed marinated pork with clams, potato, and coriander. It's a dish that can work with either white or red wines (see Table 13-14), but I prefer one of the soft, ripe and satisfying red blends from the same region.

Table 13-14 Pairing Wine with Portuguese Main Dishes

Local Dish Name (English)	Best Wine Style (Example)	Alternative Wine Style (Example)
Frango na churrasco (piri piri marinated grilled chicken)	Red: Light-bodied, bright, and zesty, low tannins (Dâo red blend)	Red: Light-bodied, bright, and zesty, low tannins (Piedmont Barbera)
Carne de porco à alentejana (pork with potatoes, clams, paprika, coriander)	Red: Full, deep, and robust, turbocharged, chewy texture (Alentejo red blend)	Red: Light-bodied, bright, and zesty, low tannins (Central Otago Pinot Noir)

Local Dish Name (English)	Best Wine Style (Example)	Alternative Wine Style (Example)
Cozido à Portuguesa (stew of beef shank, pork, blood sausage, vegetables)	Red: Light-bodied, bright, and zesty, low tannins (Dão red blend)	Red: Light-bodied, bright, and zesty, low tannins (Burgundy Pinot Noir)
Tripas à moda do porto (tripe with white beans)	White: Full-bodied, soft, wood-aged (Dão white blend)	White: Full-bodied, soft, wood-aged (Burgundy Chardonnay)
Leitão (roast suckling pig)	Red: Light-bodied, bright, and zesty (Bairrada Baga)	White: Aromatic, fruity, round (Alsace Pinot Gris)

Desserts

Eggs, crème, and sugar form the basis of many sweets. Custards in particular are very popular, especially the rich *natas do ceu,* "cream from heaven," and *pastéis de nata,* the small high-calorie custard tarts that are made in every Portuguese bakery at home and abroad. These types of desserts require very sweet wines to match, such as the excellent *Moscatél de Setúbal*, the sweet Muscat-based fortified wine from around the Setúbal Peninsula. It differs from other fortified Muscats from southern France in that it is macerated on the skins for several months and then aged for prolonged periods, sometimes up to 20 years before bottling, adding remarkable orange blossom honey and caramel complexity, well beyond the simple floral notes of fresh Muscat. Check out Table 13-15 for some wine suggestions for Portuguese desserts.

Table 13-15	Pairing Wine with Portuguese Desserts	
Local Dish Name (English)	Best Wine Style (Example)	Alternative Wine Style (Example)
Natas do ceu (heavenly cream custard)	Sweet: Fortified amber (Moscatél de Setúbal)	Sweet: Late harvest (Niagara Peninsula Icewine Vidal)
Bolo de mel (Madeira honey cake)	Sweet: Fortified amber (Malmsey Madeira)	Sweet: Late harvest noble rot (Vouvray Moelleux Chenin Blanc)
Pastéis de nata (sweet custard tarts)	Sweet: Fortified amber (Moscatél de Setúbal)	Sweet: Late harvest noble rot (Monbazillac)

Going to the Greek Isles

Greece, and more specifically the Island of Crete, is credited as the origin of the Mediterranean diet. Extra virgin olive oil; cured olives; *horta* (wild greens); aromatic herbs; legumes such as the fava bean, split pea, chickpea, and lentil; fish and seafood of every description; snails; nuts; sesame seeds; whole grains; and a few simple goat's and sheep's milk cheeses, not to mention wine, are staples of the Greek table, and now by extension, of the entire Mediterranean.

Dishes are both regional and seasonal, changing with the availability of ingredients. If your experience with Greek cuisine is limited to a handful of clichéd dishes like *souvlaki* and *gyros,* you're in for a treat when you travel to Greece, or dine in one of the many exellent *estiatorios* (Greek for *restaurant,* a little fancier than a *Taverna*) popping up worldwide. Restaurant culture is slowly catching up to the depth and diversity of the Greek home kitchen. *Tavernas* still serve traditional foods, while *estiatorios* are where culinary innovation meets time-honored preparations.

Many traditional recipes call for combinations of vegetables, beans, or rice with more expensive proteins as a means to stretch dishes. The basic grain in Greece is wheat, while principal vegetables include tomato, eggplant, potatoes, green beans, okra, green bell peppers, onion, and garlic. Oregano, mint, dill, and bay leaf occur frequently, as do thyme, basil, fennel seed, and rosemary. In Macedonia in northern Greece, sweet spices like cinnamon and clove are more prominent than elsewhere with meat dishes.

As with most Mediterranean cuisines, Greek food is very wine-friendly. Fresh, savory ingredients and simple preparations that often involve nothing more than a grill, olive oil and a squeeze of lemon, and the absence of strong spice, make Greek cuisine compatible with a wide range of wines. Considering that wine is ever-present on the Greek table, it's natural that food and wine evolved compatibility over millennia of co-existence.

Mezes: Tapas, Greek style

A typical Greek meal involves a variety of dishes set on the table at once, or in successive waves. This is the *meze* tradition, small plates of savory foods that vary in color, texture, and temperature, always shared and always accompanied by something to drink. It's the Greek equivalent of Spanish tapas, although Greeks usually eat sitting down and spend hours at the table. Wine and other alcoholic beverages play an important role, and certain mezes are designed to be either wine or ouzo-friendly. Mezes are part of the Greek way of life.

Table 13-16 highlights some of the dishes you'd likely be served in a traditional Greek taverna during an afternoon of grazing. The arrival of multiple dishes at once poses the same challenge for wine pairings here as elsewhere where set courses are not the norm, but again, considering the wine-friendliness of most preparations, one or two crisp, versatile wines can cover a lot of ground. I offer some more specific recommendations with each dish, but in practice, serving so many wines at once would be impractical. Ideally, though, serving a few wine selections at the same time is the most fun way to try out different pairings.

Table 13-16	Pairing Wine with Greek Mezes	
Local Dish Name (English)	*Best Wine Style (Example)*	*Alternative Wine Style (Example)*
Saganaki (pan-seared, brandy–flamed kefalo-tyri cheese)	White: Lightweight, crisp, and stony (Peloponnese Roditis)	White: Full-bodied, soft, wood-aged (Southern Rhône white blend)
Grilled octopus	White: Lightweight, crisp, and stony (Santorini Assyrtiko)	White: Lightweight, crisp, and stony (Rias Baixas Albariño)
Grilled calamari	White: Lightweight, crisp, and stony (Santorini Assyrtiko)	White: Lightweight, crisp, and stony (Alto Adige Pinot Grigio)
Dolmades (grape leaves stuffed with rice, raisins, pine nuts, served with tzatziki)	White: Lightweight, crisp, and stony (Robola of Cephalonia)	White: Lightweight, crisp, and stony (Casablanca Valley Sauvignon Blanc)
Keftedes (meatballs with cumin, cinnamon)	Red: Light-bodied, bright, and zesty, low tannins (Amyndeo Xinomavro)	White: Full-bodied, soft, wood-aged (California Viognier)
Fasolakia (green beans stewed with potatoes, zucchini, tomato)	Rosé: Dry (Amyndeon Xinomavro rosé)	Red: Light-bodied, bright, and zesty, low tannins (Chinon Cabernet Franc)
Skordalia (garlic and potato puree)	White: Lightweight, crisp, and stony (Retsina)	White: Lightweight, crisp, and stony (Mosel Riesling kabinett)
Tyropita (cheese in phyllo pastry)	White: Aromatic, fruity, round (Macedonia Malagouzia)	White: Traditional Method Sparkling (Champagne)
Spanakopita (spinach and feta cheese in phyllo pastry)	White: Lightweight, crisp, and stony (Mantinia Moscophilero)	White: Lightweight, crisp, and stony (Sancerre Sauvignon Blanc)

(continued)

Table 13-16 *(continued)*

Local Dish Name (English)	Best Wine Style (Example)	Alternative Wine Style (Example)
Taramosalata (a dip of cod or carp roe with mashed potatoes, lemon juice, vinegar, olive oil)	White: Lightweight, crisp, and stony (Retsina)	White: Lightweight, crisp, and stony (Clare Valley Riesling)
Melitzanosalata (egg-plant purée with garlic, lemon juice, olive oil)	White: Lightweight, crisp, and stony (Mantinia Moscophilero)	White: Lightweight, crisp, and stony (Marlborough Sauvignon Blanc)
Horiatiki (Greek salad with tomatoes, bell peppers, cucumbers, olives, feta)	White: Lightweight, crisp, and stony (Mantinia Moscophilero)	White: Lightweight, crisp, and stony (Pouilly Fumé Sauvignon Blanc)

Main courses

Traditional Greek cuisine has countless vegetarian main courses, because many of the country's culinary customs have evolved out of the Greek Orthodox calendar and its proscribed periods of fasting. All animal products and fish (but not seafood, which is bloodless) are forbidden for almost half the year for adherents to the Orthodox religion.

Meat was traditionally reserved for the Sunday meal and for festive occasions. Lamb and goat, pork (especially in rural communities), poultry, and wild game, especially game birds and hares (or rabbits today), are the main animal proteins, especially on the mainland. Fish and seafood, particularly whole grilled fish and octopus, are essential mainstays of the Greek island diet and of coastal communities. Check out Table 13-17 for some suggestions for wine with Greek main dishes.

Table 13-17   Pairing Wine with Greek Main Courses

Local Dish Name (English)	Best Wine Style (Example)	Alternative Wine Style (Example)
Moussaka (eggplant, zucchini ground meat, and potato pie casserole with béchamel)	Red: Light-bodied, bright, and zesty, low tannins (Naoussa Xinomavro)	Red: Light-bodied, bright, and zesty, low tannins (Loire Valley Cabernet Franc)

Local Dish Name (English)	Best Wine Style (Example)	Alternative Wine Style (Example)
Spetzofai (spicy lamb sausage in bell pepper, tomato, oregano sauce)	Red: Light-bodied, bright, and zesty, low tannins (Rapsani Reserve)	Red: Medium-full bodied, balanced, moderately tannic (Nemea Reserve Agiorgitiko)
Loukaniko (pork sausage, grilled)	Red: Light-bodied, bright, and zesty, low tannins (Nemea Agiorgitiko)	White: Lightweight, crisp, and stony (Santorini Assyrtiko)
Gyros (spit-roasted meat served with tzatziki)	White: Aromatic, fruity, round (Epanomi Malagouzia)	Red: Light-bodied, bright, and zesty, low tannins (Naoussa Xinomavro)
Paidakia (grilled lamb chops with lemon, oregano, salt, pepper)	Red: Light-bodied, bright, and zesty, low tannins (Naoussa Xinomavro)	White: Lightweight, crisp, and stony (Santorini Assyrtiko)
Stifado (rabbit or hare stew with pearl onion, red wine, vinegar, cinnamon)	Red: Light-bodied, bright, and zesty, low tannins (Naoussa Xinomavro)	Red: Light-bodied, bright, and zesty, low tannins (Cru Beaujolais Gamay)
Fasolada (vegetarian bean stew with tomatoes, onions, carrots, celery, and herbs, finished with olive oil)	Red: Light-bodied, bright, and zesty, low tannins (Amydeon Xinomavro)	Red: Medium-full bodied, balanced, moderately tannic (Bordeaux St. Emilion)

Desserts

Greece is well known for its confections, cakes, and cookies. Like the wealth of dishes made without animal products, a broad range of traditional Greek sweets made with olive oil evolved as a result of the fasting calendar. Phyllo filled with nuts or cream and flavored with Greek honey syrup are among the most common.

Greek honey is highly prized and is made mainly from the nectar of fruit and citrus trees: Lemon, orange, bitter orange, and pine trees, along with thyme honey are some of the best.

Greece is likewise famous for its sweet wines, some of the most ancient styles on the planet. The technique of leaving grapes to dry in the sun for several days is very likely a Greek invention, which allows water to evaporate and concentrates sugars. The result is delectably sweet, dried fruit-flavored wines with amazing complexity, well suited to the common honey and nut flavors of many desserts. Table 13-18 has my wine suggestions.

Table 13-18	Pairing Wine with Greek Desserts	
Local Dish Name (English)	*Best Wine Style (Example)*	*Alternative Wine Style (Example)*
Loukoumades (fried dough with cinnamon and honey syrup)	Sweet: Fortified/Passito amber (Samos Nectar Muscat)	Sweet: Sparkling white (Moscato d'Asti)
Halva (sesame paste confection with honey and pistachios)	Sweet: Passito (Santorini Vinsanto)	Sweet: Late harvest noble rot (Quarts de Chaumes Chenin Blanc)
Spoon sweets (preserves of seasonal fresh fruits, unripe nuts, vegetables in simple syrup)	Sweet: Fortified white (Muscat of Limnos)	Sweet: Fortified/Passito (Mavrodaphne of Patras)
Baklava (phyllo pastry filled with nuts, covered in honey)	Sweet: Fortified/ Passito (Samos Nectar Muscat)	Sweet: Fortified amber (Rivesaltes Ambré Muscat)
Galaktoboureko (phyllo pastry filled with custard, soaked in lemon-scented honey syrup)	Sweet: Fortified amber (Samos Grand Cru Muscat)	Sweet: Late harvest (Alsace Riesling Vendanges Tardives)

Chapter 14

Staying Close to Home: North America Food

● ●

In This Chapter

▶ Dining casually

▶ Heading home for the holidays

▶ Getting messy with southern-style BBQ

▶ Looking at Cajun/Creole food

▶ Combining Texas with Mexico: "Tex-Mex"

▶ Visiting the West Coast: Pacific Northwest cuisine

▶ Going north of the border: O' Canada:

● ●

*N*orth America has one of the most diverse culinary landscapes on earth. The cuisine, like the culture, is a true melting pot. Aside from traditional ethnic restaurants making food "like back home" found in virtually all urban centers, creative North American chefs have drawn upon a rich diversity of culinary influences from all corners of the globe in order to create new and unique flavor experiences. They can't rightly be counted among any existing traditions — they have become regional classics in their own right. The fusion of French Creole flavors in the southeastern United States, or Tex-Mex in the Southwest, for example, illustrate the melding of cultures to create a new category of cuisine. And North America continues to push the culinary envelope as I discuss in this chapter.

Wine culture, too, is burgeoning. The United States ranks in the world's top five wine-producing nations. And Canada, while still comparatively small, is quickly developing regional wine styles that are as distinct as the established wines of Europe. People take considerable pride in local wines, and new local food and wine pairings are continually emerging. But North Americans are spoiled for choice. Wines from every growing region in the world find their way here, and sommeliers, and you, literally have the world to play with. Some dishes are better suited to new world–style wines, and others are best with old world–style wines. The good news for you: There are no rules engraved from centuries of repetition. North Americans are adventurous, pioneer spirits at heart with a penchant for exploring new combinations. This chapter is only your starting point.

Eating Informally

Casual dining with comfort food will never go out of style — it's pure, easy enjoyment without the fuss of formal occasions. Add to it the affordability of the dishes in this section, and you can be sure that this is what most folks are eating nightly.

Wine may not be the usual choice of beverage, but a full-throttle California Zinfandel with a Good old American burger piled sky-high with toppings is a beautiful thing. Just like you have comfort food, you also have comfort wines — the bottle you reach for when you want a sure bet. More than likely, your favorite food and your favorite wine will make for a happy occasion, so technically "right" or "wrong" matches don't exist. Nevertheless, for the tasty foods in these sections, I include the wines styles that I've enjoyed alongside in the past. If the match is out of your comfort zone, give it a try, at least once. You may discover a new favorite. I find generally that the easy-going, soft, luscious, ripe, and fruit flavored wines of the new world are often the best matches for soul-satisfying foods.

Classic sandwiches

Most delis don't serve wine (or very good wine), so you may want to grab one of these sandwiches to go that I discuss in Table 14-1, and then grab a bottle of wine and head home for a living room picnic.

Table 14-1	Pairing Wine with North American Sandwiches	
Sandwich	*Best Wine Style (Example)*	*Alternative Wine Style (Example)*
Philly cheese steak (rib-eye steak, cheese, caramelized onions, sweet peppers, crusty Italian roll)	Red: Medium-full bodied, balanced, moderately tannic (Napa Valley Merlot)	Red: Light-bodied, bright, zesty, low tannins (Piedmont Barbera)
Reuben sandwich (corned beef, Swiss cheese, thousand island dressing, sauerkraut, rye bread)	White: Lightweight, crisp, and stony (Finger Lakes Riesling)	White: Full-bodied, soft, wood-aged (Sonoma Chardonnay)
California club sandwich (oven-roasted turkey, bacon, tomato, avocado, mayonnaise)	White: Aromatic, fruity, round (Mendocino Pinot Gris)	White: Lightweight, crisp, and stony (Monterey Riesling)
Pastrami on rye with mustard	White: Aromatic, fruity, round (Santa Barbara Viognier)	White: Lightweight, crisp, and stony (Niagara Peninsula off-dry Riesling)

Burgers and dogs

Burgers and beers go down nicely together, but when you're going gourmet, go for wine, too. Table 14-2 lists a few of my pairing suggestions.

Table 14-2   Pairing Wine with North American Burgers and Dogs

Burger/Hot Dog	Best Wine Style	Alternative Wine Style
Classic gourmet cheese-burger (fully dressed)	Red: Medium-full bodied, balanced, moderately tannic (California Merlot)	Red: Light-bodied, bright, zesty, low tannins (Santa Barbara Pinot Noir)
Lone Star burger (BBQ brisket, tomato, lettuce, cheese, BBQ sauce, roasted jalapenos, onion bun)	Red: Medium-full bodied, balanced, moderately tannic (Paso Robles Zinfandel)	Red: Medium-full bodied, balanced, moderately tannic (Sicily Nero d'Avola)
Burger Cubano (griddled ground beef, roast ham, onion, paprika, mojito sauce, toasted poppyseed bun)	Rosé: Dry (Central Coast Rhône style rosé blend)	Red: Medium-full bodied, balanced, moderately tannic (Maipo Valley Merlot)
Chicago-style hot dog (all beef frank, yellow mustard, white onions, sweet pickle, tomato, pickled peppers)	White: Lightweight, crisp, and stony (Marlborough Sauvignon Blanc)	White: Lightweight, crisp and stony (Columbia Valley Riesling)

Mac 'n' meatloaf

Mac 'n' cheese and meatloaf are two more classic comfort foods. Because of their usually mild flavors, both dishes are very wine friendly, as Table 14-3 shows.

Table 14-3   Wine Pairing with Two Classics

Dish	Best Wine Style	Alternative Wine Style
Lobster mac 'n' cheese (lobster, elbow macaroni, aged cheddar)	White: Full-bodied, soft, wood-aged (Russian River Valley Chardonnay)	White: Lightweight, crisp, and stony (Mosel-Saar Riesling)

(continued)

Table 14-3 *(continued)*

Dish	Best Wine Style	Alternative Wine Style
Classic mac 'n' cheese (macaroni, old cheddar, béchamel sauce)	White: Full-bodied, soft, wood-aged (Carneros Chardonnay)	White: Aromatic, fruity, round (Anderson Valley Pinot Gris)
Meatloaf (ground beef, garlic, cheddar cheese, dried herbs, black pepper)	Red: Medium-full bodied, balanced, moderately tannic (California Merlot)	Red: Medium-full bodied, balanced, moderately tannic (Carneros Pinot Noir)

Cal goes Ital

California has developed its own style of Italian cooking, thanks to many Italian immigrants and a similar Mediterranean climate with abundant fresh produce, just like Italy. Whenever tomatoes, cheese, and baked dough are involved, zesty reds are a smart choice as you can see in Table 14-4.

Table 14-4 — Pairing Wine with "Italian" Food

Dish	Best Wine Style	Alternative Wine Style
Thin crust pizza (tomato sauce, basil, mozzarella, parmesan cheese)	Red: Light-bodied, bright, zesty, low tannins (Sonoma Coast Pinot Noir)	Red: Light-bodied, bright, zesty, low tannins (Chianti Sangiovese)
Chicago deep dish pizza (3-inch crust, chunky chopped tomato, tomato sauce, mozzarella, Romano cheese)	Red: Light-bodied, bright, zesty, low tannins (Willamette Valley Pinot Noir)	Red: Light-bodied, bright, zesty, low tannins (Napa Valley Sangiovese)
"Apizza" pizza (oregano, tomato sauce, pecorino Romano cheese, anchovy, mozzarella cheese)	Red: Medium-full bodied, balanced, moderately tannic (Napa Valley Petite Sirah)	Red: Medium-full bodied, balanced, moderately tannic (Chianti Classico Sangiovese)
Calzone (zinfandel sausage, roasted red pepper, grilled eggplant, tomato, ricotta, roasted garlic, tomatoes, thyme)	White: Full-bodied, soft, wood-aged (Russian River Valley Chardonnay)	Red: Medium-full bodied, balanced, moderately tannic (Central Coast Syrah)

Heading Home for the Holidays

Holiday meals are all about family, tradition, and copious amounts of food. Each family has its favorite recipes and specialty dishes, often handed down from generation to generation, which mark these occasions with their uniqueness. And considering the infinite variations on the many holiday mealtime themes and the number of different dishes often included with each meal, no single ideal wine selection exists for any particular holiday specialty.

Budget is usually a consideration too, because the amount of wine required for a full-blown family gathering with a large number of guests (of varying degrees of interest in wine), can be considerable, too. But my advice is simple: Drink as well as you can afford to, and don't sweat it. People often feel that holidays are the time to bring out the best bottles from the cellar, and they certainly can be. But when half the family would be just as happy with a beer and the other half with anything white or red, I suggest you save the top drops for a more intimate occasion.

If the number of different plates being served is large, the guests numerous, and preferences across the board, forget the straightjacket of specific wines with specific courses, and take the *shotgun approach* instead. The holidays are about making everyone happy, so all you need do is lay out a bunch of different bottles on the table at the same time, and let family and guests taste whatever, and in whichever order they wish. If your shotgun is well loaded with buckshot and the spray goes wide enough, you'll hit at least a bull's-eye or two. In other words, if you have enough types of wine, more than likely all your guests can find one they like and that works with each dish.

No matter if some innocent dishes or wines get hurt along the way, you're having a family dinner, which isn't a life-or-death matter (at least in most homes). At my place, a myriad of dishes are thrown onto to the table at the same time, and my plate fills up with dozens of disparate and distinct flavors, making a single sniper shot tougher than picking off a wild turkey at 200 yards. I like to include a wide range of flavors and textures, while at the same time selecting wines that are versatile enough to work well with most of the dishes. I generally choose wines that are bright, fresh, with palate-cleansing acidity, minimal oak (except in the fireplace, where it belongs), light tannins that won't dry out that over-cooked bird any further, and occasionally a pinch of sweetness to take on the sweet potato or pumpkin pie.

The following sections offer a few classic holiday preparations with a couple recommended wine styles to get you going in the right direction.

Turkeys and hams

Turkey is a very lean meat and can dry out quickly if over-cooked. I find even perfectly cooked birds are best with soft, supple wines that won't further de-lubricate the palate with astringent tannins. Any color can work here — red, white, or rosé — as long as the emphasis is on a sweet, ripe fruit impression, and soft, moderate tannins, as in Pinot Noir, lighter Zinfandels, southern Rhône blends based on Grenache, juicy Spanish Tempranillo, and the like. If opting for whites/rosés, the range of possibilities is wider (no tannins to worry about), and your mom's version of stuffing and gravy can give you the cue. Just remember if the stuffing has some notable sweetness, as in lots of dried fruit, then a pinch of sweetness in the wine is a smart bet.

Traditional Easter ham is usually *wet-cured* (marinated in a saltwater solution), and then put in a smokehouse (or injected with smoke flavoring). It's often cooked with some sort of sweet element, whether that's brown sugar, honey, molasses, pineapple, or even maple syrup. So you're dealing with essentially a sweet-salty protein. The sweetness calls for a wine with a similar degree of sweetness. Acidity is also a nice contrast to salty flavors, making the ideal choice a crisp, off-dry wine as in traditional German Riesling in Spätlese ripeness, or Alsatian Pinot Gris. Plump, tropical fruit-flavored whites with a sweet impression from ripe fruit like warm climate Sauvignon Blanc, Viognier, or Chardonnay (not too oaky) also fit the bill.

Table 14-5 lists some of my wine recommendations for turkey and ham.

Table 14-5	Pairing Wine with Turkey and Ham	
Dish	*Best Wine Style*	*Alternative Wine Style*
Vermont style turkey (with sage herb gravy, rosemary-cranberry stuffing)	Red: Light-bodied, bright, and zesty, low tannins (Paso Robles Rhône blend)	Rosé: Dry (Niagara Peninsula Cabernet rosé)
Maine style turkey (whole roasted turkey, cider herb gravy, sage-herb stuffing)	White: Aromatic, fruity, round (Napa Valley Sauvignon Blanc)	White: Lightweight, crisp, and stony (Savennières Chenin Blanc)
Cajun turducken (deboned chicken, deboned duck, deboned turkey, sausage stuffing, bread crumbs, gravy)	White: Full-bodied, soft, wood-aged (Napa Valley Viognier)	White: Full-bodied, soft, wood-aged (Central Coast Roussanne/Marsanne)

Dish	Best Wine Style	Alternative Wine Style
Baked ham (smoked honey ham, garlic, Dijon mustard, brown sugar, orange zest, herbs)	White: Lightweight, crisp, and stony (off-dry) (Mosel-Saar Riesling spätlese)	White: Aromatic, fruity, round (Alsace Pinot Gris)
Baked ham (bone-in ham, molasses, brown ale, dry mustard, cider vinegar, cloves, mixed herbs, bread crumbs)	White: Aromatic, fruity, round (Alsace Late Harvest Pinot Gris)	Red: Medium-full bodied, balanced, moderately tannic (Lodi Zinfandel)

Prime rib and lamb

A simple but incredibly flavorful prime rib is the moment to pull out your top reds. It's a perfect foil; rib roasts rarely clash with any wines and synergize beautifully with well-aged, umami-rich reds. Traditionalists reach for their best Pinot, but Bordeaux and Cabernet fans are equally happy.

The flavor of lamb, whether grilled, roasted, or braised, is somewhat stronger and more particular, and usually works best with equally turbocharged, intense reds. Table 14-6 outlines a few of my wine recommendations.

Table 14-6	Pairing Wine with Prime Rib and Lamb	
Dish	Best Wine Style	Alternative Wine Style
Prime rib roast (whole prime rib, garlic, olive oil, salt, thyme, black pepper)	Red: Medium-full bodied, balanced, moderately tannic (Russian River Valley Pinot Noir)	Red: Full, deep, and robust, turbocharged, chewy texture (Barolo Nebbiolo)
Prime rib roast with red wine jus (whole prime rib, garlic, red wine, shallots, seasoning salt, bread crumbs, dried Italian herbs)	Red: Medium-full bodied, balanced, moderately tannic (Alexander Valley Cabernet Sauvignon)	Red: Medium-full bodied, balanced, moderately tannic (Clare Valley Shiraz)

(continued)

Table 14-6 *(continued)*

Dish	Best Wine Style	Alternative Wine Style
Lamb shank (braised shank, balsamic vinegar, red wine, shallots, carrots, onions, brown sugar, cider vinegar, rosemary)	Red: Full, deep, and robust, turbocharged, chewy texture (Napa Valley Cabernet Sauvignon)	Red: Full, deep, and robust, turbocharged, chewy texture (Taurasi Aglianico)
Lamb rack (pistachio crust, herbes de provence, Dijon mustard, butter, bread crumbs, black pepper)	Red: Full, deep, and robust, turbocharged, chewy texture (Barossa Shiraz)	Red: Full, deep, and robust, turbocharged, chewy texture (Châteauneuf-du-Pape)

Getting Messy with Southern-Style BBQ

Southern style BBQ is more popular now than ever before. The techniques are varied, from charbroiling to smoking, pit-cooking, and spit-roasting, but it's all about flavor turned up to eleven. In the southern United States, people approach it with quasi-religious fervor. Meats are subjected to dry rubs, wet brines, injected marinades, and lavishly doused in numberless variations on BBQ sauce. Vinegar, molasses, whiskey, Worcestershire, soy sauce, ketchup, honey, and dozens of different chile peppers are just some of the common ingredients in typical BBQ sauce, but exact recipes are kept locked up, family secrets to be handed down only to the worthy.

Southern style BBQ is tough but not impossible to enjoy with wine. The combination of spicy, sweet, tart, and hot ensures that only seriously turbocharged wines will stand up. Your best options are from the warm climates of the new world, where sunshine and heat translate to full bodied, ripe, and intensely fruity wines. This type of cooking lends itself well to heavily oaky wines. The charred flavor of barrel aging, red or white, is a nice mirror for the smoky flavor of the grill. From succulent pork spare-ribs with sweet and savory Kansas City BBQ sauce, to pulled pork with spicy, vinegar-based BBQ sauce in the Carolinas, or the smoky, zesty flavor of rosemary and mesquite smoked chicken from Texas, you have plenty of great combinations just waiting to happen — so get the coals firing.

Hog heaven

Succulent, fatty pork lends itself beautifully to southern style BBQ, with each inch of the flesh and fat able to absorb a serious amount of flavor. Most preparations are best with soft, bold reds, but don't overlook off-dry whites and rosés — even if not fashionable, the synergy is undeniable. Check out Table 14-7 for some wine recommendations with BBQ.

Table 14-7	Pairing Wine with BBQ	
Dish Name	*Best Wine Style*	*Alternative Wine Style*
BBQ pulled pork butt roast with spicy vinegar BBQ sauce (brown sugar, paprika, garlic, onion, salt, dry mustard, cider vinegar, ketchup)	Red: Medium-full bodied, balanced, moderately tannic (Paso Robles red Rhône blend)	Red: Light-bodied, bright, zesty, low tannins (Santa Barbara Pinot Noir)
Memphis pork shoulder with tomato-chile pepper Worcestershire BBQ sauce (cumin, paprika, garlic, sage, ginger, dry mustard)	Red: Full, deep, and robust, turbocharged, chewy texture (Amador County Zinfandel)	Red: Medium-full bodied, balanced, moderately tannic (Maipo Valley Carmenere)
Jerk rubbed pork ribs with tamarind BBQ sauce (allspice, scotch bonnets, sage, cinnamon, nutmeg, brown sugar, onion, tamarind, raisins, molasses, ginger, garlic)	Red: Full, deep, and robust, turbocharged, chewy texture (Dry Creek Valley Zinfandel)	Red: Medium-full bodied, balanced, moderately tannic (Santa Barbara Grenache, Syrah, Mourvedre)
Charcoal and lava rock pit-roasted Kailua pig (whole roasted pig with Hawaiian clay sea salt wrapped in banana leaves)	Red: Medium-full bodied, balanced, moderately tannic (Central Coast Syrah)	Red: Light-bodied, bright, zesty, low tannins (Central Otago Pinot Noir)

Steering in the right direction

The expensive cuts of beef are mostly reserved for simple steakhouse-style grilling. But southern BBQ specialists know that the off-cuts are the most flavorful and perfect for the southern treatment. As you'd expect, medium-full bodied and robust, turbocharged reds are your best ally with these dishes, as Table 14-8 shows.

Table 14-8	Pairing Wine with BBQ Steaks	
Dish Name	*Best Wine Style*	*Alternative Wine Style*
Carson City marinated BBQ tri-tip beef steak (soy sauce, balsamic vinegar, brown sugar, garlic, crushed dry chile peppers, lime)	Red: Medium-full bodied, balanced, moderately tannic (Napa Valley Merlot)	Red: Medium-full bodied, balanced, moderately tannic (Eden Valley Shiraz)

(continued)

Table 14-8 *(continued)*

Dish Name	Best Wine Style	Alternative Wine Style
Oak smoked beef brisket with dry spice rub and beer (paprika, jalapeno, cider vinegar, brown sugar, black pepper)	Red: Medium-full bodied, balanced, moderately tannic (Central Coast Syrah)	Red: Light-bodied, bright, zesty, low tannins (Sonoma Pinot Noir)
Dry rubbed charcoal roasted beef ribs (white vinegar, garlic, oregano, celery seed, paprika, chili powder, black pepper)	Red: Full, deep, and robust, turbocharged, chewy texture (Napa Valley Cabernet Sauvignon)	Red: Full, deep, and robust, turbocharged, chewy texture (Tuscany Cabernet or Sangiovese)
Slow charcoal roasted Louisiana rubbed beef brisket with tangy sauce (ketchup, pineapple juice, corn syrup, apple juice, brown sugar, chili flakes, Worcestershire, liquid smoke)	Red: Full, deep, and robust, turbocharged, chewy texture (Dry Creek Valley Zinfandel)	Red: Medium-full bodied, balanced, moderately tannic (Montepulcinao D'Abruzzo)

'Cueing up the chicken

Chicken is the great flavor canvas. It's pretty neutral without any treatment, which is why it makes such a great foil for the flavors of BBQ. If you're cooking at home, track down a free-range, heritage breed chicken that hasn't been injected with water (to make it heavier and therefore more expensive) for best results. The best wine matches are driven by the marinade, brine, rub, or glaze; all colors can work, though make sure they're at the upper end of the flavor intensity scale. Table 14-9 offers some wine suggestions.

Table 14-9 — Pairing Wine with BBQ Chicken

Dish Name	Best Wine Style	Alternative Wine Style
Vinegar-brined, spit-roasted whole BBQ chicken with sweet and sour BBQ sauce (garlic, sage, rosemary, lemon zest)	Red: Light-bodied, bright, zesty, low tannins (Oregon Pinot Noir)	Rosé: Dry (California rosé blend)

Dish Name	Best Wine Style	Alternative Wine Style
Mississippi root beer BBQ chicken with habanero BBQ sauce (root beer, vinegar, molasses, garlic, ketchup, paprika, dry herbs, onion, habanero chile, black pepper)	White: Aromatic, fruity, round (Central Coast Viognier)	White: Full-bodied, soft, wood-aged (Colchagua Valley Chardonnay)
Louisville bourbon BBQ chicken (Kentucky bourbon, butter, tomato sauce, molasses, dry mustard, onion, garlic)	White: Lightweight, crisp, and stony, off-dry (Finger Lakes off-dry Riesling)	White: Lightweight, crisp, and stony (Mosel Riesling Spätlese)

Heading to N'awlins: Cajun/Creole Country

Cajun and Creole cooking stand out as some of North America's most distinctive regional cuisines. Cajuns, as they're affectionately known, are descendants of French colonists who first settled in Acadia, a colony of New France in the Eastern Canadian Maritimes. Creole is a generic term that refers to foreign settlers from outside of the United States.

The holy trinity of both Cajun and Creole is the combination of onion, celery, and bell pepper. Creative cooks in the region had to rely on local vegetables and proteins, including alligator, possum, and crawfish.

Despite their distant European heritage, new world–style wines are usually best suited to the boisterous aromas, textures, and flavors of Cajun and Creole cooking.

Rajun' Cajun

Cajun cuisine stems mainly from rustic Provencal French cooking. *Roux,* a flour-based thickener used for sauces and soups, is cornerstone of Cajun cooking. You can find it in everything from gumbo to étouffée and an assortment of chowders. The frequent inclusion of cayenne pepper calls for off-dry wines, though soft, forwardly fruity whites and reds with their own vaguely sweet impression can fit the bill. Check out Table 14-10 for some examples.

Table 14-10	Pairing Wine with Cajun Cuisine	
Dish Name	*Best Wine Style*	*Alternative Wine Style*
Cajun crawfish étouffée (crawfish tails, rice, bell pepper, celery, garlic, roux, onions, cayenne, parsley)	Rosé: Off-dry (Paso Robles Syrah)	White: Aromatic, fruity, round (Argentina Torrontés)
Cajun blackened salmon filet with Cajun lemon rice (salmon filet, rice, lemon zest, paprika, onions, cayenne, scallions, basil)	Red: Light-bodied, bright, zesty, low tannins (Carneros Pinot Noir)	White: Lightweight, crisp, and stony (Rias Baixas Albariño)
Cajun spicy shrimp (shrimp, paprika, tomatillo, thyme, butter, oregano, garlic, cayenne)	White: Aromatic, fruity, round (Washington State Riesling)	Rosé: Off-dry (California white Zinfandel)
Cajun maque choux with boudin noir and corn (blood sausage, corn, butter, black forest ham, poblano chile, herbes de Provence, plum tomatoes, cilantro, white pepper)	White: Aromatic, fruity, round (Alsace Pinot Gris)	Rosé: Dry (Sonoma County Merlot)

The Creole effect

Creole cuisine is a distinct style combining French, Spanish, Portuguese, Caribbean, African, and Native American influences. French Creole cooking in particular gives a nod back to Europe, with many dishes originally conceived by experienced French cooks who had fled France during the French Revolution and settled in Louisiana. Classic Creole dishes include jambalaya, shrimp Creole, and trout meuniere, as well as side dishes like dirty rice, stewed okra, and maque choux. White wines generally fair best, with aromatic, fruity, and round styles most capable of handling the bold and occasionally spicy flavors of Creole cooking. Refer to Table 14-11 for some wine recommendations.

Table 14-11	Pairing Wine with Creole Cuisine	
Dish Name	*Best Wine Style*	*Alternative Wine Style*
Creole chicken gumbo (roux, bacon, bell pepper, andouille sausage, shrimp, crab, garlic, okra, tomato, file powder)	White: Aromatic, fruity, round (Central Coast Viognier)	Rosé: Dry (Tavel Grenache/Cinsault)
Sausage and shrimp Creole jambalaya (tasso sausage, paprika, cumin, tomatoes, bell peppers, brown rice, shrimp, scallions)	White: Aromatic, fruity, round (Argentina Torrontés)	White: Aromatic, fruity, round (Willamette Valley Pinot Gris)
Creole crab and okra dip (crab, garlic, bell peppers, okra, cayenne, mayonnaise, chives, lemon pepper)	White: Aromatic, fruity, round (Mendocino Gewürztraminer)	White: Lightweight, crisp, and stony (Muscadet Melon de Bourgogne)
Creole beef casserole (ground beef, cheddar cheese, roast potatoes, ketchup, brown sugar, creole seasoning, cayenne pepper, goldfish crackers)	Red: Light-bodied, bright, zesty, low tannins (Sonoma Pinot Noir)	White: Aromatic, fruity, round (Alsace Gewürztraminer)
Creole trout meuniere (flour, butter, shallots, lemon juice, green brined peppercorns, parsley)	White: Lightweight, crisp, and stony (Columbia Valley Riesling)	White: Full-bodied, soft, wood-aged (Santa Ynez Valley Viognier)

Creole sweets

With the French culinary heritage came a love of sweets, so desserts are a big part of the Creole repertoire, and include the now famous classics such as bananas foster, beignets, and pecan pie.

Most Creole sweets are extremely sweet, so ensure that you select an equally sweet wine from the upper end of the intensity scale to handle the sugar. Table 14-12 offers some wine suggestions.

Table 14-12	Pairing Wine with Creole Desserts	
Dish Name	**Best Wine Style (Example)**	**Alternative Wine Style (Example)**
Bananas foster (bananas, butter, allspice, nutmeg, rum, orange zest, banana liqueur)	Sweet: Noble rot (Sauternes)	Sweet: Noble rot (Tokaj Aszú 5 Puttonyos)
Pecan pie (pie crust, sugar, pecans, corn syrup, eggs, vanilla extract)	Red: Sweet fortified (California Zinfandel)	Sweet: Fortified amber (Oloroso Dulce)
Chocolate beignets (bitter chocolate, whipping cream, corn syrup, puff pastry, sugar, eggs)	Red: Sweet fortified (Banyuls Grenache)	Red: Sweet fortified (Late bottled vintage Port)

Blending Texas with Mexico: Tex-Mex

You can argue that Tex-Mex cuisine is the most popular locally created cuisine in North America. Thousands of restaurants across the continent, including several successful fast-food chains, serve Tex-Mex style food. The name comes from the Texas/Mexican Railway completed in 1875, while the style of food melds the flavors of Mexico and bordering US states.

Texas Style: Chili, nachos, and fajitas

Tex-Mex food features beans, beef, and spices, usually smothered in melted cheese and sour cream and served with some sort of soft or crisp tortilla. Dishes like chili con carne, nachos, and fajitas are all Tex-Mex in origin, though many confuse them with authentic Mexican cuisine. The use of spice in Tex-Mex, such as cumin and coriander, also isn't typically Mexican, but rather borrowed from different cuisines altogether.

As with Mexican cooking, the bold flavors and heavy texture of Tex-Mex food are best with robust, abundantly fruity and full-bodied wines — a classic matchup of the heavyweight category. Both Texas and Mexico produce wines in this style, so you can experiment with some new classic regional food and wine pairings. Table 14-13 lists some wine recommendations.

Table 14-13	Pairing Wine with Traditional Tex-Mex	
Dish Name	*Best Wine Style*	*Alternative Wine Style*
Five-alarm chili con carne (beef chuck, ancho, poblano, jalapeño, habanero, chipotle, cumin, garlic, tomatoes, cilantro, lime, queso)	Red: Medium-full bodied, balanced, moderately tannic (Montague County Syrah)	Red: Medium-full bodied, balanced, moderately tannic (Rioja Joven Tempranillo or Garnacha)
Turkey, corn, and bean chili (ground turkey, black beans, pinto beans, corn, onion, jalapeño, cumin, oregano, tomato, epazote, Monterey Jack)	Red: Medium-full bodied, balanced, moderately tannic (Paso Robles red Rhône blend)	Red: Medium-full bodied, balanced, moderately tannic (Chateauneuf-Du-Pape Syrah, Grenache, or Mourvedre)
Beef fajitas (flank steak, southwest spice, avocado, cheddar cheese, onions, bell peppers, refried beans, pico de gallo, scallions, flour tortillas)	Red: Light-bodied, bright, zesty, low tannins (Central Otago Pinot Noir)	Red: Light-bodied, bright, zesty, low tannins (Dolcetto D'Alba)
Corn tortilla nachos (corn tortilla chips, chicken, guacamole, black olives, Monterey jack cheese, jalapeños, tomato salsa, sour cream, cilantro)	White: Lightweight, crisp and stony (Sonoma County Sauvignon Blanc)	White: Lightweight, crisp and stony (Alto Adige Pinot Grigio)
Tuna and black bean quesadilla (tuna steak, black beans, corn, onions, jalapeños, Monterey Jack cheese, queso fresco, cilantro, cumin, flour tortilla)	White: Aromatic, fruity, round (Texas Roussanne)	White: Aromatic, fruity, round (Argentina Torrontés)
Seven-layer bean dip (avocado, mayonnaise, taco seasoning, refried beans, tomatoes, cilantro, scallions, black olives, Cheddar, sour cream, cayenne)	White: Aromatic, fruity, round (Napa Valley Sauvignon Blanc)	White: Aromatic, fruity, round (Columbia Valley Riesling)

Baja California Dreamin'

Texas may be the dominant state, but Arizona, New Mexico, and Baja (lower) California have also influenced the cuisine. Check out Table 14-14 for some wine suggestions. Remember to select wines, whether red, white, or rosé, with bold new world–fruity flavors.

Table 14-14	Pairing Wine with Baja-Mex Dishes	
Dish Name	*Best Wine Style*	*Alternative Wine Style*
Pulled pork tamales with tomatillo salsa (pork shoulder, masa, chipotle, corn, raisins, lime juice, cilantro, tomatillo)	White: Lightweight, crisp, and stony (Columbia Valley Riesling)	Red: Medium-full bodied, balanced, moderately tannic (Côtes du Rhône)
Chicken chimichangas (chicken, rice, enchilada sauce, jack cheese, black olives, refried beans, jalapeño, cilantro, sour cream, Cheddar)	White: Aromatic, fruity, round (Anderson Valley Gewürztraminer)	White: Aromatic, fruity, round (Margaret River Semillon/Sauvignon)
Fish tacos (mahimahi, corn tortillas, key limes, oregano, cumin, cayenne, tomatoes, arugula, cilantro, serrano, rice)	White: Aromatic, fruity, round (Willamette Valley Pinot Gris)	Rosé: Dry (Côtes De Provence)
Baja tortilla soup (corn tortilla, tomatoes, pasilla chili, onion, chipotle, cilantro, avocado, sour cream, Oaxacan cheese)	Red: Medium-full bodied, balanced, moderately tannic (Sonoma County Merlot)	White: Aromatic, fruity, round (Casablanca Valley Sauvignon Blanc)

West Coast: Pacific Northwest Cuisine

The Pacific Northwest refers to the US states of Oregon, Washington, and Alaska, as well as the Canadian province of British Columbia. These regions share the Pacific Ocean and all it has to offer, as well as a strong culinary influence from Asia due to significant immigration in recent years.

This area is lush, dense, and wild with plenty of untouched coastline. In addition to the ocean, the region's lakes, streams, and rivers are rich with fish, while the land bears fruit orchards and a cornucopia of vegetables, both wild and cultivated. This is a true farm-to-table region, at the forefront of organic cultivation and sustainability, with a goal to ensure that future generations can enjoy the same bountiful offerings.

Oregon, Washington, and British Columbia are all significant wine producers, and the philosophy of going local whenever possible applies to wine here as well. The sommeliers of the Pacific Northwest never miss an opportunity to showcase local wines, and you have lots to choose from, from rich opulent reds to lightweight, aromatic whites, sparkling and Icewines.

Down by the seashore

Seafood is king in the Pacific Northwest. You frequently come across wild salmon, sable fish (black cod), oysters, and other shellfish, such as Dungeness crab, sea urchin, and a variety of clams. Cooking techniques vary, but cedar planking, smoking, stone cooking, and charbroiling are extremely popular. High-impact cooking methods applied to fish, like char-broiling and cedar planking, can swing the pairing to red, but for the most part, crisp and aromatic whites are most comfortable at the table. Table 14-15 offers some wine recommendations.

Table 14-15   Pairing Wine with Pacific Northwest Fish Dishes

Dish Name	Best Wine Style	Alternative Wine Style
Oyster chowder (Pacific oysters, butter, bacon, potatoes, corn, bell pepper, celery, parsley)	White: Aromatic, fruity, round (Okanagan Valley Pinot Gris)	White: Lightweight, crisp, and stony (Columbia Valley Riesling)
Cedar plank salmon (Pacific salmon, lemons, dill, parsley, brown sugar, thyme, white pepper)	Red: Light-bodied, bright, zesty, low tannins (Willamette Valley Pinot Noir)	Red: Light-bodied, bright, zesty, low tannins (Barbera d'Asti)
Pan-fried smelts	White: Lightweight, crisp, and stony (Okanagan Valley Riesling)	White: Aromatic, fruity, round (Yakima Valley Roussanne/Marsanne)
Cornmeal crusted hama hama oysters with garlic aïoli	White: Lightweight, crisp, and stony (Oregon unoaked Chardonnay)	White: Aromatic, fruity, round (Willamette Valley Pinot Gris)
Smoked Alaskan halibut with wildberry relish (wild Pacific halibut, lingonberry, melonberry, thyme, orange zest)	White: Aromatic, fruity, round (Okanagan Valley Gewürztraminer)	White: Aromatic, fruity, round (Napa Valley Sauvignon Blanc)
Salmon and wild beet asparagus salad (salmon red and golden beets, asparagus tips, sour cream-horseradish dressing, watercress)	White: Aromatic, fruity, round (Napa Valley Sauvignon Blanc)	White sparkling: Lightweight, crisp, and stony (Okanagan Valley Chardonnay)

Got game?

Game meats are plentiful in the Pacific Northwest, with moose, elk, caribou, bear, and deer appearing on many restaurant menus. Mushrooms, too, are big business. This region produces the best and greatest variety of wild mushrooms in North America, including the highly prized and very expensive matsutake Japanese mushroom. Many wild plants and herbs are also cultivated here for both culinary and medicinal purposes. Game calls for flavorful, robust reds for the most part, and you can find plenty on the West Coast to choose from. Table 14-16 provides a few wine suggestions.

Table 14-16	Pairing Wine with Pacific Northwest Game	
Dish Name	*Best Wine Style*	*Alternative Wine Style*
Roast squab with apple and leeks (squab, leeks, apples, rosemary, mustard, fennel, ginger)	Red: Light-bodied, bright, zesty, low tannins (Willamette Valley Pinot Noir)	Red: Medium-full bodied, balanced, moderately tannic (Okanagan Valley Syrah)
Wild elk and blueberry sausage (elk roast, blueberries, rosemary, garlic, bacon, onion, red wine, juniper berry)	Red: Medium-full bodied, balanced, moderately tannic (Washington State Syrah)	Red: Medium-full bodied, balanced, moderately tannic (Washington State Merlot)
Venison shepherd's pie (venison, mashed potatoes, thyme, onion, carrot, peas, tomato, Gruyère cheese)	Red: Medium-full bodied, balanced, moderately tannic (Okanagan Valley Cabernet blend)	White: Full-bodied, soft, wood-aged (Okanagan Valley Chardonnay)
Alaskan ale-battered mushrooms with dill aïoli (local ale, button mushrooms)	White: Lightweight, crisp, and stony (Columbia Valley Riesling)	White: Full-bodied, soft, wood-aged (Santa Barbara white Rhône blend)

O Canada: Going North of the Border

Canada is more of a mosaic then a melting pot, with cultures retaining much of their distinctive heritage. But a blending of the edges, mixed with availability of foods and marked seasonal variation, has resulted in a distinctive, regionally-based style of cooking that continues to evolve. Quebec maintains a strong French influence, while cuisine from Ontario and the Prairie provinces derives from a mixture of ethnic backgrounds, including the First Nations. The food and wine scene here is thriving and growing rapidly; Toronto and Montreal are some of the best dining cities in the world.

When dining *à la Canadienne*, don't forget to consider some of the excellent wines produced in Canada. Over the last 30 or so years, wine production and culture have developed rapidly, all within the cool climate context that characterizes Canada's growing regions.

Le Quebecois

Quebec's food culture is tied to the old world more so than anywhere else in Canada; it's an artisan culture with a serious love of gastronomy. Much like northern France, traditional Québecoise cuisine is high in fat, drawing on hog, duck, and cow alike, which is no doubt due in part to the cold winters of Québec, where, at least historically, the often brutal conditions made calorie count important: the more, the more likely you could survive.

Quebec is famous for its *tourtière* (meat pie), *poutine* (french fries covered in meat gravy and cheese curds), habitant pea soup, maple syrup, and hundreds of artisan cheese producers creating some of the best raw milk cheeses in North America.

Maple syrup is one of the oldest culinary traditions in Quebec. Many gastronomic festivals are timed around the annual collection of maple syrup, beginning in early spring when sap starts to flow. Many Quebecers venture out to these sugar shacks to enjoy everything maple syrup, including eggs, ham, and bean dishes doused in the sweet, spicy, golden nectar. But if heading to the backwoods to collect sap is not your thing, fear not. The restaurant culture in Québec is well developed, ranging from high-end, elegant restaurants with a European feel, to chic bistros and boisterous casual eateries. You're likely to also get a free education on wine when dining out, because Québec also has one of the most evolved wine cultures on the continent, with trained sommeliers being the norm rather than the exception in most dining spots.

Substantial wines, both red and white, are called into action with these rib-sticking dishes. Refer to Table 14-17 for some wine recommendations.

Table 14-17	Pairing Wine with Québec Cuisine	
Dish Name	*Best Wine Style*	*Alternative Wine Style*
Quebecois habitant pea soup (yellow peas, ham hocks, onion, celery, carrot, savory, Sherry)	White: Full-bodied, soft, wood-aged (Niagara Peninsula Chardonnay)	White: Aromatic, fruity, round (Alsace Pinot Gris)
Pork and veal tourtière (diced pork, veal, beef, garlic, onion, sage, thyme, clove in pastry crust)	Red: Medium-full bodied, balanced, moderately tannic (Okanagan Valley Syrah)	Red: Medium-full bodied, balanced, moderately tannic (Chateauneuf-du-Pape)
Poutine Canadienne (Yukon Gold potatoes, cheese curds, beef gravy, salt, pepper)	Red: Light-bodied, bright, and zesty, low tannins (Prince Edward County Pinot Noir)	Red: Light-bodied, bright, and zesty, low tannins (Beaujolais Villages Gamay)
Montreal baked beans (pork fat, navy beans, onions, celery, ketchup, molasses, dry mustard, maple, rosemary)	Red: Medium-full bodied, balanced, moderately tannic (Chateauneuf-du-Pape)	Red: Medium-full bodied, balanced, moderately tannic (Ribera del Duero Tempranillo)
Roast Québec lamb with apple cider maple glaze (with, maple syrup, apple cider, orange zest, mint, pink peppercorn)	White: Aromatic, fruity, round (off-dry/ late harvest) (Alsace Gewürztraminer)	Off-dry: Cider (Québec sparkling hard cider)

Ontario and the Prairies

Ontario is Canada's most populous province and also its most multicultural. The capital city, Toronto, is a vast cultural mosaic consisting of many ethnic neighborhoods featuring authentic Italian, Chinese, Indian, Greek, Portuguese, Polish, Vietnamese, Jamaican, Latino, Ukrainian, and many other cuisines from around the world. Chefs here thus draw on many inspirations to create their unique dishes, and slowly but surely a local Ontarian cuisine is coming into focus.

Alberta is Canada's cattle ranching capital, supplying the rest of the country with top quality beef. This land-locked province relies heavily on beef, simply prepared, for much of its protein.

There's of course much more to the Canadian wine industry than Icewine. Ontario, in particular, is becoming known for its fine, cool climate–style wines that are highly versatile at the table. Chardonnay and Riesling lead the way for whites, while the Pinot Noir and Cabernet Franc are my picks for red grapes, with occasional excellent Bordeaux-style blend. Look at Table 14-18 for some specific recommendations.

Table 14-18	Pairing Wine with Other Canadian Cuisine	
Dish Name	*Best Wine Style*	*Alternative Wine Style*
Pickled northern Ontario pike with fiddleheads (vinegar, salt, sugar, pickling spice, mushrooms, chiles)	White: Lightweight, crisp, and stony (Niagara Peninsula dry Riesling)	White: Lightweight, crisp, and stony (Prince Edward County Chardonnay)
Pan-seared foie gras with Icewine-poached peaches (with pearl onion, tarragon, thyme)	Sweet: Late harvest (Niagara Peninsula vidal [oak aged])	Sweet: Noble rot (Sauternes)
Alberta beef stew (blade roast, onion, potato, bacon, dried herbs, cinnamon, red wine, carrots, rutabaga)	Red: Medium-full bodied, balanced, moderately tannic (Okanagan Valley Cabernet blend)	Red: Medium-full bodied, balanced, moderately tannic (Burgundy Pinot Noir)
Bison medallions with roasted mushrooms (bison tenderloin, mushrooms, sage, garlic, red wine)	Red: Medium-full bodied, balanced, moderately tannic (Okanagan Valley Syrah)	Red: Medium-full bodied, balanced, moderately tannic (Barossa Valley Shiraz)
Braised pork ribs with wheat beer honey glaze (spareribs, beer, brown sugar, honey, cayenne, garlic, mustard, thyme)	Red: Light-bodied, bright, zesty, low tannins (Okanagan Valley Pinot Noir)	White: Lightweight, crisp, and stony (Mosel Riesling spätlese)
Saskatoon spinach and fennel salad (spinach, fennel bulb, flax seeds, paprika, Saskatoon berries, pecans)	White: Aromatic, fruity, round (Okanagan Valley aromatic white blend)	White: Aromatic, fruity, round (Niagara Peninsula Sauvignon Blanc)

Wines from Down Under: Australia

If you're in North America, you may want to consider some Australia wines. Grapevines arrived in Australia with the first fleet of British prisoners in 1788, landing near what is Sydney today in the state of New South Wales. Winemaking expertise in the penal colony was in short supply to say the least, but the arrival of European free settlers in search of gold in the 1800s ensured that grapevines survived and thrived. Australia experienced a massive boom in exports in the 1980s, 1990s, and the early part of this century, spurred on by technical proficiency, clever marketing, and fruity, sunshine-filled wines with broad consumer appeal. The creation of regional blends from across vast stretches of southeastern Australia allowed for both quantity and consistency in style — a recipe for success.

Today the Australian wine scene has diversified immensely, and the country is no longer defined by inexpensive wines with cute labels. There are vineyards throughout the southern and western states of Australia, but the main action is in South Australia. This is where you'll find some of Australia's best-known wine regions, such as the Barossa Valley, McLaren Vale, and Coonawarra. Although a wide variety of grapes are grown, South Australia is best known for its bold, rich, ultra-ripe style of Shiraz wines that fit into the full-bodied, turbocharged category to be sure. I find these excellent when there are equally bold flavors (curries, charcoal-grilled meats) on the table. Slightly cooler Coonawarra is the source of some of Australia's best Cabernet Sauvignon, especially from vineyards within the small cigar-shaped patch of soil called *terra rossa* (red earth, colored by high iron content). South Australia also produces excellent dry Riesling, mainly from the Clare and Eden Valleys. The style is dry, crisp, and stony, with flavors and unique lime-scented, like lime cordial. These Rieslings can age magnificently.

Lovers of Chardonnay and Pinot Noir should seek out wines from the state of Victoria. The cooler areas along the coast of the Bass Straight, such as the Mornington Peninsula and a little farther inland in the Yarra Valley, are excellent sources of refined, food-friendly wines with a little more heft than classic Burgundy but a little less forwardness then typical California-style Pinot and Chardonnay. Western Australia accounts for a mere 5 percent of the country's annual grape crush, but small quantities belie the large reputation that the classic Bordeaux-style blends, red and white, and Chardonnay, enjoy internationally, particularly from the region of Margaret River. The sommelier's choice, however, goes to the remarkable Semillons from the Hunter Valley in New South Wales. When young, they're searingly dry and acidic, but in time (ten years or so), they blossom into some of the most amazing white wines in the southern hemisphere.

Chapter 15

Warming Up to Northern Europe: Land of Butter and Animal Fat

In This Chapter

▶ Dining in northern France

▶ Exploring culinary Italy, north of Rome

▶ Eating in Germanic central Europe

▶ Pub hopping in the United Kingdom

*T*his chapter looks at the cuisine of northern Europe. This is the land where butter and animal fat are used for cooking instead of olive oil, prevalent in the Mediterranean. This chapter looks at northern France and Italy, as well as Germany, Austria, Switzerland, and the United Kingdom. As with the rest of the chapters in Part IV, this chapter isn't a comprehensive look at all the traditional dishes in this part of the world, but rather a sampling of foods that you'd find both when traveling in the region or back home in a regionally inspired restaurant (or in your own kitchen, too).

In some cases, the wine match may come from the geographic context of the dish. It doesn't take a master sommelier to match *Boeuf Bourguignon* with a bottle of red Burgundy or *Brasato al Barolo*, beef braised in Barolo wine, with a bottle of the same. But the farther north you travel in Europe, the more likely you are to find beer, hard cider, mead, and spirits traditionally served at the table where wine isn't produced. In the absence of tried-and-true regional food and wine pairings, I make some suggestions drawing from the broad world of wine now available to consumers in every corner of the planet.

Bonjour: Looking At Northern France and Its Cuisine

By general but unofficial consensus, France can be neatly divided by the Loire River, which runs for 1,000 kilometers from its source in the Massif Central near the Rhône River first northward, and then westward all the way to Nantes on the Atlantic coast. The weather, language, produce, wine, and the cuisine all take on a decidedly more northern feel north of the Loire. Regionally, this means Normandy and Brittany in the northwest, Burgundy and Alsace in the east, and from the central Loire Valley to Nord Pas de Calais, France's northernmost point bordering Belgium. (I cover southern France in Chapter 13.)

Differentiating between northern and southern French cooking

Judging by local markets and restaurant menus alone, you'd hardly believe you're in the same country when traveling between northern and southern France. The north is all about green pasture and grass-fed cattle, beef, butter, cream, cow's milk cheese, cold water crustaceans and fish, and orchard fruits, not to mention beer and cider. As you'd expect, the historical availability of these ingredients drives the traditional local cuisines, and heavier, cream-based dishes reflect the cooler climate.

As you move south, the temperature rises, the sun shines more brightly, and the growing season is much longer. Only sheep and goats can survive the arid, rocky conditions here. And where olive trees thrive, olive oil is king. In the south, the cooking is lighter, driven by fresh produce and minimal handling.

France is united by wine, a proud cultural patrimony that is shared by all its citizens. North or south, wine is used both in cooking and in washing down the results of your labor.

Satisfying soups and sandwiches

Soups and stews are important dietary staples in northern France. Recipes are passed down through the generations and are as much a family tradition as they are a way of life.

Probably the most famous contribution to the world's soup repertoire is the classic French onion soup from Alsace, now popular in both fine dining restaurants and casual pubs worldwide. During the cold winter months, very few things warm the body and soul more than a piping hot bowl of soup with a warm, crusty baguette, and, of course, a glass of wine. Table 15-1 reviews some wine pairings with French soups and sandwiches.

Table 15-1	Pairing Wine with French Soups and Sandwiches		
Region	*Local Dish Name (English)*	*Best Wine Style (Example)*	*Alternative Wine Style (Example)*
Alsace	Soupe à l'oignon (onion soup with butter, beef stock, cognac, French bread, Gruyère cheese, parsley)	White: Aromatic, fruity, round (Alsace Pinot Gris)	White: Full-bodied, soft, wood-aged (Paso Robles Roussanne)
Lorraine	Soupe aux haricot verts (green beans, smoked bacon, onion, potatoes, cream, parsley)	White: Lightweight, crisp, and stony (Alsace Riesling)	Rosé: Dry (Tavel Grenache)
Champagne-Ardenne	Champagne joute (stewed ham, bacon, sausage, and chicken with carrots, turnips, potatoes, cabbage)	White: Aromatic, fruity, round (Alsace Pinot Gris)	Red: Medium-full bodied, balanced, moderately tannic (Burgundy Pinot Noir)
Paris Ile de France	Croque monsieur (ham, Emmental, and gruyere cheese on toasted buttered brioche)	White: Aromatic, fruity, round (Alsace Gewürztraminer)	White sparkling: (Champagne)

Meat, poultry, and game

When it comes to meat cookery, the French literally wrote most of the book. From slow, one-pot succulent braises and stews to the currently popular *sous vide* (boil-in-a-bag) technique, and rich Sunday roast dinners to poaching in fat for confit — the French know how to maximize the succulent, savory, umami taste of protein. These techniques and their resulting dishes are also infinitely wine-friendly, something that every French cook worth his salt would have in mind.

Expect everything from woodland game birds to beef, duck, chicken, rabbit, venison, and hare to find its way into the copper-bottomed brazier or cast iron enameled terrine or mold. Table 15-2 lists some wine pairings with common French meat dishes.

When braising meat "à la Française" — in wine — save some for your glass. Alternatively, braise with something similar but less expensive than what you serve at the table. For example, use a generic Bourgogne Rouge for your boeuf Bourguignon, and serve a better quality, village level red Burgundy or better at the table.

Table 15-2	Wine Pairings with French Meat Dishes		
Region	**Local Dish Name (English)**	**Best Wine Style (Example)**	**Alternative Wine Style (Example)**
Alsace	Alsace baeckeoffe (lamb, pork, and beef casserole stew cooked in wine with carrot, leek, French herbs)	White: Aromatic, fruity, round (Alsace Gewürztraminer)	Red: Medium-full bodied, balanced, moderately tannic (Burgundy Pinot Noir)
Burgundy	Boeuf bourguignon (beef braised red burgundy with potatoes, carrots, onion, garlic, bouquet garni)	Red: Medium-full bodied, balanced, moderately tannic (Burgundy Côte de Nuits Pinot Noir)	Red: Full, deep, and robust, turbocharged, chewy texture (Châteauneuf-du-Pape)
Burgundy	Coq au vin (rooster [chicken] braised in red burgundy, bacon, mushrooms, pearl onions, garlic, carrots, bouquet garni)	Red: Medium-full bodied, balanced, moderately tannic (Burgundy Pinot Noir)	Red: Light-bodied, bright, zesty, low tannins (Cru Beaujolais Gamay)
Loire Valley	Le Mans rillettes de porc (terrine of pork belly, lean ham, rendered pork fat, coriander seeds, thyme, garlic, and peppercorns — served with baguette and cornichon)	White: Lightweight, crisp, and stony (off-dry) (Vouvray demi-sec Chenin Blanc)	Red: Light-bodied, bright, zesty, low tannins (Chinon Cabernet Franc)
Normandy	Civet de cerf (venison braised in orange juice, red wine and beef broth, with red currants, orange zest, juniper, parsley)	Red: Full, deep, and robust, turbocharged, chewy texture (St. Estèphe Bordeaux Blend)	Red: Full, deep, and robust, turbocharged, chewy texture (Taurasi Aglianico)

Fish and shellfish

Brittany and Normandy have significant fishing industries, with Brittany alone accounting for 80 percent of France's shellfish harvest. Oysters, crabs, lobster, scallops, langoustine, mussels, and winkles are plentiful in this region, in addition to a number of classic preparations such as *moules marinières* (mariner's mussels), cooked in white wine, cream, and garlic. Turbot and especially sole are also specialties from the sea, with the latter featured in the simple but timeless preparation called *sole meunière,* "miller's sole," so named for the dusting of flour on the fish before it's pan-fried in butter with lemon juice and black pepper.

Light, crisp, dry wines with mouth-watering acids, as well as fuller, more aromatic wines pair well with the salty, briny, and delicate flavors of the many types of shellfish. The Loire Valley and Alsace have much to offer in these categories, but you can choose from a vast array of similar styles made worldwide. Table 15-3 identifies some wine pairings for common French seafood dishes.

Table 15-3	Pairing Wine with French Seafood Dishes		
Region	*Local Dish Name (English)*	*Best Wine Style (Example)*	*Alternative Wine Style (Example)*
Paris Ile de France	Cuisses de grenouille (frogs' legs dredged in flour and fried with garlic, butter, parsley sauce)	White: Lightweight, crisp, and stony (Sancerre Sauvignon Blanc)	White: Lightweight, crisp, and stony (Marlborough Sauvignon Blanc)
Normandy	Flétan aux crevettes et crème fraîche (poached flounder in a sauce of prawns, mussels, cider, butter, chanterelles, lemon, crème fraîche with fingerling potatoes)	White: Lightweight, crisp, and stony (Alsace Riesling)	White: Lightweight, crisp, and stony (Loire Valley Chenin Blanc)
Normandy	Sole meunière (fried sole with butter, lemon juice, black pepper, parsley)	White: Full-bodied, soft, wood-aged (Puligny-Montrachet Chardonnay)	White: Full-bodied, soft, wood-aged (Mornington Peninsula Chardonnay)

(continued)

	Table 15-3 *(continued)*		
Region	*Local Dish Name (English)*	*Best Wine Style (Example)*	*Alternative Wine Style (Example)*
Brittany	Moules marinières (mussels with garlic, shallots, parsley, thyme, white wine, cream, served with crusty loaf)	White: Lightweight, crisp, and stony (Muscadet)	White: Aromatic, fruity, round (Entre-Deux-Mers Sauvignon/ Semillon)
Brittany	Cotriade (mixed fish stew with potatoes, poured over a toasted baguette)	White: Lightweight, crisp, and stony (Vouvray Sec Chenin Blanc)	White: Aromatic, fruity, round (Wachau Grüner Veltliner)

Desserts — a visit to the patisserie

The French repertoire consists of an astonishing array of elaborate preparations including decadent pies, cakes, truffles, tarts, éclairs, crêpes, and custard-based desserts like the universal crème brûlée. Northern France is particularly well known for desserts containing butter and cream, considering its important dairy farming industry. Table 15-4 is barely the icing on the cake of the range on offer, but it includes some of the standard classics you can find in French bistros worldwide.

France also has a wide range of sweet wines to propose with dessert. Late harvest and noble rot wines are specialties of Bordeaux, the Loire Valley, and Alsace, while sweet fortified wines are produced throughout the south, especially in the Languedoc-Roussillon.

Table 15-4	Pairing Wine with French Desserts		
Region	*Local Dish Name (English)*	*Best Wine Style (Example)*	*Alternative Wine Style (Example)*
Various	Crème caramel (cream custard topped with caramel sauce)	Sweet: Late harvest noble rot (Sauternes)	Sweet: Passito style (Vin Santo di Toscana)
Various	Crème brulée (cream custard topped with hard caramelized sugar)	Sweet: Late harvest noble rot (Sauternes)	Sweet: Fortified white (Muscat De Beaumes de Venise)

Region	Local Dish Name (English)	Best Wine Style (Example)	Alternative Wine Style (Example)
Paris Ile de France	Tarte tatin (upside down caramelized apple tart)	Sweet: Late harvest noble rot (Côteaux du Layon Chenin Blanc)	Sweet: Late harvest noble rot (Rheingau Riesling beerenauslese)
Lorraine	Tarte à la rhubarbe (rhubarb tart, pastry crust, caster sugar, vanilla, eggs, cream, milk	Sweet: Late harvest Icewine (Niagara Peninsula Cabernet Franc)	Sweet: Sparkling red (Brachetto d'Aqui)
Various	Île flottante ("floating Island"; meringue atop crème anglaise)	Sweet: Late harvest noble rot (Barsac)	Sweet: Late harvest Icewine (Niagara Peninsula Vidal)
Paris	Crèpes suzette (crèpes with caramelized butter and sugar sauce, orange juice and zest, flambéed in grand marnier liqueur)	Sweet: Late harvest (Alsace Gewürztraminer Vendanges Tardives)	Sweet: Passito style (Santorini Vinsanto Assyrtiko blend)
Various	Charlotte aux fraise (layered sponge cake with strawberry purée, custard)	Sweet: Fortified red (Banyuls Grenache)	Sweet: Late harvest Icewine (Niagara Peninsula Cabernet Franc)

Scoping Out Northern Italy and Its Food

Northern and southern Italian cooking is dramatically different. While wheat and dry pasta reign supreme in the south, rice, corn, and potatoes, risotto, polenta, gnocchi, and fresh egg pasta are the focus in the north. French and Germanic influences are keenly observed in the north, as opposed to the Arabic and Moorish-informed dishes of the south. And where the south calls for olive oil, the north cries for butter, with many recipes calling for it to both start and finish a dish. Northern cooks also use less tomato, relying more on *brodo* (meat broth), or wine to moisten dishes. These are just a handful of the differences.

In the following sections, I look at several classic preparations from the rich lands north of Rome. Many of the ingredients — Parmigiano-Reggiano, prosciutto di Parma, bologna, and aged balsamic vinegar, for example — are all familiar and are all produced in the north.

Northern Italy is incredibly rich in wine, too, producing some of the best and most food-friendly wines anywhere. (I've often said that if I had to choose only one place in the world to eat and drink, it would be Piedmont.) Here you can find such well-known wines as Gavi, Dolcetto, and Barbera from various appellations, as well as Barbaresco and Barolo, Valpolicella and Amarone, Chianti, Brunello di Montalcino, and Vino Nobile di Montepulciano to name just a few.

Though regional differences drive cuisine and wine styles, wine and food pairing knows no arbitrary political boundaries. Classic regional matches of course exist, with recipes and wine production methods tested and refined over centuries to work together. But you're not bound to any traditions. Countless wines from other regions and other countries are available that can harmonize with regional Italian specialties. So use the classics as a starting point, but experiment, too. I'm sure a Renaissance man (or woman) would have done the same thing given the opportunities that you have.

Soups

Italian soups are hearty and rustic meals unto themselves. Whereas elsewhere it seems somehow odd to drink liquid while eating liquid, Italians are comfortable drinking wine with their hearty soups — in fact one wouldn't do without it. I suggest you follow suit with my suggestions in Table 15-5. Popular dishes from the north include minestrone and *pasta e fagiole*, both based on beans and both eminently wine-friendly.

Table 15-5	Pairing Wine with Italian Soups		
Region	*Local Dish Name (English)*	*Best Wine Style (Example)*	*Alternative Wine Style (Example)*
Tuscany	Pasta e fagiole (cannellini bean soup with macaroni, olive oil, garlic, onion, tomato paste, ham trotter, herbs, chicken stock)	Red: Light-bodied, bright, zesty, low tannins (Chianti Sangiovese)	Red: Medium-full bodied, balanced, moderately tannic (Burgundy Pinot Noir)
Emilia-Romagna	Zuppa di pesce (fish stew of mullet, scorpion fish, squid, octopus, and turbot with tomatoes, garlic, parsley, olive oil, black pepper)	White: Lightweight, crisp, and stony (Verdicchio dei Castelli di Jesi)	White: Aromatic, fruity, round (Soave Garganega)

Region	Local Dish Name (English)	Best Wine Style (Example)	Alternative Wine Style (Example)
Liguria	Minestrone alla genovese (pasta and bean soup with tomato, carrots, celery, basil, thyme, parsley, broth, Parmigiano-Reggiano)	White: Aromatic, fruity, round (Colli di Luni Vermentino)	White: Aromatic, fruity, round (Alto Adige Pinot Grigio)

Pasta, gnocchi, polenta, and risotto

Pasta asciuta (dried pasta made from durum wheat, also known as semolina) is popular all over Italy, but is more of a southern specialty. In the north, *pasta fresca* (fresh, egg-based pasta) is the forte. Many Italians consider the Romagnoli of Emilia-Romagna to be the best pasta makers of Italy, especially of fresh, thick *tagliatelle, pappardelle,* and lasagna noodles. Stuffed pastas come in the form of *tortellini* (belly button) or *cappelletti* (little hats), as well as *ravioli* and *agnolotti.*

The north's repertoire of sauces extends beyond the traditional tomato-based sauces of the south, opening the door to more varied wine pairings, and white wines come into play more frequently. Even with stuffed pasta, I find the sauce to be the driving force behind a good match. With mushroom-stuffed ravioli in a cream sauce, for example, I suggest a substantial, wood-aged white. But with the same ravioli in a red (tomato) sauce, I'd opt for an earthy, zesty red. Likewise, when pairing with dishes based on potato *gnocchi* (dumplings), polenta (corn grits), or risotto (a rice-based dish), it's all about the sauce/main ingredients, so use that as your starting point. I point out some suggestions in Table 15-6.

Table 15-6	Pairing Wine with Italian Pasta and Other Starches		
Region	Local Dish Name (English)	Best Wine Style (Example)	Alternative Wine Style (Example)
Emilia-Romagna	Cappelletti romagnoli (cappelletti pasta stuffed with ricotta, nutmeg, ground chicken, Parmigiano-Reggiano, lemon rind, parsley served in chicken broth)	White: Lightweight, crisp, and stony (Albana di Romagna)	White: Full-bodied, soft, wood-aged (Russian River Valley Chardonnay)

(continued)

Table 15-6 *(continued)*

Region	Local Dish Name (English)	Best Wine Style (Example)	Alternative Wine Style (Example)
Emilia-Romagna	Spaghetti bolognese (spaghetti in meat sauce)	Red: Medium-full bodied, balanced, moderately tannic (Sangiovese di Romagna)	Red: Full, deep, and robust, turbocharged, chewy texture (Barolo Nebbiolo)
Liguria	Gnocchi al pesto (potato gnocchi in fresh basil, garlic and olive oil purée with cheese)	White: Lightweight, crisp, and stony (Riviera Di Ponente Pigato)	White: Lightweight, crisp, and stony (Hunter Valley Semillon)
Piedmont	Agnolotti al plin (fresh pasta stuffed with veal, and vegetables, in sage-butter sauce)	White: Aromatic, fruity, round (Roero Arneis)	White: Full-bodied, soft, wood-aged (Adelaide Hills Chardonnay)
Valle d'Aosta	Polenta ricca (polenta with Gruyère, fontina, whole milk, butter, salt, parsley, white pepper)	White: Aromatic, fruity, round (Valle d'Aosta Petite Arvine)	White: Aromatic, fruity, round (Friuli Pinot Grigio)
Lombardy	Risotto Milanese (carnaroli rice, bone marrow, butter, white wine, saffron, chicken broth, Parmigiano-Reggiano, black pepper)	Red: Light-bodied, bright, zesty, low tannins (Valpolicella)	White: Aromatic, fruity, round (Soave Garganega)

Meat, poultry, and game

Beef, pork, lamb, chicken, rabbit, and many types of game including wild boar, pheasant, hare, and even horsemeat, are all on the menu in northern Italy. Cured meats and sausages are a staple and are served as an accompaniment, on their own or incorporated within the dish itself. Chopped raw beef tartar-style with shaved white truffles is a classic preparation of the Piedmont region. Many sauces are meat-based, as in the classic Bolognese that originates in

Bologna in Emilia Romagna. Stews, whole roasts, and charbroiled items, such as lamb, goat, and various cuts of beef, round out typical menu items.

Because preparations vary so widely, virtually all the dry red wine styles come into play, and even some fuller, wood-aged whites. The braised and slow-cooked meat dishes generally shift into more robust reds, while white meat preparations favor zestier reds or full whites. Refer to Table 15-7 for the specifics with each listed dish.

Table 15-7	Pairing Wine with Italian Meat Dishes		
Region	*Local Dish Name (English)*	*Best Wine Style (Example)*	*Alternative Wine Style (Example)*
Veneto	Fegato alla Veneziana (calf's liver with slow-stewed onion, white wine, sage)	White: Aromatic, fruity, round (Soave Classico Garganega)	Red: Light-bodied, bright, and zesty, low tannins (Côtes du Rhône)
Piedmont	Carne cruda (chopped raw beef tenderloin seasoned with white truffle, garlic, anchovy, parsley, lemon)	Red: Medium-full bodied, balanced, moderately tannic (Barbaresco Nebbiolo)	White: Aromatic, fruity, round (Roero Arneis)
Lombardy	Ossobuco con porcini (braised veal shanks with porcini mushroom sauce)	Red: Full, deep, and robust, turbo-charged, chewy texture (Valtellina Superiore Nebbiolo)	Red: Full, deep, and robust, turbo-charged, chewy texture (Amarone della Valpolicella)
Lombardy	Cappone con le noci (poached capon with walnut and bread stuffing)	White: Full-bodied, soft, wood-aged (Terre di Franciacorta Chardonnay)	Red: Medium-full bodied, balanced, moderately tannic (Burgundy Pinot Noir)
Veneto	Pastissada di caval (horsemeat stew with bay, nutmeg, clove)	Red: Full, deep, and robust, turbo-charged, chewy texture (Amarone della Valpolicella)	Red: Full, deep, and robust, turbocharged, chewy texture (Châteauneuf-du-Pape)

(continued)

Table 15-7 *(continued)*

Region	Local Dish Name (English)	Best Wine Style (Example)	Alternative Wine Style (Example)
Piedmont	Lepre al vino rosso (rabbit braised in red wine with bacon, cinnamon, juniper, savory herbs)	Red: Medium-full bodied, balanced, moderately tannic (Barbera d'Alba)	Red: Light-bodied, bright, zesty, low tannins (Central Coast Pinot Noir)
Tuscany	Bistecca alla fiorentina (charcoal-grilled Chianina beef T-bone steak)	Red: Full, deep, and robust, turbo-charged, chewy texture (Brunello di Montalicno)	Red: Full, deep, and robust, turbo-charged, chewy texture (Napa Valley Cabernet Sauvignon)

Fish and seafood

Northern Italy boasts a wide selection of saltwater and freshwater fish. You can find shellfish, eels, sardines, sea bass, and river fish, such as trout and bream, in regional restaurants. Fish stews are popular on the coast.

Northern Italy has an ample supply of fresh, crisp whites as well as lighter reds to match the seafood dishes of the region, with many variations to choose from. Table 15-8 lists some of the classic local pairings.

Table 15-8   Pairing Wine with Italian Seafood Dishes

Region	Local Dish Name (English)	Best Wine Style (Example)	Alternative Wine Style (Example)
Veneto	Sarde in saor (fried sardines in sauce of onions, red wine vinegar, pine nuts, raisins, flour, lemon, parsley, served cold)	Sparkling: Dry (Prosecco Brut)	White: Lightweight, crisp, and stony (Bianco di Custoza Trebbiano blend)

Region	Local Dish Name (English)	Best Wine Style (Example)	Alternative Wine Style (Example)
Liguria	Filetto di orata alla ligure (sea bass with potatoes, pine nuts, green olives, lemon, basil, white wine, olive oil)	White: Aromatic, fruity, round (Riviera di Ponente Vermentino)	White: Aromatic, fruity, round (Campania Falanghina)
Veneto	Calamari fritti alla padella (pan-fried squid with olive oil, breadcrumbs, rosemary, red onions)	White: Lightweight, crisp, and stony (Alto Adige Pinot Grigio)	White: Lightweight, crisp, and stony (Sancerre Sauvignon Blanc)
Friuli – Venezia Giulia	Cernia al burro (grouper in lemon-garlic butter sauce)	White: Full-bodied, soft, wood-aged (Colli Orientali del Friuli white Blend)	White: Aromatic, fruity, round (Austria Grüner Veltliner)

Desserts — the dolci effect

The north is home to many sweet classics like *zuccotto* (sponge cake), *tiramisù* (layered espresso cake), and *Piedmontese zabaglione* (sweet egg custard). The repertoire of sweet wines is no less varied. The lineup includes many passito-style (made from partially dried grapes) wines, such as the Vin Santo of Tuscany and the *reciotos* of the Veneto (Valpolicella and Soave), as well as the sweet sparkling wines of Pidemont, Moscato d'Asti, and Brachetto d'Acqui. Table 15-9 provides a few wine suggestions for Italian desserts.

Table 15-9	Pairing Wine with Italian Desserts		
Region	Local Dish Name (English)	Best Wine Style (Example)	Alternative Wine Style (Example)
Veneto	Tiramisù (layered espresso cake)	Sweet: Passito red (Recioto della Valpolicella)	Sweet: Fortified amber (Rutherglen Muscat)

(continued)

Table 15-9 *(continued)*

Region	Local Dish Name (English)	Best Wine Style (Example)	Alternative Wine Style (Example)
Tuscany	Zuccotto (semi-frozen sponge cake with brandy, ice cream, topped with chocolate, whipped cream)	Sweet: Passito white (Vin Santo di Toscana)	Sweet: Late harvest noble rot (Tokaji Aszú 5 puttonyos)
Lombardy	Panettone (sweet bread with candied citrus fruit, raisins)	Sweet: Sparkling (Moscato d'Asti)	Sweet: Passito white (Vin Santo di Toscana)
Piedmont	Zabaglione con marsala (cooked, whipped egg yolks, with sugar, marsala, vanilla)	Sweet: Passito white (Recioto di Soave)	Sweet: Fortified amber (Marsala Superiore)

Going Germanic with German Cuisine

Germany, Austria, and Switzerland represent the heartland of German-speaking Europe. This is the land of sausages and cured meats. In fact, Germany and Austria alone have more than 1,600 types of sausage.

All three are significant wine-producing countries, especially Germany and Austria, whose wines are exported worldwide. Both red and white wines from this cool zone are generally fresh, crisp, and high acid, making them particularly food-friendly and appropriate pairings for the many rich, high-fat local dishes. Riesling and Grüner Veltliner are the most important varieties. German Riesling is often off-dry and light-bodied (warning: exceptions!), while Austrian Riesling is mostly dry and fuller bodied. Grüner is Austria's flagship grape and is a superbly versatile variety; Chasselas is Switzerland's, usually fresh and unoaked.

Cured meats — sausages and forcemeats

Cured meats and sausages are a Germanic specialty, made predominantly from pork. The salty, fatty taste of sausages works well with crisp whites and light reds with minimal oak. Table 15-10 lists some wine pairings for cured meats.

Table 15-10	Pairing Wine and Germanic Cured Meats		
Country (Region)	*Local Dish Name (English)*	*Best Wine Style (Example)*	*Alternative Wine Style (Example)*
Germany (Bayern)	Sülze (headcheese: pig's head, tongue, onion, dried apricot, black pepper, allspice, vinegar, aspic jelly, parsley)	White: Aromatic, fruity, round (Alsace Gewürztraminer)	White: Full-bodied, soft, wood-aged (Condrieu Viognier)
Germany (Baden-Wurttemburg)	Weisswurst (white sausage: minced veal, ground pork, bacon, parsley, lemon, mace, cardamom, ginger, onion, white pepper)	White: Lightweight, crisp, and stony (Baden Pinot Gris)	White: Aromatic, fruity, round (Alsace Pinot Blanc)
Austria (Salzburg)	Bosna (bratwurst sausage: ground pork and beef)	Red: Light-bodied, bright, zesty, low tannins (Carnuntum Zweigelt)	Red: Medium-full bodied, balanced, moderately tannic (Côtes du Rhône)
Switzerland (Geneva)	Papet vaudois (vaudois leek hotpot: smoked vaudoise [pork sausage] and fribourg [double smoked pork sausage] in soup)	White: Lightweight, crisp, and stony (Valais Chasselas)	White: Aromatic, fruity, round (Alsace Pinot Gris)

Salads and fondue

Salads from Germany and Austria usually contain root vegetables, such as carrots, turnips, or beets, making them more like slaw in consistency. Raw apples, cucumber, cabbage, and winter squash are also used frequently, adding acidy and earthy-sweetness. The majority of such recipes, as with most salads, are best with fruity, aromatic, and high acid whites, or light, zesty reds. Table 15-11 previews some wines to pair with Germanic salads.

Consider how tart the dressing is when selecting your match: The more tart, the higher acid wine you need. Salads consisting of cured meats, sausages, and cold cuts can work with more substantial (but likely not turbocharged) reds. The Swiss classic fondue — vegetables, and/or meat dipped in melted cheese, white wine, and spices — is served locally with Chasseslas, Switzerland's most widely planted white grape, but most aromatic whites will do.

Table 15-11	Pairing Wine with Germanic Salads		
Country (Region)	*Local Dish Name (English)*	*Best Wine Style (Example)*	*Alternative Wine Style (Example)*
Germany (Baden-Wurttemburg)	Würstsalat (sausage salad with lyoner and stadwurst, onions, pumpkinseed oil, gherkins, radishes, parsley, chives)	Red: Light-bodied, bright, zesty, low tannins (Baden Pinot Noir)	White: Lightweight, crisp, and stony Pfalz Riesling kabinett)
Austria (Burgenland)	Salat aus grünen bohnen (green bean salad with bacon, red onion, dill, pumpkinseed oil, cider vinegar)	White: Lightweight, crisp, and stony (Steiermark Sauvignon Blanc)	White: Lightweight, crisp, and stony (Colli Orientali del Friuli Friulano)
Switzerland (Fribourg)	Fondue (Gruyère, Vacherin Fribourgeoise and Emmental cheese, white wine, garlic, kirsch, black pepper, paprika, nutmeg)	White: Aromatic, fruity, round (Valais Chasselas)	White: Aromatic, fruity, round (Alsace Pinot Gris)

Meat, fowl, and game

Roasted, grilled, and stewed meats, meat pies, and casseroles are very popular within these countries' cuisines. Pork is the mostly widely used meat, though game, poultry, beef, and lamb have their place in the culinary repertoire. Offal, used in many traditional recipes, is currently enjoying a renaissance in popularity. Table 15-12 shows some wines to go with common Germanic meat dishes.

Pick a wine for meat dishes based on the preparation method and sauce rather than the meat. Boiled or braised red meats are often better with rich, barrel-fermented, or aromatic white wines than red, especially if the sauce has cream or wild mushrooms in it.

Table 15-12	Pairing Wine with Germanic Meat Dishes		
Country (Region)	*Local Dish Name (English)*	*Best Wine Style (Example)*	*Alternative Wine Style (Example)*
Germany (Rhineland-Pfalz)	Sauerbraten (roast-brined beef, with cider vinegar, red vinegar, cloves, juniper, mustard seed, sugar, gingersnaps, raisins)	Red: Light-bodied, bright, zesty, low tannins (Baden Pinot Noir)	Red: Medium-full bodied, balanced, moderately tannic (Rioja Reserva)
Germany (Niedersachsen)	Jäger schnitzel (hunter's cutlet: breaded-fried pork cutlet, with mushroom and bacon sauce, sour cream, chives)	White: Full-bodied, soft, wood-aged (Burgundy Chardonnay)	Red: Light-bodied, bright, zesty, low tannins (Ahr Pinot Noir)
Germany (Saxony-Anhalt)	*Huhnerfrikassee* (chicken fricassee with leek, celery, carrot, mushrooms, clove, nutmeg, white wine, egg yolk, whipping cream)	White: Full-bodied, soft, wood-aged (Baden Pinot Gris)	White: Full-bodied, soft, wood-aged (Burgundy Chardonnay)
Austria (Vienna)	Tafelspitz (boiled tri-tip beef round served with apple and horse-radish sauce)	White: Aromatic, fruity, round (Wachau Grüner Veltliner)	Red: Medium-full bodied, balanced, moderately tannic (Burgunland Blaufränkisch)

(continued)

Table 15-12 *(continued)*

Country (Region)	Local Dish Name (English)	Best Wine Style (Example)	Alternative Wine Style (Example)
Austria (Upper Austria)	Hasenpfeffer (wild hare braised in red wine, with juniper, smoked bacon, mushrooms, brandy)	Red: Full, deep, and robust, turbocharged, chewy texture (Mittelburgenland Blaufränkisch)	Red: Full, deep, and robust, turbocharged, chewy texture (Dry Creek Valley Zinfandel)
Austria	Wiener schnitzel (breaded and fried veal escalope)	White: Lightweight, crisp, and stony (Austria Grüner Veltliner)	White: Lightweight, crisp, and stony (Mosel Riesling kabinett)
Austria	Rindsrouladen (beef rolls with gherkin and carrot stuffing in mustard sauce)	White: Aromatic, fruity, round (Wachau Grüner Veltliner)	White: Full-bodied, soft, wood-aged (Niagara Peninsula Chardonnay)
Austria	Geröstete kalbsleber (sautéed calf's liver)	White: Aromatic, fruity, round (Kamptal Grüner Veltliner)	Red: Light-bodied, bright, and zesty (Cru Beaujolais Gamay)
Austria	Fleischlaberl (minced beef or veal rissoles)	White: Lightweight, crisp, and stony (Wachau Riesling Smaragd)	White: Aromatic, fruity, round (Colli Orientali del Friuli Pinot Grigio)
Switzerland (Luzern)	Chügelipastete (savory meat pie with sweetbreads, ground veal, butter, onion, mushrooms, parsley, heavy cream)	White: Full-bodied, soft, wood-aged (Russian River Valley Chardonnay)	Red: Medium-full bodied, balanced, moderately tannic (Bordeaux Merlot)

Desserts

Cakes, flans, and tarts laden with fruit, nuts, and cheese are very popular sweets in all three countries. Austria in particular has a rich pastry and confectionary tradition. The capital Vienna is filled with decadent pastry shops. On the streets and at fairs, tortes and doughnut-like balls *(krapfen)* filled with jam, jelly, or Bavarian cream are hugely popular, as are thin pancakes and waffles covered with powdered sugar and syrup. Table 15-13 lists some wine pairings with Germanic desserts.

All three countries are significant producers of sweet wines, particularly Germany, where sweet wines are made in virtually all wine-growing regions from a variety of grapes, especially Riesling. The Burgenland around Lake Neusiedle southeast of Vienna is the place to search for excellent quality and value, late harvest, noble rot sweet wines in Austria.

Table 15-13	Pairing Wine with Germanic Desserts		
Country (Region)	*Local Dish Name (English)*	*Best Wine Style (Example)*	*Alternative Wine Style (Example)*
Austria (Vienna)	Sacher torte (bittersweet chocolate layer cake with apricot jam, chocolate icing)	Sweet: Late harvest noble rot (Burgenland trockenbeerenauslese)	Sweet: Late harvest noble rot (Tokaji Aszú 6 puttonyos)
Germany (Nordrhein-Westfalen)	Butterküchen (butter cakes with almond flakes, cinnamon)	Sweet: Late harvest, noble rot (Germany Riesling auslese)	Sweet: Fortified white (Muscat de Beaumes de Venise)
Austria (Salzburg)	Kaiserschmarrn (sweet pancake with apples, kirsch, lingonberry jam, icing sugar)	Sweet: Late harvest noble rot (Burgenland Chardonnay [auslese])	Sweet: Late harvest (Mosel Riesling auslese)
Germany (Baden-Wurttemburg)	Schwarzwälder kirschtorte (black forest cake: layered chocolate cake with cherries, whipped cream)	Sweet: Sparkling red (Brachetto d'Aqui)	Sweet: Fortified red (Banyuls Grenache)
Austria (Vienna)	Altwiener apfelstrüdel (apple strudel)	Sweet: Late harvest noble rot (Burgenland beerenauslese)	Sweet: Passito style (Vin Santo di Toscana)

Jolly Good! Eating in the United Kingdom and British Cuisine

Cuisine in the United Kingdom (also known as British food) covers the cuisines of England, Scotland, Ireland, and Wales. UK chefs have come a long way from boiled beef and brown vegetables; there has been a bona fide culinary revolution led by celebrity chefs like Jamie Oliver and Gordon Ramsay, and Michelin stars are now as common as fish and chips.

Yet when people abroad think of British food, pub grub like meat pies, bangers and mash, and fish and chips still come to mind, as do traditional hearty English breakfasts and roast beef with Yorkshire pudding. Well, the pub has gone upscale. Gastro-pubs are now serving far more refined fare and elegant twists on traditional preparations. Considering its colonial history and recent rise in immigration, it's not surprising that British cuisine, like North American cuisine, is heavily influenced by ethnic foods, especially Indian food. Anglo-Indian hybrid dishes, such as the fiery *phaal* curry, have become traditional classics in their own right. Middle Eastern, Southeast Asian, East Asian, and Mediterranean influences are also frequently observed.

Although England has its own thriving wine industry (check out the sparkling wines), wine from every corner of the planet is available in the UK. The wine trade here developed hundreds of years ago with ties to countries like France (especially Bordeaux) and Portugal (especially Port and the Douro Valley). As such, British sommeliers have the world at their disposal; the breadth is easily observed on the top wine lists across the region.

Brunching in the British Isles

Brunch is an institution in the British Isles. Besides the well-known bacon, eggs, and bangers, dishes like *bubble and squeak* (leftover shallow-fried Saturday dinner), black pudding, potato farl, *haggis* (stuffed sheep's bladder), white pudding (oatmeal pudding), and *boxty* (Irish potato pancakes) are served from coast to coast. As for brunch wine selections, the timeless classic is Champagne — never a bad choice. But I provide some alternatives in Table 15-14.

Table 15-14		Pairing Wine with a British Brunch	
Region	*Dish*	*Best Wine Style (Example)*	*Alternative Wine Style (Example)*
England	Smoked cod, basmati rice, hardboiled eggs, heavy cream, cayenne, saffron, curry powder	White: Aromatic, fruity, round (Alsace Gewürztraminer)	White sparkling: Lightweight, crisp, and stony (Penedès Cava)
Scotland	Smoked salmon hash with potatoes, fennel, tarragon	White sparkling: Lightweight, crisp, and stony (Vouvray Brut Chenin Blanc)	White: Aromatic, fruity, round (Marlborough Sauvignon Blanc)
Ireland	Corned beef hash, fried eggs	White: Full-bodied, soft, wood-aged Burgundy Chardonnay Meursault)	Red: Medium-full bodied, balanced, moderately tannic (Paso Robles Zinfandel)
Wales	Sheppard's pie with goat cheese, leeks	White sparkling: Lightweight, crisp, and stony (Alsace Riesling)	White: Lightweight, crisp, and stony (Marlborough Sauvignon Blanc)

Traditional holiday meals

Holiday feasts, such as Christmas and Easter, are taken seriously in Great Britain. Mild but flavorful traditional dishes like roast beef and Yorkshire pudding are also perfect foils to show off special bottles, particularly for intimate gatherings. When the entire extended family and/or friends are in the house, I usually mix up the wine selections and let guests try a number of different bottles. Table 15-15 looks at some of my wine suggestions.

Table 15-15	Pairing Wine with British Holiday Meals		
Region	**Local Dish Name (English)**	**Best Wine Style (Example)**	**Alternative Wine Style (Example)**
England	Roast beef, Yorkshire pudding, roasted vegetables, red wine jus	Red: Medium-full bodied, balanced, moderately tannic (Pomerol Merlot)	Red: Medium-full bodied, balanced, moderately tannic (Burgundy Côte de Nuits Pinot Noir)
Scotland	Cooked partridge with scotch broth, barley, sage, beans	White: Full-bodied, soft, wood-aged (Russian River Valley Chardonnay)	Red: Light-bodied, bright, and zesty (Central Otago Pinot Noir)
Ireland	Irish mincemeat pies (egg, butter, raisins, currants, beef suet, brown sugar, nutmeg, citrus zests, apples, black pepper)	Rosé: Sparkling (Penedès Cava Rosado)	White: Full-bodied, soft, wood-aged (Mornington Peninsula Chardonnay)
Wales	Welsh lamb cawl (Welsh lamb, bacon, leek, cabbage stew)	Red: Light-bodied, bright, zesty, low tannins (Willamette Valley Pinot Noir)	Red: Medium-full bodied, balanced, moderately tannic (Rioja Reserva)

Meat, fish, and game

British meat dishes consist primarily of large roasts or preparations in the form of pies, casseroles, and stews. Beef is the most popular meat, with lamb, chicken, pork, and goat also appearing. Wild game, such as squab, partridge, hare, venison, and boar are often treated to slow cooking in stews and braises. Fish is popular in coastal regions; you'll find salmon, trout, sole, pike, turbot, halibut, and other flatfish in markets and on restaurant menus. With so many choices, there's no single wine style to match, so Table 15-16 gives you some options.

Table 15-16	Pairing Wine with British Meat and Fish		
Region	*Local Dish Name (English)*	*Best Wine Style (Example)*	*Alternative Wine Style (Example)*
England	Steak and kidney pie with mushrooms, bacon, peas	Red: Medium-full bodied, balanced, moderately tannic (Burgundy Côte de Nuits Pinot Noir)	Red: Full, deep, and robust, turbocharged, chewy texture (Châteauneuf-du-Pape)
England	Wild boar civet (boar braised in red wine and sherry vinegar with bacon potatoes, carrots, onions, leeks, juniper, rosemary, thyme, cinnamon, fennel seed, clove)	Red: Medium-full bodied, balanced, moderately tannic (Cahors Malbec)	Red: Medium-full bodied, balanced, moderately tannic (Barbaresco Nebbiolo)
Scotland	Haggis (sheep stomach, heart, lungs, liver, tongue, suet, oatmeal, onions, beef stock, nutmeg, mace)	Red: Light-bodied, bright, zesty, low tannins (Santa Lucia Highlands Pinot Noir)	White: Full-bodied, soft, wood-aged (Northern Rhône Rousanne)
Scotland	Roasted venison with celeriac, woodland mushrooms, cream	Red: Full, deep, and robust, turbocharged, chewy texture (Amarone della Valpolicella)	Red: Full, deep, and robust, turbocharged, chewy texture (Taurasi Aglianico)
Ireland	Potato-cheddar crusted halibut with spinach	White: Full-bodied, soft, wood-aged (Central Coast Roussanne)	White: Aromatic, fruity, round (Wachau Grüner Veltliner)
Wales	Eog cothi pob (baked salmon with butter, cucumber, lemon juice, egg yolk, lemon zest, cayenne)	White: Aromatic, fruity, round (Alsace Pinot Gris)	White: Lightweight, crisp, and stony (Savennières Chenin Blanc)

Desserts

Desserts in the UK are highly seasonal. The summer brings fresh fruit to the table in the form of trifle, panna cotta, and summer fruit puddings and gelatins. Winter brings warm preserved fruit crumbles, cobblers, and succulent, savory bread puddings, including the classic English treat — spotted dick, a suet pudding with dried fruits, milk pastry, and brown sugar served with custard. Table 15-17 gives you some wine options to go with your desserts.

Table 15-17	Pairing Wine and British Desserts		
Region	*Local Dish Name (English)*	*Best Wine Style (Example)*	*Alternative Wine Style (Example)*
England	Trifle (sponge cake with strawberries, almonds blueberries, bananas, orange juice, whipping cream, maraschino cherries, vanilla pudding)	Sweet: Sparkling (Moscato d'Asti)	Sweet: Fortified white (Mistelle) (Muscat of Limnos)
Scotland	Sticky toffee and malt scotch pudding	Sweet: Passito (Vin Santo di Toscana)	Sweet: Fortified red (Tawny Port 20 years)
Ireland	Steamed chocolate and whisky pudding	Sweet: Fortified red (Late bottled Vintage Port)	Sweet: Fortified/ Passito amber (Rutherglen Muscat)
Wales	Pwdin afal brandi (apple brandy pudding with molasses, suet, brandy, graham cracker, vanilla, ginger, cream)	Sweet: Fortified amber (Malmsey Madeira)	Sweet: Late harvest Icewine (Niagara Peninsula Vidal)

Chapter 16

Venturing to Eastern Europe: Those Lovely Light Dishes

In This Chapter

▶ Recognizing pairings with Polish and Eastern European food

▶ Contemplating food and wine pairings with Hungarian food

. . . .

*E*astern European cuisine is hearty. You can put thoughts of dieting aside when traveling through this region; starch, protein, and fat are the order of the day, useful for getting through cold winters and long days in the fields. For this chapter, I focus on a couple of the more prevalent national specialties from Poland and Hungary, because the scope of this book doesn't allow for a full review of all nations in the region. At the risk of offending many people, I'd say that the cuisine of Poland shares many similarities with neighboring countries like Ukraine and Russia, while Hungarian cuisine, quite distinctive on its own (and widely exported around the world — at one point in the 20th century, goulash was ranked in the top five most popular dishes in the United States), has likewise also influenced, and been influenced by its neighbors. Between these two countries, you can find variations on many Eastern European specialties.

Considering the prevalence of preserved foods in this part of the world, such as pickles and pickled vegetables with lots of vinegar, wine is often a tough match. Beer and spirits like vodka have traditionally been the beverages of choice, though just because wine isn't as traditional doesn't mean it can't work. You have access to infinitely more wines than the average Eastern European citizen from not so long ago, so perhaps it's just more a question of discovering the new possibilities.

Considering Poland and Polish Food

Polish cuisine is rich in meat and starches. Dill, caraway, and sour cream are common flavorings, and sauerkraut, beets, pickles, kohlrabi, mushrooms, and smoked sausages are everywhere. Most meals begin with a soup, such as borscht, followed by appetizers like various cured meats, fish, or vegetables.

The main course consists of boiled or roasted meat or poultry with sides of boiled potatoes or *kasza* (most often kasha, or buckwheat groats, but can also refer to any cereal in general) with its unique, nutty flavor — one of the most emblematic cereals that has been part of Slavic cuisine for a thousand years.

Soups and starters

Barszcz, more commonly known as *borscht,* is an Eastern European classic. You can find many variations on the theme of beetroot soup: served hot or cold, with yogurt, sour cream, kefir; with potatoes, carrots, cabbage, or other vegetables; tomatoes, with or without meat, finished with dill and/or parsley. Each region has its own version, but the main taste element in virtually all variations is the earthy sweetness of the beets themselves and the tang of vinegar, making an off-dry, high acid wine a suitable choice. Versions with more dairy cream can handle more full-bodied styles. Alternatively, an earthy, beetroot-flavored new world–Pinot with its own sweet fruit can do nicely.

Match vinegary starters like pickled herrings with high acid wines for best harmony.

Table 16-1 reviews some pairings for wine and common Polish starters and soups.

Table 16-1	Wine Pairings with Polish Starters and Soups	
Dish name	*Best Wine Style*	*Alternative Wine Style*
Borscht (beetroot soup with sour cream)	White: Aromatic, fruity, round (Mosel Riesling kabinett)	Red: Light-bodied, bright and zesty (Barbera D'Asti)
Krupnik (barley soup with vegetables, smoked meat)	White: Aromatic, fruity, round (Alsace Pinot Gris)	Red: Light-bodied, bright, and zesty (Austria Zweigelt)
Grochówka (thick pea soup)	White: Aromatic, fruity, round (Tokaji dry Furmint)	White: Dry, fortified (Oloroso Sherry)
Zupa grzybowa (mushroom soup with cream)	White: Dry, fortified (Oloroso Sherry)	White: Full-bodied, soft, wood-aged (Yarra Valley Chardonnay)
Śledzie w śmietanie (herring in sour cream with onion)	Sparkling: Dry (Prosecco Brut)	White: Lightweight, crisp, and stony (Muscadet)
Boczek ze śliwką (bacon-wrapped prunes)	Rosé: Dry (Navarra Tempranillo or Garnacha)	Red: Light-bodied, bright, and zesty (Valpolicella Ripasso)

Main courses

Typical Polish main courses are easier to pair with wine then traditional beer and vodka consumption would imply. The absence of hot spice (except occasionally horseradish) expands the possibilities. You want to echo the sweet elements of honey or fruit used in sauces with the sweetness in wine — an impression of sweetness from ripe fruit or actual residual sugar. The sour nature of pickled vegetables like sauerkraut, as well as the rich fattiness of pork or sausages, for example, needs wines with a nice bite of acidity. Table 16-2 gives a range of traditional dishes with suitable wines and styles.

Table 16-2	Pairing Wine with Polish Main Dishes	
Local Dish Name (English)	*Best Wine Style (Example)*	*Alternative Wine Style (Example)*
Golonka w piwie (pork knuckle in beer sauce)	White: Aromatic, fruity, round (Tokaji Furmint)	White: Lightweight, crisp, and stony (Chablis or unoaked Chardonnay)
Kiełbasa smażona (fried smoked sausages)	Red: Light-bodied, bright, and zesty (Barbera D'Asti)	White: Lightweight, crisp, and stony, off-dry (Rheingau Riesling spätlese)
Żeberka w miodzie (spare pork ribs in honey)	White: Aromatic, fruity, round (off-dry) (Tokaji late harvest Furmint)	White: Lightweight, crisp, and stony (off-dry) (Mosel Riesling spätlese)
Bigos (sauerkraut with various meats and sausages)	White: Aromatic, fruity, round (Baden Pinot Gris)	White: Lightweight, crisp, and stony (Burgundy Chardonnay)
Gołąbki (cabbage stuffed with meat and rice, served with tomato sauce)	Red: Light-bodied, bright, and zesty (Central Otago Pinot Noir)	Red: Medium-full bodied, balanced, moderately tannic (Hungary Kékfrankos)
Łosoś (baked salmon in dill sauce)	White: Aromatic, fruity, round (Marlborough Sauvignon Blanc)	White: Full-bodied, soft, wood-aged (Napa Valley Sauvignon Blanc)
Pierogi ruskie (dumplings filled with cheese and potatoes, boiled then fried in butter, onion)	White: Aromatic, fruity, round (Badacsony Pinot Gris)	White: Lightweight, crisp, and stony (Mosel Riesling kabinett)

Desserts

Poland shares many desserts with its neighbors. Fried dough, fruit-based preparations, walnuts, poppy seed and raisin fillings, and cakes of all kinds, especially cheesecake (*sernik*), are very popular. Table 16-3 lists some of the classics and my wine suggestions.

Table 16-3	Pairing Wine with Polish Desserts	
Local Dish Name (English)	*Best Wine Style (Example)*	*Alternative Wine Style (Example)*
Makowiec (poppy seed cake with raisins, walnuts)	White: Sweet fortified (Oloroso Dulce Sherry)	Sweet: Late harvest noble rot (Tokaji Aszú 4 or 5 puttonyos)
Sernik (cheesecake with vanilla, raisins, orange peel)	Sweet: Late harvest noble rot (Tokaji Aszú 5 puttonyos)	Sweet: Passito (Passito di Pantelleria)
Faworki (light fried pastry dusted with powdered sugar)	Sweet: Sparkling (Moscato d'Asti)	Sweet: Late harvest (Muscat Beaumes De Venise)
Kutia (sweet wheatberry pudding with poppy seeds, nuts, raisins, honey)	Sweet: Fortified red (Tawny Port)	Sweet: Passito (Vin Santo di Toscana)

Scoping Out Hungary and Hungarian Edibles

Hungary's cuisine is as colorful and varied as its thousand-year history. Although the language may be impenetrable to foreigners, the cuisine can often be identified by the brownish-red tinge of paprika used in countless preparations. Paprika comes in both sweet (*csemege*) and hot (*csipös*) versions, so be sure to check the label or with your purveyor or waiter before proceeding. Onions and lard are the other two pillars of Hungarian cuisine, with the combination of this trilogy forming the first steps of many recipes.

Like other parts of Eastern Europe, a classic meal starts with a soup, followed by a main course and dessert. In many instances, the soup is the heartiest course containing the protein, while the second course is lighter and complementary, as in the typical menu of *halászlé,* fishermen's soup with hot paprika, followed by *túrós csuszá,* noodles with a type of cottage cheese and bacon. Aside from the many meat-based dishes, Hungary is also known for its fresh garden vegetables, which many dishes and side dishes reflect.

Tracing goulash's origins

The term *gulyás* (goulash) means literally "shepherd" or "herdsman," and the origins of the dish can be traced back to the ninth century. Wandering shepherds cubed up their meat and cooked it with onion in a heavy iron kettle over an open fire, slowly stewing the dish until all the liquid had evaporated. The remnants were further dried in the sun, and then stored in a bag made of sheep's stomach. This instant meal could then be reheated as needed with a little water: More water made *gulyásleves* or goulash soup; less water resulted in *gulyáshus* or goulash meat, more like a thick stew than a soup. This distinction is still made today.

Wine is an important part of Hungarian gastronomic culture, with more than a thousand years of wine-producing experience. During the Soviet era and the implementation of the command economy within the Eastern Block, Hungary was designated as a wine-producing nation, charged with supplying the Soviet Empire with wine. As such, wine is a larger part of Hungarian culture than it is in many other Eastern European countries.

Soups and stews

Soups are an essential part of a Hungarian meal; it's unheard of for a traditional meal to go without. The repertoire is vast and varied, with multiple recipes for every type of meat, vegetable, and legume available in the country. Many are hearty enough to be a main course on their own, especially if the recipe calls for some kind of noodle or dumpling.

Stews are likewise essential, especially the most famous traditional dish of all called *gulyás* (goulash). *Pörkolt* is a similarly thick meat stew made with larger pieces of meat, in which paprika (sweet or hot), onion, bacon, or lard are mandatory. The main difference between pörkolt and *paprikás* (literally "paprika-ed") is that the latter is finished with sour cream, and that beef, mutton, game, goose, and duck are more common for pörkolt, while chicken and veal are the standards for paprikás.

Regardless of the particular preparation, most gulyás, pörkolt, and paprikás dishes are well-suited to medium-full bodied red wines. The spicier versions need sweet-fruited, full-bodied, new world–style reds, while the sweeter or sour cream-cut versions are equally good with lighter styled reds too. Refer to Table 16-4 for some suggestions.

Table 16-4	Pairing Wine with Hungarian Soups and Stews	
Local Dish Name (English)	*Best Wine Style (Example)*	*Alternative Wine Style (Example)*
Gulyásleves (beef soup with onion, potato, peppers, caraway, paprika)	Red: Medium-full bodied, balanced, moderately tannic (Egri Kékfrankos)	Red: Medium-full bodied, balanced, moderately tannic (Napa Valley Merlot)
Halászlé (fish soup with hot paprika)	Red: Light-bodied, bright and zesty (Szekszárdi Kadarka)	Red: Light-bodied, bright, and zesty (Marlborough Pinot Noir)
Jókai bableves (bean soup with smoked pig's feet, sausage, pork ribs, paprika)	Red: Full, deep, and robust, turbocharged, chewy texture (Villány Cabernet blend)	Red: Full, deep, and robust, turbocharged, chewy texture (Maipo Valley Cabernet Sauvignon)
Zöld bab főzelék (thick green bean stew with dill)	White: Aromatic, fruity, round (Tokaji Harslévelú)	White: Aromatic, fruity, round (Alsace Gewürztraminer)
Vaddiszno pörkölt (wild boar ragù)	Red: Full, deep, and robust, turbocharged, chewy texture (Villány Cabernet Franc)	Red: Full, deep, and robust, turbocharged, chewy texture (Brunello di Montalcino)
Csirkepaprikás (chicken stew with sweet paprika, sour cream)	Red: Medium-full bodied, balanced, moderately tannic (Egri Kékfrankos)	Red: Medium-full bodied, balanced, moderately tannic (Chile Carmenere)

Main courses

Table 16-5 lists some traditional Hungarian dishes that would be served as main courses. Most contain ingredients that are considered *Hungaricum*, an unofficial term applied to typically Hungarian food products, animal breeds, and occasionally even customs. *Téli szalami* (winter salami), paprika (both the fresh red, yellow, and green peppers, as well as the ground red spice), and *liba máj* (goose liver) are just some of the specialties considered Hungaricum. Goose liver in Hungary is usually less fatty than French foie gras, and is traditionally served with a glass of sweet Tokaji.

By luck or design, two of the traditional Hungarian red grape varieties, Kékfrankos (also known as Blaufränkisch) and Kadarka, both have a distinctive herbal-peppery profile, plus crisp acidity that makes them natural partners with rich, paprika-based meat dishes and zesty tomato and fresh pepper preparations.

Table 16-5	Pairing Wine with Hungarian Main Dishes	
Local Dish Name (English)	*Best Wine Style (Example)*	*Alternative Wine Style (Example)*
Töltött káposzta (cabbage stuffed with rice, ground pork, beef)	Red: Light-bodied, bright, and zesty (Soproni Kékfrankos)	Red: Light-bodied, bright, and zesty (Barbera D'Asti)
Töltött paprika (bell peppers stuffed with tomato, ground veal, pork)	Red: Light-bodied, bright, and zesty (Szekszárdi Kadarka)	Red: Light-bodied, bright, and zesty (Chinon Cabernet Franc)
Lecsó (stewed peppers, tomatoes, onions)	Red: Light-bodied, bright, and zesty (Egri Kékfrankos)	Rosé: Dry (Côtes de Provence)
Túrós csusza (egg noodles with fresh ewe's cheese, bacon)	White: Aromatic, fruity, round (Badacsony Pinot Gris)	White: Aromatic, fruity, round (Wachau Grüner Veltliner)
Liba máj (roast goose liver)	Sweet: Late harvest noble rot (Tokaji Aszú 3 puttonyos)	Sweet: Late harvest noble rot (Côteaux du Layon Chenin Blanc)
Paprikás krumpli (potato stew with paprika and sweet veal sausages)	Red: Light-bodied, bright, and zesty (Egri Kadarka)	Red: Medium-full bodied, balanced, moderately tannic (Crozes-Hermitage syrah)
Hortobágyi palacsinta (savory crepes filled with veal paprikás stew, sour cream)	Red: Light-bodied, bright, and zesty (Egri Bikavér red blend)	Red: Medium-full bodied, balanced, moderately tannic (Niagara Peninsula meritage)
Rakott krumpli (layered potato casserole with hardboiled eggs, ham, sausage, sour cream)	Red: Light-bodied, bright, and zesty (Villány Kékfrankos)	Red: Medium-full bodied, balanced, moderately tannic (Russian River Valley Pinot Noir)

Desserts

Hungary has a rich tradition of sweets. No visitor to a Hungarian house escapes before the hosts brings out a selection of cakes or pastries, usually accompanied by strong espresso coffee, sweet dessert wine, or *pálinka* (fruit brandy). Many recipes were adapted from Austrian pastries, which were in turn brought from the French Court. Hungary's sweet, nobly rotten Tokaji Aszú is of course the mandatory match for just about every dessert served in the country, but you're allowed a little more flexibility in your choices. Check out Table 16-6 for some wine suggestions with Hungarian desserts.

Getting your sweet on: Noble Tokaji

Tokaji Aszú is Hungary's, and one of Europe's, most famous sweet wines with 500 years of history. It's made in the northeastern corner of the country around the town of Tokaj, at the confluence of the Tisza and the Bodrog Rivers. The humidity caused by the proximity of water causes noble rot, *botrytis cinerea*, to settle in the vineyards with amazing regularity each autumn, shriveling and concentrating grapes. These dried, so-called *aszú* berries of mainly the Furmint, Hárslevelú, and Muscat varieties are then harvested in containers called *puttony* (hoppers) and macerated in a dry base wine (or still fermenting wine) from the same vintage. The addition of the sugar-rich Aszú grapes prolongs the fermentation of the base wine, and additional flavor is gently extracted. After a short period, the whole mixture is pressed, and the wine is run into barrels where it continues fermenting and aging. But the sugar concentration is so great that the fermentation invariably stops before the wine is dry.

The ratio of aszú berries added to the base wines determines the sweetness level in the finished wine: The greater the number of *puttony*, the sweeter the wine. Tokaji Aszú wines are labeled as either 3, 4, 5, or 6 *puttonyos*. *Esszencia* is the amazingly rich and sweet wine made from pure Azsú grapes, without any base wine. All Aszú wines are aged for long periods (minimum two years in oak barrels), and thus develop an intriguing spicy, nutty taste alongside that of quince paste and dried apricots. *Tokaji kesöi szuretelésu*, or late harvest wines, are made from the same grapes affected by botrytis, but are usually aged in stainless steel and bottled young, and are thus fresher and fruitier. When considering alternative wines from around the world to match with Hungarian desserts beyond Tokaji, consider the style I recommend in the nearby tables: Aszú or late harvest (that is, oak aged sweet wine or unoaked).

Table 16-6	Pairing Wine with Hungarian Desserts	
Local Dish Name (English)	*Best Wine Style (Example)*	*Alternative Wine Style (Example)*
Gundel palacsinta (Gundel-style crepes filled with walnuts, in chocolate-rum sauce, flambéed)	Sweet: Late harvest noble rot (Tokaji Aszú 6 puttonyos)	Sweet: Fortified red (Tawny Port 10 or 20 years)
Dobos torta (sponge cake layered with chocolate butter cream, caramel glaze)	Sweet: Late harvest noble rot (Tokaji Aszú 6 puttonyos)	Sweet: Fortified red (Banyuls Grand Cru Grenache)
Almas rétes (apple strudel)	Sweet: Late harvest (Tokaji Furmint late harvest)	Sweet: Late harvest noble rot (Quarts de Chaumes Chenin Blanc)

Local Dish Name (English)	Best Wine Style (Example)	Alternative Wine Style (Example)
Somlói galuska (Somló-style trifle with layered chocolate and vanilla sponge cake, vanilla custard, raisins, walnuts, chocolate sauce, rum, whipped cream)	Sweet: Late harvest noble rot (Tokaji Aszú 6 puttonyos)	Sweet: Passito (Mavrodaphne of Patras)
Madártej (meringue on vanilla custard)	Sweet: Late harvest (Tokaji Furmint late harvest)	Sweet: Sparkling white (Moscato D'Asti)
Mákos beigli (poppy seed roll)	Sweet: Late harvest noble rot (Tokaji Aszú 4 puttonyos)	Sweet: Passito (Tuscany Vinsanto)

Chapter 17

Bringing On the Spice: Asia

*T*his chapter covers a lot of ground: all of Southeast Asia and its amazingly diverse and flavorful cuisine. You need to keep a couple points in mind as you read through the following sections:

✔ Although a real culture of wine consumption is growing in these countries, it remains in the very early stages of development, which means that access to wines is limited, with the exception of some of the major urban centers. You can apply much of the advice in this chapter to the exported versions of these cuisines, offered in Asian restaurants (eat-in and take-out) the world over, where you're more likely to encounter some of the recommended wines. Home cooks now also have better access to the unusual ingredients called for in Asian dishes, making experimentation at home another enjoyable way to experience the flavors of Asian cuisine and wine.

✔ Another important consideration is the fact that Asian dining culture dictates the serving of multiple dishes at once, which makes a single wine match difficult to pull off. (I outline some strategies for dealing with multiple dishes in Chapter 4.) Another option, and one that I often practice, is to bring several bottles to the table at the same time. This way you can try different combinations and go with the ones that work. Choose two or more of the wine styles that I recommend in these tables with the range of dishes being served. A few extra glasses are also helpful when you're taking your fun really seriously.

Delving Into Southeast Asia

Southeast Asian cuisine offers an incredible range of cooking styles and ingredients, born of the exchange between the diverse cultures of the region. Much of the cuisine centers on a bowl of rice, a symbol of prosperity, but beyond this staple product, you can find a vast array of foods that are both friendly and challenging to pair with wine.

A whole range of exotic spice previously unknown in the West, such as peppercorns, nutmeg, cloves, and vanilla, originated in Southeast Asia, not to mention an amazing range of tropical fruits. From basic cooking methods, such as a chicken satay skewered on a sugar cane spear and grilled over charcoal and coconut husks, to the more complex preparation of giant snapper with a fish curry paste wrapped in banana leaves and cooked *hāngi* method in the ground with heated stones, Southeast Asia has a deep repertoire of methods and a wealth of flavors.

And you don't need to travel to the region to experience it; you can find Southeast Asian cuisine in major urban centers around the world. You may, however, have to bring your own wine when dining out, because for the most part, such restaurants have yet to embrace the Eurocentric focus on wine.

The dishes featured in these sections, which focus on the countries of Malaysia, Singapore, the Philippines, and Indonesia, often pair best with lighter, crisper, aromatic whites or rosés made with little or no oak aging. Hot chile peppers are prevalent in most dishes, encouraging perspiration and making high temperatures easier to endure. Serving wines relatively cold offers effective, if temporary, relief from the heat of spice, while off-dry or medium-dry wines (still or sparkling) also mitigate the burn. Because *capsaicin* — the compound that gives peppers their burn — is soluble in alcohol, wines with moderately high alcohol can help, but only up to about 14 percent or so; beyond that, alcohol can add its own fuel to the fire. The presence of carbon dioxide in bubbly wines can also increase the burn (beer isn't a great option for this reason, other than for its cold temperature).

Starters, soups, salads, satay, sambal

You can find a riot of flavors and textures in Southeast Asian starters, so stick with versatile wines (think crisp and little/no oak or tannins). These small bites don't usually last very long on the table, so going for wine by-the-glass when dining out is a smart option. A crisp, still, or sparkling white can get you through most bites, especially with a pinch of residual sugar. Table 17-1 outlines some wine pairings for popular Southeast Asian starters.

Table 17-1	Pairing Wine with Southeast Asian Starters		
Country of Origin	**Local Dish Name (English Name)**	**Best Wine Style (Example)**	**Alternative Wine Style (Example)**
Malaysia	Sambal asam sate (beef satay with tamarind, chile dip)	White: Full-bodied, soft, wood-aged (Northern Rhône white blend)	White: Lightweight, crisp, and stony, off-dry (Mosel Riesling)
Singapore	Chun juan (vegetable spring rolls)	White: Lightweight, crisp, and stony (Loire Valley Sauvignon Blanc)	White: Lightweight, crisp, and stony sparkling (Anderson Valley Traditional Method)
Singapore	Popiah (baked spring roll with shrimp, sausage)	White: Lightweight, crisp, and stony (South Australia Riesling)	Red: Light-bodied, bright, zesty, low tannins (Piedmont Barbera)
Indonesia	Cumi-cumi isi (shrimp- stuffed squid in coconut sauce with cori-ander leaf)	White: Aromatic, fruity, round (Paso Robles Marsanne/ Roussanne)	White: Full-bodied, soft, wood-aged (California Fumé Blanc)
Bali	Sate udang (spice paste prawn satay)	White: Lightweight, crisp, and stony (Mosel-Saar Riesling kabinett)	White: Lightweight, crisp, and stony (Santorini Assyrtiko)

Rice, noodles, stir-frys, and laksa

Rice, noodles, and dumplings are ubiquitous and range from a simple bowl of steamed white rice to a complex noodle preparation with more than 30 ingredients. Focus on the food's driving ingredients, and think of the wine as an accent to complement the dish. Wines with some residual sugar (off-dry, medium-dry, or an impression of sweetness, see Chapter 12), and ripe orchard and tropical fruit flavors served cold usually fare well. Table 17-2 gives you some wine pairings suggestions for Southeast Asian rice and noodle dishes.

Table 17-2		Pairing Wine with Southeast Asian Rice and Noodle Dishes	
Country of Origin	*Local Dish Name (English Name)*	*Best Wine Style (Example)*	*Alternative Wine Style (Example)*
Malaysia	Bihun goreng (fried rice noodles with egg, chile, sausage, shrimp, lime, sprouts)	White: Lightweight, crisp, and stony (South Australia Riesling)	Red: Light-bodied, bright, zesty, low tannins (Beaujolais Gamay)
Malaysia	Epok-epok (fried dumplings with pork, anchovy, coconut)	White: Full-bodied, soft, wood-aged (Stellenbosch Chenin Blanc)	White: Aromatic, fruity, round (Argentina Torrontés)
Singapore	Xia mian (yellow egg noodles with pork, shrimp, soy, chile, spinach)	White: Aromatic, fruity, round (Okanagan Valley Gewürztraminer)	Rosé: Off-dry (Chile Cabernet rosé)
Indonesia	Nasi goreng (fried rice with egg, chicken, shrimp, chile, scallion)	White: Lightweight, crisp, and stony (Marlborough Sauvignon Blanc)	White: Aromatic, fruity, round (Wachau Grüner Veltliner)
Indonesia	Pais udang (shrimp stir-fry with chile, galangal, basil, lime)	White: Lightweight, crisp, and stony (Sancerre Sauvignon Blanc)	Rosé: Dry (Rioja rosado)
Indonesia	Nasi kuning (yellow turmeric rice with coconut, cinnamon leaf)	White: Aromatic, fruity, round (Alsace Gewürztraminer)	White: Lightweight, crisp, and stony (Friuli Sauvignon Blanc)

Curries and stews

For a one-dish meal, you can't beat the all-encompassing flavors, textures, and aromas in the slow-braised curries and stews from Southeast Asia.

Serve ripe, full-bodied wines with intense, sweet fruit flavors, and even those with an impression of sweetness or actually off-dry, with the equally intense flavors of curries and stews. Rich whites and opulent, plush reds in the new world–style are the order of the day. The sweet spice of barrel-aged whites can also be an effective, complementary match with many coconut-based curries. Table 17-3 highlights some wine pairings with curries and stews.

Table 17-3   Pairing Wine with Southeast Asian Curries and Stews

Country of Origin	Local Dish Name (English Name)	Best Wine Style (Example)	Alternative Wine Style (Example)
Malaysia	Daging masak asam (braised beef curry in tamarind with lemongrass)	White: Aromatic, fruity, round (Alsace Gewürztraminer)	Red: Medium-full bodied, balanced, moderately tannic (Burgundy 5+ years)
Malaysia	Gulai tumis (tamarind fish curry with shallots, candlenuts, lemongrass, coconut, lime leaf)	White: Aromatic, fruity, round (Willamette valley Pinot Gris)	White: Full-bodied, soft, wood-aged (Santa Ynez Valley Viognier)
Singapore	Bei gu pa shi shu (braised shiitake and black mushroom stew in brown sauce with garlic)	Medium-dry fortified amber: (Oloroso Sherry)	White: Aromatic, fruity, round off-dry (Alsace Pinot Gris)
Singapore	Hong shao e rou (slow braised 5-spiced goose with tofu)	White: Full-bodied, soft, wood-aged (Condrieu Viognier)	White: Aromatic, fruity, round, medium-dry (Tokaji Aszú 3 puttonyos)
Philippines	Humba (braised pork belly with vinegar, soy, black beans, palm sugar, star anise)	White: Full-bodied, soft, wood-aged (Napa Valley Chardonnay)	Red: Light-bodied, bright, zesty, low tannins (Veneto Valpolicella)
Indonesia	Be celeng base manis (braised pork in sweet soy with fried shallots, chiles)	White: Aromatic, fruity, round (Alsace Gewürztraminer)	Red: Light-bodied, bright, zesty, low tannins (Santa Barbara Pinot Noir)
Indonesia	Kambing mekuah (Balinese lamb curry with lemongrass, coconut, cardamom)	White: Full-bodied, soft, wood-aged (Central Coast Viognier)	White: Off-dry, late harvest, barrel-aged (Tokaji Szamorodni Furmint)

Sweets, pastries, and desserts

Candlenuts, coconut, and gingko nuts make frequent appearances in Southeast Asian desserts, making them amazingly wine-friendly.

Southeast Asian desserts tend to be less sweet than typical western desserts, which opens up the possible pairings to a wider range of wines. Broaden your horizons and think of some wines you normally wouldn't consider with western desserts. While still following the cardinal rule of selecting a wine that's at least as sweet as the dish served, some sweet-savory desserts can pair beautifully with wines that are just off-dry or medium-dry; relatively few require the richest and sweetest styles, though these can also work. Off-dry Riesling auslese or Alsatian whites with a pinch of residual sugar can harmonize beautifully, especially with their aromatics as exotic as an Asian fruit and spice market. Table 17-4 offers some wine pairings with Southeast Asian desserts.

Table 17-4	Pairing Wine with Southeast Asian Sweets		
Country of Origin	*Local Dish Name (English Name)*	*Best Wine Style (Example)*	*Alternative Wine Style (Example)*
Malaysia	Nangka lemak (jackfruit in coconut milk)	Sweet: Icewine (Niagara Peninsula Vidal Icewine)	Sweet: Late harvest (Burgenland blend beerenauslese)
Malaysia	Mangkok kueh (steamed sweet rice cakes)	Sweet: Late harvest (German Riesling auslese)	Sweet: Sparkling (Moscato d'Asti)
Singapore	Wo bing (lotus paste pancakes with cream)	Sweet: Late harvest (Tokaji late harvest Hárslevelú)	Sweet: Late harvest passito (Sicily Passito di Pantelleria Zibibbo)
Philippines	Bibinkang galapoong (coconut rice cake)	Sweet: Late harvest noble rot (Monbazillac)	Sweet: Late harvest (Niagara Peninsula Vidal)

Delving Into Mainland Southeast Asia

The Southeast Asian mainland, including Thailand, Vietnam, Cambodia, Laos, and Burma, is a land of true fusion cuisine. Bordering countries have influenced each other for centuries, either as occupiers or traders. You can find the culinary marks of China, India, Malaysia, Portugal, and Mongolia from the more distant past, and more recently, France's significant culinary influence in Vietnam during its occupation in the late forties and early fifties.

The style of cuisine is as varied as the landscape. Rice is still a staple, both sticky and long-grained, but it's accompanied by a seemingly endless array of ingredients. Don't be surprised to find things like frogs, insects, river catfish, green papaya, fermented shrimp paste, and orchard fruits on your plate — few edible things are left untouched.

In the next sections I concentrate on the foods of Thailand and Vietnam, the countries whose cuisines have been most widely exported around the world.

Snacks and street foods

The streets of this region are packed with food stands and hawker's stalls; watch out, too, for whizzing motorized vending bikes, all serving up some amazing food experiences. The concept of street foods is originally Chinese, introduced here in the 1800s. Over time, demand grew, and simple offerings like green papaya or melon salads made way for more complex offerings such as curries, salads, stir-frys, noodles, and pastries. Imagining this region today without its vibrant street food scene is difficult. And the concept is gaining popularity in other parts of the world, too.

You won't likely find many wines to choose from when snacking on the streets of Asia, so use the examples in Table 17-5 as guidelines for similar dishes served in Asian restaurants around the world (though I've enjoyed some memorable street food parties in China, it took some work to gather the wines). Generally, light, crisp, and/or effervescent wines, with maximum versatility fit the bill. Dry or off-dry rosé is also a great option, providing a fruity contrast to the penetrating, pungent flavors of these small bites.

Table 17-5	Pairing Wine with Southeast Asian Snacks		
Country of Origin	*Local Dish Name (English Name)*	*Best Wine Style (Example)*	*Alternative Wine Style (Example)*
Thailand	Kao dtang nar dtang (rice cakes with chile, prawn, pork sauce)	White: Aromatic, fruity, round (Willamette Valley Pinot Gris)	White: Lightweight, crisp, and stony off-dry sparkling (Prosecco)
Thailand	Tort man pla (fried curried fish cakes with kaffir lime)	White: Lightweight, crisp and stony (Wachau Grüner Veltliner)	White: Aromatic, fruity, round (California Viognier)

(continued)

Table 17-5 *(continued)*

Country of Origin	Local Dish Name (English Name)	Best Wine Style (Example)	Alternative Wine Style (Example)
Vietnam	Báhn guốn (steamed rice noodle wraps filled with pork, prawn, wood ear mushrooms)	White: Aromatic, fruity, round (Alsace Gewürztraminer)	White: Aromatic, fruity, round, off-dry (Anjou Chenin Blanc)
Vietnam	Báhn khoái (happy hue pancake stuffed with pork belly, prawn, sprouts, mushroom)	White: Lightweight, crisp, and stony sparkling (Champagne)	White: Lightweight, crisp, and stony sparkling (Carneros Traditional Method)

Soups, salads, and sandwiches

Soups in this region can make a satisfying one-dish meal, such as the rich and varied *phở* of Vietnam. These are choose-your-own rice noodle soups into which diners can add chicken or beef prepared various ways (rare, meatballs, cooked flank, and so on) along with things like tendon and tripe, vegetables, fresh bean sprouts, and Thai basil. Phở has become so popular that you'll find phở restaurants in urban centers around the world. If you plan to drink wine with your phở, go easy on the spicy chile condiment sitting on every table.

Accompanying salads often employ shredded coconut, rice, cool sliced vegetables, and pickles — natural cooling agents — to mitigate the burn of fiery chiles in main dishes. Chefs from this region are masters in balancing sweet and heat and use a deft touch to ensure the palate isn't overwhelmed.

The best-known sandwich in the region is the *banh mi* or Saigon sub, introduced by the French during the colonial period. This sandwich is an airy baguette with assorted cold cuts, pork liver pate, sausage, cucumber, pickled carrots, fresh coriander butter, and mayonnaise. Table 17-6 identifies some wine suggestions for these types of dishes.

Table 17-6   Pairing Wine with Southeast Asian Soups and Salads

Country of Origin	Local Dish Name (English Name)	Best Wine Style (Example)	Alternative Wine Style (Example)
Thailand	Yam kai (chicken and papaya salad with coriander, fish sauce, lime, chile)	White: Lightweight, crisp, and stony (Niagara Peninsula Riesling)	White: Aromatic, fruity, round (Argentina Torrontés)
Thailand	Yam puu mamuang (crab and green mango salad)	White: Lightweight, crisp, and stony (Marlborough Sauvignon Blanc)	White: Aromatic, fruity, round (Austria Grüner Veltliner)
Vietnam	Phở bò hà nội (beef noodle soup with scallion, coriander, chile, lime)	White: Aromatic, fruity, round (Alsace Gewürztraminer)	Rosé: Dry (Côtes de Provence)
Vietnam	Phở gà (chicken noodle soup with basil, lime, chile, fresh coriander)	White: Aromatic, fruity, round (Casablanca Valley Sauvignon Blanc)	White: Aromatic, fruity, round (Willamette Valley Pinot Gris)
Vietnam	Banh mi (Saigon sub baguette with ham, sausage, headcheese, mayo, butter, coriander)	White: Lightweight, crisp, and stony (Niagara Peninsula Riesling)	Rosé: Off-dry (Napa Valley White Zinfandel)

Curries, noodles, and rice

Getting through a Thai or Vietnamese meal without at least one fierce curry, spicy noodle, or rice-based dish is indeed rare. Thai and Vietnamese restaurants abroad typically list dozens of variations on the theme.

When considering the match, you can most often forget the protein and focus almost exclusively on the sauce. Whether it contains beef, chicken, pork, shrimp, or anything else is a secondary consideration, because frequently the same sauce is used for all. Wine pairing with these complex flavors is a challenge, but not impossible. The heat and pungency can easily turn refined and delicate wines invisible: The sweet-sour-hot balance makes lean and firm wines even leaner and harder. So focus instead on either light, fruity, and aromatic, or even off-dry whites and rosés, such as Viognier, Pinot Gris, Grüner Veltliner, Riesling, and Albariño, or match power with power by selecting a bold, rich, ripe, and fruit-forward new world–style wine (without too much oak and not more than about 14 percent alcohol), such as red Zinfandel, new world Pinot Noir, Australian Shiraz, Chilean Cabernet Sauvignon, Argentine Malbec, or southern Rhône Grenache-based blends. Refer to Table 17-7 for some wine suggestions for these dishes.

Table 17-7 Pairing Wine with Southeast Asian Curries and Noodles

Country of Origin	Local Dish Name (English Name)	Best Wine Style (Example)	Alternative Wine Style (Example)
Thailand	Kuaytiaw phat thai (rice noodles with prawn, peanut, lime, chile, egg, coriander)	White: Lightweight, crisp, and stony (Mantinia Moscophilero)	White: Aromatic, fruity, round (Friuli Sauvignon Blanc)
Thailand	Khao sawy (chang mai noodles with chicken, chile paste, coconut, lime)	White: Lightweight, crisp, and stony (Clare Valley Riesling)	White: Aromatic, fruity, round (Paso Robles Roussanne)
Thailand	Kaeng phanaeng neua (red curry beef with coconut, fish sauce, lime, tamarind, coriander)	White: Aromatic, fruity, round (Alsace Gewürztraminer)	Red: Medium-full bodied, balanced, fruity, supple (Central Otago Pinot Noir)
Vietnam	Xoi (sticky rice with mung beans, peanuts, coconut)	White: Aromatic, fruity, round (Rias Baixas Albariño)	White: Lightweight, crisp, and stony (Austrian Riesling)
Vietnam	Bò xào lan (glass noodles with beef, red curry, coconut, chile, lemongrass, lime)	White: Aromatic, fruity, round (Santa Ynez Viognier)	Red: Medium-full bodied, balanced, fruity, supple (Sonoma Pinot Noir)
Vietnam	Cari ga (yellow curry with chicken, potato, coriander, lime)	White: Aromatic, fruity, round (Alsace Pinot Gris)	White: Lightweight, crisp, and stony (Sonoma Sauvignon Blanc)

Meat, fish, and game

In Southeast Asia, meat is still considered a luxury. Meat generally refers to pork and chicken; beef is far less common, and other red meats like lamb and large game are very rare indeed, though you'll occasionally come across more exotic meat dishes in restaurants abroad.

With thousands of miles of coastline on the other hand, fish and seafood are staples of the diet. Both saltwater and freshwater bodies of water are fished daily. Shrimp and squid are plentiful, along with lake perch, catfish, bass, carp, and mackerel. The ancient preservation techniques of salt curing, pickling, and smoking are used extensively, and thus make their way into traditional recipes. Table 17-8 lists some pairing possibilities.

Table 17-8	Pairing Wine with Southeast Asian Meat Dishes		
Country of Origin	*Local Dish Name (English Name)*	*Best Wine Style (Example)*	*Alternative Wine Style (Example)*
Thailand	Puu phat phong karii (cracked crab with coconut curry, lime, coriander)	White: Aromatic, fruity, round (Okanagan Valley Pinot Planc)	White: Lightweight, crisp, and stony, off-dry (German Riesling spätlese)
Thailand	Nok gradtaa thawt (fried quail with palm sugar, soy, garlic)	White: Aromatic, fruity, round (Wachau Grüner Veltliner)	Red: Light-bodied, bright, zesty, low tannins (Santa Barbara Pinot Noir)
Thailand	Kai yaang (lemongrass marinated whole grilled chicken)	White: Lightweight, crisp, and stony (South Australia Riesling)	White: Lightweight, crisp, and stony (Santorini Assyrtiko)
Vietnam	Tom nướng dầu hào (chargrilled jumbo prawns in oyster sauce)	White: Lightweight, crisp, and stony (Margaret River Sauvignon Blanc/ Semillon)	White: Lightweight, crisp, and stony (Loire Valley Chenin Blanc)
Vietnam	Thit kho khom (caramelized pork with sweet pineapple)	White: Full-bodied, soft, wood-aged (Napa Valley Chardonnay)	White: Aromatic, fruity, round, off-dry (Alsace Pinot Gris late harvest)

Sweets, pastries, and desserts

Sweets aren't so much the typical conclusion to a meal as they are a snack to be enjoyed throughout the day. Desserts and sweets are usually simple preparations ranging from fried bananas in sweetened coconut milk to ice cream on a baguette covered with condensed milk and palm sugar syrup. Street vending carts offer flavored shaved ices or black sticky rice wrapped in banana leaves sweetened with mango and palm sugar. But after a spicy meal, a cool, sweet taste sensation can be a welcomed experience, and served with a cool sweet wine, life gets even better. Remember that the wine you select should be sweeter than the dessert. Refer to Table 17-9 for some suggestions.

Table 17-9	Pairing Wine with Southeast Asian Sweets		
Country of Origin	*Local Dish Name (English Name)*	*Best Wine Style (Example)*	*Alternative Wine Style (Example)*
Thailand	Khao neeo see dam (black rice pudding with mango, strawberry, palm sugar, coconut)	Sweet: Icewine (Niagara Peninsula Cabernet Franc)	Sweet: Sparkling (Piedmont Brachetto d'Acqui)
Thailand	Sangkaya fak thawng (pumpkin with egg custard, cinnamon)	Sweet: Late harvest (Mosel-Saar Riesling spätlese)	Sweet: Fortified amber (Santorini Vinsanto)
Vietnam	Chè bắp dì tám (sweet corn, sticky rice pudding)	Sweet: Icewine (Niagara Peninsula Vidal)	Sweet: Fortified white (Muscat de Beaumes de Venise)
Vietnam	Dau xanh vung (deep fried sesame dumplings)	Sweet: Late harvest (Mosel Riesling, auslese or sweeter)	Sweet: Late harvest, noble rot (Barsac)

Focusing on China and Regional Chinese Cuisine

The wok and cleaver may symbolize the Chinese kitchen, but China has one of the richest and most diverse culinary traditions in the world. In fact, there's no such thing as Chinese food, but rather a regional tapestry of varying cuisines driven by local ingredients and cooking styles that have arisen over some 7,000 years of history.

In the next sections I explore the four most influential and commonly known regional cuisines of China: Szechuan, Cantonese, Mandarin, and Hunan. You can typically find restaurants serving these cuisines abroad, though you may have to bring your own wine.

Eyeing the flavors of Szechuan (Sichuan) cuisine

Szechuan cuisine originates from the province of the same name in south-western China. It's best known for its bold, spicy, and pungent flavors derived from a heavy reliance on garlic, chile, fermented black bean, sesame paste, and the stinging Szechuan peppercorn. Pickling, salting, and drying are frequently used techniques, and there's almost always chile oil involved. You also frequently encounter star anise, fennel seed, and ginger, among others.

Favored cooking techniques include stir-frying, steaming, and braising; the wok is indispensable. Beef is the favored protein in Szechuan cooking, and no part of the animal is ever wasted.

Eyeing the flavors of Cantonese cuisine

Originating in the southeastern coastal province of Guangdong (also known in English as Canton) near Hong Kong, Cantonese cuisine is the best-known Chinese food in the western world, thanks to significant emigration from the region. Chinatowns from Toronto to San Francisco to Melbourne offer largely Cantonese food.

Cantonese cuisine is well-balanced, rarely greasy, and notably less spicy than Szechuan or Hunan. *Dim sum,* small, bite-sized or individual portions of food served in steamer baskets or on small plates, is a Cantonese creation. Aside from coriander, few other herbs are used, another point of difference from neighboring cuisines. Condiments such as hoisin (a typical Cantonese dipping sauce), oyster, plum, sweet and sour sauce, and black bean paste are relied upon to provide much of the flavor for sauces, glazes, and braising liquids.

Eyeing the flavors of Beijing (Mandarin) cuisine

Beijing cuisine is better known to the rest of the world as Mandarin cuisine. It had a great influence on Chinese Imperial cuisine, reserved for society's upper classes. Cooks from all over China vied for the opportunity to come to the Forbidden City to cook for the courtiers of the royal family and supreme officials. Many regional cuisines have thus influenced Mandarin food.

The most emblematic dishes are Peking duck and hot and sour soup. Main flavorings include dark soy sauce, roasted sesame oil, fermented tofu, and scallions. Roasting and barbecuing are popular cooking methods.

Eyeing the flavors of Hunan cuisine

Hunan cuisine is among the spiciest, most colorful, and most aromatic regional cuisines in China. It incorporates a large array of ingredients and techniques: Stewing, pot roasting, frying, smoking, and braising are all used. Dishes are made fiery hot by the addition of pure chile, while garlic, and shallots to add supporting flavor to braising liquids and sauces. Hunan cuisine is very seasonal, ranging from heavy and hearty in the cold months to light and even chilled preparations in the summer. Hunan cuisine has contributed more than 4,000 dishes to China's culinary repertoire.

A word on wine with Chinese Cuisine

Chinese dishes often contain multiple ingredients that wreak havoc on wine. Chile peppers, vinegars, pickled ingredients, as well as fermented bean pastes, fish, and tofu can pose a real challenge, and in most cases, your best reds and whites should be left in the cellar (or pause between bites and sips).

The other challenge is that a traditional Chinese meal usually means multiple dishes on the table at once, with a wide-ranging spectrum of flavors and textures. Rather than search for the perfect pairing, the best tactic is to select one or more versatile wines. In general, white and rosé wines tend to work better with most styles of Chinese cuisine, especially off-dry, fruity styles. Remember that for the spiciest Hunan and Szechuan dishes, fuller bodied, fruit-forward wines with a pinch of sweetness (or impression of sweetness) and 13.5 to 14 percent alcohol, served very cool, such as Gewurztraminer, Viognier, Pinot Gris, or Grüner Veltliner, all mitigate the burn and refresh the palate. If you must serve a red, opt for light, zesty, low-tannin, and low/no oak wine, such as Gamay, Pinot Noir, Zweigelt, Barbera, Tempranillo, Frappato, or Valpolicella, served chilled.

For the generally lighter, less pungent flavors of Cantonese and Mandarin cuisines, especially steamed or delicately poached seafood items, crisp, dry, stony wines like Pinot Grigio, Riesling, unoaked Chardonnay, or Chenin Blanc can enhance the flavor of the food. For umami-rich dishes like steamed clams with black beans, avoid tannic reds and opt instead for a chilled Mosel Riesling, crisp Chablis, Tavel rosé, or similar, for best chances of success.

For richer braised meat dishes with more earthy flavors like *Xiaoxing wine* (a Sherry or dry Madeira-like grain-based wine) and ginger-braised veal cheeks, a silky-rich, new world–style Pinot Noir, or generous Argentine Malbec works. For heartier roasted dishes where the toasty flavor of wood-aged wines can be echoed, try an Aussie Shiraz or Spanish Rioja.

Dim sum, snacks, and soups

This section offers a glimpse at a few of the more wine-friendly dishes out of hundreds that are rolled around dim sum halls or served as lighter bites in restaurants. As with all Chinese meals, these plates all hit the table in quick succession or simultaneously, so use the suggested wine style pairings offered in Table 17-10 as general guidelines as to which types are likely to work best across several plates. When in doubt, go for a soft, slightly off-dry bubbly like Prosecco for maximum versatility.

Table 17-10	Pairing Wine with Chinese Dim Sum		
Culinary Style	*Dish Name*	*Best Wine Style (Example)*	*Alternative Wine Style (Example)*
Szechuan	Spicy braised shrimp with ginger, soy, Xiaoxing wine, chile bean paste, scallion	White: Lightweight, crisp, and stony (Marlborough Sauvignon Blanc)	Rosé: Dry (Rioja rosado)
Cantonese	Har gau (wheat starch dumplings with shrimp, scallion)	White: Lightweight, crisp, and stony (Alsace Pinot Blanc)	White: Lightweight, crisp, and stony, sparkling rosé (Carneros traditional method)

(continued)

Table 17-10 *(continued)*

Culinary Style	Dish Name	Best Wine Style (Example)	Alternative Wine Style (Example)
Cantonese	Siu mai won ton dumplings with ground pork, shrimp, wood ear, scallion	White: Lightweight, crisp, and stony (Clare Valley Riesling)	White: Lightweight, crisp, and stony, sparkling (Penedes Cava)
Cantonese	Steamed scallops in black bean sauce with ginger, garlic, scallion	Rosé: Off-dry (new world off-dry rosé)	Red: Light-bodied, bright, zesty, low tannins (Beaujolais Villages)
Mandarin	Jiaozi pork and cabbage dumpling with chile dipping sauce, scallions	White: Lightweight, crisp, and stony sparkling (Prosecco)	White: Lightweight, crisp, and stony (Mosel Riesling Kabinett)
Hunan	Scallop soup with ham, mushroom, dinger, scallion, sesame	White: Full-bodied, soft, wood-aged (Napa Valley Sauvignon Blanc)	White: Aromatic, fruity, round (Austria Grüner Veltliner)

Poultry and meat

For the poultry and meat dishes listed in Table 17-11, focus on the sauce/principal ingredients rather than the protein. It's the rich array of flavorings used that will make or break the match.

Table 17-11 **Pairing Wine with Chinese Meat Dishes**

Culinary Style	Dish Name	Best Wine Style (Example)	Alternative Wine Style (Example)
Szechuan	Kung pao chicken (with chiles, peanuts, vegetables)	White: Lightweight, crisp, and stony (Wachau Grüner Veltliner)	White: Aromatic, fruity, round (Santa Ynez Viognier)

Szechuan	Dry shredded beef with ginger, garlic, pepper paste, carrot, chile, scallion	Red: Medium-full bodied, balanced, moderately tannic (Sonoma Pinot Noir)	White: Full-bodied, soft, wood-aged (Bordeaux Blanc Semillon)
Cantonese	Sweet and sour pork with pineapple, green pepper, onion	White: Lightweight, crisp, and stony off-dry (Niagara semi-dry Riesling)	White: Aromatic, fruity, round (Anjou Blanc Chenin Blanc)
Cantonese	Steamed spareribs with fermented black beans, chile pepper	White: Full-bodied, soft, wood-aged (Sonoma Chardonnay)	Red: Medium-full bodied, balanced, moderately tannic (Victoria Shiraz)
Mandarin	Peking duck with pancakes, spring onions, hoisin sauce	White: Lightweight, crisp, and stony (Marlborough Sauvignon Blanc)	Red: Full, ripe, and fruity (Russian River Pinot Noir)
Hunan	General Tao's breaded chicken with dark soy, ginger, garlic	White: Aromatic, fruity, round (Santa Barbara white Rhône blend)	Rosé: Dry (Côtes de Provence)

Fish and seafood

As with meat dishes, focus more on the accompanying sauce and principal flavorings, rather than the particular fish when choosing your wine pairing. Chinese fish and seafood dishes are rarely simple or subtle preparations, so you'll need to engage aromatic and crisp whites and rosés, as well as sparkling wines to make it all work. Table 17-12 lays out some popular fish and seafood dishes with suitable wine styles to match.

Table 17-12	Pairing Wine with Chinese Fish Dishes		
Culinary Style	*Dish Name*	*Best Wine Style (Example)*	*Alternative Wine Style (Example)*
Szechuan	Braised carp in spicy sauce of chile bean paste, black fungus, scallion	White: Aromatic, fruity, round (Austria Grüner Veltliner)	Rosé: Dry (Côtes de Provence)
Szechuan	Fried lobster with chile-peanut sauce, sesame, garlic, scallion, ginger	White: Aromatic, fruity, round (Chile aromatic blend)	White: Lightweight, crisp, and stony, off-dry (Alsace Riesling)
Cantonese	Steamed sea bass with sesame, ginger, peppercorn, fresh coriander	White: Lightweight, crisp and stony (Sonoma Sauvignon Blanc)	White: Aromatic, fruity, round (McLaren Vale Roussanne)
Cantonese	Curried crab with bean thread noodles, scallion, ginger	White: Lightweight, crisp, and stony (Austria Riesling)	White: Aromatic, fruity, round (Willamette Valley Pinot Gris)
Mandarin	Crispy fried lake perch with sweet and sour sauce	White: Lightweight, crisp, and stony (Vouvray demi-sec Chenin Blanc)	White: Lightweight, crisp, off-dry sparkling (Prosecco)
Hunan	Crispy fried snapper with mushroom soy, chile, carrot, scallion, bamboo shoot, fresh coriander	White: Lightweight, crisp, and stony (Sancerre Sauvignon Blanc)	White: Lightweight, crisp, and stony (South Australia Riesling)

Rice and noodles

China has a huge repertoire of rice and noodle dishes, many of which can be surprisingly wine-friendly, especially with softer, aromatic wines both white and occasionally red. Table 17-13 shows a few popular dishes along with their best wine matches.

Table 17-13   Pairing Wine with Chinese Rice and Noodles

Culinary Style	Dish Name	Best Wine Style (Example)	Alternative Wine Style (Example)
Szechuan	Egg noodles with beef, star anise, bok choy, tomatoes, bean paste, fresh coriander	White: Aromatic, fruity, round (Wachau Grüner Veltliner)	Red: Light-bodied, bright, zesty, low tannins (Carneros Pinot Noir)
Cantonese	Bean thread noodles with curried crab, garlic, fresh coriander	White: Aromatic, fruity, round (Greece Malagouzia)	Rosé: Off-dry (new world, soft, and fruity rosé)
Cantonese	Stir-fried glutinous rice with Chinese sausage, dried shrimp, bacon, garlic, scallions	White: Lightweight, crisp and stony (Napa Valley Fume Blanc)	Rosé: Dry (Rioja Grenache)
Cantonese	Fried pork chow mein with black mushroom, bean sprouts, chives, ginger	White: Aromatic, fruity, round (Alsace Gewürztraminer)	White: Full-bodied, soft, wood-aged (Chile Viognier)
Mandarin	Egg fried rice with green peas, shallot, sesame, scallions	White: Aromatic, fruity, round (Argentina Torrontés)	White: Full-bodied, soft, wood-aged (Santa Barbara Chardonnay)
Mandarin	Fried rice with lop cheung sausage, egg, oyster sauce, garlic	White: Aromatic, fruity, round (Central Coast Pinot Gris)	White: Off-dry, lightweight, crisp, and stony (Mosel Riesling spätlese)
Hunan	Shredded chicken fried rice with egg, chile, soy, sesame, scallion	White: Off-dry, lightweight, crisp, and stony (Mosel Riesling spätlese)	White: Aromatic, fruity, round (Alsace Gewürztraminer)
Hunan	Rice noodles with chile fried beef, eggplant, pickled radish, scallion, soy, sesame, ginger	White: Aromatic, fruity, round (New Zealand Gewürztraminer)	Rosé: Dry (Pinot Noir rosé)

Vegetable-based dishes

Vegetarians are happy in China, because Chinese cuisine offers one of the most creative and flavorful repertoires of non-meat dishes anywhere. Stick to crisp and aromatic whites and zesty reds for the most part. Table 17-14 lists a few popular vegetable-based dishes with suitable wine pairings.

Table 17-14		Pairing Wine with Chinese Vegetarian Dishes	
Culinary Style	*Dish Name*	*Best Wine Style (Example)*	*Alternative Wine Style (Example)*
Szechuan	Spicy cucumber, baby eggplant, red pepper, dried chile, scallion	White: Aromatic, fruity, round (South Africa Sauvignon Blanc)	White: Lightweight, crisp and stony (Vinho Verde Alvarinho)
Szechuan	Spicy bean curd rolls with carrot, bean sprouts, vinegar dip	White: Lightweight, crisp and stony (Eden Valley Riesling)	Rosé: Off-dry (California white Zinfandel)
Cantonese	Wok fried bean curd with sesame oil, garlic chives, red bean paste	White: Aromatic, fruity, round (Wachau Grüner Veltliner)	Red: Light-bodied, bright, zesty, low tannins (California Grenache)
Mandarin	Bamboo shoots with mushroom, garlic, garlic chives	White: Aromatic, fruity, round (Okanagan Valley aromatic blend)	Rosé: Dry (new world fruity rosé)
Hunan	Wok-fried spicy cucumber with dried prawns	White: Lightweight, crisp, and stony (Marlborough Sauvignon Blanc)	White: Aromatic, fruity, round (Barossa Viognier)

Venturing to Japan and Japanese Cuisine

Japanese cuisine is founded on impeccable ingredients and meticulous preparation. Seemingly simple items like sushi take years to learn to prepare; a sushi chef must train under a master for at least ten years before being considered proficient. Although the West has influenced Japanese cuisine (most notably after the Meji Restoration Period of 1868 when the Emperor lifted the ban on red meat and promoted a new cuisine known as *Yōshoku*, a Japanese form of European cuisine), it still retains its staunchly traditional approach and quasi-religious devotion to purity.

The umami-taste sensation was brought to light and defined in Japan (refer to Chapter 2 for details), and remains a critical element in most dishes. The Holy Trinity of Japanese food ingredients is considered to be

- ✔ Miso (fermented soy bean paste)
- ✔ Bonito (dried, smoked tuna shavings used for *dashi* broth)
- ✔ Yuzu (a small Japanese type lemon with piercing aromas)

All three figure prominently in many recipes. In essence, Japanese food is a deceivingly simple cuisine that delivers complex tastes, textures, and flavors. And more importantly, it's also the most generally wine-friendly Asian cuisine, given the Japanese focus on purity of flavor and general avoidance of hot spice (aside from wasabi).

The delicate and pure flavors of Japanese cuisine are best highlighted by equally pure and delicate wines. Light, crisp, unoaked selections are your best allies at the Japanese table, including dry sparkling wines. When serving red, look for older bottles in which the astringent bite of tannin will have softened into a silky texture, yet still braced by acids (and avoid heaps of wasabi). The approach of pairing based on relative weight usually works best. Try sushi or sashimi with a lean, crisp, white or sparkling wine, such as Riesling or Champagne; move up the intensity scale to *yakitori* (grilled skewered meat) accompanied by a lightly oaked Chardonnay or silky Pinot Noir, and step it up another level with a dish such as charbroiled mushroom-stuffed quail, paired with a medium-full balanced red like Nero d'Avola from Sicily.

Maki sushi, nigiri sushi, and sashimi

The image of sliced raw fish, seaweed, and rice is inextricably linked to Japan, even if sushi is originally a Chinese concept. Chinese monks originated the idea of pressing fish together with rice and seaweed as a means of preservation in the days before refrigeration. The technique took hold and flourished in Japan, and by the end of the Edo Period (the mid-1800s), it was refined into the artful, varied, fastidiously prepared food that is familiar today. Considering that sushi is almost invariably ordered as a platter (or a boat) containing various types of fish, shellfish, and other more exotic ingredients, pairing wines to individual types of sushi is impractical. Table 17-15 suggests both the best general style categories of wine, as well as a couple of personal favorite wines to serve with a typical sushi platter containing several types. But ultimately the range of possibilities is broad.

Unlike sushi, which incorporates rice, sashimi is straight sliced raw fish, usually served with soy sauce and wasabi. Sashimi, too, is generally ordered as a platter with various types of fish, so again specific recommended pairings are of little practical use. The sensible strategy is to select a versatile wine that can cover the range of flavors, textures, and oil contents of multiple fish.

Rolls are more complex preparations involving multiple ingredients including avocado, various vegetables, egg, and spicy mayonnaise along with some type of fish or shellfish. The spicier the roll, the tougher the match, but as with sushi and sashimi, because rolls are usually part of a larger meal, a flexible wine such as one of those I suggest here is a smart choice.

Table 17-15 — Pairing Wine with Japanese Sushi and Sashimi

Local Dish Name (English Name)	Best Wine Style (Example)	Alternative Wine Style (Example)
Nigiri-zushi moriawase (nigiri sushi set, including items like maguro (tuna), unagi (eel), suzuki (sea bass), hamachi (yellowtail), tako (octopus)	White: Lightweight, crisp, and stony sparkling (Champagne blanc de blancs or other traditional method sparkling; also Prosecco Brut)	White: Aromatic, fruity, round (Austria Grüner Veltliner)
Sushi moriawase (combo maki/nigiri sushi set, including cucumber, salmon, tuna, shrimp rolls)	White: Lightweight, crisp, and stony (Mosel-Saar Riesling kabinett)	White: Aromatic, fruity, round (Friuli Pinot Grigio)
Tsukuri moriawase (assorted lean sashimi set, including ebi (shrimp), o'hyou (halibut), ma-dai (snapper), hamachi (yellowtail))	White: Lightweight, crisp, and stony (Rias Baixas Albariño; Loire Valley Chenin Blanc; Muscadet)	White: Lightweight, crisp, and stony (Vinho Verde)
Tsukuri moriawase (assorted fatty sashimi set, including otoro (tuna belly), saba (mackerel), sake (salmon), hotate (scallop))	White: Lightweight, crisp, and stony (Marlborough Sauvignon Blanc)	Red: Light-bodied, bright, zesty, low tannins (Carneros Pinot Noir)
Special hard rolls (including futomaki (salmon roll), spider roll (soft shell crab roll))	White: Aromatic, fruity, round (Central Coast Viognier)	White: Lightweight, crisp, and stony (Rias Baixas Albariño)
Uni (sea urchin)	White: Aromatic, fruity, round (Alsace Gewürztraminer)	White: Lightweight, crisp, and stony (Rias Baixas Albariño)

Rice and noodles

The Japanese are noodle eaters. Many types such as *ramen, shiritaki, sōmen, udon, hirasume,* and the popular *soba* (buckwheat) noodles are appreciated in a variety of preparations, from ice cold to chilled, deep-fried, or steeped in broth. Noodles are a significant part of the daily Japanese diet. Rice, too, is of course very popular and culturally significant; Japanese samurai were paid in *koku,* originally a measure of rice sufficient to feed one person for a year.

As with most relatively neutral starches, wine pairings for Japanese noodles and rice dishes are dictated by what they're dressed and served with. Considering that soy sauce and sesame oil, and mushrooms and broth (umami-rich things) are common accompaniments, you want to avoid big, tannic red wines. Umami-rich foods enhance their astringency and harden the texture. Mature red wines, crisp whites, or succulent, sweet-fruited whites are safe options. Table 17-16 provides some wine suggestions.

You won't find much synergy between broth-based noodle preparations and wine. The liquid will be mostly gone from your mouth by the time you reach for a sip (getting both wine and liquid soup to mingle in your mouth at once is tough). Thus the wine acts more as a palate refresher or interlude between spoonfuls, and you needn't fuss too much about the perfect pairing. Dry fortified wines like Sherry and Madeira, on the other hand, can provide some complementary pleasure with their generous mouth-feel and body (plus they're seemingly richer in umami than most wines, which enhances the broth's savory side, as it does with traditional beef consommé).

Table 17-16   Pairing Wine with Japanese Rice and Noodle Dishes

Local Dish Name (English Name)	Best Wine Style (Example)	Alternative Wine Style (Example)
Kaki-agé donburi (tempura prawn rice bowl with shoyu)	White: Lightweight, crisp, and stony (Vinho Verde)	White: Lightweight, crisp, and stony (Chablis Chardonnay)
Tori gohan (chicken breast with rice, shiitake mushroom)	White: Lightweight, crisp, and stony (Alsace Pinot Blanc)	White: Lightweight, crisp, and stony (Napa Valley Sauvignon Blanc)
Umi no sachi no udon (cold seafood udon with mussels, clams, prawns, broccoli)	White: Lightweight, crisp, and stony (Sancerre Sauvignon Blanc)	White: Aromatic, fruity, round (Santa Barbara County Viognier)

(continued)

Table 17-16 *(continued)*

Local Dish Name (English Name)	Best Wine Style (Example)	Alternative Wine Style (Example)
Kinoko ramen (ramen noodles with kombu broth and forest mushrooms)	Dry fortified white: (Fino Sherry)	Red: Light-bodied, bright, zesty, low tannins (Santa Lucia Highlands Pinot Noir)
Hiyamugi (cold noodles with shrimp, mushrooms, dashi egg)	White: Aromatic, fruity, round (Wachau Grüner Veltliner)	White: Lightweight, crisp, and stony (Columbia Valley Riesling)
Zarusoba (buckwheat noodles with nori seaweed)	White: Lightweight, crisp, and stony (Muscadet)	Late harvest: medium-dry (German/Austrian Riesling)

Izakaya cuisine: Tempura, robata, yakitori, kushiyaki

The popularity of *izakayas* outside of Japan has exploded in the last decade. The word *izakaya* itself is a compound of two Japanese words: *I*, meaning "to stay," and *sakaya*, a "saké shop." Originally a simple sake drinking hole that served limited food, the izakaya has evolved to become what you'd call today a sort of Japanese-style gastro-pub offering mostly snacks ranging from traditional things like *yakitori* (skewered meat), *robata* (food charbroiled over a pit), and *sashimi* (sliced raw fish), to more complex dishes with a little Euro-Japanese fusion influence. The izakaya boom has taken hold in the West, and new establishments are popping up in urban areas at a fast pace. Table 17-17 previews a few wine suggestions with classic izakaya food.

Table 17-17	Pairing Wine with Japanese Izakaya Dishes	
Local Dish Name (English Name)	Best Wine Style (Example)	Alternative Wine Style (Example)
Ebi mayo (shrimp tempura with spicy mayonnaise)	White: Lightweight, crisp, and stony (Chablis)	White: Lightweight, crisp, and stony, sparkling) (Champagne rosé)
Takoyaki (deep-fried octopus balls with scallion, Worcestershire mayo)	White: Lightweight, crisp, and stony (Vinho Verde Alvarinho)	White: Aromatic, fruity, round (Santorini Assyrtiko)

Local Dish Name (English Name)	Best Wine Style (Example)	Alternative Wine Style (Example)
Tai no kaisen salad (sea bream salad with shaved daikon, carrot, ponzu dressing)	White: Lightweight, crisp, and stony (Marlborough Sauvignon Blanc)	White: Aromatic, fruity, round (Willamette Valley Pinot Gris)
Uzura no kinoko zume (charbroiled mushroom stuffed quail with gingko nuts, balsamic)	Red: Medium-full bodied, balanced, moderately tannic (Sicily Nero d'Avola)	Red: Light-bodied, bright, zesty, low tannins (Valpolicella)
Yakitori (chicken and leek skewers with mirin-soy glaze)	White: Full-bodied, soft, wood-aged (White Rioja Crianza)	Red: Medium-full bodied, balanced, moderately tannic (Central Otago Pinot Noir)
Negi pon (skewered pork loin with scallion, ponzu)	White: Lightweight, crisp, and stony (Friuli Pinot Grigio)	White: Full-bodied, soft, wood-aged (White Burgundy Chardonnay)
Gindara saikyo (black cod with sweet white miso)	White: Full-bodied, soft, wood-aged (Burgundy Chardonnay (Meursault))	White: Full-bodied, soft, wood-aged (Sonoma Coast Chardonnay)
Wafu supearibu (soy grilled spareribs)	Red: Light-bodied, bright, zesty, low tannins (Sonoma Pinot Noir)	White: Aromatic, fruity, round (Wachau Grüner Veltliner)
Asari no suimono mizo jitate (littleneck clams in miso broth)	White: Full-bodied, soft, wood-aged (Russian River Chardonnay)	White: Aromatic, fruity, round (Alsace Pinot Gris)

Sweets and desserts

Like savory Japanese dishes, desserts are clean yet intricate, and usually reflective of the seasons. *Agar agar,* a gelatin derived from seaweed, is commonly used to firm up many of the jellies, sauces, pastry fillings, and confectionaries. The Japanese are very fond of the plum *(boshi),* and when pickled, it's used for a multitude of dessert preparations including ice cream, fillings, sauces, and jellies. You can frequently encounter other ingredients, such as cherries, chestnuts, green tea, pears, and chocolate. The popular favorite green tea ice cream, on the other hand, numbs the palate with cold, making wine (or anything else) tough to really synergize, so enjoy separately. Check out Table 17-18 for some wine pairing suggestions with desserts.

Table 17-18	Pairing Wine with Japanese Desserts	
Local Dish Name (English Name)	**Best Wine Style (Example)**	**Alternative Wine Style (Example)**
Hakuto no jeli yose (white peach jelly)	Sweet: Late harvest (Mosel-Saar Riesling)	Sweet: Icewine (Niagara Peninsula Riesling)
Limushi no imo an ikomi (sticky rice cakes with sweet yams)	Sweet: Fortified amber (Oloroso Dulce Sherry)	Sweet fortified: Amber (California Orange Muscat)
Kanten yose (seasonal fruit in jelly)	Sweet: Icewine (sparkling) (Niagara Peninsula Riesling)	Sweet: Sparkling (Piedmont Moscato d'Asti)
Ichigo no garutan (strawberry gratin)	Sweet: Sparkling (Piedmont Brachetto d'Acqui)	Sweet: Icewine (Niagara Peninsula Cabernet Franc Icewine)

Sampling Korea and Korean Offerings

Korean cuisine has been less widely exported than Chinese and Japanese cuisine, though it is growing in popularity. If you've experienced it, you'll probably conjure up flavorful images of barbecued meats *(bulkogi)* surrounded by plates of spicy pickled vegetables (cucumber, Napa cabbage, radishes, scallions, among others) collectively known as *kimchi,* which automatically arrive at your table to accompany the rest of the meal.

Korean cuisine offers up an abundance of salty, sweet, hot, sour, and savory tastes. Ingredients, such as soy sauce, sugar, rice vinegar, salt, garlic, sesame, chile, soybean paste, and hot chile pepper paste play a primary flavoring role in many dishes. Korean cooking differs from other Asian cuisines in its reliance on the uniquely Korean condiment called *gochujang* (or *kochujang*), a savory, fiery hot paste made from red chile, glutinous rice, fermented soybeans, and salt, naturally fermented over several years in earthen pots stored outdoors. Like elsewhere in Asia, rice is a dietary staple, also doubly useful to mitigate intense spice.

Korean food poses a challenge for wine pairing on two levels. Traditional meals incorporate several main dishes served at once, surrounded by a wide assortment of side dishes called *banchan.* With so many different tastes, textures, and flavors on the table at once, finding a single wine that will sing with everything is tough. Furthermore, the near-ubiquitous combination of hot and sour (pickled foods) is a killer for most wine. The best strategy is to focus on the main dishes and not get distracted by the side dishes nor reach for a sip of wine straight after a bite of kim chi. I've found bold, rich, ripe reds and whites to be most effective in handling the savory dishes like bulkogi, especially Rhone-style white blends and spicy, zesty, jammy reds like Aussie Shiraz and California Zinfandel — just remember to keep these lightly chilled for maximum enjoyment when the spice is turned up. Semi-sweet, late harvest whites fare even better, though are tough to enjoy throughout an entire meal.

Rice, porridge, and noodles

Rice isn't indigenous to Korea and was quite expensive when it was first imported. Over time it became the principal starch, but cooks frequently mixed it with other grains, such as millet and barley, to stretch availability. This is evident in popular dishes like *boribap,* rice cooked with barley. Rice or rice flour also finds its way into many other preparations including griddle cakes, pancakes, congee, or gruel, occasionally mixed with vegetables, seafood, and meats to make a complete, satisfying one-pot meal. Noodles are also relatively new to mainstream Korean cuisine, having been reserved almost exclusively for special occasions before World War II. Noodles are mostly used in hot broths with assorted flavorings and ingredients. Refer to Table 17-19 for some wine suggestions.

Table 17-19   Pairing Wine with Korean Rice and Noodle Dishes

Local Dish Name (English Name)	Best Wine Style (Example)	Alternative Wine Style (Example)
Bibim bap (rice medley with shredded beef, shiitake, carrot, egg, sprouts, hot sauce)	White: Full-bodied, soft, wood-aged (Paso Robles Rhône style white blend)	Red: Medium-full bodied, balanced, moderately tannic (Central Coast Syrah)
Bi bim guk su (spicy cold somen noodles with cucumber, kimchi, pear, sesame oil)	White: Aromatic, fruity, round (Alsace Gewürztraminer)	White: Aromatic, fruity, round (Wachau Grüner Veltliner)
Bi bim naeng myeon (spicy buckwheat noodles with egg, cucumber)	White: Off-dry, light-weight, crisp, and stony (Vouvray demi-sec Chenin blanc)	White: Aromatic, fruity, round (off-dry) (Alsace Pinot Gris)
Japchae myeon (glass noodles with ground pork, shiitake, carrot, soy, chile paste, garlic, scallions)	White: Full-bodied, soft, wood-aged (Burgundy Chardonnay)	Rosé: Dry (Tavel Grenache)

Korean barbeque and braised dishes

Korean BBQ is the most well-known (and exported) style of Korean cuisine. The most popular restaurants abroad are *bulkogi* (meaning "fire meat"), where you sit at a table with your own griddle to cook an assortment of thinly sliced marinated meats served with a variety of side dishes — interactive dining at its finest. In addition to bulkogi, stewed meat and seafood dishes are also usually served as part of the main meal to add contrast to the flavor of grilled foods. Table 17-20 has some wine suggestions for Korean barbeque.

Table 17-20	Pairing Wine with Korean Barbeque	
Local Dish Name (English Name)	*Best Wine Style (Example)*	*Alternative Wine Style (Example)*
Dak nal ke jo tim (spicy chicken wings with honey-pepper BBQ sauce)	White: Lightweight, crisp, and stony, off-dry (Alsace Riesling)	Red: Full, deep, robust, turbocharged, chewy texture (Napa Valley Zinfandel)
Samgyeopsal gui (charbroiled pork belly with chile, honey, hot pepper, mushroom, soy)	Red: Medium-full bodied, balanced, moderately tannic (Maipo Valley Cabernet Sauvignon blend)	Red: Full, deep, robust, turbocharged, chewy texture (Barossa Shiraz)
Soegogi gui (grilled beef with cucumber, garlic, mushrooms, pepper paste, soy sauce)	Red: Light-bodied, bright, zesty, low tannins (Marlborough Pinot Noir)	White: Full-bodied, soft, wood-aged (Rhône Valley white blend)
La kalbi (BBQ ribs with Korean pear, honey, soy, sesame)	Red: Full, deep, robust, turbocharged, chewy texture (Dry Creek Valley Zinfandel)	White: Full-bodied, soft, wood-aged (Carneros Chardonnay)
Bulkogi (marinated, grilled rib-eye steak with soy, garlic, ginger, sesame)	Red: Full, deep, robust, turbocharged, chewy texture (Napa Valley Cabernet Sauvignon)	Red: Medium-full bodied, balanced, moderately tannic (Argentina Malbec)

Looking Closer at the Indian Subcontinent

The Indian subcontinent, which includes Bangladesh, Pakistan, Sri Lanka, and India, is a vast region with more than 1.5 billion people where many culinary philosophies coexist. Internationally, the cuisine is usually lopped under the generic name of Indian food, but from such a large and populous area, regional variations abound. Like the many dialects of the area, the cuisine can vary from city to city and even from village to village.

Similarities between regions also exist, particularly in the importance placed on the use of abundant and varied spicing. Subcontinental food is deeply complex with multiple layers of aroma and flavor; chefs here spend a lifetime perfecting the right admixture of spice in blends like *garam masala* and curry powder, often closely guarded family secrets. Each spice blend has a purpose, used to enhance aroma, color, or taste, and even the order in which spices are added have a dramatic effect on the outcome of the dish.

Rather than divide by country, I delve into the food of this region in the following sections by dish type such as curries or rice-based dishes, much as you would see on a typical Indian restaurant menu.

A word on wine with foods of the subcontinent

Wine rarely springs to mind when considering what to drink with Indian food. Most people consider the abundant spice and heat a bad match for wine, and reach for beer instead. But unlike the fiery and pungent foods from some other parts of the world, the mark of excellent Indian cuisine is a balance of flavors, aromas, and tastes. Sweet, sour, bitter, salty, and hot are combined to balance one another, and dishes are rarely dominated by any single taste. And balanced dishes, no matter what level of flavor intensity, can be successfully paired with the right wine. Many of the herbs and spices used, such as cardamom, ginger, turmeric, clove, star anise, and coriander, find their counterparts in wine. I can't help but think that if India had been colonized by the Portuguese or Spanish instead of the British, then wine would be more commonly served alongside Indian food. The growing interest in wine in this part of the world, as well as the development and expansion of India's own homegrown wine industry will surely see wine more often on Indian tables.

Common wisdom has it that off-dry aromatic whites are the safest bets with Indian cuisine, and indeed this is often, if not always, the case. The burn of spice is most effectively handled by sweetness, or the impression of sweetness (ripe fruit) along with cold serving temperature (refer to Chapter 2 for more information). Capsaicin, the compound that gives chiles their burn, is also soluble in alcohol, meaning that higher alcohol wines, up to about 14 percent, not only have the weight to match heavy Indian dishes, but they're also more effective at cooling the fire.

I find the most effective overall strategies are matching weight with weight, and contrasting flavors (refer to Chapter 5). Indian food is quite rich with often high fat content (through the use of cream, yogurt, clarified butter), requiring wines of equally substantial body to match, while ripe fruit flavors provide a pleasant contrast to deep, earthy spices, much like the fruit chutneys served alongside Indian dishes. Complementary matches can also work; *sotolone,* the very potent aromatic compound chiefly responsible for the pungent, earthy-sweet flavor of curries, is also found in some wines, especially older, barrel-aged wines, and wines aged under a veil of yeast like the *Vin Jaune* of the Jura region in France.

Avoid, bone-dry, dusty, astringent, and very oaky red wines with Indian foods. The spice and heat make them taste even more bitter, harder, and mouth-puckering, and crush any delicacy or nuance.

Tiffin: Light meals and snacks

Tiffin is a term used today to describe any light meal or snack. The word came into use in British India between the 1600s to 1900s and derives from the English slang word *tiffing* meaning "taking a drink or small sip," sort of the equivalent of afternoon tea. Today, typical tiffins include *dosas* (fermented crepe or pancake made from rice batter or black lentils), *idlis* (steamed batter cakes), *samosas* (a stuffed, deep-fried pastry), *kofta* (the Indian equivalent of the meatball, also made with seafood or vegetables), *pakora* (fritters, usually with onion), *tikka* (chunks of skewered meat or fish cooked in a tandoor oven), and many more. In India, tiffin also refers to a lunch that's packed in a three-tiered metal lunch box, also known by the same name.

Champagne and sparkling wines are a fine match for most tiffin, especially demi-sec (rosé) sparkling, with its pinch of residual sweetness. Table 17-21 lists some additional wine suggestions for these dishes.

Table 17-21	Pairing Wine with Indian Snacks		
Country of Origin	*Local Dish Name (English Name)*	*Best Wine Style (Example)*	*Alternative Wine Style (Example)*
India	Samosa (deep-fried pastries filled with potato, pea, coriander)	White: Lightweight, crisp, and stony (sparkling) (Prosecco)	White: Aromatic, fruity, round (Wachau Grüner Veltliner)
India	Kofta (lamb meatballs with garlic, chile, yogurt, cumin, mint)	White: Full-bodied, soft, wood-aged (Sonoma Chardonnay)	White: Aromatic, fruity, round (Alsace Gewürztraminer)

Country of Origin	Local Dish Name (English Name)	Best Wine Style (Example)	Alternative Wine Style (Example)
India	Aloo ki tikki (fried potato cakes with turmeric, chile, chaat masala)	White: Aromatic, fruity, round (Alsace Dry Muscat)	White: Full-bodied, soft, wood-aged (Northern Rhône white blend)
Pakistan	Anokhay kabaab (minced beef kebabs with cumin, potato, mint)	White: Full-bodied, soft, wood-aged (Napa Valley Fumé Blanc)	Red: Medium-full bodied, balanced, moderately tannic (Barossa shiraz)
Bangladesh	Haleem (fried chicken and lentil balls with fresh ginger, onion)	White: Lightweight, crisp, and stony (Mosel-Saar Riesling) kabinett	White: Full-bodied, soft, wood-aged (Napa Valley Chardonnay)

Curries

The word *curry* causes some confusion. People in India today use it to mean simply "gravy," but it has come to be applied to a wide variety of heavily-sauced dishes. Curry is believed to derive from the Tamil word *kaari,* meaning literally "sauce," but it applies to any main course to be eaten with rice.

Indian curries are made by cooking fish or meat and/or vegetables along with assorted spices, seasoning, and thickening agents to create a deeply layered dish. They come under many names; just watch out for the ones labeled *vindaloo* or *phaal,* the hottest of the curry family.

Aside from rice, a popular accompaniment for curries is fresh-baked *naan,* flat bread made with yogurt, egg, and ghee, cooked in a clay oven *(tandoor),* best used to sop up the thick sauce left in the bottom of the curry bowl and temper the burn. Other assorted unleavened breads such as *roti, paratha* (made with ghee and flour, rolled and folded numerous times to create a light flaky texture), or *chapati,* flat, whole wheat bread cooked in a skillet, are also frequently served with curries.

If you insist on drinking wine with the most highly spiced curries at the upper end of the intensity scale like Goan vindaloos, I'd go with full-bodied, fruit-forward, new world–style reds with ripe, well-rounded tannins and ample black fruit flavors. Although this match may not be perfect, big plush reds are about the only wines that can stack up against the penetrating taste, flavor, and burn of such curries. Australian Shiraz, and Californian Zinfandel, Chilean Cabernet or Carmenere, Argentine Malbec, southern Portuguese red blends, and fruity Spanish Tempranillos, for example, stand up well. And one last tip: Serve your whites cold and your reds chilled for maximum harmony and enjoyment. Table 17-22 covers some wine suggestions for these dishes.

Table 17-22	Pairing Wine with Indian Curries		
Country of Origin	*Local Dish Name (English Name)*	*Best Wine Style (Example)*	*Alternative Wine Style (Example)*
India	Rogan josh (braised mutton with yogurt, tomato, ghee, fresh coriander, cardamom)	White: Full-bodied, soft, wood-aged (Santa Barbara County Viognier)	Red: Medium-full bodied, balanced, moderately tannic (Sonoma County Zinfandel)
India	Murgh makhani (butter chicken with chile, ghee, cumin, clove, yogurt, lime, tomato)	White: Full-bodied, soft, wood-aged (Napa Valley Chardonnay)	White: Aromatic, fruity, round (Alsace Gewürztraminer)
India	Bhuna gosht (lamb curry with fried spices, chile ginger, lime, tomatoes, yogurt, fresh coriander)	White: Full-bodied, soft, wood-aged (Santa Barbara Viognier)	Red: Light-bodied, bright, zesty, low tannins (Ribera del Duero Tempranillo joven)
India	Ras chawal (fish curry with lime, turmeric, chile, cashew, garlic, fennel, fresh coriander)	White: Aromatic, fruity, round (Marlborough Sauvignon Blanc)	White: Full-bodied, soft, wood-aged (Southern Rhône white blend)
India	Vindaloo (pork curry with red chile spices, garlic, tamarind, vinegar, onion, jaggery)	Red: Full, deep, and robust, turbocharged, chewy texture (Amador County Zinfandel)	Red: Full, deep, and robust, turbocharged, chewy texture (Barossa Valley Grenache or GSM blend)

Country of Origin	Local Dish Name (English Name)	Best Wine Style (Example)	Alternative Wine Style (Example)
India	Nalli korma (braised lamb shank with cashew, saffron, green chile, masala, yogurt, cardamom)	Red: Full, deep and robust, turbocharged, chewy texture (Napa Valley Merlot)	Red: Full, deep and robust, turbocharged, chewy texture (South Australia Shiraz)
India	Phaal (beef curry with dried chiles, scotch bonnets, tomato, coconut, fennel, ginger)	Red: Full, deep and robust, turbocharged, chewy texture (Barossa Valley Shiraz)	White: Off-dry, late harvest (Alsace Pinot Gris late harvest)
Bangladesh	Do piazz (beef curry cooked with onion, garlic, chile, clove, tamarind, ginger, cardamom)	Red: Full, deep, and robust, turbocharged (McLaren Vale Shiraz/Viognier)	Red: Medium-full bodied, balanced, moderately tannic (Douro Valley red blend)

Vegetables and legumes

The subcontinent may well have the most developed and complex vegetarian cuisine in the world. Driven by both religious beliefs as well as shortage of meat, Indian cooks have learned to be creative with vegetables and legumes, and they have plenty to choose from; the sheer variety available is staggering. As a result, an ingenious approach has evolved for preparing, cooking, and presenting vegetables, with as much focus and attention paid, and as complex textures and flavors created, as for any animal protein-based dishes.

Legumes, including split beans, peas, and lentils, are collectively referred to as *dhal.* Dhals are prepared to the consistency of soup, or thicker and chunkier like a puree, and everywhere in between. Preparation methods and cooking times have an immense effect on the taste, flavor, texture, and aroma of the finished dish, with cooking times ranging from as little as 20 minutes to as long as 20 hours at low temperatures. Dhals can be full meals on their own, but are most often part of a larger range of dishes.

Medium-full bodied aromatic whites, such as Grüner Veltliner, Alsatian-style Gewürztraminers and Pinot Gris, Argentine Torrontés, Viognier (California, Rhône Valley, Chile), and most Rieslings with firm acids, residual sugar, and crisp, penetrating flavors are among your safest bets for the intense aromatics of Indian vegetarian main courses. Table 17-23 lists some wine suggestions.

Table 17-23	Pairing Wine with Indian Vegetarian Dishes		
Country of Origin	*Local Dish Name (English Name)*	*Best Wine Style (Example)*	*Alternative Wine Style (Example)*
India	Aloo gobi (mustard roasted potato, cauliflower, and tomatoes with masala, ginger)	White: Aromatic, fruity, round (Okanagan Valley aromatic white blends)	White: Lightweight, crisp, and stony (Mosel-Saar Riesling kabinett)
India	Saag paneer (fresh pressed Indian cheese with spinach, green peas, fenugreek, garlic, masala)	White: Aromatic, fruity, round (Alsace Pinot Gris)	White: Full-bodied, soft, wood-aged (Condrieu Viognier)
India	Chana masala (chickpeas stewed in yogurt, chile, masala, tamarind, ginger, onion, fresh coriander)	White: Aromatic, fruity, round (Wachau Grüner Veltliner)	White: Aromatic, fruity, round (Rueda Verdejo)
India	Toor dhal (yellow lentils with spices, curry leaf, tomatoes, molasses)	White: Aromatic, fruity, round (Alsace Gewürztraminer)	White: Full-bodied, soft, wood-aged (Jura Chardonnay)
Pakistan	Dahi baingan (eggplant with yogurt, chile, cumin, cardamom, fresh coriander)	White: Lightweight, crisp, and stony (Mosel-Saar Riesling spätlese)	White: Aromatic, fruity, round (California Viognier)

Rices and grains

The subcontinent is rich in rice and grains. Basmati is the most widely encountered, but it's just one of several dozens of long and short-grained varieties of rice, a daily staple served alongside curries and other dishes. The list of specialty rice dishes is long, but each falls into two main categories:

✔ Biryanis are made from plain or fried rice cooked separately from curry, spices, meats, eggs, or vegetables.

✔ Pulaos are plain or fried rice cooked together with all the other spices, seasonings, and ingredients.

Many other savory dishes are made from grains, such as semolina and sevian noodles, made from wheat flour.

Follow the general pairing advice outlined in the section above on vegetarian dishes. Crisp and/or aromatic whites and rosés are widely applicable, although occasionally wood-aged whites can be better matches when ingredients like cashews are added. Table 17-24 focuses on some wines for these dishes.

Table 17-24	Pairing Wine with Indian Rice Dishes		
Country of Origin	*Local Dish Name (English Name)*	*Best Wine Style (Example)*	*Alternative Wine Style (Example)*
India	Vegetable biryianni (basmati rice with onion, assorted vegetables, cardamon, turmeric)	White: Aromatic, fruity, round (Mantinia Moscophilero)	White: Aromatic, fruity, round (Austria Sauvignon Blanc)
Pakistan	Methi pulao (stir-fried basmati rice with tomato, garlic, chile, turmeric)	White: Aromatic, fruity, round (Wachau Grüner Veltliner)	White: Lightweight, crisp, and stony (Mantinia Moscophilero)
Bangladesh	Bhuna khichdi (stir-fried yellow lentil and rice with boiled eggs, clove, chile)	White: Lightweight, crisp, and stony (Austria Riesling)	White: Aromatic, fruity, round (Alsace Gewürztraminer)
Sri Lanka	Kahabath (coconut fried rice with lemongrass, turmeric, cinnamon, curry leaf)	White: Full-bodied, soft, wood-aged (California Viognier)	Rosé: Dry (Tavel Grenache)

Sweets, desserts, and pastries

Mithai is the Hindi-Urdu word that means "sweet food." Desserts and sweets from the subcontinent are an essential part of every meal, though not only for hedonistic reasons. Sweets are often served to aid digestion and are consumed after very spicy meals to help revive the palate and restore equilibrium. It's quite amazing how well a sweet rice and coconut pudding with rose water and raisins can help soothe the tongue's trigeminal nerve (which detects the burn of spice) after an encounter with a fierce vindaloo.

Milk, condensed milk, and sugar form the basis of many sweets, often elegantly decorated with cardamom, colored candy sprinkles, raisins, almonds, pistachios, cashew nuts, and dried fruit, such as guava, pineapple, mango, melon, orange, and cherry. Some of the more popular desserts include *barfi*, a sweet confectionary made from condensed milk with sugar and pistachios; *jalebi*, deep-fried batter dipped in sugar syrup; and *kulfi*, frozen milk or cream, flavored with sugar and spice. Table 17-25 lists some wine pairings for Indian deserts.

Table 17-25	Pairing Wine with Indian Desserts		
Country of Origin	*Local Dish Name (English Name)*	*Best Wine Style (Example)*	*Alternative Wine Style (Example)*
India	Rossogollas (sweetened fresh cheese with pistachios in sugar-milk syrup)	Sweet: Passito (Muscat of Samos)	Sweet: Fortified amber (Oloroso Dulce Sherry)
India	Halva (grated carrots with milk, ghee, sugar, raisins, cardamom, shaved almond)	Sweet: Fortified amber (Sicily Marsala)	Sweet: Icewine (Niagara Peninsula Vidal, oak aged)
India	Barfi (pistachio cake with cardamom, ghee, cloves, sugar, milk)	Sweet: Noble rot (Burgenland beerenauslese)	Sweet: Late harvest/passito (Sicily Moscato)
Pakistan	Akhrot ka halwa (pureed walnut cake with condensed milk, saffron)	Sweet: Noble rot (Tokaji Aszú 5 puttonyos)	Sweet: Fortified amber (Mavrodaphne of Patras)
Pakistan	Bas bussa (semolina cake with coconut, almond)	Sweet: Noble rot (Sauternes)	Sweet: Fortified red (Tawny Port)
Sri Lanka	Wellawahum (coconut-stuffed crepes with cardamom, brown sugar)	Sweet: Passito (Santorini Vinsanto)	Sweet: Noble rot (Burgenland Ausbruch)

Chapter 18

Visiting the Land of Chiles: Mexico and South America

*L*atin America, stretching from the US border to Patagonia, is dominated by the Spanish language of its colonizers, with the notable exceptions of Brazil (Portuguese) and the Caribbean (English, French, and Dutch, among others). Yet despite the European background, outside of a couple of countries like Argentina, Uruguay, and Chile, wine isn't the first thought at dinner time. As with other cuisines that evolved without a true wine culture alongside, there's no reason why you can't enjoy Latin American food with wine.

Finding a selection of suitable wine options can be a challenge when traveling through these regions, especially when you venture beyond major cities and resorts, though the good news is that many traditional Latin American foods are now widely exported. Specialty shops and restaurants are popping up across North America and elsewhere, serving both vibrant Latin American ex-pat communities and adventurous locals. So you can enjoy many great Latino food and wine pairings closer to home, too. This chapter focuses specifically on Mexico and South America.

Going South across the Border: Mexico

Authentic Mexican cuisine is celebrated for its bright, vibrant colors, pungent flavors, and contrasting textures. The term "Mexican food" is somewhat misleading, belying a much more complex patchwork of regional cooking styles. Although Spanish is the most widely spoken language and used for all official functions, the Mexican government recognizes no fewer than 68 indigenous Amerindian languages — just to give you an idea of the complexity of the nation's fabric and culinary heritage.

Beer and tequila/mezcal (and the cocktails made from them) are usually the beverages of choice with Mexican food, though I suspect that has as much to do with cultural conditioning as compatibility. The cuisine of Mexico in fact lends itself well to wine pairings. The degree of spicy heat in most dishes is seldom as fiery as many Asian cuisines, and it comes naturally tempered by cheese, cream, or other heat-curbing ingredients. Considering the ubiquity of the lime, served alongside innumerable dishes to brighten flavors and freshen the palate with its saliva-inducing acidity, there's surely a place for crisp, high acid whites, served well-chilled, which act themselves like a squeeze of lime. Think crisp Riesling, Sauvignon Blanc, or unoaked Chardonnay along with anything else in the same style category, and you're in the right field. Fuller-bodied, creamy, and even oak-aged whites work well with richer fish and pork dishes, as well as those containing a lot of cheese or cream.

For reds, softer, new world–style Pinot Noir and fruity Zinfandel, for example, as well as plush southern Rhône-style red blends fare quite well with roasts, grilled meats, and earthier vegetarian dishes based around legumes and savory, lightly bitter tastes. As with other spicy cuisines, if burning chile is a principal part of the dish, leave the delicate, leaner, bone-dry, more astringent old world–style reds in the cellar for another day.

Appetizers: Soups, salads and starters

Regional cuisine notwithstanding, certain ingredients come up time and again in Mexican recipes, especially limes, tomatoes, onions, coriander (also known as *cilantro*), and *queso fresco,* a mild, soft, fresh cheese (usually cow's and/or goat's milk) that's used to top all manner of tortilla preparations. It's also crumbled in soups and salads because its fat content can temper the sting of chiles. And of course the chile pepper (most famously jalapeño, though dozens of other varieties are also cultivated) is an integral part of the Mexican culinary repertoire.

Having several dishes on the table to start a traditional Mexican meal is common. If that's the case, and you're going with only one wine, select something versatile. Table 18-1 walks you through some specific food and wine pairings for common Mexican starters.

Table 18-1	Finding Wine Pairings with Mexican Appetizers	
Dish Name	*Best Wine Style (Example)*	*Alternative Wine Style (Example)*
Guacamole (mashed avocado with onion, tomato, jalapeño, cilantro, lime)	White: Lightweight, crisp, and stony (Marlborough Sauvignon Blanc)	White: Full-bodied, soft, wood-aged (Carneros Chardonnay)

Dish Name	Best Wine Style (Example)	Alternative Wine Style (Example)
Chiles en nogada (shredded chicken stuffed poblano chile with pomegranate seeds, walnut cream sauce)	White: Aromatic, fruity, round (Aromatic White Blends)	White: Full-bodied, soft, wood-aged (South Australia Riesling)
Chiles rellenos (cornmeal breaded chile peppers stuffed with queso fresco cheese, shredded pork)	White: Aromatic, fruity, round (Austria Grüner Veltliner)	White: Aromatic, fruity, round (Alsace Gewürztraminer)
Pozole (dried corn, pork, and chicken soup with avocado, red onion, cilantro)	White: Aromatic, fruity, round (Chile Viognier)	Fortified: Dry white (Fino Sherry)
Flautas (deep fried tortilla rolls stuffed with chicken or beef, black beans, queso cheese)	Red: Medium-full bodied, balanced, moderately tannic (Paso Robles Zinfandel)	Red: Medium-full bodied, balanced, moderately tannic (Ribera del Duero Tempranillo)
Tamales (masa corn flour loaf stuffed with pork filling, steamed in a corn husk)	Dry rosé: (Tavel Grenache)	White: Sparkling lightweight, crisp, and stony (Spanish Cava)
Empanada (baked pastry turnovers stuffed with pulled beef, green peas, queso)	Red: Medium-full bodied, balanced, moderately tannic (Mendoza Malbec)	Red: Medium-full bodied, balanced, moderately tannic (South Australia Shiraz/Viognier)
Gordita (deep-fried masa harina pastry corn cake stuffed with cheese, meat, beans, potato)	White: Full-bodied, soft, wood-aged (White Bordeaux Semillon)	White: Lightweight, crisp, and stony sparkling (Traditional Method Sparkling)
Ensalada de nopales (cactus salad with tomato, queso añejo, cilantro, lime, onion, olive oil)	White: Lightweight, crisp, and stony (Casablanca Valley Sauvignon Blanc)	White: Aromatic, fruity, round (Campania Falanghina)
Ensalada de aguacate con naranja (avocado and orange salad with cilantro)	Rosé: Off-dry (Sonoma white Zinfandel)	White: Lightweight, crisp, and stony (Napa Valley Sauvignon Blanc)

Meat and seafood

Pork is the most common meat throughout Mexico, though beef is also popular in the north. As you'd expect, the cities, towns, and villages dotting the Pacific and Caribbean coastlines have the freshest seafood. Light, zesty, fruity reds like Gamay or Barbera can be effective for both meat and fish dishes, based on tomatoes and sweet peppers (as in Veracruz style), especially when served with a light chill. Table 18-2 lays out wine pairings for popular meat and seafood dishes in Mexico.

Table 18-2   Pairing Wine with Mexican Meat and Seafood Dishes

Dish Name	Best Wine Style (Example)	Alternative Wine Style (Example)
Cabrito (BBQ kid goat steak with lime, olive oil, salt)	White: Aromatic, fruity, round (Sonoma Sauvignon Blanc)	Red: Light-bodied, bright, zesty, low tannins (Chianti Sangiovese)
Mixiote (pit BBQ cubed whole roast chicken with pasilla chile, cumin, marjoram, garlic, clove)	White: Full-bodied, soft, wood-aged (Chile Viognier)	White: Lightweight, crisp, and stony (Rueda Verdejo)
Birria (lamb and dried roasted pepper stew with corn tortillas, onions, cilantro)	Red: Medium-full bodied, balanced, moderately tannic (Central Coast Syrah)	Red: Medium-full bodied, balanced, moderately tannic (Barossa Shiraz)
Albóndigas (veal and lamb meatballs with vegetables in tomato broth)	Red: Light-bodied, bright, zesty, low tannins (Chianti Sangiovese)	Red: Medium-full bodied, balanced, moderately tannic (Sicily Nero d'Avola)
Carnitas (braised pork soft tacos with tomato, cilantro, avocado, refried beans, coriander, lime)	White: Lightweight, crisp, and stony (Mosel Riesling kabinett)	White: Aromatic, fruity, round (Alsace Pinot Gris)
Atun con marinada de chile y jengibre (chile-marinated, grilled tuna steak with ginger)	Rosé: Dry (Grenache-based)	Red: Light-bodied, bright, zesty, low tannins (Niagara Peninsula Pinot Noir)
Trucha en macadamia (baked trout in macadamia sauce)	White: Aromatic, fruity, round (Central Coast Chardonnay, no oak)	White: Lightweight, crisp, and stony (Loire Valley Chenin Blanc, off-dry)
Arroz Veracruz a la rumbada (Veracruz seafood rice with shrimp, octopus, crab, clams, onion, tomatoes, parsley)	Red: Light-bodied, bright, zesty, low tannins (Ribera del Duero Joven Tempranillo)	Red: Medium-full bodied, balanced, moderately tannic (Guadaloupe Valley Zinfandel)

Dish Name	Best Wine Style (Example)	Alternative Wine Style (Example)
Pargo rojo empapelados (red snapper in parchment with garlic, tomatoes, cilantro, olive oil)	White: Lightweight, crisp, and stony (Bío-Bío Valley Riesling)	White: Lightweight, crisp, and stony (Marlborough Sauvignon Blanc)
Pescado en verde (whole sea bass in green chile-cilantro salsa)	White: Aromatic, fruity, round (Argentina Torrontés)	White: Lightweight, crisp, and stony (Vinho Verde Loureiro)
Bacalao a la vizcaina (cod-fish with tomatoes, olives, chiles)	White: Lightweight, crisp, and stony (Rias Baixas Albariño)	White: Aromatic, fruity, round (Alto Adige Pinot Grigio)
Salmon pibil Yucatán (salmon baked in banana leaves with achiote, orange, cumin, cinnamon, garlic, allspice)	White: Full-bodied, soft, wood-aged (Chile Viognier)	Red: Light-bodied, bright, zesty, low tannins (Veneto Valpolicella)

Starches, legumes, grains, and vegetables

Beans and corn are staple starches, used to make a vast array of flours, pastes, doughs, breads, and meals, not to mention corn oil. Vegetarian dishes based on potatoes, various chile peppers, and mushrooms, among other bountiful vegetables, are common. Table 18-3 walks you through suggested wine pairings for some common vegetarian Mexican dishes.

Table 18-3   Pairing Wine with Mexican Vegetarian Dishes

Dish Name	Best Wine Style (Example)	Alternative Wine Style (Example)
Frijoles negros (baked black beans with onions, peppers, chiles, cilantro)	Red: Light-bodied, bright, zesty, low tannins (Willamette Valley Pinot Noir)	Red: Medium-full bodied, balanced, moderately tannic (Côtes du Rhône)
Lentejas Oaxaqueñas (Oaxacan-style stewed lentils with garlic, onion, pineapple, tomato, allspice)	White: Aromatic, fruity, round (Columbia Valley Riesling)	White: Aromatic, fruity, round (Alsace Pinot Gris)
Frijoles refritos (pureed pinto beans with onions, wax chiles)	Red: Medium-full bodied, balanced, moderately tannic (Chinon Cabernet Franc)	Red: Light-bodied, bright, zesty, low tannins (Marlborough Pinot Noir)

(continued)

Table 18-3 (continued)

Dish Name	Best Wine Style (Example)	Alternative Wine Style (Example)
Arroz rojo con queso y rajas (red rice casserole with poblano chiles, epazote, jack cheese)	White: Aromatic, fruity, round (Austria Grüner Veltliner)	White: Full-bodied, soft, wood-aged (Barossa Viognier)
Patatas en aguacate vinagreta de limón (potatoes in avocado lime vinaigrette, cilantro, chile)	White: Lightweight, crisp, and stony (South Australia Riesling)	White: Aromatic, fruity, round (Alsace Gewürztraminer)
Empanadas de papa (potato patties with cheese, chard, cilantro)	White: Full-bodied, soft, wood-aged (Casablanca Valley Chardonnay)	White: Aromatic, fruity, round (Alsace Pinot Gris)
Tacos con setas, espinacas, y queso (mushroom and spinach tacos with queso, epazote, garlic, red mole chili sauce	Red: Light-bodied, bright, zesty, low tannins (Rioja Joven Tempranillo/ Garnacha)	Red: Light-bodied, bright, zesty, low tannins (Niagara Peninsula Pinot Noir)
Chiles poblanos con salsa (roasted poblano chilies with tomato, corn salsa)	White: Full-bodied, soft, wood-aged (Napa Valley Viognier)	Red: Light-bodied, bright, zesty, low tannins (Leyda Valley Pinot Noir)

Desserts and sweets

Mexican sweets can be as colorful as the country's savory dishes. In fact, you can often see ingredients cross over from savory to sweet with different preparations, such as rice, avocado, pumpkin, and sweet potato, just as some ingredients normally associated with sweets find their way to the savory side, like chocolate in mole sauce. The full range of sweet wine styles pair with Mexican desserts, though I find well-aged and/or fortified wines to be the most constant table companions. Table 18-4 lists some food and wine matches for common Mexican desserts.

Table 18-4	Pairing Wine with Mexican Desserts	
Dish Name	Best Wine Style (Example)	Alternative Wine Style (Example)
Helado de aguacate (avocado ice cream)	Sweet: Late harvest (auslese) (Mosel-Saar Riesling)	Sweet: Fortified white (white Port)

Dish Name	Best Wine Style (Example)	Alternative Wine Style (Example)
Flan de calabaza (pumpkin flan with walnuts, vanilla)	Sweet: Passito (Sicily Moscato di Patelleria)	Sweet: Fortified white, aged (Bual Madeira)
Pay de limon con tequila (tequila lime pie with cracker crust)	Sweet: Sparkling white (Moscato d'Asti)	Sweet: Late harvest noble rot (Sauternes Semillon/ Sauvignon)
Budin de camote (sweet potato pudding with coconut vanilla cream)	Sweet: Passito (Tuscany Vinsanto)	Sweet: Late harvest (Burgenland auslese)
Piña y fresa drepes dulces (pineapple and strawberry-stuffed sweet crepes with lemon sauce)	Sweet: Sparkling (Prosecco dry)	Rosé: Lightweight, crisp, and stony (Piedmont Brachetto d'Aqui)
Pacana tarta con fechas (pecan tart with dates, cinnamon, vanilla, coffee, honey syrup)	Sweet: Late harvest (Tokaji Aszú 5 puttonyos)	Sweet: Fortified amber (Oloroso Dulce Sherry)
Budín de pan de plátano (plantain bread pudding with pine nuts, chocolate drizzle)	Sweet: Fortified red (Banyuls or Tawny Port)	Sweet: Fortified aged Sherry (Oloroso Dulce Sherry)
Buñuelos de manzana con canela banana azúcar (apple banana fritters with cinnamon sugar, jalapeño caramel)	Sweet: Icewine (Niagara Peninsula Vidal Icewine)	Sweet: Late harvest (Mosel Riesling beerenauslese)

South America: Land of Potatoes, Avocados, Raw Fish, and Grass-Fed Beef

Much of South America is covered by dense tropical jungles or the high mountain peaks of the rugged Andes Mountains. Major exceptions are the vast Central Valley of Chile, a fertile agricultural paradise, and the immense plains, or *pampas,* of Southern Brazil and Argentina that are home to huge cattle ranches. Corn, beans, chile peppers, nuts, avocados, tomatoes, quinoa, yucca, tropical fruits, and dozens of types of potatoes are the main indigenous staples. But the merging of old and new worlds beginning in the 16th century brought both European ingredients and culinary philosophies to South America, fused with later waves of immigrants from Africa and other parts of the Americas. These sections explore this enormous continent and its signature culinary specialties, born of this synthesis of worlds. And with gastronomy going ever more global, restaurants featuring South American dishes around the world are popularizing this "Nuevo Latino" cuisine, one of the hottest 21st century culinary trends.

South America is a major player in the world of wine. Argentina, Chile, Uruguay, and Brazil all make exportable quantities of *vino*. (Argentina is the world's fourth or fifth largest wine producer, depending on the harvest.) And though the culture of pairing food and wine generally isn't as developed as it is in the old world, and per capita wine consumption (with the exception of Argentina and Uruguay) is relatively low, it's not surprising that the people here have a good sense of the alchemy between food and wine. This will only continue to develop as wine culture evolves.

The fertile vineyards of Chile's Central Valleys and the high elevation vineyards of Mendoza, Argentina with their sun-soaked vines, produce wines of bold, fruity flavors as dramatic as an Andean vista, and ripe, generously proportioned body. This style of wine is well suited to the fresh, bright, straightforward, but pronounced flavors of the continent's culinary specialties. Generous, sweet fruit flavors and herbal nuances also work well with the fresh sauces like *chimichurri* and *salsa verde* and *rojo* (mildly spiced, uncooked vegetable and herb-based sauces) that often accompany roasted and grilled meats and fish. And as winegrowers push ever farther to the continent's cooler terroirs as in Coastal Chile, Patagonia, the high elevation sites of northern Argentina, and the rolling hills of Uruguay and southern Brazil, the range of styles and flavors will continue to grow. These fresher, crisper wines with subtle fruit flavor are the ones to look for to pair with South America's abundant seafood, salads, and other zesty plates.

Soups, ceviche, salads, and starters

Of all South American dishes, perhaps none is more emblematic than *ceviche* (sometimes spelled *cebiche* or *seviche*). Ceviche is a raw seafood preparation using lime (or lemon) juice to marinate and cook fish or shellfish, which must be impeccably fresh. Several nations in the region lay claim to the origins of ceviche, but ownership remains hotly disputed.

In any case, hundreds of variations exist; most incorporate some form of chile, onion, coriander/cilantro, salt, and raw vegetables, along with just about anything that swims or lives in water. Ceviche is a perfect summertime dish — light and refreshing — especially when washed down by a crisp unoaked white from one of the newer, cooler vineyard areas of South America. Table 18-5 identifies some wine pairings with common South American starters.

Table 18-5	Pairing Wine with South American Starters		
Country of Origin	Dish Name (English)	Best Wine Style (Example)	Alternative Wine Style (Example)
Brazil	Salada de batata com atún (potato salad with tuna, mayonnaise, parsley)	White: Lightweight, crisp, and stony (Casablanca Valley Sauvignon Blanc)	White: Aromatic, fruity, round (Marlborough Pinot Gris)
Argentina	Ensalada de palmitos primavera (spring hearts of palm salad with chopped egg, beets)	White: Full-bodied, soft, wood-aged (Mendoza Chardonnay)	White: Full-bodied, soft, wood- aged (Napa Valley Viognier)
Peru	Ceviche de atún con Limon (tuna with chili, lime, cilantro, corn)	White: Lightweight, crisp, and stony (Chile Leyda Valley Sauvignon Blanc)	White: Lightweight, crisp, and stony (Patagonia Sauvignon Blanc)
Peru	Ceviche pez espada (marinated sword-fish with red onions, cilantro, lime juice)	White: Lightweight, crisp, and stony (Casablanca Valley Sauvignon Blanc)	White: Lightweight, crisp, and stony (Vinho Verde Alvarinho)
Peru	Ceviche de corvina (marinated sea bass with onion, celery, chile pepper, cilantro)	White: Lightweight, crisp, and stony (Bío-Bío Valley Riesling	White: Lightweight, crisp, and stony (Santorini Assyrtiko)
Venezuela	Croquetas de atún (tuna croquettes with lime, mayonnaise)	White: Lightweight, crisp, and stony (Bío-Bío Valley Riesling)	White: Lightweight, crisp, and stony (Limarí Valley Sauvignon Blanc)
Chile	Ceviche pez espada (swordfish ceviche with red onion, avo-cado, lime, cilantro)	White (Casablanca Valley Sauvignon Blanc)	White: Lightweight, crisp, and stony (Finger Lakes Riesling)
Ecuador	Ceviche de pulpo (marinated octopus salad with orange, lime, red onion)	White: Aromatic, fruity, round (Leyda Valley Sauvignon Blanc)	White: Aromatic, fruity, round (Alsace Pinot Gris)

Meat and seafood

Both meat and seafood play a large role in the diets of South Americans. Chile and Peru in particular are known for their seafood, because they're situated at the edge of the Pacific where the icy Humboldt Current brings a plentiful diversity of fish, most famously sea bass.

Argentina, Uruguay, and Brazil, on the other hand, are expert meat eaters. The *asado,* a term used for both the event itself and for an assortment of mostly red meats, especially grass-fed beef, sausages, and other items grilled over an open fire or coal pit on a *parilla* (grill), is an Argentine institution, invariably accompanied by copious amounts of strong red Malbec. In Brazil, the asado is called *churrasco,* often served in a restaurant called a *rodízio,* where waiters bring skewered meats to carve at the table for guests. Plates are kept full until the diners wave the red flag when they can eat no more. Table 18-6 offers wine pairings with common South American meat and seafood dishes.

Table 18-6   Pairing Wine with South American Meat and Seafood

Country of Origin	Dish Name (English)	Best Wine Style	Alternative Wine Style
Brazil	Feijoada (clay pot beef, pork, and bean with garlic, spice)	Red: Medium-full bodied, balanced, moderately tannic (Brazil Merlot/blends)	Red: Medium-full bodied, balanced, moderately tannic (California Zinfandel)
Brazil	Bacalhau ao forno (baked salted codfish with tomato, olives, onions)	White: Full-bodied, soft, wood-aged (Mendoza Chardonnay)	Red: Medium-full bodied, balanced, moderately tannic (Chile Carmenere)
Argentina	Costillas con chimichurri (braised beef ribs with chimichurri)	Red: Medium-full bodied, balanced, moderately tannic (Mendoza Malbec)	Red: Light-bodied, bright, zesty, low tannins (Patagonia Pinot Noir)
Peru	Mejillones con cal y chiles (mussels in tomato broth with chilies, lime, corn)	White: Lightweight, crisp, and stony (Bío-Bío Valley Riesling)	White: Lightweight, crisp, and stony (Rias Baixas Albariño)
Peru	Cerdo cocido con cerveza y cilantro (beer braised pork shoulder with red pepper, cilantro)	White: Lightweight, crisp, and stony (Casablanca Valley Sauvignon Blanc)	Red: Light-bodied, bright, and zesty, low tannins (Loire Valley Cabernet Franc)

Country of Origin	Dish Name (English)	Best Wine Style	Alternative Wine Style
Venezuela	Pargo al horno con cilantro (baked red snapper in lemon-cilantro sauce)	White: Lightweight, crisp, and stony (Elquí Valley Sauvignon Blanc)	White: Lightweight, crisp, and stony (Rueda Verdejo)
Chile	Curanto (stewed mussels, clams, sausage, and potato in tomato broth with garlic bread)	Red: Medium-full bodied, balanced, moderately tannic (Maipo Valley Merlot)	Red: Light-bodied, bright, zesty, low tannins (Valpolicella corvina/rondinella)
Ecuador	Biche de pescado (Fish stew with chickpeas, peanuts, corn, yucca)	White: Aromatic, fruity, round (Chile aromatic white blends)	White: Lightweight, crisp, and stony (Vouvray chenin blanc)

Empanadas, arepas, and other snacks

The empanada is a satisfying snack, eaten at virtually any time of day, and is featured in fiestas throughout South America. The name itself derives from the Spanish *empanar,* meaning to coat in bread. And although Spanish colonizers did bring the empanada to South America, the dish is hardly a uniquely Spanish concept.

In South America, the empanada (called *pastel* in Brazil) is a fiercely regional product, with each country claiming its own, superior version. The correct degree of juiciness is a hotly contested aspect, while size and cooking method (baked, fried) vary from region to region even within the same country. Stuffings also differ greatly, and can include vegetables, seafood, ground beef, hard-boiled eggs, raisins, and olives, among many other ingredients.

The beef debate: Grass versus grain?

Grass-fed beef is believed to be better for you than grain-fed beef, because it contains less saturated fat and more omega-3 fatty acids. It's also leaner and cooks more quickly than the marbled, grain-fed type. Most importantly, its lean but umami-rich taste works with a variety of wine styles, from light and zesty reds (which can otherwise get lost in the intramuscular fat of grain-fed beef) to fully turbocharged reds that synergize the taste of charred barrels and charred meat. Grass-fed beef isn't even a bad match with crisp whites, whose acid is like the essential dash of white or red vinegar found in an asado's traditional accompanying salsa, chimichurri.

The *arepa* is a specialty of Venezuela and Colombia. It's an unleaven patty made from cornmeal or flour, and baked, fried, grilled, or even boiled, and then stuffed or topped with a variety of ingredients.

You don't need to fuss too much about what to drink with any of the snacks in Table 18-7. The empanada and arepa are casual foods, eaten on the street, during fiestas, or as a quick snack between meals, but I provide some options to consider. I also include some other regional specialties that you're likely to come across throughout South America.

Table 18-7	Pairing Wine with South American Snacks		
Country of Origin	*Dish Name (English)*	*Best Wine Style*	*Alternative Wine Style*
Brazil	Empanadinhas de palmito *(empanadas with hearts of palm)*	White: Full-bodied, soft, wood- aged (Central Valley Chardonnay)	White: Lightweight, crisp, and stony (Mosel Riesling)
Argentina	Empanada Mendocina (Mendoza-style empanadas with ground beef, olives, hard-boiled eggs)	Red: Light-bodied, bright, zesty, low tannins (Patagonia Pinot Noir)	Red: Medium-full bodied, balanced, moderately tannic (Mendoza Malbec)
Peru	Humitas con pasta de aji (fresh corn tamales with tomato chile pepper paste)	White: Full-bodied, soft, wood- aged (Limarí Valley Chardonnay)	White: Aromatic, fruity, round (Rueda Verdejo)
Venezuela	Arepa de pabellon criollo (shredded beef corn cake filled with beans, rice, plantain)	Red: Medium-full bodied, balanced, moderately tannic (Rapel Valley Carmenere)	White: Aromatic, fruity, round (Chile Rhône-style white blend)
Chile	Empanada con pino (Chilean empanada with beef, onions, raisins, black olives, hard-boiled egg)	White: Aromatic, fruity, round (Leyda Valley Sauvignon Blanc)	Red: Medium-full bodied, balanced, moderately tannic (Elquí Valley Syrah)

Vegetables, starches, and grains

Among South America's many contributions to the culinary world, you'd have to rank the potato and the tomato as the two most important. The potato originates in southern Peru and northwestern Bolivia, where more than a thousand species are still in existence, if not available in the supermarket. In most cuisines, the potato is looked upon more as a staple starch than something to savor, but the variety of flavors and textures is astonishing. People treat it as a relatively neutral canvas to showcase other ingredients; on its own, the potato pairs happily with many wine styles.

The tomato, too, is believed to come from the Peruvian highlands, but spread quickly throughout Latin America. The characteristic aspect of the tomato in all its many varieties is relatively high acidity and fine sweet-sour balance. Most tomato-based dishes are best served with wines of at least equal acidity, because soft, low acid wines usually seem overly flabby with zesty tomato dishes. Table 18-8 lists several popular bean, rice, quinoa, and other dishes that are eaten as main courses or served alongside meats and seafood.

Table 18-8	Pairing Wine with Vegetarian Dishes		
Country of Origin	**Dish Name (English)**	**Best Wine Style**	**Alternative Wine Style**
Brazil	Arroz con pequí (Brazilian style rice with soari nut (an edible fruit))	Red: Light-bodied, bright, zesty, low tannins (Patagonia Pinot Noir)	Red: Light-bodied, bright, zesty, low tannins (Chianti Sangiovese)
Argentina	Berenjenas en escabeche (marinated eggplant with oregano, garlic, vinegar)	White: Aromatic, fruity, round (Patagonia Sauvignon Blanc)	White: Lightweight, crisp, and stony (Alto Adige Pinot Grigio)
Argentina	Tomates rellenos con arroz (rice stuffed tomatoes with peas, olives, parsley)	Red: Light-bodied, bright, zesty, low tannins (Mendoza Bonarda)	Red: Light-bodied, bright, zesty, low tannins (Piedmont Barbera)

(continued)

Table 18-8 (continued)

Country of Origin	Dish Name (English)	Best Wine Style	Alternative Wine Style
Peru	La quinoa con pepino, tomate y menta (quinoa with cucumber, tomato, mint, parsley, chiles)	White: Lightweight, crisp, and stony (Elquí Valley Sauvignon Blanc)	White: Lightweight, crisp, and stony (Sancerre Sauvignon Blanc)
Venezuela	Caraotas negras (black beans with tomato, onion, chili, cilantro)	Red: Medium-full bodied, balanced, moderately tannic (Rapel Valley Carmenere)	Red: Light-bodied, bright, zesty, low tannins (Santa Barbara Pinot Noir)
Chile	Porotos quebra-dos (green bean, pumpkin, corn stew)	White: Aromatic, fruity, round (Chile Viognier)	White: Full-bodied, soft, wood-aged (Casablanca Valley Chardonnay)
Chile	Lima guiso de judías (lima bean casserole with tomato, corn, peppers)	White: Lightweight, crisp, and stony (Bío-Bío Valley Riesling)	White: Full-bodied, soft, wood-aged (Souther Rhône white blend)

Desserts and sweets

South Americans, especially Argentineans, are fond of sweets, especially Italian-style ice cream. Another specialty, *alfajores* (caramel cream or other type of jam or chocolate sandwiched between two sweet biscuits and covered in white or dark chocolate), is originally of Spanish-Moorish origin. Like the empanada, alfajores come in many regional variations across Latin America. Sweet wines aren't a specialty of this region, though you can find some. Table 18-9 lists some sweet wine suggestions from around the world, though if you can find a similar style made locally, I'd give it a try.

Table 18-9	Pairing Wine with South American Desserts		
Country of Origin	*Dish Name (English)*	*Best Wine Style*	*Alternative Wine Style*
Brazil	Cassata de abacaxi (pineapple cassata with ladyfingers, coconut, condensed milk)	Sweet: Late harvest (Alsace Gewürztraminer Vendanges Tardives)	Sweet: Late harvest (Mosel-Saar Riesling auslese)
Brazil	Cuca de banana (banana buttermilk cake with vanilla)	Sweet Icewine (Niagara Peninsula Riesling Icewine)	Sweet: Passito (Tuscany Vinsato)
Argentina	Buñuelos de manzana (apple fritters with icing sugar)	Sweet: Late harvest (Mosel-Saar Riesling auslese)	Sweet: Iced Cider (Québec cidre de glace)
Argentina	Arroz con leche (rice pudding with raisins, cinnamon, cream)	Sweet: Fortified white (Muscat de Beaumes de Venise)	Sweet: Fortified amber (Sicily Malvasia delle Lipari)
Peru	Helado de lúcuma (lucuma ice cream, a native tropical fruit)	Sweet: Sparkling (Moscato d'Asti)	Sweet: Fortified white (Muscat de Beaumes de Venise)
Venezuela	Dulce de leche pionono (jelly roll sponge cake with caramel icing)	Sweet: Noble rot (Tokaji Aszú 5 puttonyos)	Sweet: Fortified amber (Douro Valley Tawny Port)
Chile	Mil hojas de manjar (caramel raspberry napoleon with pastry cream)	Sweet: Fortified red (Douro Valley Late Bottled Vintage Port)	Sweet: Fortified red (Banyuls Grenache
Argentina	Alfajores (shortbread sandwich cookie filled with vanilla, milk caramel)	Sweet: Passito (Recioto di Soave)	Sweet: Passito (Muscat of Samos)

Chapter 19

Sampling the Flavors of the Middle East and North Africa

*T*he countries in the Middle East and North Africa have a rich gastronomic heritage. And in some cases, they have centuries, if not millennia, of wine-producing history. For many and varied socioeconomic and religious reasons, wine today is rarely a focus in this part of the world, especially where Islam is the dominant religion. This of course has nothing to do with wine compatibility with traditional dishes, and you can enjoy plenty of great pairings. Although many of these countries don't usually serve wine in public, the Middle Eastern–inspired restaurants (and take-out venues) in other parts of the world allow you to play around with these pairings.

This chapter looks at a cross section of the foods found throughout the southern and eastern Mediterranean, along with some of the best wine matches that I've experienced. As with other chapters in these parts, I offer the best local matches where possible, and failing that, some of the best options from the rest of the wine-producing world.

Sampling the Flavors of the Fertile Crescent

The semicircular region embracing the eastern Mediterranean was once dubbed the Fertile Crescent for its rich, fertile lands conducive to agriculture. Most likely, the first permanent settlements of nomadic tribes heading west from Asia lived there. Many important foods originated here, such as wheat, pistachios, figs, and pomegranates. But as far as I'm concerned, the greatest contribution from this part of the world was the discovery of fermentation, some 7,000 years ago. Wine and beer both made their debuts here.

Middle Eastern food is popular internationally, from simple *shawarma, falafel,* and kebab houses to more elaborate restaurants. Aside from being tasty, Middle Eastern food is also good for you. Studies have shown that this grain and vegetable-rich diet can reduce the risk of heart-related illnesses, cancer, and Alzheimer's disease.

Although not particularly well known as a wine-producing region, Israel, Lebanon, and Turkey all have thriving local wine industries. And Middle Eastern cuisine is likewise wine-friendly for the most part, with predominantly fresh, savory, earthy flavors and modest use of hot spice (aside from *harissa,* a typically North African chile pepper sauce) that leaves plenty of room to play with a wide array of whites, rosés, and reds. I find that the bold, forwardly fruity flavors of new world–style wines to be especially well-suited to vibrant Middle Eastern flavors.

The following sections discuss popular dishes and the some wine pairings that can make your Middle Eastern and North African meals more memorable.

Starters, soups, and appetizers

In this part of the world, casual dining with multiple dishes on the table is the rule rather than the exception. A selection of the dishes in this section can make for a full meal. Refer to Chapter 4 for strategies when casual communal dining is the order of the day. Table 19-1 identifies some common starter dishes from Lebanon, Turkey, and Israel with specific wine pairings.

Table 19-1	Pairing Wine and Starters in the Fertile Crescent		
Country of Origin	*Local Dish Name (English Name)*	*Best Wine Style (Example)*	*Alternative Wine Style (Example)*
Lebanon	Fattoush (pita with romaine, tomato, cucumber, peppers, onion, mint)	White: Lightweight, crisp, and stony (South Australia Riesling)	White: Aromatic, fruity, round (Casablanca Valley Sauvignon Blanc)
Lebanon	Fatayer (phyllo triangles with spinach, pine nuts, butter)	White: Full-bodied, soft, wood-aged (Burgundy Chardonnay)	White: Lightweight, crisp, and stony (Marlborough Sauvignon Blanc)
Turkey	Kiymali lahana sarmasi (rice-stuffed collard greens with ground beef, tomato, parsley)	White: Lightweight, crisp, and stony (Rias Baixas Albariño)	Red: Light-bodied, bright, zesty, low tannins (Chianti Classico Sangiovese)

Country of Origin	Local Dish Name (English Name)	Best Wine Style (Example)	Alternative Wine Style (Example)
Turkey	Tavuk cigeri kavurmasi (fried chicken livers with lemon, cayenne)	White: Off-dry, lightweight, crisp, and stony (Mosel Riesling spätlese)	Dry: Rosé (Tavel Grenache or Cinsault)
Israel	Gefilte (poached fish dumplings with matzoh, eggs, onions)	White: Aromatic, fruity, round (Israeli Viognier)	White: Aromatic, fruity, round (Stellenbosch Chenin Blanc)

Meats

Lamb and mutton are the principal meats in the Middle East, followed by chicken; pork is limited due to the dietary restrictions of both Muslims and Jews. Skewered meat (kebabs) and meatballs (kafta) are common. Table 19-2 suggests some pairings for common meat dishes and wine.

Table 19-2	Fertile Crescent Meat and Wine Pairings		
Country of Origin	Local Dish Name (English Name)	Best Wine Style (Example)	Alternative Wine Style (Example)
Lebanon	Lubee (lamb stew with green beans, rice, cinnamon, tomato)	Red: Light-bodied, bright, zesty, low tannins (Valpolicella)	White: Aromatic, fruity, round (Santorini Assyrtiko)
Lebanon	Kafta (ground lamb meatballs with parsley, cayenne, allspice)	Red: Medium-full bodied, balanced, moderately tannic (Aglianico del Taburno)	White: Full-bodied, soft, wood-aged (Condrieu Viognier)
Lebanon	Shawarma (chicken wrap with tomato, lettuce, yogurt, tahini, garlic, parsley, lemon, onion)	White: Full-bodied, soft, wood-aged (Niagara Peninsula Chardonnay)	Rosé: Off-dry (Cabernet rosé)
Turkey	Fistikli kebap (mutton and pistachio meatballs with cumin, chili powder)	Red: Medium-full bodied, balanced, moderately tannic (Paso Robles Zinfandel)	Red: Light-bodied, bright, zesty, low tannins (Rioja, Crianza Tempranillo)

(continued)

Table 19-2 *(continued)*

Country of Origin	Local Dish Name (English Name)	Best Wine Style (Example)	Alternative Wine Style (Example)
Turkey	Kiremitte tavuk (chicken baked on clay tile with peppers, garlic)	White: Lightweight, crisp, and stony (Austria Riesling)	Red: Light-bodied, bright, zesty, low tannins (Central Coast Pinot Noir)
Turkey	Etli bakla (stewed lamb with fava beans, garlic, yogurt	Red: Light-bodied, bright, zesty, low tannins (Carneros Pinot Noir)	White: Full-bodied, soft, wood-aged (Mâcon Chardonnay)
Israel	Cholent (brisket stew with potato, paprika, eggs, onion, barley	Red: Light-bodied, bright, zesty, low tannins (Israeli Galilee Barbera)	White: Full-bodied, soft, wood-aged (Napa Valley Chardonnay)
Israel	Kishke (beef sausage with matzoh meal, spices)	Red: Light-bodied, bright, zesty, low tannins (Israeli Pinot Noir)	Rosé: Dry (Côtes de Provence)

Vegetables, grains, and rice

The Middle East, much like parts of Asia, relies on wheat and rice as its main staples. Barley, cracked wheat, and couscous (a product made from semolina) along with many types of bread are essential items. Other common ingredients in this area include milk, yogurt, and cheese, an array of spices, nuts, beans, pulses, and vegetables such as tomatoes, eggplants, onions, peppers, squash, and cabbage. Table 19-3 highlights a few vegetable, grain, and rice dishes with wine pairing suggestions.

Table 19-3   Pairing Wines with Vegetarian Items

Country of Origin	Local Dish Name (English Name)	Best Wine Style (Example)	Alternative Wine Style (Example)
Lebanon	Falafel (fried chickpea balls with garlic, cumin, coriander, parsley)	White: Aromatic, fruity, round (Wachau Grüner Veltliner)	White: Lightweight, crisp, and stony (Rias Baixas Albariño)

Country of Origin	Local Dish Name (English Name)	Best Wine Style (Example)	Alternative Wine Style (Example)
Lebanon	Malfouf mehshi (rice-stuffed cabbage rolls with paprika, garlic, mint, cumin, pomegranate)	White: Aromatic, fruity, round (Alto Adige Pinot Grigio)	Red: Medium-full bodied, balanced, moderately tannic (Chinon Cabernet Franc)
Turkey	Kabak patates mucveri (zucchini and potato fritters)	White: Lightweight, crisp, and stony (Santorini Assyrtiko)	White: Sparkling, lightweight, crisp, and stony (Traditional sparkling)
Turkey	Kuskonmaz kavur-masi (asparagus with eggs, onion, black pepper)	White: Lightweight, crisp, and stony (Franken Silvaner)	White: Aromatic, fruity, round (Austria Grüner Veltliner)
Israel	Kugel (potato, egg noodle, zucchini casserole)	White: Lightweight, crisp, and stony (Rias Baixas Albarino)	White: Aromatic, fruity, round (Alsace Pinot Gris)
Israel	Latka (potato pan-cakes with onion, sour cream, apple sauce)	White: Sparkling, lightweight, crisp, and stony (Traditional Method sparkling)	White: Aromatic, fruity, round (Southern France Viognier)

Sweet confections

Desserts in this part of the world are for the most part a little less sweet, and certainly less dependent on cream and eggs, than typical North American desserts. Nuts and exotic spices play a feature role, which makes for great pairing potential with sweet wines aged for prolonged periods in wood before bottling, which develop their own exotic spicy-nutty notes. Table 19-4 gives you some ideas for pairing wine and this region's desserts.

Table 19-4	Pairing Wine with Desserts		
Country of Origin	Local Dish Name (English Name)	Best Wine Style (Example)	Alternative Wine Style (Example)
Lebanon	Mahallebi (milk and corn pudding with pis-tachio, cinnamon syrup)	Sweet: Passito (Passito di Pantelleria)	Sweet: Noble rot (Sauternes)

(continued)

Table 19-4 *(continued)*

Country of Origin	Local Dish Name (English Name)	Best Wine Style (Example)	Alternative Wine Style (Example)
Lebanon	Namoora (coconut cake with yogurt, almonds, lemon icing)	Sweet: Late harvest (Moscato de Setúbal)	Sweet: Late harvest (Burgenland white blend auslese)
Lebanon	Sfouf (semolina milk cake with turmeric, pine nuts)	Sweet: Passito (Recioto di Soave Garganega)	Sweet: Fortified amber (Sicily Malvasia delle Lipari)
Turkey	Cezerye (Turkish delight with hazelnuts, coconut, carrot)	Sweet: Fortified amber (Jerez Oloroso Dulce)	Sweet: Fortified amber (Rivesaltes Ambré)
Turkey	Muhallebili incir tatlisi (dried fig milk pudding with rice flour, walnuts, vanilla)	Sweet: Fortified red (Tawny Port)	Sweet: Icewine (Niagara Peninsula Vidal)
Turkey	Uzumlu cevizli kek (raisin walnut cake with orange, cinnamon, walnuts, cherry syrup)	Sweet: Noble rot (Tokaji Aszú 5 puttonyos)	Sweet: Fortified red (Banyuls Grenache)
Israel	Rugelach (turnovers with cream cheese, walnuts, apricot preserves, cinnamon)	Sweet: Late harvest Passito (Passito di Pantelleria)	Sweet: Fortified red (Tawny Port)
Israel	Halvah (ground sesame paste and honey loaf)	Sweet: Passito (Tuscany Vin Santo di Toscana)	Sweet: Passito (Muscat of Samos Grand Cru)

Sampling the Flavors of Morocco, Egypt, Algeria, and Tunisia

Picture bustling spice markets, rocky coastlines, dessert oases, and rows of date palms, and you're imagining this region, known as the Maghreb Union. The cuisine of North Africa, including Morocco, Egypt, Algeria, and Tunisia, blends Arabian influence with the traditional regional Berber cuisine, the original inhabitants of North Africa west of the Nile. This area also has many influences from various Mediterranean invaders and European traders and travelers, evident through various ingredients and cooking methods still in use today. Egyptian cuisine, for example, shows heavy Ottoman/Turkish influence, while Algeria and Tunisia have more French and Italian influences.

Farther west, Spain and Portugal influence Moroccan cuisine, which has become the most well known international North African cuisine.

The sweet-savory combination of tastes in many North African dishes are well-suited to bold, fruity, new world–style reds, whites, and rosés. Avoid serving bone-dry, tannic reds and high acid whites with any dishes containing sweet elements, which render the wine even more tart and/or astringent. (I don't list native food names here because they don't translate well.)

Starters, soups, and appetizers

Table 19-5 looks at food and wine pairings for starting dishes in North Africa.

Table 19-5	Pairing Wine with North African Starters		
Country of Origin	*Local Dish Name (English Name)*	*Best Wine Style (Example)*	*Alternative Wine Style (Example)*
Morocco	Phyllo meat pie with shredded chicken, ginger, almonds, turmeric, cinnamon	White: Aromatic, fruity, round (Alto Adige Pinot Grigio)	White: Full-bodied, soft, wood-aged (Napa Valley Chardonnay)
Morocco	Beef kebabs with garlic, pepper, parsley, coriander, cumin rub	Red: Light-bodied, bright, zesty, low tannins (Northern Rhone Syrah)	Red: Medium-full bodied, balanced, moderately tannic (Mendoza Malbec)
Morocco	Eggplant salad with garlic, lemon juice, tomato, black olives	Rosé: Dry (Bandol Rosé)	Red: Light-bodied, bright, zesty, low tannins (Rioja Crianza, tempranillo
Egypt	Chicken and rice soup with cinnamon, cardamom, sumac, garlic, parsley	White: Aromatic, fruity, round (Central Coast white Rhône Blend)	Rosé: Dry (Tavel Grenache, Cinsault)
Algeria	Egg and meatball soup with saffron, almonds, cilantro, parsley, lemon	White: Full-bodied, soft, wood-aged (Carneros Chardonnay)	White: Lightweight, crisp, and stony (Sancerre Sauvignon Blanc)
Tunisia	Tuna and eggplant salad with tomato, oregano, garlic, crumbled feta	White: Lightweight, crisp, and stony (South Australia Riesling)	Rosé: Dry (Provence Rosé)

Meat, fish, and game

Staple proteins of the Maghreb include beef, lamb, and goat, usually served alongside couscous, dates, nuts, various oils, and a rich assortment of fruits and vegetables. Aromatic herbs and spices are liberally used, including cumin, cardamom, cinnamon, paprika, ginger, sumac, nutmeg, mint, and parsley. In general, foods are rarely spicy-hot, with the exception of dishes using the famous *harissa* spice paste (pepper, garlic, chile, coriander, and caraway). Sweet and savory tastes often share the same plate; dried fruits (apricots, dates, raisins) are frequently cooked along with meats, as in the regionally emblematic dish called *tajine,* named for the conical earthenware vessel in which it is cooked. Table 19-6 shows some wine pairings with some common North African meat and fish dishes.

Table 19-6	North African Wine and Meat Pairings		
Country of Origin	*Local Dish Name (English Name)*	*Best Wine Style (Example)*	*Alternative Wine Style (Example)*
Morocco	Slow cooked lamb tajine with apricots, raisins, preserved lemon, saffron, paprika, ras el hanout	Red: Full, deep and robust, turbocharged (Paso Robles Zinfandel)	White: Aromatic, fruity, round (Central Coast Viognier
Morocco	Whole roasted lamb with lemon, salt	Red: Medium-full bodied, balanced, moderately tannic (Coonawarra Cabernet Sauvignon)	Red: Light-bodied, bright, zesty, low tannins (Naoussa Xinomavro)
Morocco	Shrimp, swordfish, and calamari with cellophane noodles, tomato	White: Aromatic, fruity, round (Friuli Pinot Grigio)	Red: Light-bodied, bright, zesty, low tannins (Barbera d'Asti)
Egypt	Sweet potato beef pie with garlic, onion, nutmeg, allspice, cinnamon, bread crumbs	Red: Medium-full bodied, balanced, moderately tannic (Napa Valley Merlot)	Red: Light-bodied, bright, zesty, low tannins (Willamette Pinot Noir)
Egypt	Lamb meatballs with parsley, cumin, pine nuts, yogurt, lemon	Red: Full, deep, robust, turbocharged (Barossa Shiraz)	Red: Medium-full bodied, balanced, moderately tannic (Bordeaux St. Emilion)

Country of Origin	Local Dish Name (English Name)	Best Wine Style (Example)	Alternative Wine Style (Example)
Egypt	Roasted chicken with allspice, garlic, chile, walnuts, pomegranate	White: Aromatic, fruity, round (Fiano di Avellino)	White: Lightweight, crisp, and stony (Greece Moscophilero)
Algeria	Chicken couscous with garlic, chick-peas, cinnamon, zucchini, peppers, turnip, cayenne	Red: Light-bodied, bright, zesty, low tannins (Beaujolais Villages Gamay)	White: Aromatic, fruity, round (Wachau Grüner Veltliner)
Tunisia	Whitefish stew with potato, harissa, tomato, parsley, mint, garlic	Rosé: Dry (Côtes de Provence)	White: Aromatic, fruity, round (South Africa Chenin Blanc)

Vegetables, starches, and grains

As in much of the Mediterranean, vegetables, starches, and grains make up the majority of the daily diet — animal protein is less regularly consumed. Clever combinations of herbs, oils, and spices make for compelling flavor experiences, which can also create magic with wine. Table 19-7 gives you a few wine pairings with some common North African vegetarian dishes.

Table 19-7	North African Wine and Vegetarian Pairings		
Country of Origin	Local Dish Name (English Name)	Best Wine Style (Example)	Alternative Wine Style (Example)
Morocco	Couscous with stewed carrots, peppers, chick-peas, olive oil, lemon	Red: Light-bodied, bright, zesty, low tannins (Beaujolais Villages Gamay)	White: Aromatic, fruity, round (Wachau Grüner Veltliner)
Morocco	Fava beans with lemon, parsley, olive oil, paprika	White: Lightweight, crisp, and stony (Malborough Sauvignon Blanc)	White: Aromatic, fruity, round (Alsace Pinot Gris)

(continued)

Table 19-7 (continued)

Country of Origin	Local Dish Name (English Name)	Best Wine Style (Example)	Alternative Wine Style (Example)
Morocco	Stewed lentils in tomato sauce with cumin, saffron, garlic, cilantro	Red: Light-bodied, bright, zesty, low tannins (Barbera d'Asti)	White: Lightweight, crisp, and stony (Alto Adige Pinot Grigio)
Egypt	Fava bean and chickpea patties with scallion, yogurt, garlic, dill, parsley	White: Lightweight, crisp, and stony (Columbia Valley Riesling)	White: Full-bodied, soft, wood-aged (Limarì Valley Chardonnay)
Egypt	Lemon garlic potato and bean salad with olive oil, parsley, sumac	White: Aromatic, fruity, round (Loire Valley Chenin Blanc)	White: Lightweight, crisp and stony (Sonoma Sauvignon Blanc)
Algeria	Potato stew with cumin, paprika, lentils, tomato paste	White: Aromatic, fruity, round (Willamette Valley Pinot Gris)	White: Aromatic, fruity, round (Wachau Grüner Veltliner)
Tunisia	Swiss chard, lentils and chickpeas with tomato paste, garlic, lemons	White: Lightweight, crisp, and stony (Chablis Chardonnay)	Red: Light-bodied, bright, zesty, low tannins (Niagara Pinot Noir)

The sweet shop

This part of the world is rich in sweet confections. Most desserts incorporate nuts, dried fruits, and honey, often wrapped with the ultra thin and light phyllo type of pastry. Table 19-8 highlights some wine pairings with popular North African desserts.

Table 19-8	North African Wine and Vegetarian Pairings		
Country of Origin	*Local Dish Name (English Name)*	*Best Wine Style (Example)*	*Alternative Wine Style (Example)*
Morocco	Phyllo-wrapped banana and apricots with almonds, cinnamon, honey	Sweet: Fortified white (Muscat de Rivesaltes)	Sweet: Passito (Sicily Passito di Pantelleria)
Morocco	Baked date cakes with yogurt, cinnamon, vanilla, sesame, orange water	Sweet: Fortified red (Tawny Port)	Sweet: Late harvest/ Noble rot (Tokaji late harvest)
Morocco	Almond milk pudding with crushed pistachios, rosewater	Sweet: Icewine (Niagara Peninsula Vidal)	Sweet: Fortified white (Samos Nectar)
Egypt	Coconut almond pound cake with dates, raisins	Sweet: Fortified amber (Jerez Oloroso Dulce)	Sweet: Fortified amber (Rutherglen Muscat)
Egypt	Apricot mousse with cottage cheese, honey	Sweet: Passito (Recioto di Soave)	Sweet: Passito: (Muscat of Rio Patras)
Algeria	Crispy fried donut balls with lemon honey syrup, icing sugar	Sweet: Sparkling white (Moscato d'Asti)	Sweet: Late harvest (Niagara Peninsula Riesling late harvest)
Tunisia	Layered phyllo with honey-poached figs, apricot, cardamom, walnuts	Sweet: Noble rot (Tokaji Aszú 5 puttonyos)	Sweet: Fortified red (California Zinfandel Port-style)

Wines of South Africa: 350 years young

South Africa recently celebrated 350 years of winemaking; the first wine grapes were pressed in Cape Town on February 2, 1659, according to the diary of Jan van Riebeeck, the Dutch colonial administrator who founded Cape Town in 1682. Centuries of ups and downs later, the South African wine industry finally entered the modern age after severe international trade sanctions against the pro-apartheid government were lifted in the wake of the first democratic elections in 1994.

As a first-time visitor to the winelands of the Cape, you'll be struck by the staggering beauty of the area, among the most picturesque wine-growing regions in the world. You'll see rugged granite-capped mountains sitting atop ancient crumbled shales and sandstones, rising up to more than 3,000 feet from the shores of False Bay just a dozen miles to the south. Across the western horizon stands the unmistakable landmark of Table Mountain, with its near-permanent wisps of cloud covering the leveled summit like a 1960s Beatles mop-top. Inland and to the north you'll see vine-covered slopes and lush green valleys covered with beautiful and infinitely varied native flowers. The Cape Floral Kingdom is the smallest yet richest of the six recognized floral kingdoms in the world. The Cape alone contains more biodiversity than the entire northern hemisphere, some 9,600 unique species.

Two oceans temper the hot African sun: the Southern and the Indian Oceans. Constant breezes cool vineyards each afternoon, where grapes grow in some of the oldest vineyard soils in the world, up to 500 million years. More than half of wine production is red, with the region of Stellenbosh leading the way in international recognition. South Africa is closely tied to excellent quality Cabernet Sauvignon and Bordeaux-style blends, which sit stylistically midway between the bold fruitiness of new world–style reds and the restrained structure and earthy flavors of old world wines. Rhône grapes, both red and white, as well as the uniquely South African specialty Pinotage are worth seeking out, especially when the BBQ (called a braai in Afrikans) is fired up.

You can find lively, zesty, green pepper–scented Sauvignon Blancs from the coolest zones of the Cape, namely Constantia, Walker Bay, and around Africa's southernmost point, Cape Agulhas. The insider's choice, however, is Chenin Blanc. Once used exclusively for brandy production, a vast supply of old vineyards are now crafting wines of amazing depth, concentration, and minerally flavors. Most Chenin Blancs are barrel-aged; you should consider them whenever the food calls for pairing with substantial wood-aged whites.

Chapter 20

The Classic Pairing: Wine and Cheese

In This Chapter

▶ Appreciating cheese in all its varied glory

▶ Matching wines with all different types of cheese

▶ Setting up a wine and cheese party

Supposed to be the foolproof partnership, wine and cheese is really a minefield. So many wines crumple into a quivering heap before the fatty, salty, pungent profile of many cheeses. To make the sommelier's life harder, a cheese board usually contains a range of cheeses (as it should) from mild to stinky, goat to cow's milk, so you just can't find a single type of wine that will run the table and make all the cheeses happy.

This chapter gives you all the details about avoiding the pitfalls and making successful wine and cheese pairings. I slice up the vast world of cheese into a few manageable bites of major styles and recommend general wine styles with each, along with some specific recommendations. Think of them as starting points, which can get you thinking along the right lines when you're looking for the right wine with any cheese.

I also provide suggestions for a couple of turnkey wine and cheese parties: the casual affair and the serious affair. I let you know which cheeses and wines to buy, and how to set it up so that you look like you've been doing it for years.

Wine and Cheese: The Complex and Paradoxical Relationship

Few edible products share as many similarities as wine and cheese. Both were discovered accidentally several thousand years ago, and people haven't stopped trying to perfect them since. They're both converted from a relatively simple raw material (grape juice and milk) into a marvelously complex product with a bewildering array of flavors. The region of production greatly influences the final outcome, and both wine and cheese making require no small measure of human skill to get it right. So it's no surprise that wine and cheese are like kindred spirits, each capable of making the other greater, or tearing each other apart.

The world of wine and cheese is fascinating and complex. I know people who have dedicated their lives to cheese, as many have to wine, so obviously I can't cover all the possibilities in a few pages. I do look at some of the factors that affect the taste, texture, and flavor of cheese. I then categorize the major cheese styles and provide wine pairing advice for each.

Appreciating the complexity of cheese

Just as wine is complicated, cheese, too, is a crazy world that you could spend years studying to try to grasp. So many variables make cheese such a wonderfully diverse product, and a little bit of background information goes a long way to increasing your appreciation. The main factors affecting the flavor profile of cheese (like wine) are

- Raw material
- Production methods
- Age

The following sections explain these three factors in a little more detail.

What you start with

Consider just a few of the variables with cheese production: Milk may come from cow, sheep, goat, water buffalo, or even yak. It can be collected from a morning or an evening milking, or from a combination of both. It may be taken during the summer months of high-mountain pasture feeding, or during the winter months of farmyard dining. The milk may be skimmed of its cream content or have cream added to it. Factors that influence the flavor of the raw material include the quality of the milk, its richness, its acid content, and the breed of animal.

What you do

The complex world of cheese also includes the variance in production methods: the amount of *rennet* (an extract used in cheese making to curdle milk) used; whether the milk is pasteurized or not; the way the cheese is pressed; the heating of the curds; the temperature; the degree of salting; the number of times the cheese is turned from one side to another while it is maturing; the length and location of maturation; how the cheese is brushed, scraped, or washed, as well as various other possible flavor additions. The possible flavor additions include wine, beer, spirits, spices, ashes, herbs, and leaves to name but a few, and they can impact significantly on the aroma, flavor, and texture, and therefore, the best style of wine to match.

I briefly explain all these variances just in case the pairing recommendations I suggest in the following sections aren't perfect. Just know that it's not me. The cheese has changed.

Flavor intensity varies considerably depending on how mature the cheese is: the older, the stinkier (if it smells like ammonia, toss it out). Unpasteurized, artisanal, farmhouse cheeses also have a much stronger flavor profile than pasteurized supermarket cheeses. Your wine choice should also climb the scale of intensity to make the match work. For instance, young, mild, pasteurized cheddar will be fine with an inexpensive, moderately complex, soft red. Serious, well-aged, crumbly farmhouse cheddar from unpasteurized milk, on the other hand, would crush all but the sturdiest of reds — think of matching intensity with intensity.

Thousands of cheeses are made worldwide, with more and more local, artisanal, and farmhouse cheeses popping up every year. I obviously don't have enough room to list them all here. If you don't see the name of your cheese in the following lists in each section (I list only some of the classic, widely recognized types, such as Brie and Camembert under the "soft, bloomy rind" category) and aren't sure which category it belongs to, check with your cheese purveyor. He or she can tell you what type it is so you know what category of wine to go sifting through for the best match.

Though most people think of red wine first with cheese, white wine and even off-dry or medium sweet wines (and sparkling wines) are much more versatile and make for better general matches. If you're going with just one wine for a range of cheeses, an off-dry wine like Chenin Blanc or Riesling is your safest choice.

To rind or not to rind

Many foodies in the cheese world debate whether you should or you shouldn't eat the rind. One thing people agree on is that you avoid the inedible types, such as wax, cloth, bark, plastic, or other inorganic materials (don't laugh, it's been done), but on all the other types, not even the experts agree. As with all matters of taste, it depends on the type of cheese, the type of rind, and your personal taste preferences. Some rinds that form naturally over long periods of ripening, such as on aged Parmesan, are too hard to eat.

The bloomy rind on cheeses, such as Brie and Camembert, encouraged by spraying the cheese with edible mold spores, is usually pretty mild, and most people are happy to eat it. The rind on washed rind cheeses, on the other hand, such as Münster, Époisses, Limberger, or Taleggio, are usually much more intensely flavored — that's the point of repeatedly bathing the cheese in various types of briny solutions. Some find the flavors objectionable, while others love the pungency, just as some love chile peppers and others can't tolerate the spice. For me it depends mostly on how mature the cheese is: Even the bloomy rind on a piece of Brie can get pretty pungent as the cheese ages. And the rind usually causes the most problems for wine matching. So if I'm looking for better synergy between wine and cheese, I sometimes cut off the rind and just eat the paste, especially if it has started to develop the scent of ammonia, a sign of advanced maturity. But if I'm not drinking, I leave on the rind until it's ready to crawl off on its own.

Matching with soft, fresh cheeses

Some examples of soft, fresh cheeses include cottage cheese, ricotta, fromage blanc, fromage frais, and queso fresco. These fresh cheeses are mild in flavor. They'll work, or at least not clash, with most wines.

The best wine-style category for these cheeses includes lightweight, crisp, and stony whites or light-bodied, bright, and zesty, low tannin reds.

Matching with goat's cheese

Although many types of goat's milk cheeses are available, ranging from fresh to firm, I find in general that the tangy acidity (goat's milk has a higher fatty acid content than cow's milk cheese) of cheeses, such as Crottin de Chavignol, St. Maure, Chabichou, or anything called *chèvre,* calls for a wine with equally vibrant acidity. Unoaked whites, including lightweight, crisp, and stony whites, work best. The Loire Valley, famous for its goat's milk cheeses, also produces a range of crisp whites that work beautifully with them. Sancerre and Pouilly Fumé are the big guns made from Sauvignon Blanc, but dozens of less expensive options like Reuilly or Quincy or Sauvignon de Touraine are suitable. Dry Vouvray made from Chenin Blanc is also fine, as are other similar wines from around the world.

If the goat's cheese is firm and well-aged, you can stay in the same zone, but increase the intensity with something like a Sauvignon Blanc from Marlborough, New Zealand. Crottin de Chavignol and Sancerre is *the* regional match.

Matching with soft, bloomy rind cheese

Soft ripened cheeses, such as Camembert, Brie, Explorateur, and Chaource, are sprayed or dusted with a (good type of) mold and left to ripen. They come in varying degrees of richness, usually designated as single, double, or triple cream, (which have 50, 60, and 70 percent butterfat, respectively).

Some of the best wine style categories include medium- to full-bodied, soft, wood-aged whites or light-bodied, bright and zesty, low tannin reds. The richer the cheese, the richer and more full-bodied the wine should be. Brie and Camembert work well with soft, round, slightly buttery Chardonnay and dry fruity rosés. Light, soft, fruity reds are also generally simpatico, such as Gamay (Beaujolais), new world–Pinot Noir (such as from New Zealand, Ontario, or Chile). If it's a runnier, riper version, increase the intensity to Sonoma, Carneros, or Oregon Pinot Noir, or softer, gently oaky Merlot, for example. Triple cream Explorateur is delicious with Blanc de Blancs Champagne. Chablis and Chaource is a classic regional match.

Matching with soft, washed rind cheese

Washed-rind cheeses are regularly bathed with brine, beer, cider, wine, brandy, or oils during the ripening period. This practice encourages bacterial growth that allows the cheese to ripen from the outside in. Some of the milder examples of soft, washed rind cheese include Vacherin Mont d'Or, Livarot, Pont l'Évèque, Reblochon, and Taleggio. Some of the more pungent examples include Epoisses, Münster, Limberger, and Liederkranz.

Pour full-bodied complex, aromatic, round, spicy whites with milder types, such as Gewürztraminer, richer Pinot Gris, Viognier, or southern French white blends. You may try intensely flavored, medium- to full-bodied reds, such as Merlot, old-vine Zinfandel, southern Rhône Valley blends, or Shiraz. The more pungent, "I-can-smell-you-from-across-the-room" types crush any unsuspecting, delicate wines. They're a tough match at the best of times. Try off-dry or semi-sweet wines, such as demi-sec Vouvray or Alsatian vendanges tardives (late harvest). Münster with Alsatian Gewürztraminer is supposed to be a classic local pairing, but I find it has to be a really rich Gewürz and a younger, not so pungent Münster to really work. With really ripe and stinky cheeses like Epoisses, give up on wine and switch to spirits like fruit eau-de-vie (a clear fruit distillate). *Marc de Bourgogne* is the real insider's matchup.

The riper the cheese, the more intense the flavor of the rind will be. Some folks enjoy the pungent bacterial flavor of the rind, while others can do without. But in many cases, the rind clashes with wine, not the milder paste itself. If you find that the rind kills the match and you still want to enjoy wine alongside, just cut the rind off. (See the nearby sidebar for the lowdown on rinds.)

Matching with semi-soft cheeses

The category of semi-soft cheeses includes a wide variety ranging from mostly mild and nutty to occasionally more pungent and aromatic, such as Fontina, Havarti, Morbier, Jarslberg, Emmenthal, Monterey Jack, Port Salut, Oka, Gouda, and Edam. The milder (younger) versions are fairly friendly with wine, and soft fruity reds provide a good match. Try new world, delicately oaked Merlot, Pinot Noir, Zinfandel, and similar, medium-full bodied, fruity, balanced, moderately tannic reds. Medium-bodied, soft, and fruity whites are another way to go.

Matching with semi-hard and hard cheeses

Semi-hard and hard cheeses provide an opportunity to showcase some heavy-hitting, high quality, mature red wines. Some examples of these cheeses include Manchego, Pecorino, Parmigiano-Reggiano, Crotonese, Gouda, Cheddar, Tomme, Raclette, Comté, Cantal, Provolone, Gruyère, and

Mimolette. The combination of moderate fat content, sharp, pungent flavor and crumbly texture calls for full-bodied, deep and robust, turbocharged, chewy and tannic reds, such as Cabernet Sauvignon (and blends), Amarone della Valpolicella, Barolo/Barbaresco, Brunello di Montalcino, Douro Valley reds, and Tempranillo-based wines from Rioja and Ribera del Duero. You see how this type of cheese actually softens tannic reds, creating a smoother, creamier texture — a win-win pairing. Try also dry fortified amber wine, such as Oloroso Sherry or Marsala Vergine, for an unusual but superb combination.

The older the cheese is, the harder the texture and the greater the concentration of umami. I find really old cheese matches beautifully with very mature wines, especially old fortified wines that have spent a long time in barrel and have developed their own engaging nutty flavors and umami character. Try dry Amontillado or Oloroso Sherry with a 12-month aged Manchego for a real treat. Old vintage Champagne with its nutty flavors is an unexpected but delicious match with aged Parmigiano-Reggiano.

Matching with blue-veined cheeses

The intense saltiness and pungent flavors of blue cheese, which includes such examples as Stilton, Roquefort, Gorgonzola, Cabrales, and St Agur, wreak havoc on dry whites and reds, but make a brilliantly contrasting match with sweet wines. Both red and white, fortified, and late harvest/botrytis-affected sweet wines can be called into action. The saltier and more intense the cheese, the sweeter the wine should be. Try Icewine, select late harvest wines, sweet Chenin Blanc, such as Côteaux du Layon or Vouvray Moêlleux, Sauternes, Tokaji Aszú, Port, Banyuls, and fortified Muscats from the south of France like Rivesaltes or Beaumes de Venise, or the raisiny Muscats of Rutherglen in Australia. Roquefort with Sauternes and Port with Stilton are the arch-classic, textbook matches.

Setting Up for a Wine and Cheese Party

You like hosting get-togethers, but you're never sure exactly what cheese and wine to serve. I'm here to help. These sections offer easy setup guidelines for two practical wine and cheese parties: the casual affair and the formal, do-it-right type.

No matter what type of affair, when purchasing cheese, shop at a specialty cheese store whenever possible. Just as buying wine at the general store is risky business, buying cheese in a shop where it's an afterthought doesn't usually yield the best results. Also be sure to serve all cheeses at room temperature. Cheeses served straight from the fridge deliver only a fraction of their potential flavor, just as serving wines too cold kills much of their enticing aroma and flavor.

Doing wine and cheese without the fuss: The casual affair

The world of cheese is as vast and varied as the world of wine, so you want to avoid falling into easy traps. One trap that many people fall into is that they set out too many different types of cheese for the party, making it impossible for any single wine to work well. But serving a different wine for every cheese isn't exactly practical either in most cases. So here are some tips for setting up a casual but successful (free of natural disasters) wine and cheese party:

- ✔ **Select four or five different cheeses, making sure to cover several of the basic categories.** Select younger, milder versions of each, such as a young, mild bloomy rind cheese instead of a fully ripe, runny Camembert, or a young, semi-hard Cheddar instead of a dry, hard, crumbly, pungent, farmhouse Cheddar.

- ✔ **Set out two to three different wines and let guests discover the good and bad matches.** The good news is that there won't be any really bad matches, just some combinations that are better than others. Whites are generally more versatile with cheese, so be sure to have a crisp, dry, or off-dry white on hand, such as an off-dry Riesling, Sauvignon Blanc, uno-aked or gently oaky Chardonnay, Alsatian-style Pinot Gris, Vouvray demi-sec, and the like. Because you also need red, pick a smooth, soft, fruity, crowd-pleasing red, such as Spanish Tempranillo, a southern Rhône blend, or softer (inexpensive) new world Cabernet, Merlot, or Malbec.

Fussing for the right wine and cheese matches

If you're focused on getting a more formal event right, set up stations, each with a different cheese and wine combo. Encourage your guests to make their way around the room and try each different wine and cheese together.

Ideally, guests should try in the order I recommend in the following list, but don't bully them too much. Remember for stand-up affairs you need extra glasses, because some people will insist on a fresh glass with each type, especially if they're moving from big red back to light white. If it's a sit-down dinner party, make sure that everyone has a glass of each wine and be clear about which wine to try with each cheese.

Because you're going all the way, be sure to select top-quality, artisanal cheeses; no plastic-wrapped supermarket cheese, please. Local, unpasteur-ized farmhouse cheeses would be an extra nice touch.

Buying on apples, selling on cheese

An old Bordeaux adage goes straight to the heart of food and wine pairing theory: "Buy on apples and sell on cheese." The merchants of Bordeaux wine had figured out how to identify the best wines made locally, and then how to make them more appealing in order to re-sell them to consumers by using a simple food-and-wine pairing trick. In this case, sweet apple makes all wines taste more bitter and tart, and Bordeaux was indeed often bitter (tannic) and relatively high acid, especially when young. So the merchants ate a slice of apple before tasting a sample, and if the wine was *still* good, then it was worth buying.

On the other side, the right cheese, with its salt, fat, and protein content, has the effect of softening wines, especially tannic reds. So serving a little nibble of cheese along with the sample to unsuspecting retail customers was a sure-fire way to make all wines taste richer, rounder, smoother, and more appealing — the deal was as good as sealed.

Here's a classic setup:

- **Table 1:** Semi-firm goat's cheese plus Sancerre (or other crisp, dry Sauvignon Blanc)

- **Table 2:** Soft, bloomy rind cheese, such as Brie or Camembert plus Mâcon Villages or other lightly oaked Chardonnay

- **Table 3:** Soft, washed-rind cheese, such as Reblochon or Münster plus full-bodied, aromatic white, such as Alsatian Gewürztraminer

- **Table 4:** Hard cheese, such as Parmigiano-Reggiano plus Amarone or other full-bodied red wine

- **Table 5:** Blue cheese, such as Roquefort, Blue d'Auvergne, Gorgonzola plus Port or other sweet wine like Sauternes or Icewine

Part V

Party Time! Pairing with Friends . . . and Professionals

The 5th Wave   By Rich Tennant

GRICHTENNANT

"This one's earthy but light, with undertones of blackberry, vanilla, and Scotchgard."

In this part . . .

The enjoyment of food and wine happens in many places, and under many circumstances. This part looks at how to maximize the food and wine experience when dining out, throwing a party, and hosting a dinner at home. I share my experience on how to spot wine-friendly restaurants, and after you're inside, how to order off the list to get the best value, and how to get the most out of your server. I also take you on a little trip inside the mind of a sommelier that shows you how to ensure more enjoyment.

I'm frequently asked about parties: which type of wines to serve; what style, region, and color; how much of each to buy; what order to pour them in; and maybe even when to stop pouring. From large-scale gatherings to intimate family dinners, each situation is a little different. I tell you what I've discovered over the years about hosting the show, including what every sommelier (and host) should know about serving alcohol.

And after all this, if you're still interested in the sommelier profession, this part contains a chapter on becoming a sommelier. Here you can find out what it means, what it takes, and what the possibilities are after you get there. There might be a new career waiting for you.

Chapter 21

Dining Out: Finding Places That Appreciate Wine

In This Chapter

▶ Locating wine-savvy restaurants

▶ Gaming the wine list and beating the odds

▶ Leveraging the sommelier

In order to have a great food and wine experience when dining out, you have to be in the right place. Plenty of restaurants with excellent food exist, but oftentimes the wine program seems to be a bit of an afterthought or haphazardly thrown together. You may still have a great experience, but the odds are against it. By the same token, lots of serious, wine-focused restaurants and bars have lousy food (though fewer on average, because serious wine folks also usually like to eat well and thus serve good food). The quality of the food and service is tough to ascertain from a brief walk-by, but I've discovered over time how to spot the more serious wine places where the odds are in your favor, as well as the telltale signs of places best avoided, and I share those secrets with you in this chapter.

After you're in a promising restaurant, you want to make sure you order the right wine. If the list is large and full of unfamiliar names, places, and grapes, where do you start? How do you know which wines offer the best value, the most wine for your money? If you don't already know what you want to drink when you sit down, then this chapter is for you. It's packed with tips on maximizing your dining experience. Having put together dozens of wine lists, I have plenty of tips on how to read one and where to find the top values. And having worked the floor in many restaurants, I can share all the questions and information I hoped to get from guests in order to be able to match them with what they'd be happiest drinking.

Knowing How to Spot Wine-Savvy Restaurants

I've spent a lot of time traveling around the world and eating out in cities that I'm not familiar with. The best strategy when trying to pick a place to eat out is to ask a trusted local. I find winemakers in particular to be the best resource for great restaurants because great winemakers aren't only great drinkers, but they're also usually great eaters as well. *Sommeliers* (professionals trained in beverage knowledge and service), are usually happy to recommend other restaurants in the same town or region, the sort of places they would go on their nights off. You want to make sure you visit these places as well.

What do you do in the absence of a trustworthy recommendation? You can still increase the odds of landing in a wine-savvy restaurant by knowing how to spot the telltale signs. In these sections, I share a few clues that I've picked up over time that indicate the establishment takes its wine program a little more seriously than the average.

Looking for wine cues on the walk-by

Restaurants with a wine focus are usually easy to identify from a brief bit of background research or even from a 20-second walk-by on the street. Essentially, you want to seek out restaurants that do the following:

Employ a sommelier/wine director

A restaurant that's willing to incur the extra expense of a dedicated sommelier or wine director is obviously serious about wine, and has made it a key part of the overall food and beverage strategy. Restaurants that employ sommeliers usually capitalize on the fact and advertise it somewhere, such as on the wine list and/or website. They also usually make it part of the general promotional material along with the name of the chef. Otherwise, short of asking whether the restaurant employs a sommelier, look for the telltale sign of a certified sommelier wearing a pin on his or her lapel with some kind of vinous motif, like a bunch of grapes or the head of Bacchus, Roman god of wine.

Have high-quality, polished glassware

Take a quick glance at the place settings or the back bar area as you stroll by and peak your head in the window (or look at images on the restaurant's website). What do you see? Are wine glasses on the tables? Does the restaurant have a large supply of glassware at the bar? If not, keep walking. If glasses are on the tables or behind the bar, what are they like? Quality glassware is one of the most conspicuous and obvious signs that a restaurant cares about wine. Refer to Chapter 8 where I discuss how the type of glass a wine is served in does indeed make a difference, and savvy restaurateurs know it.

A gorgeous, shapely crystal stem is the single most effective way to enhance the wine experience and makes the ordinary look (and even taste) a little more extraordinary. Good glassware isn't cheap. It can cost four or five times more than standard, industrial, banquet-type wine glasses (and many times more than that), not to mention that breakage through careless handling by servers is more or less a given. Having high-quality glassware is a significant, and on-going, investment. So any restaurant that has invested in proper stem-ware — relatively large bowl with tapered, (unrolled) rim, tall, and elegant — is making a serious effort.

Post the wine list

Look to see that the restaurant posts its wine list or part of it on its web-site or outside with the menu. Doing so means that the restaurant is proud enough of the list to want to publicly display it and wants to use it to draw in patrons (a pathetic list of four selections would have the opposite effect).

Posting the wine list can also mean that the pricing is fair. Restaurants with atrociously high mark-ups rarely make their lists available for viewing outside the establishment; it's too easy in the days of instant access to information to do some quick price checking and referencing. They also know that after you're already seated and settling in for the meal, you're much less likely to get up and leave when you see the wine list. If a restaurant practices fair pricing, however, capitalizing on the fact to encourage potential patrons to walk in is smart.

Have prominent visual displays of wine

If customers see visible wine racking or bins, wine cabinets, a glassed-in show cellar, and large format bottles (magnums, double magnums, and larger) in a conspicuous location like on the bar, they are much more likely to buy. Restaurant patrons are notoriously bad about knowing what they want. They know they're hungry and thirsty, but they rarely know ahead of time exactly what they will eat and drink. Visual cues are therefore very pow-erful (as are verbal suggestions).

Seeing a cellar full of fine wine or bottles prominently displayed gets you thinking about ordering wine. If the restaurateur were smart enough to build an expensive wine display of some kind, and even lose a few seats on the floor in order to accommodate the display, then I'd wager that he or she has also invested money and effort in filling the cellar with appropriate bottles and spent some time considering which wine goes best with each dish.

Care about storage and preservation

Nothing sends a clearer message that wine is taken seriously than the sight of a temperature-controlled wine fridge (or cellar) or wine preservation and dispensing unit like the Enomatic machine or Le Verre de Vin, which protect open wines from oxidizing too quickly. Proper wine storage and service tem-perature, along with some means of protecting wines, are very good signs.

Include suggested wines with dishes on the menu

Seeing a food menu that lists suggested wine pairings (even if it's a pairing I wouldn't go for) always reassures me. Devising pairings for each menu item takes extra time, effort, and money. It also means more frequent reprints of the menu because wines come in and out of stock. These suggestions mean that someone has taken the trouble to think about, and maybe even test out the right match, and wants to make the guests' wine selections easier and more foolproof as well as enhance the overall dining experience (not to mention boost wine sales). Only wine-savvy restaurants give this added touch.

Offer a prix fixe menu with a wine pairing option

Devising a full *prix fixe menu* (a set number of specific courses) with a wine pairing optional add-on takes effort. For the diner, it's a great way to avoid the fear-fraught process of choosing the right wines to match each dish. When the restaurant says "trust me," I'm often willing to give it a go, at least once.

Serve a large number of wines by the glass

Offering guests a wide range of wines by the glass is risky. If open bottles don't sell quickly, they spoil, which means profits literally poured down the sink. Only confident sommeliers in wine-savvy establishments with well-trained staff can pull off a robust by-the-glass program. You want to be there. This is also a great way for you to try and discover new wines, like a wine course without the homework.

List wine specials online or on a chalkboard

A chalkboard is a simple, inexpensive, yet effective way to refresh the selection continually, or complement the selection on the main, printed wine list. Think of the chalkboard as the sommelier's playground. The modern version of the chalkboard is the electronic wine list, which, if set up properly, is the ultimate tool for the sommelier.

Of all of the sommelier's regular duties, keeping the wine list up-to-date and free of errors and out-of-stock items is the biggest headache. The larger the list is, the bigger the headache is. The task can be so onerous that the sommelier is actually discouraged from changing the list. He or she can fall into the trap of listing only regularly available, large brands and/or re-ordering the same wines over and over again, which isn't necessarily a bad thing, but the world of wine is constantly changing and evolving, with new wines coming into every market regularly. If part of the sommelier's job description includes discovering new and exciting wines and food pairings, and then sharing them with customers, then the carved-in-stone wine list is an obstacle.

Use social media to advertise new wine arrivals

The "if you build it they will come" promotional strategy has seen countless restaurants go out of business. If a restaurant is serious about wine, then it lets people know! If I see an establishment promoting new wines by the glass, recent arrivals, new pairings, or whatever else related to food and wine on its Facebook page, via Twitter, or through any other modern form of communication, then that restaurant probably takes the substance of its wine program seriously enough to consider a visit.

Spotting the danger signs

Identifying the places where you're least likely to have a great wine (and food) experience is just as easy. If an interesting, well-thought-out, and passionately assembled wine list is what you're after, then you may want to avoid restaurants with:

- **Plastic-laminated wine menus:** Being handed a plastic wine list is like the kiss of death. I appreciate the expense of reprinting menus. Although using plastic-laminated menus may even make sense in a restaurant where finger food is served (nobody likes to find the sticky rib sauce from the previous dinner on the list), to me it's generally a sign of giving up. The restaurant is saying: "Here's our list, it never changes, we've given up trying to improve and evolve, and we don't care to discover anything new and share it with you." Laminating is a pain and costs money, so usually when you coat something in plastic, you don't intend to change it anytime soon, like carving the list in stone. The restaurant loses all flexibility to offer new and exciting finds to its customers. The list carved in stone is a dead list.

- **No vintages listed on the wine list:** The *vintage* — the year in which the grapes were grown — is important in the world of wine, even if most people can't (and shouldn't) possibly know what the weather was like every year in every winegrowing region of the world. That's the sommelier's job. A restaurant that doesn't list vintages along with the name of the wine either doesn't care about the variations in style and flavor profile from year to year, or more likely, has opted to list a bunch of cookie-cutter style brands that are designed in a boardroom, not in a vineyard with the help of Mother Nature, and which probably don't change much from year to year anyway. It also means that the restaurant doesn't care much for the customer who cares about vintage, which is to say, anyone who takes wine seriously. If I'm looking for an interesting wine experience, I stay away from these types of places.

- **Spelling errors and missing information on the list:** As with missing vintages, abundant spelling errors, missing producer names, mismatched wines and regions, and other presentation mistakes are signs of carelessness. For the wine-savvy diner, they're also danger signs.

- **Prominent alcohol manufacturers' advertising:** These can include branded menu covers, flashing neon signs, branded table tent cards advertising wine, and so on. Translation: The restaurant has sold out. Free umbrellas and wine list covers come with a quid pro quo: We give you this, you give us that. This usually means some kind of deal on minimum number of *placements,* that is, a guarantee of a certain number of the advertiser's brands listed on the wine list and/or by-the-glass list. Again, nothing is inherently evil about getting a little help from your preferred suppliers with the setup and day-to-day running costs of a restaurant, which are significant, but it also means that someone else is in charge of the wine program. And that someone has only one agenda: to sell more of his or her brands. It has nothing to do with the suitability of wines for the establishment or the compatibility with the food. All else equal, a place that has turned over its program to a vendor/advertiser isn't where I go for a great food and wine experience.

Reading a Wine List: What a Casino and Restaurant Have in Common

You found what appears to be a restaurant that cares about wine. You settle in and prepare for a great wine and food experience. But the wine list is so large and full of names, some familiar, some vaguely familiar, and lots that you've never seen or heard of before. What's the next step?

One of the best ways to get a firm grasp on the wine list is to read the wine list like a sommelier does. A sommelier must put together a list that maximizes revenues for the restaurant and offers a selection that will make guests happy, while still satisfying his or her passion for wine. Assembling a good wine list is an art. In the following sections, you get an inside look at how it's done and where to find the best odds and which "games" to avoid if you're after top value. Although this analogy isn't perfect, wine programs and casinos do share some common ground.

Choosing wine on a restaurant list is a lot like gambling in a casino. Just as smart gamblers know the strategic ways to bet and which games to avoid altogether to come out on top, smart diners, even without intimate knowledge of the wine list, can tip the odds in their favor of getting the most wine for the money. A little inside understanding about how wine programs are assembled will go a long way to making you a smarter and more successful diner.

A restaurant, like a casino, is an entertainment business that generates revenue from its patrons: The latter offers the thrill of gambling, the former the pleasure of eating and drinking. In each case, the thrill or pleasure is offered in many forms: The casino offers various games, the restaurant various menu items.

In the following sections, I put you in the mind of the creator of the wine list so you can see it from his or her perspective, and show you how wine programs and casinos, believe it or not, share some common aspects. I offer some tips on beating the house — that is, maximizing your chances of getting the most for your money.

Getting the most bang for your buck

In a casino, each game has an inherent advantage that favors the house, called the *house edge*, which is what the casino expects to take in from each game, and it varies from game to game. Basic statistical analysis reveals, for example, that keno has one of the highest house advantages at a whopping 25 percent. That means the house profits $25 for every $100 wagered overall. Double odds craps and blackjack, on the other hand, are where the smart money is wagered. These games have a house edge of just .6 percent and .8 percent respectively, bringing in just 60 and 80 cents per $100. Gambling specialists also know that a skilled blackjack player can not only eliminate the house edge, but also even shift the edge in his favor.

Similarly, every product listed on a restaurant menu has a house edge; each is priced to make money, but the percentage varies from item to item. Some items have higher cost margins, some lower. I'm referring to what the house takes as a percentage. For example, a well-aged 24-ounce bone-in rib-eye may seem expensive at $60, but it's probably the best relative value on the

menu — the wholesale cost of the item might be $30, meaning that the cost margin is 50 percent, which is very high by industry standards. The restaurant only doubles its money, before paying all the other operating expenses. But fully half of what you pay goes directly to product, not profit. Compare with a bowl of spaghetti at $15: It's cheaper, but a much lower relative value. It probably costs less than $3 to make, yielding a cost margin of just 20 percent. Most of your money goes to the house, not the noodles.

When dining out, all things being equal, I'm after the best relative values on the wine list. I want the largest percentage possible of my money going to the wine, not the house. As with food, cost margins vary from wine to wine (in a well-run establishment), ranging from as low as 15 to 20 percent (500 to 600 percent over cost) for the most aggressively marked up, to more than 50 percent (less than 200 percent mark-up). The game is to know which wines are likely to have the keno house advantage, and which the blackjack.

Don't play (or drink) keno

Every wine program, like casinos, needs cash generators, which I refer to as the kenos on the wine list. They're the popular mainstream grapes and wine styles that sell themselves, the ones that *must* be on the list. In a well-run restaurant, these wines, like the game of keno in a casino, have the biggest *house edge* (biggest mark-up), and they subsidize the rest of the wine program (and keep the restaurant afloat). The sommelier knows they will outsell everything else, so this is where profits are maximized.

A combination of factors can identify these kenos, such as

✔ **Temptingly priced just above the entry-level price point on the list:** For example, if the cheapest bottle listed is $30, the kenos sit around the $35 to $40 mark. Consumer psychology dictates that the cheapest stuff doesn't sell as well as items priced just above the bottom end. Position 3 or 4 on a wine list organized by ascending price is highly coveted by wine suppliers. And remember that in general, all the bottles at the lower end of the price scale almost always offer the worst odds.

✔ **Popular/fashionable grapes or places that you've heard of:** The wine world is daunting, and familiarity is comforting. Restaurants prey on your weakness for something recognizable and *en vogue*. Counter intuitively (and despite my later point in this list), this strategy can even apply to popular, well-known brands in some instances. People often overpay for something that's familiar, even when they know what the regular retail price is.

✔ **Not from well-known or readily available producers:** This is key. You can't easily price reference a keno, because it won't be available at every supermarket or corner wine shop. The smart sommelier can find an inexpensive example of a popular grape, such as Pinot Grigio, Chardonnay, Merlot, or Cabernet Sauvignon, from a source you don't have easy access to, and list it with a healthy mark-up, banking on the popularity of the grape. If you want popular, you'll pay.

✔ **Scorned by sommeliers:** Despite their profitability, sommeliers (as long as the sommelier isn't the owner) usually look down at keno wines. If the sommelier or server subtly rolls his or her eyes or thinly disguises disdain when you order the wine, there's a good chance it's a keno.

Bad gamblers play keno. Avoid wines made from popular grapes, places, and wineries priced just above the entry point, and which may cause a barely susceptible display of contempt when ordered. (Refer to the nearby sidebar that explains how bad the odds are with keno.)

Seek the unknown

The flipside to avoiding kenos that I mention in the previous section is to find the blackjacks of the wine list. The *blackjacks* have the lowest house edge and best odds for you. They're usually the wines you've never heard of. Seek out the odd, strange, or seemingly out of place listings. They're there for a reason, and chances are they'll at least be worth trying. Ask the sommelier for assistance (refer also to the later section, "Relying on Your Sommelier/Server" for more details).

Consider the mentality of the sommelier. She spends a lot of time tasting wine and quickly grows tired of mainstream, popular brands and overly fashionable grapes. She's always seeking something new, unusual, interesting, from unknown grapes or places; expanding her horizons; and indulging her passion. This is what keeps the job exciting, what quickens the pulse. She doesn't get much enjoyment from cranking the cork on the hundredth bottle of Pinot Grigio or doing inventory at 3 a.m.

Although such obscure wines often offer better value, that is, more flavor and character for the money, the sommelier also knows that unknown wines don't sell. Yet she can't help herself — the wine is just too cool not to list. So she adds it, but at a very reasonable mark-up to entice you to explore and to ensure that it doesn't suck up inventory dollars and space for too long. After all, what's the point of listing an obscure, poor-quality wine at an inflated price? The keno wines will subsidize them.

Know what's supposed to sell, and avoid it

You want to find the odd ducks on the list: the wines, even if well known, that seem out of place. Look for what you'd expect to find on the list. For example, a steakhouse is expected to list big Cabernets or a pizzeria Chianti or Valpolicella. These wines are the main sellers and source of profit, the categories where the odds of hitting a keno are highest. Playing here is playing right into the hands of the house.

But a well-curated program run by a passionate sommelier invariably has some wines that don't really fit in with the general theme of the wine list and restaurant. They may be included because of the sommelier's personal passion, or area of expertise, or because they were just too good to pass up. Look for suspiciously incongruous wines, such as a long list of Champagnes at a sports bar or a collection of crisp, dry whites at a steakhouse. There's really no operational reason for such wines to be on a list; they take up space and cost money in inventory. But they're there because someone's passionate about them and likely priced to move, lest the sommelier lose her job.

Buy local

No matter where you are, if wine grows locally, more than likely it offers some of the best odds on the list. Sommeliers are generally proud and excited to share local wines with guests, and in order to encourage sales, the prices are made attractive. If you really want to drink Bordeaux in Burgundy, or Napa in Niagara, well then, you'll pay the best odds to the house.

Steer clear of Monte Carlo

Self-evident but worth mentioning nonetheless is the observation that some operations are more expensive to run than others. In Monte Carlo casinos, for example, the stakes are high — no $1 minimum blackjack tables there. It's expensive to be in Monte Carlo. You don't go unless you can afford it, and you're not after value. Similarly, if it's pure value in the glass (and not all the confounding factors surrounding it) that you want, then avoid the gastronomic palaces. The more ostentatious the restaurant, the more the odds are stacked against you.

The ultra-luxury restaurants in prime locations, with a celebrity chef and everything from valet parking to linen tablecloths and crystal stemware, add to the minimum required profit per square foot. A certain wine in one of these places is necessarily more expensive than the exact same wine in a casual wine bar on the edge of town. I'm not knocking high-end restaurants; this strategy applies only to finding the best odds for value wine.

Slow-paced dining = higher house edge

To find the best odds for value wine, you also want to avoid small restaurants with slow-paced service. Consider this: Blackjack is played fairly swiftly; a good dealer averages about 60 hands per hour. Roulette, on the other hand, is a slower paced game, averaging only about 30 rounds per hour. The inherent house edge must therefore reflect the speed of the game (5.6 percent for double zero roulette versus 0.8 percent for blackjack) if the same profit per hour per square foot is to be realized. The slower the game, the more the house expects to make per wager. Restaurants operate in the same way, or go out of business.

If the establishment is the type where a guest can dine leisurely over several hours and the house doesn't expect to *turn the table* (seat multiple parties at the same table over the course of the evening), then the minimum profit per guest must necessarily be higher to generate sustainable profits. You want to avoid one-turn restaurants when seeking high relative value wines.

In other words, most deliberately slow-paced restaurants offer the worst odds out of necessity. Because fewer people are dining, each person has to pay more. The restaurant compensates for this by having an excellent selection, fine stemware, knowledgeable servers, and so on, so that you still feel you're getting your money's worth, even when you're paying much more for the same bottle of wine than in a more casual, faster-paced eatery, where greater volume affords lower margins per customer.

Educate yourself to improve the odds

Players who take the time to educate themselves about which games have the best odds and then master the basic strategy are the ones most likely to walk away winners. Uninformed players who don't know how to do basic odds calculations are going to lose. They play keno or the one-arm bandits, the slot machines, engineered to relieve them of excess coin (contrary to popular belief, the odds don't improve the longer you play; they're identical and long, each time you pull the lever). Diners familiar with current trends in the wine world, principal grape varieties, and general pricing for the wines of the major regions, and who are able to identify unusual listings or groups of listings on a wine list are more likely to spot the wines that deliver the most for their money.

No gambling system is foolproof, and the house always wins. Recreational players don't mind parting with a small sum, rationalizing the experience as the price paid for a little fun. Your goal as a diner should be to leave the restaurant feeling that the meal was worth every penny or even more. In that case, you both win.

Relying on Your Sommelier/Server

Another way to find wine value is to go directly to the server or sommelier and ask for a recommendation. Many people still feel a little trepidation when speaking to a sommelier, fearing that the sommelier's goal is to extract as much money from them as possible. That may once have been true, but it's less and less so.

If you're in the right establishment, someone will be on the floor who knows what he is talking about and willing/able to help. In the following sections, I offer some tips on how to spot an informed sommelier and how to know when you're about to be had. I also offer advice on how to get the most out of your sommelier, to help him help you find the wines that you're after, or to perhaps introduce you to something new that you're likely to enjoy. Just as there's an art to serving, there's also an art to dining. And knowing what questions to ask and what information to share can go a long way to ensuring a great experience every time.

Knowing what to ask the sommelier

The modern sommelier is on your side — there to make you happy — so don't be afraid to ask for advice. When dining out, most professional sommeliers I know are happy to defer to the house sommelier, so why wouldn't you? No one knows more about the specific wines on the list and what works best with each dish than the person who works there nightly. By asking the right questions and providing some useful information, you can help him out. Here are some tips:

Don't be afraid to talk price

Everyone has a price range they're comfortable with so don't fret about talking about price. Many people still feel shy about discussing money, especially in front of guests. As I sommelier, I was always relieved when the guest gave me a price range to work with, saying something like, "I like to spend between X and Y." This kind of statement avoids any ambiguity and embarrassment later on and saves time. So don't be shy; there's nothing shameful about saying about much you're willing to spend.

On the other hand, a well-trained sommelier isn't likely to directly ask how much you want to spend if you don't offer the information. That too can be awkward and put off the guest. She won't know in most cases who's at the table and whether you're comfortable discussing price in front of them. The sommelier can rely on some subtle tactics to find out, such as recommending three wines in three different price brackets, ensuring with a finger gesture that your attention is drawn to the price posted on the wine list, and waiting to see which option you're more drawn too. If you experience this, you're likely in good hands.

Providing price parameters becomes even more important when giving the sommelier *carte blanche* to select a wine to match your meal. If such a request gets into the wrong hands without any limits, you're just asking to get fleeced. You're paying, so you're in charge. Take control of the situation.

Give as much information as possible

Make sure you tell the server or sommelier as much information as possible. The more you can share about what you like, the more likely you are to get it. If you liked a certain type of wine before, mention that fact. Even something as basic as "I prefer red to white" is at least a helpful starting point. If you don't enjoy a certain wine style, make sure you say so, as in "I don't like dry wines, or astringent wines, or acidic wines or high alcohol wines." This critical information can help the sommelier pick what's right for you.

Tell the server what you usually drink

Most diners are intimidated of *wine speak*. They aren't comfortable with the complex technical and esoteric terminology that wine experts frequently fling about. Rather than risk looking foolish, they opt not to say anything at all. To get around this, rather than struggling to describe the style of wine that you like, simply tell the sommelier which specific wines you like to drink. You can be as detailed as a particular vintage and appellation that you remember, as in, "I loved the 2009 Château X from Bordeaux," or something more broad such as "I'm into California Cabernet or Sauvignon Blanc." If remembering wines or grapes is a challenge, or pronunciation embarrasses you, snap a photo of your favorite labels on your mobile device and show them.

A good sommelier can immediately pick up on this valuable information and guide you in the right direction. If she gives you a puzzled look or blank stare, on the other hand, that means trouble. You may need to ask for a server who knows, or revert to the strategies that I describe in the "Reading a Wine List: What a Casino and Restaurant Have in Common" section earlier in this chapter.

Ask your sommelier what she is most excited about

If your sommelier looks reasonably competent and enthusiastic, try asking what her latest discoveries are. Nothing will make a sommelier happier than the chance to talk about something she loves, and at the same time, lessen the odds of considering you merely as a means to an end (a larger wad of cash in the pocket at the end of the night). Passionate sommeliers live to talk about their latest finds, the new vintage, producer, region, or grape that got them excited. This is your chance for a little free education, and who knows, you may just find something new that you'd never have considered ordering on your own.

Often, but not always, the sommelier's suggestions will be interesting, unusual, seemingly out-of-place wines on the list at fair prices, or at least good relative value (refer to the earlier section, "Seek the unknown").

If the sommelier jumps straight to the most expensive bottle on the list claiming it's her latest *fave,* retake control of the situation and lay down some firm guidelines on price.

Ask your sommelier to pair wines to your food

Giving the sommelier a chance to dazzle with her wine knowledge and ability to make perfect pairings increases your odds of a great experience. Because the goal is to impress you, the sommelier will do everything in order to make that happen, including offering you the best values on the list, giving a free education on food and wine compatibility, and maybe even opening bottles for you that aren't usually available by the glass. As usual, you should give the sommelier parameters on pricing and any restrictions on wines you don't care for upfront.

Spotting the ruse: Warning signs

Identifying the ruse — a mercenary server out to up-sell you at all costs or otherwise guide you in the wrong direction — isn't always easy. Here I provide some additional red flags to look for:

✔ **Servers, bartenders, or sommeliers that talk and don't listen:** If you've ever worked in the service and hospitality industry, you know how to be a good listener. Unless you have an established relationship with the server and he already knows your preference and price comfort zone, the only way for him to find out is by discreetly asking a few questions, by engaging in conversation, and then by listening to what you have to say. If he talks without listening and without asking any questions, I get concerned. How can the server possibly know what I like and how much I'm willing to pay?

If you ask for a recommendation without providing any of the information listed in the previous section, "Knowing what to ask the sommelier," and the server doesn't ask you for any further information, and then says: "I've got just the thing for you," it's more than likely just the thing that *the server* wants to serve you.

- **Servers, bartenders, or sommeliers who only recommend one wine**: Good sommeliers give multiple options, especially if a price range hasn't already been established. Giving options is the only discreet way to find your comfort zone, for style as well as price. It also shows that the sommelier is comfortable with the wine list. Servers and bartenders who offer only a single recommendation likely don't know their stuff. Ill-trained staff tend to always recommend the same wine to everyone, at all times, mostly because it's the only wine they know, or it's the one they like to drink at the end of their shift. That doesn't necessarily mean that the wine is a poor selection and that you won't enjoy it, but the odds are against you.

- **Servers, bartenders, or sommeliers who make up stuff:** Nobody wants to appear ignorant, but one of the basic tenets of hospitality is never to lie to a guest. A good server or bartender is trained to apologize and go find someone who knows the answer to a guest's question if he doesn't. There are a hundred excuses to make stuff up: It's a busy night, there's no time to find the right answer, they didn't want to jeopardize their tip, and so on, but no excuse is good enough. Knowing when a server is lying isn't always obvious, but you can look for clues, such as perceptible hesitation, avoidance of direct eye contact, shifting of weight from one leg to another leg, and vague, off-the-point answers. If you observe any of these signs, then the server is probably lying (or just incompetent). If you get the feeling that the server doesn't know what he is talking about, ask to speak to someone else, or revert to other strategies.

Chapter 22

Dining In: Becoming the Perfect Host

*H*osting at home is no easy task. Whether you've invited friends, family, or other guests, putting on a successful dinner party takes some forethought, organization, and more than a little skill to pull it off. I can't help you with the cooking and cleaning, but I can share some pointers about wine.

In this chapter, I look at which wines to serve to diverse crowds, knowing that different occasions require different wines. I include tips about serving at different types of parties, from the casual stand-up cocktail party to the formal sit-down, multicourse dinner. I also offer some advice on bringing wine to somebody else's house for dinner (or what to bring instead of wine).

And because being a good host also means being a responsible host (and good guests are likewise responsible guests), I provide some background details on standard drink sizes, calculating your blood alcohol content, and recognizing the visual signs of the progressive effects of intoxication. All well-trained servers, bartenders, and sommeliers have this training, and it's worth your having a basic understanding of it.

Matching Your Guests with Wine

A party calls for libations. And to get a party right, wine has to be in the mix. But just as certain foods call for certain wines, different types of social gatherings require a tweak to the selections. The appropriate quantity, style, and price all change with the crowd and the occasion. In theses sections, I take you through a few common scenarios and offer some tips on becoming a savvy sommelier for your own parties.

Selecting wines for the large affairs

For large affairs, corporate events, office mixers, big weddings, and any other type of event where you don't know or can't remember half the guests' names, play it safe and stick with the mainstream: nothing idiosyncratic or overly dramatic. The more character the wine has, the less likely it is to appeal to everyone.

Avoid excessive oak, alcohol, acidity, tannins, or violently aromatic wines. Well-known regions and grapes are key. You don't want the guests wondering why such an unusual wine was selected. For reds, err on the side of more full-bodied, such as warm climate Cabernet Sauvignon, Merlot, Syrah/Shiraz, or Malbec. For whites, low or unoaked Chardonnay, Pinot Grigio, and Sauvignon Blanc are safe choices. For bubbles, Cava or Prosecco do the job, unless you're working with a Champagne budget. Your budget and the type of food being served ultimately drive the specific types of wines you select.

To maximize your bang for the buck, spend a few cents less on wine and a few more on the glassware, if you're renting. Nothing ruins the experience of a decent wine like those thick-rimmed, old-style balloon glasses, while even an average wine tastes better in a classy glass (refer to Chapter 8 for basic stemware types, sizes, and shapes). For casual stand-up affairs, count on needing 1.5 glasses per person (that's 150 glasses for 100 people, for example, for a reception-type event), and encourage reusing/rinsing. More formal, sit-down, multi-wine events require one glass per person per wine.

Buying for the intimate gathering of friends or family

When you are just having a few close friends and/or family members over for an intimate gathering, you can really shine as a wine-savvy host. Toss all safe picks out the window and dazzle your friends with your latest cutting-edge finds.

Do a little bit of research and arm yourself with a few third-party reviews, just in case anyone challenges your sophisticated, jet-setting selections, and drop a line about the rarity or the up-and-comingness of each wine as you pull it out. Avoid the expected grapes and regions for a real night of exploration.

For sparkling, skip the big brands and go with grower Champagne or other traditional method sparkling wine from off the beaten path. For whites, look for insider's picks such as Austrian Grüner Veltliner, Spanish Albariño or Verdejo, Chardonnay from Canada, Argentine Torrontés, white blends from the Roussillon in Southern France, the Alentejo in Portugal, Clare or Eden Valley Riesling in South Australia, or one of those weird, orange-colored wines made in amphorae in Friuli in northeastern Italy.

For reds, consider Loire Valley Cabernet Franc and Beaujolais, especially from the natural wine movement (minimal intervention in the winery), Malbec from Patagonia instead of Mendoza, Central Coast California Rhône-style blends, Agiorgitiko or Xinomavro from Greece, Tasmanian Pinot Noir, or Saperavi from Georgia, to name a few fun possibilities. Go to a trusted source to find these wines and others like them.

This occasion should be about sharing something new and learning together. More than likely, not everyone will appreciate all the wines, but your guests will appreciate the extra effort you've made to introduce them to something different; unusual/obscure wines also score points among wine aficionados.

Bringing wine to someone's house

Friends ask you to dinner. You're not sure what type of wine to bring as a gift. Unless you know what your host prefers, I suggest that you stick with the classics because they're safe and always appreciated.

So what are the classics? Well, if you've never heard of the wine, then it's probably not a classic. The majority of self-proclaimed serious wine drinkers drink red wine, so think red. Your most solid red options are big, full-bodied wines with household names like Napa Valley Cabernet Sauvignon, Amarone, Chianti Classico, Brunello, Barolo, Barossa Valley Shiraz, Burgundy, or Bordeaux (just remember, it starts with a "B" and you're ahead of the game). They're some of the blue chips of the red wine world.

You may decide to go with sparkling wine, which most people appreciate, even those who don't really like bubbles — it just seems more sophisticated. In this case, go with Champagne (I've yet to see somebody frown when receiving real Champagne). Premium California sparkling or another well-respected traditional method sparkling also fits the bill.

If your hosts prefer white wine, go with Sancerre, white Burgundy, higher end ($20 or more) California Chardonnay, or a well-respected local wine producer — people most often appreciate the fact that you support local (quality) wineries.

When you're looking for wine to gift, you aren't looking for value. The wow factor is more important. Stay away from obscure wines, even if they're a great value. The host may not recognize how great a value it is and just think you gifted an inexpensive bottle. But if the host is a wine buff, then he or she will be pleased if you can introduce a new wine. Providing a little background on whatever you bring is a nice touch. You may bring a third-party review of the wine or some information gathered from the winery's website. This extra effort can go a long way and impress your host.

What's the etiquette for bringing wine?

Selecting wine to bring to somebody's house for dinner can cause as much anxiety as hosting the party. With close friends, bringing the right wine may be a tad easier. You usually know each other well enough to communicate and plan in advance without any embarrassment, and you probably have a decent idea what type of wine your host likes. But the etiquette becomes less certain the less you know your hosts. And when invited to dine with perfect strangers, there's a deep social vacuum on the correct approach. How much do you spend? Should you bring one bottle or two? Should you insist on having your special wine opened that evening (because you were hoping to have a glass, too), even if it doesn't match with the food?

If you bring wine, then be prepared to spend about the average price for a main course in a fine dining establishment for one bottle. Spending any more may make your host feel awkward, as if the cheaper wine they plan on serving is beneath you, and any less is, well, less. Remember, your host easily can check prices online without much effort. Bring one bottle per couple, which is about equivalent to

what you'll consume over the course of the evening; more just looks like you want to booze it up. But don't expect to drink the wine you bring. In fact, insist that it's a gift for the host and not to be opened. A gracious, savvy host will likely crack it anyhow, especially if it looks better than what the host is serving, and if not, then you knew what to expect. If you really want to drink the wine you bring, then bring two bottles (two different types look better), and state clearly which one is to be shared tonight and which is a gift for the host to enjoy another time.

If you're really stuck, you can dodge the whole wine dilemma and bring a potted flower instead (cut flowers die; potted plants remind your hosts of your thoughtfulness forevermore). You may also consider a specialty, nonperishable food product, such as an exotic extra-virgin olive oil; rare wine vinegar; single origin chocolate (minimum 66 percent cacao content; milk chocolate is for toddlers); freshly roasted whole coffee beans (never pre-ground) from an exotic country (also fair trade, just in case your hosts are activists); special, loose leaf tea; or premium jams — are all good bets. The more exotic, the better you look.

Deciding On Quantity and Color

Knowing how much wine to buy for certain types of parties is one of the sommelier's crucial skills and sometimes not easy for the everyday party planner. So when figuring out how much and what type of wine to have for a social event, you have to consider how many people will be there, what type of event it will be, and the likely consumption; afternoon garden parties are evidently different from night weddings. The type of people and the average age of those who will be at the gathering are also important considerations. And remember: Having too much wine on hand is much better than too little.

You walk a fine line between making everyone satisfied and happy, and not pressuring anyone to go overboard and overserving. Running out of booze, on the other hand, is a surefire way to end the party early (which could also be part of your strategy). The challenge in determining appropriate quantities for purchase lies in the fact that each person has a different capacity, tolerance, and desire to drink alcohol. Having a trained server or sommelier at the party who knows how to pick up on subtle signals and body language (the pleading eyes that say "no more!") is a smart move if you're taking it really seriously.

In the next sections, I look at a few common types of gatherings and offer some guidelines on quantities and color split to purchase based on my experience. Keep in mind that these quantities also vary from country to country, because different cultures have varying degrees of fondness for alcohol. For some, drinking wine is a way of life; for others it's a very special occasion.

Stand-up cocktail parties and receptions

Stand-up cocktail parties and receptions usually include a full bar with beer, wine, and mixed drinks that lasts only a couple of hours, with minimal food and/or hors d'oeuvres served. In this situation, count on about one-quarter to one-third bottle per person total. If it's a male-heavy crowd, expect more beer and less wine to be consumed, the reverse if women outnumber the men. If wine is the only alcoholic beverage being served, increase the quantities to at least one-third bottle per person.

The average age of the group is also a factor. Your body's ability to metabolize alcohol decreases with age (along with the desire to consume), so if you're dealing with a thirty-something crowd, increase the quantities, or count on a little less consumption per person for Baby Boomers.

Sit-down meals

Sit-down affairs occur over a prolonged period usually with a full meal, which means that people typically consume more wine than at stand-up affairs. I usually count on at least a half bottle per person total over the course of the meal, regardless of how many different wines are served, or a little more if it's a serious wine-drinking crowd.

If you're serving specific wines with each course, then you need at least 2 ounces (60 ml) per person for a proper tasting portion, though you can adjust the serving size for each wine so that the total amount of wine served over the course of the meal equals about 12 to 14 ounces (one-half bottle — a standard 750ml bottle holds just under 25 ounces). For example, if you're serving a three-course meal with a wine for each course, then three 4-ounce glasses will be about right. If it's a seven-course meal, then 2-ounce pours are sufficient.

Just remember that you almost always need more of the reception/first wine served, because guests usually consume the first beverage faster than subsequent drinks, and you may need refills. You also need a larger than average pour of the main course wine, because the main course is usually the largest plate and takes longer to eat, with more sips in between. People quickly consume small appetizers, soups, and salads, so you need less wine with these courses. A 2-ounce pour of sweet wine at the end of the meal or with dessert is also usually sufficient.

Getting down the red-to-white ratio

Unless it's a set meal with pre-determined specific wines for each course, red beats white in most other self-serve or open bar–type events. If it's cool outside, make the split one-quarter white to three-quarters red. If appropriate attire is linens and summer dresses, make it one-third white/rosé to two-thirds red. If sparkling wine is in the mix, make sure you have enough on hand to pour everyone at least one proper 5-ounce glass, which means one bottle for every five guests.

Don't forget about the serving temperature (see Chapter 8 for serving wine at its intended temperature for guidance), especially if the event is an outdoor summer event in hot weather. If so, you need ice buckets (or fridges) for the red wines as well.

Recognizing the Effects of Alcohol

Alcohol plays an important and common role in social gatherings. This undoubtedly has much to do with the fact that people are programmed to seek pleasure, not pain, and one of alcohol's agreeable effects is body relaxation. The neurons of people under the influence of alcohol transmit electrical signals in an alpha wave–pattern, similar to what is observed when the body is relaxed without any self-medication.

Drinking alcohol may also have something to do with people's inherent shyness and lack of self-confidence. Blood alcohol content (BAC) between 0.03 and 0.12 can cause an overall improvement in mood and possible euphoria, and increase self-confidence and sociability. Many people would consider these positive developments, especially in a social setting.

But remember that being a good host also means being a responsible host. A large part of that responsibility is making sure guests don't overconsume. Aside from unpleasant situations, in most countries the host is legally responsible for his or her guests. Make sure you know a little about the effects of alcohol so you can recognize the signs of intoxication (most professional servers of alcohol are legally required to take a training course on the subject), as well as how many drinks it takes to get there. These sections outline how a standard drink is defined in the United States, how to roughly calculate a person's blood alcohol content, and some of the observable effects of alcohol at different concentrations.

Calculating your BAC

BAC is a measure of how much alcohol is in your blood system. Your BAC increases when your rate of consumption exceeds your liver's ability to process and eliminate alcohol from your system. BAC is calculated as a percentage of alcohol in the blood. For example, a BAC of 0.10 means that your blood contains 0.10 percent (one tenth of one percent) alcohol by volume. (The legal limit in the United States to operate a vehicle is 0.08.) The precise calculation of BAC varies greatly by individual and depends on such multiple factors as gender, weight, ethnic background, rate of consumption, and type of drink, as well as how much food, if any, is consumed alongside (which slows down the rate of absorption into the bloodstream).

The most effective hangover cure is prevention. A *hangover* is essentially the result of the diuretic effects of alcohol (it causes urination), which in turn causes dehydration that leads to retracting brain tissues that leads to headaches, among other unpleasant feelings. Drinking one glass of water for every standard drink you consume is your best anti-hangover strategy.

As a very rough guideline, a person can eliminate from the body the alcohol contained in one standard drink in about one hour. Drinking faster than this increases your BAC. For instance, two 5-ounce glasses of Champagne within one hour puts me in the euphoric zone (0.02 to 0.03 BAC), while a third, puts me over 0.05 BAC, at which point it's illegal to drive in most countries.

Observing the effects of alcohol

A host needs to pay attention to how the people at the gathering are behaving. As the host, you may not be able to know a person's BAC, but you can watch behavior changes to identify when a person is inebriated. Here are some behavioral changes associated with BAC levels.

- ✔ 0.010–0.029: Average individual appears normal

- ✔ 0.030–0.059: Mild euphoria, relaxation, joyousness, talkativeness, decreased inhibition

- ✔ 0.06–0.09: Blunted feelings, lack of inhibition, extraversion

- ✔ 0.10–0.19: Overexpression, emotional swings, anger or sadness, boisterousness, decreased libido

- ✔ 0.20–0.29: Stupor, loss of understanding, impaired sensations

- ✔ 0.30–0.39: Severe central nervous system depression, unconsciousness, possible death

- ✔ 0.40–0.49: General lack of behavior, unconsciousness, possible death

If you notice a guest getting more and more inebriated, you can politely suggest that he or she slow down alcohol consumption, and/or switch to water or other nonalcoholic beverages. Contrary to popular belief, coffee, tea, and other caffeinated beverages don't reduce your BAC and sober you up, though they can buy some time to allow the BAC to naturally drop to safer levels. If the guest is driving, suggest leaving his or her vehicle and taking a taxi home. As an extreme measure, you can conveniently run out of alcoholic beverages to serve. Remember that in a restaurant, the server, bartender, and proprietor are legally required to stop serving inebriated customers; the same law applies to party hosts as well.

Chapter 23

So You Want to Be a Sommelier

*Y*ou may be wondering what being a sommelier really means. Maybe you imagine that being sommelier means leading a glamorous life, traveling the world's great wine regions, wining and dining all the way, meeting fascinating people, and living like a rock star. Well, it's not quite like that. Although most sommeliers I know rarely complain about their job, the job description does include plenty of hard grunt work, long days, short nights, and administrative drudgery — it's not all swirling and sipping.

What's great is how the profession has evolved so dramatically in the last couple of decades. What was once a very specific role has blossomed into a world of different opportunities. The possibilities for a certified sommelier are incalculably greater today than they were just 20 years ago, when few people had even heard of the title. The public perception of sommeliers has also changed significantly, moving away from the image of a snooty old man in a tuxedo out to extract as much money from your wallet as possible, to one of youthful, passionate individuals out to share their love of wine and food, ensure your happiness at all costs, and help to create the most memorable dining experiences possible.

The good news is that anyone can become a sommelier. Some people have a misperception that you have to have a super nose and palate in order to make the grade. But in reality, training yourself to detect, recognize, and describe the great number of aromas and textures encountered in wine is more about hard work, discipline, and a good memory. *Supertasters* (people particularly sensitive to taste sensations) may have an advantage (refer to Chapter 2 for more details), but without enough practice and especially experience, you'll lack the context and the memory bank of smells and tastes necessary to really get to the top of the class. The good news is the homework required to develop your reference bank is not so bad.

This chapter gives you the inside scoop on what it means to be a sommelier today. Here I tell you about the requirements for the different qualification levels of the Court of Master Sommeliers, the world's foremost teaching and certification body, and what it takes to reach the highest level. By the end of this chapter, you may be ready to drop everything and enroll in a sommelier course tomorrow. (I've taught many folks working on their second and third careers as sommeliers.)

Knowing What a Sommelier Is All about in Today's World

The word *sommelier* is a regularly mispronounced French word for someone who is trained in the knowledge and service of beverages, and the pairing of food and beverages, usually working in a restaurant. (The correct pronunciation is so-meh-lee-*ay*.) Several theories regarding the origins of the word exist, but it most likely derives from the old Provençal word "saumalier," which means a pack animal driver, later applied to the officials transporting supplies to the royal courts of France using pack animals. You can only imagine how important the regular supply of wine was to the royal courts. The *saumalier* brought the wine.

Although the sommelier designation immediately brings wine to mind, it actually involves a lot more. Besides a working knowledge of the world's major wine regions, grape varieties, wine styles, important producers, and vintages, a well-trained sommelier also needs to be versed in beer types, spirits, classic cocktails, sake, coffee, tea, and even mineral waters. What's more, a modern sommelier's skills must also extend to product procurement and storage, inventory management, overseeing and training other staff members, and customer service and sales, not to mention occasionally mopping up the washrooms and taking out the recycling. The ultimate goal of the sommelier is to ensure customer satisfaction while maximizing profitability for the establishment.

The following sections explain more in depth the different types of jobs held by today's sommelier and the differentiation between a sommelier and a master sommelier.

Seeing the possibilities of being a sommelier

Today's qualified sommelier can choose from a wide range of job titles and responsibilities. Although the traditional picture of a sommelier working in a restaurant, managing the wine program, and working the floor, selling and serving wine still represents the majority today, the possibilities for a well-trained, knowledgeable sommelier have expanded considerably. The following are some of the different roles and jobs that sommeliers hold in today's marketplace beyond the historical restaurant role:

- ✔ **Representative for wine distributors or wineries:** These sommeliers work for wine importing and distribution companies, training and teaching other employees about wine, and selling it to other sommeliers/wine buyers working in restaurants.

- ✔ **Wine director:** This sommelier holds the position of executive sommelier or wine director, jobs that didn't exist only a few years ago. Like executive chefs who are responsible for the overall running of food services (who rarely actually cook themselves), wine directors work from the top down and oversee the entire beverage program of a restaurant or group of restaurants or hotels, managing a team of servers or sommeliers (and rarely actually work on the floor).

- ✔ **Restaurant or winery consultant:** Many sommeliers work as consultants who offer services to restaurants, helping them shape their beverage program to meet market needs and train staff, and also to wineries, assisting with the creation of different wines, blends, and brands.

- ✔ **Winemaker:** A number of sommeliers have become winemakers themselves, applying their vast knowledge of not just grapes, regions, and wine styles, but also markets and consumer preferences and food compatibility to develop their own range of successful wines.

- ✔ **Writer/reviewer/host:** A growing number of sommeliers are writers for newspaper and magazine columns, reviewing and reporting on wine, and are also authors of books on wine, food and wine pairing, and other related subjects. Others host radio and television shows related to wine, food, and travel.

- ✔ **Tour guide:** Capitalizing on the explosion of interest in wine country travel, some sommeliers organize and lead guided trips to wine regions around the world, educating and entertaining along the way.

- ✔ **Speaker/entertainer:** Many sommeliers are hired to host tastings and dinners for corporate and private groups, and to speak at conferences and wine festivals.

These are just some of the possibilities. You can see that the professional opportunities for a sommelier are greater than ever before, and there's never been a better time to be in the business.

Comparing sommelier versus master sommelier

The professional designation of *sommelier* alone isn't protected, as, say, medical doctor (MD) or chartered accountant (CA) are, which have common national standards. Hundreds of institutions and organizations around the world offer sommelier courses, and some are obviously more serious than others, which means that the sommelier designation is only as worthy as its source. In fact, anyone can call him or herself a sommelier without any legal repercussions, with or without any training.

Perusing the origins of the Court of Master Sommeliers

The Court of Master Sommeliers was established to encourage improved standards of beverage knowledge and service in hotels and restaurants. Education was then, and remains today, the Court's charter. The first successful Master Sommelier examination was held in the United Kingdom in 1969. By April 1977, the Court of Master Sommeliers was established as the premier international examining body.

Individuals who successfully complete all parts of the Master Sommelier diploma are expected to uphold the accepted ethics and standards of the Court of Master Sommeliers. Recipients of the diploma are required to sign an agreement binding them to the code of ethics and conduct of Master Sommeliers.

According to the Court of Master Sommeliers, "The Master Sommelier diploma . . . guarantees to a potential employer that a candidate is among the most qualified in the industry, with outstanding tasting and evaluation skills, wine knowledge and outstanding abilities in service and beverage department management." Only about 200 people are Master Sommeliers worldwide.

The designation *Master Sommelier,* on the other hand, is a trademarked designation protected internationally by law. Only those individuals who pass the final examinations of the Court of Master Sommeliers are awarded this title. As such, this title has become the gold standard in the industry. Each person who holds this title has achieved the same level of proficiency and mastery of the field. Check out `http://www.mastersommeliers.org` for more in-depth information about the Court of Master Sommeliers, including its standards and expectations.

Grasping the Hard Work: Details and More Details

You may wonder how you get to the stage where you can take advantage of the opportunities of being a modern sommelier. And the answer, as with any worthwhile endeavor, is some hard work. In the next sections, I take you through the standard requirements of the job, including the practical requirements of the Court of Master Sommeliers and its four levels of qualification.

Before pouring your first glass: In the beginning

Prior to pursuing the sommelier designation, you want to make sure you are prepared for your journey. Before you begin, I suggest you have the following to help along the way:

✔ **Sincere passion for wine:** This really is the only prerequisite to becoming a sommelier. You have to love everything about wine — the broad range of aromas, flavors, and tastes coaxed out of grapes grown in different regions and made with varying philosophies and technical expertise, for example, among other aspects.

✔ **Basic science knowledge:** Understanding how plants grow can help you understand the impact that different climates, soils, and vine-growing methods have on grapes and ultimately on wine. *Fermentation* is a study in chemistry, so a grasp of what is going on in the fermentation tank and later on as wine ages, can put you in a better position to understand the influence that various winemaking decisions have on wine style. Geology gives you insight into what the vine roots are anchored in and how soils and subsoils change from region to region, even vineyard to vineyard.

✔ **A solid grounding in history and geography**: You may wonder, what does history have to do with wine? History goes a long way to explain why certain grapes grow where they do, how wine styles evolved to become classics, and how wine and food are intimately woven into culture. And of course geography is critical — my geographical view of the world is based on grape-growing regions, and where grapes don't grow, things get a little fuzzy.

✔ **A basic grasp of foreign languages:** Having a basic understanding of foreign languages, such as French, Spanish, Italian, and German, is also helpful because a good percentage of the world's wine production comes from countries that speak those languages. Knowing how to read wine labels in several languages is definitely useful.

So you can see that *sommellerie* is a rich field of study that goes far beyond recognizing the smell of a peach or a cherry.

Climbing the four levels of qualification for the Court of Master Sommeliers

Every organization is a little different, but the vast majority of them offer several levels of qualification. The Court of Master Sommeliers has the four following levels:

Introductory sommelier course

The first of four required steps to become a Master Sommelier is the introductory sommelier course. The course doesn't require any hard prerequisites, but a minimum of three years in the wine business or service industry is strongly recommended. A team of Master Sommeliers give an intensive two-day survey course to intro candidates, covering the world of wines and spirits, as well as wine service and especially blind wine tasting. The candidates take a multiple-choice theory exam of 70 questions at the end of the second day. The goal of this course is to give wine and hospitality professionals a solid wine tasting ability and a thorough review of the world of wines and spirits at the highest professional standards.

Passing this course doesn't mean you can call yourself a certified sommelier! To use this designation you must complete level two.

Certified sommelier examination

The certified sommelier examination is a one-day affair in three parts: a blind tasting of two wines, a written theory examination, and a practical service examination. This examination has no lectures or tastings. You're expected to come prepared, appropriately dressed, and equipped for professional wine service.

For the tasting, you have to describe and identify the two wines, selected from anywhere in the world, though representing a classic regional style and grape variety. The written theory covers the world of wine, spirits, beer, cocktails, sake, and service with emphasis on the world's wine appellations and their grape varieties. The practical service exam tests your skills on either sparkling wine service or decanting service. Candidates are also evaluated on their knowledge of aperitifs, cocktails, food and wine pairing, proper service temperature of wine and beverages, as well as their ability to communicate and sell.

Advanced sommelier examination

At this stage things get more serious, and it's time to break out the cue cards, sticky notes, endless charts, tables, diagrams, and other memory aids. In order to take the advanced sommelier examination, the Court's examination committee and the director of education identify qualified candidates from their applications via a selection process. The candidate must also have passed the certified level before being considered. You're required to submit details of your work in the trade, letters of recommendation, and answers to a brief questionnaire.

Similar aspects of the profession are evaluated at the advanced level as at the certified exam level, but the advanced exam is much, much tougher. It's geared to folks with extensive wine service experience. Three days of intensive lectures and tastings are followed by a three-part exam given over two days. Candidates are tested on practical restaurant wine service and salesmanship, written theory, and an oral blind tasting of six wines.

A minimum score of 60 percent in all three sections is needed to pass. After you pass the advanced, you're on to the next step: the Master Sommelier diploma.

Master Sommelier diploma

The Master Sommelier diploma is the ultimate professional credential worldwide. The diploma examination consists of three parts: an oral theory examination, an oral blind tasting of six wines, and a practical wine service examination, all delivered in front of a panel of Master Sommeliers.

Like the leap from the certified to the advanced level, the diploma exam takes it to another level — anything related to the service and hospitality industry is fair game. Candidates need to show up for the examination dressed in professional working attire and better not have forgotten their corkscrew or any other tools of the trade. During the examination you'll be required to "exhibit a high standard of both technical and social skills," and "demonstrate the courtesy and charm of a Master Sommelier." Because salesmanship is a big part of the job, you also have to be able to sell snow to the Eskimos, too, or at least convince several Master Sommeliers that the Chablis is a good match with the oysters.

Passing the advanced is a prerequisite to apply to sit the Master Sommelier exam. But just getting there is far from enough; the pass rate at the final level is only about 10 percent.

Aside from some helpful general knowledge of history, geography, chemistry, biology, geology, language, and culture, here's the concrete lowdown in three parts on what would be required of you to achieve the Master Sommelier diploma. For full details, visit `www.mastersommeliers.org/Pages.aspx/Master-Sommelier-Diploma-Exam`.

Part 1: Restaurant wine service and salesmanship

Part 1 of the requirements for the Master Sommelier diploma focuses on restaurant wine service and salesmanship. They include being able to do the following:

- ✔ Discuss, recommend, and serve aperitifs, displaying a thorough knowledge of their ingredients and production methods as well as the ability to serve them correctly

- ✔ Select, prepare, and position glassware necessary for the service of all beverages in the lounge, restaurant, or private function room

✔ Discuss the menu content and wine list, recommending wines to accompany a wide range of foods; displaying a sound knowledge of the products, their vintages, and characteristics

✔ Present, offer, prepare, (decanting when necessary), and serve wines, demonstrating a high degree of efficiency and proficiency

✔ Present, offer, prepare, and serve brandies, liqueurs, and other spirits, including knowledge of the proper serving portions for each

✔ Handle questions and complaints with skill, elegance, and diplomacy

Part 2: Theory

Part 2 of the requirements for the Master Sommelier diploma focuses on theory and what the sommelier needs to know. They include being able to do the following:

✔ Speak with authority on the wine areas of the world and their products

✔ Know the principal grape varieties used in winemaking and the areas of the world where they are cultivated

✔ Answer questions on international wine laws, including the European Community, United States, Australia, and other global wine regions

✔ Display knowledge of fortified wines, their vinification, storage, and handling

✔ Describe the various methods of distillation and the making of spirits and liqueurs, as well as the process of making beers and ciders and the reasons for the variations in style between different products

✔ Understand cigar production, with special reference to Havanas

✔ Discuss how the products (all beverages, cigars) should be properly stored to ensure that they remain in the optimum condition

Part 3: Practical tasting

The tasting examination is scored on the candidate's verbal abilities to clearly and accurately describe six different wines within 25 minutes. In addition to the style description, you must identify for each wine the

✔ Grape variety(ies)

✔ Country of origin

✔ District and appellation of origin

✔ Vintage

✔ Quality level

Traveling, Tasting, and Eating: The Not-So-Hard Work

Aside from the rigorous study needed to pass the courses to be a sommelier, the journey also is a lot of fun. In fact, nothing can replace firsthand experience. In this case, experience means dedicated travel, and eating and drinking with a little extra attention — things people don't mind so much doing. You can of course also enjoy exploring wine without going through the trials of obtaining some kind of certification — you will still come out richer for the experience.

Traveling the wine regions of the world

Regularly traveling to wine-producing regions is an essential part of the job. There's no better way to keep on top of changes and developments. The world of wine is in constant flux: producers appearing and disappearing, new vineyards planted and old ones ripped out, new regions discovered, old varieties recovered, advancements in technologies or ancient techniques re-embraced, and, of course, different weather conditions from year to year that affect wine quality and style. You are always learning — wine is a lifelong pursuit.

No amount of reading can replace the firsthand experience of walking through a vineyard, seeing the vines, kicking the dirt, feeling the breeze, observing the angle of the sun, and talking directly to the people who grow and transform the grapes into wine. If I had any advice for aspiring sommeliers or even someone who just wants to find out more and enjoy wine a little more, I suggest they travel as much and as often as possible. Really serious people should consider working a harvest at a winery, which is an invaluable experience. And wineries rarely pass up on free help (don't expect to get paid much, if anything at all!).

Eating and drinking with care

Getting into the habit of paying a little more attention to what you're eating and drinking can go a long way to making you a better sommelier. This advice may seem self-evident, but you can easily get caught up in the moment of a meal and forget to focus, at least for a moment, on what exactly is going on in your mouth.

Don't make eating and tasting a chore, but focus your mind on your nose and taste buds long enough to help build your reference bank of information and experience. This can enable you to make better intuitive food and wine pairing choices down the road. So go ahead; you have the perfect excuse to make a nice meal and crack a good bottle of wine: You're studying.

Part VI
The Part of Tens

In this part . . .

Think of this part like a support hotline. Need a versatile, foolproof red or white wine to match with a bunch of different foods? Or, are you wondering what dish will make that special bottle taste even more special? I have ten suggestions for wines that are always friendly to food and ten suggestions for foods that never fail to flatter wine. These have worked for me in the past, and they'll work for you.

Chapter 24

Ten Food-Friendly Wines

I lay out ten grapes and/or wines in this chapter that I've almost always found friendly at the table. You should be able to find them at your local shop without too much trouble. I reference these grapes most often in Part IV of this book, where I match dishes from around the world with wines. They're also great options when throwing a party with lots of different passed hors d'oeuvres, a well-stocked buffet, or a family-style meal when multiple dishes hit the table at once and a specific wine with each dish is impractical.

The most versatile wines are often also the cheapest. The more you pay, the more character, complexity, and stuffing you can find (or would expect to find). But more distinctive, concentrated, and structured red or whites are also less versatile with food. As with people, the stronger the personality, the more polarizing they are. So don't be ashamed. For these suggestions, go cheap or go home.

Unoaked Chardonnay

Chardonnay is one of the most malleable grapes around. It can be beaten into a number of different styles, from light, citrusy, and lean, to full-on rich, buttery, and oaky. The lighter end of the scale, exemplified by Chablis (France), is where you can find the most food-versatile styles. Salads, seafood, shellfish, poultry, pork, and fresh and soft ripened cheeses are all fair game. Look to other cool climate Chardonnays, such as New Zealand, Tasmania, Canada, Sonoma Coast (California), Oregon, or the coastal zones of Chile, for other variations on the theme.

Sauvignon Blanc

Sauvignon Blanc is a popular example of fresh, crisp, lean, and clean white wine, especially when grown in cool regions like Sancerre in the Loire Valley. It's most frequently unoaked (the oaked versions are often called Fumé Blanc outside the Loire), with zesty acids and inviting herbal-citrus-green apple flavor, which makes it like a squeeze of lemon on your food. It grows widely outside of France, so look to other cool regions for other food-friendly examples such as Marlborough in New Zealand or the coastal valleys of Chile.

Pinot Gris (Pinot Grigio)

Pinot Gris, also known as Pinot Grigio in Italian, is one of the world's most popular white grapes. The Alsatian Gris style is richer and more full-bodied, somewhere between Riesling and Gewürztraminer in weight, occasionally with a pinch of sweetness. This makes it a great match with lightly spiced dishes such as Southeast Asian green and yellow curries, or Chinese sweet-hot dishes. The extra heft allows it to travel up the intensity scale from seafood to poultry, pork and beyond, roasted and grilled. Italian-style Pinot Grigio is usually lighter and leaner, making it applicable anywhere crisp dry whites are called for. Elsewhere around the world, follow the naming (Gris versus Grigio) for an idea of the style the winemaker was after.

Riesling

Riesling is another great white wine option, especially German Riesling. In fact, a secret society of German Riesling lovers lives throughout the world. They're not easy to spot on the street, but you can identify them by how they refer to themselves: *sommelier*. I've yet to meet a savvy sommelier who doesn't have a disproportionate love for German Riesling. For one, it's among the most *terroir*-driven wines on earth (tastes like the place it comes from). It's also low alcohol (so you can drink a lot of it and still make it to the work the next day), and it's among the most versatile wines around. I refer to the types with a miraculous combination of fully ripe fruit and a pinch of residual sugar, which creates an illusion of sweetness that quickly vanishes as acidity comes shimmering down the palate.

Considering the prevalence of sweet-sour-salty-hot tastes in modern cuisine (think Asian or fusion cuisine), Riesling's sugar and high acid is the ultimate antidote. Even subtly flavored dishes come to life under Riesling's spell, thanks to the kick of acid. Mosel kabinett or spätlese-level ripeness is the archetype, though hundreds of other examples are available from around the world. Dry Riesling, such as those from the Clare and Eden Valleys in South Australia, Alsace, Austria, Finger Lakes in New York State, and the Niagara Peninsula in Canada are also wickedly food-friendly.

Champagne

The granddaddy of all food-friendly wines is Champagne from France. Take a quick poll of sommeliers around the world about what their foolproof, back-up plan for any dish imaginable is, and I would wager the majority say *champers* (that's sommelier talk for Champagne). When your situation looks hopeless, as though no wine in the world could possibly match a dish, you can always rely on champers.

When the plate has 12 different and distinct elements like a musical cacophony, Champagne can harmonize them all. With the unique combination of light, lean body, low alcohol, and high acid, plus no small measure of yeasty-toasty-savory flavor intensity, all punctuated by carbon dioxide, you have the perfect storm of elements to satisfy a long list of food requirements.

The only area I see Champagne falling short in is with strongly spiced dishes (which are tough on any wine), because carbon dioxide heightens the burn. Other than that, how can you not be happy drinking Champagne? (In a pinch, other traditional method sparkling wines work.)

Pinot Noir

Pinot Noir is the sommelier's red ace in the hole, the Swiss Army knife of wines that can handle just about any situation. Styles vary considerably from region to region, but no matter where it's from, Pinot produces a wine of relatively low tannin and high acid. Burgundy, France, is the holy land of Pinot where it's styled light and lean (except the expensive stuff, which is serious), but you can find it from just about everywhere that's cool enough (and many places that are too warm) to grow it.

When the table of four orders a fish, a chicken, a steak, and a salad, and you all want one wine to share, what does the sommelier recommend? Pinot Noir.

Gamay

Gamay is often considered a second-string grape, living in the shadow of Pinot Noir. But there's been a bit of a renaissance of late in its region of origin — the Beaujolais in eastern France — and the quality has never been better. Producers around the world have also been inspired to up their game. At its best, Gamay is a deliciously red with a structure built on acids rather than tannins, with plenty of come-hither appeal. Even the so-called Crus of Beaujolais, ten subregions that produce more distinctive versions, are incredibly adaptable at the table. From fish to salads to poultry and red meat, Gamay has your back.

Barbera

Barbera is northern Italy's juicy, zesty, serve-by-the-carafe red. Tannins are always low (unless it's been tortured with 200 percent new oak aging) and acidity high, making it a perfect, multipurpose table companion. The wines from Asti in Piedmont are particularly juicy. Serve with a slight chill for even more versatility.

Valpolicella

Valpolicella is the Veneto's (Italy) contribution to the sommelier's arsenal of lightish, fruity, easy-drinking reds. It's generally a blend of the grapes Corvina, Rondinella, and Molinara, though the recipe varies from producer to producer. For maximum versatility, make sure it's straight up valpo and not the richer, more raisined (and more expensive) version called Valpolicella Ripasso.

Dry Rosé

Crisp, fruity, bone-dry rosé is among the most adaptable wines you can find. If it weren't for the lingering impression that all pink wines are soft and sweet, it would be far more popular. To be sure you're getting an authentic dry version, start in the region that makes a specialty out of rosé: Provence in southern France. Regardless of the particular blend of grapes used, these wines have a unique combination of berry and citrus/apple flavors and a pleasant herbal tinge, like the perfumed air of the Mediterranean itself, which allows them to cross over between red– and white–wine friendly dishes. It handles salad vinaigrettes with ease and takes on mildly spicy Indian or West Indian curries, Asian dishes, or Latin American heat without blushing. It's like a diplomatic passport, making you untouchable and able to travel anywhere.

Chapter 25

Ten Foods That Flatter Wine

In This Chapter

▶ Noting some foods that highlight red wines

▶ Finding foods that enhance white wines

In this chapter I suggest ten foods that make good wines taste even better: five dishes for reds and five for whites. These foods are friendly enough to match with a wide range of wine styles, but where appropriate I mention specific wines that really sing with the dish. Some dishes are familiar fare, but I've also included a few specialty items for more exceptional occasions. Remember that to maximize the enjoyment of a special bottle, foods that are outside of your regular daily menu can add to the special feeling.

To make red wines shine, *umami* (savory) is the key taste element. It tends to bring out the best in balanced reds. You want to avoid high acid foods for the most part (except in tomato sauce, which pairs beautifully with zesty reds); acid has the effect of making reds harder, dryer, and more astringent, which isn't particularly flattering. Avoid sweet foods for the same reason, as well as really spicy dishes that numb the taste buds too much for you to enjoy the finer nuances of top red wine.

Whites on the other hand need no softening, so you can focus more on flavor and texture synergy or contrast. If you're preparing at home, taste the wine first and adapt the recipe to echo any of its flavors in the dish, such as swinging your herb marinade for roast chicken to complement a wine's particular herbal profile.

When showing off a wine is the goal, keep the food simple. Two to three elements on a plate are more than enough; busy plates with multiple elements, tastes, and textures are distracting and detract from the wine. The first five foods are best for red wines, and the last five are best for white wines.

Roast Beef

The combination of protein, fat, salt, and umami, without the distraction of complicated sauces, is a perfect foil to showcase that special red. Roast beef is particularly tasty with aged reds, because the flavors are subtle and straightforward enough not to challenge the delicacy of older wines. Rare roast beef can handle more substantial, chewy reds, but longer cooking dries out the meat and is better suited to softer, fruitier styles.

Wild Mushroom Risotto

Rice is an excellent neutral backdrop to showcase other ingredients. In this case, it's the earthy, woodsy flavors of wild mushrooms, including truffles, in wild mushroom risotto that makes red wines shine. In fact, mushrooms of all kinds tend to enhance just about any type of wine. Umami is again the protagonist taste sensation, which is especially amazing with old Pinot Noir or Barolo/Barbaresco (Nebbiolo-based reds from Piedmont, Italy). The rice does its part texturally, creating a creamy texture (when properly prepared, not mushy) as the starches are released by continual stirring, which snaps the edge off of any lingering astringent tannins in the wine.

Braised Red Meat

Braised meat dishes are wine-friendly in general, simmered for hours until the collagens break down into a deliciously soft texture. Tougher cuts of meat, such as lamb shank and shoulder or beef ribs and cheeks, make for particularly delicious braises. A little more unusual but equally tasty is oxtail, which is particularly gelatinous and has an intense, sweet-umami taste that beautifully frames up red wines. I find that mature wines that have lost their tannins, or young, plush, softer style reds are best with braised dishes, because the meat itself has lost its tannin-taming power. The fat has been absorbed into the braising liquid, and the proteins have been broken down. But ultimately, no red wine will disagree with braised meat.

Roast Game Birds

Special wines call for foods that are also special — something that's outside of your weekly culinary repertoire; it makes the entire occasion seem that much more out of the ordinary. Game birds, such as duck, pheasant, partridge, guinea fowl, grouse, snipe, goose, or wild turkey, likely fall into the unusual food category, but when oven-roasted, they're another favorite to show off great reds. Game birds just seem to have the right admixture of gamey, sweet-earthy flavor, protein, and fat (mostly from the skin) that synergizes with so many reds. The meat is lean, which is why they have to be aged (hung) to allow the meat to break down before cooking, and carefully prepared without overcooking, or alternatively braised slowly for hours.

Try game birds with mature reds for a real treat, though all but the biggest jammy-oaky styles will show beautifully.

Parmesan or Aged Manchego Cheeses

Hard cheeses, such as Parmesan and aged Manchego, are brilliant for taking the edge off robust reds. Salt and fat knock the astringent bite out of tannins, creating a luxurious, smooth mouth-feel, which lets the fruit shine. Umami is likewise a key sensation that makes mature reds look especially fine. There's no better way to end a meal than with a superb bottle of mature red wine (but not too old and delicate) and a chunk of unadorned, top-grade Parmigiano. For something a little different, try Vintage Champagne, a surprising but brilliant match with well-aged Parmigiano.

Herb-Roasted Chicken

A joke in the sommelier world says that when in doubt, recommend the chicken; it's always a perfect match. True enough, chicken, especially the breast, is a very neutral protein. It's the cooking method or marinade or accompanying sauce that swings the match to various reds or whites.

Roasted with an earthy mushroom sauce would be better with an earthy red, but when marinated in a mixture of aromatic herbs and white wine, the dish naturally swings to aromatic whites. With herb-roasted chicken, the delicate flavor of the meat lets the wine shine, while the herbs pick up and amplify the herbal nuances in the white wine. Resinous herbs (rosemary, bay, thyme) can favor barrel-aged whites, and sweet herbs (basil, tarragon, parsley, chervil, and so on) are best with unoaked whites.

Veal Schnitzel or Scaloppini

Breaded, fried veal is a great foil for crisp white wines. The meat's flavor is subtle and delicate and doesn't interfere, while the crust's crisp texture cries out for an equally snappy, crispy wine. In Vienna they show off Grüner Veltliner, but you can show off any low/no oak, zesty white or sparkling wine.

You can prepare veal scaloppini without the breading to match just about any wine, such as with a citrus beurre blanc to match with citrusy whites like Chablis, or with mushroom sauce for barrel-fermented whites.

Scallops, Lobster, and Langoustines

Luxury shellfish served on special occasions is the perfect excuse to bring out your best whites. Preparations vary, but top-notch barrel-fermented Chardonnay, such as white Burgundy (Puligny-Montrachet or Meursault) or any one of dozens of new world equivalents is a lovely, textbook match to these rich, implicitly sweet foods, especially if the dish includes any butter or cream.

Think outside the box to discover some new classics. I've reveled with barrel-fermented Assyrtiko from Santorini, minerally whites from Mount Etna in Sicily, and old bush vine Chenin Blanc from South Africa, to name but a few.

Rabbit Braised in White Wine and Sage

Another unusual but wine-friendly protein is rabbit. Like chicken, rabbit is a blank canvas; the preparation determines the best wine match. A red wine braise turns it more red-friendly, but this classic white wine and sage braise is a fine match for all but the oakiest of white wines. With rabbit, I go with a white that harmonizes with the terpene family of flavors (see Chapter 5 for more on terpene aromas and flavors), such as Pinot Gris/Grigio or Riesling. For something a little different, try Moscophilero from Greece or a Torrontés from Argentina.

Gourmet Grilled Cheese

Grilled cheese sandwiches don't usually bring wine to mind, but they have a remarkable affinity for milder reds, and especially full-bodied whites. Take your Sunday brunch uptown with a gourmet grilled cheese; I like to use *challah* bread (made with egg yolks, which tints the bread yellow and gives it a fluffy texture) and a more flavorful cheese such as *Gruyère* (a semi-hard cow's milk cheese from Switzerland; no plastic-wrapped cheese slices please!). Pair it with a full-bodied, oak-aged white such as a Chardonnay from Sonoma County or a classic white Burgundy. You'll find that the crisp texture of the sandwich contrasts nicely with the supple wine, while the buttery flavor (no margarine!) complements the lactic-buttery profile of the wine. If it's a really upscale occasion, bring out the Champagne.

Index

• X •

• Y •

• Z •

EDUCATION, HISTORY, & REFERENCE

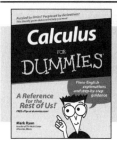

978-0-7645-2498-1

978-0-470-46244-7

Also available:

- Algebra For Dummies 978-0-7645-5325-7
- Art History For Dummies 978-0-470-09910-0
- Chemistry For Dummies 978-0-7645-5430-8
- English Grammar For Dummies 978-0-470-54664-2
- French All-in-One For Dummies 978-1-118-22815-9
- Statistics For Dummies 978-0-7645-5423-0
- World History For Dummies 978-0-470-44654-6

FOOD, HOME, & MUSIC

978-1-118-11554-1

978-1-118-28872-6

Also available:

- 30-Minute Meals For Dummies 978-0-7645-2589-6
- Bartending For Dummies 978-0-470-63312-0
- Brain Games For Dummies 978-0-470-37378-1
- Cheese For Dummies 978-1-118-09939-1
- Cooking Basics For Dummies 978-0-470-91388-8
- Gluten-Free Cooking For Dummies 978-1-118-39644-5
- Home Improvement All-in-One Desk Reference For Dummies 978-0-7645-5680-7
- Home Winemaking For Dummies 978-0-470-67895-4
- Ukulele For Dummies 978-0-470-97799-6

GARDENING

978-0-470-58161-2

978-0-470-57705-9

Also available:

- Gardening Basics For Dummies 978-0-470-03749-2
- Organic Gardening For Dummies 978-0-470-43067-5
- Sustainable Landscaping For Dummies 978-0-470-41149-0
- Vegetable Gardening For Dummies 978-0-470-49870-5

GREEN/SUSTAINABLE

978-0-470-59896-2

978-0-470-59678-4

Also available:
- Alternative Energy For Dummies 978-0-470-43062-0
- Energy Efficient Homes For Dummies 978-0-470-37602-7
- Global Warming For Dummies 978-0-470-84098-6
- Green Building & Remodelling For Dummies 978-0-470-17559-0
- Green Cleaning For Dummies 978-0-470-39106-8
- Green Your Home All-in-One For Dummies 978-0-470-59678-4
- Wind Power Your Home For Dummies 978-0-470-49637-4

HEALTH & SELF-HELP

978-0-471-77383-2

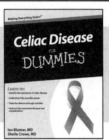

978-0-470-16036-7

Also available:
- Body Language For Dummies 978-0-470-51291-3
- Borderline Personality Disorder For Dummies 978-0-470-46653-7
- Breast Cancer For Dummies 978-0-7645-2482-0
- Cognitive Behavioural Therapy For Dummies 978-0-470-66541-1
- Emotional Intelligence For Dummies 978-0-470-15732-9
- Healthy Aging For Dummies 978-0-470-14975-1
- Neuro-linguistic Programming For Dummies 978-0-470-66543-5
- Understanding Autism For Dummies 978-0-7645-2547-6

HOBBIES & CRAFTS

978-0-470-28747-7

978-1-118-01695-4

Also available:
- Bridge For Dummies 978-1-118-20574-7
- Crochet Patterns For Dummies 97-0-470-04555-8
- Digital Photography For Dummies 978-1-118-09203-3
- Jewelry Making & Beading Designs For Dummies 978-0-470-29112-2
- Knitting Patterns For Dummies 978-0-470-04556-5
- Oil Painting For Dummies 978-0-470-18230-7
- Quilting For Dummies 978-0-7645-9799-2
- Sewing For Dummies 978-0-7645-6847-3
- Word Searches For Dummies 978-0-470-45366-7

HOME & BUSINESS COMPUTER BASICS

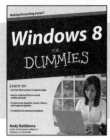

978-1-118-13461-0

978-1-118-11079-9

Also available:
- Office 2010 All-in-One Desk Reference For Dummies 978-0-470-49748-7
- Pay Per Click Search Engine Marketing For Dummies 978-0-471-75494-7
- Search Engine Marketing For Dummies 978-0-471-97998-2
- Web Analytics For Dummies 978-0-470-09824-0
- Word 2010 For Dummies 978-0-470-48772-3

INTERNET & DIGITAL MEDIA

978-1-118-32800-2

978-1-118-38318-6

Also available:
- Blogging For Dummies 978-1-118-15194-5
- Digital Photography For Seniors For Dummies 978-0-470-44417-7
- Facebook For Dummies 978-1-118-09562-1
- LinkedIn For Dummies 978-0-470-94854-5
- Mom Blogging For Dummies 978-1-118-03843-7
- The Internet For Dummies 978-0-470-12174-0
- Twitter For Dummies 978-0-470-76879-2
- YouTube For Dummies 978-0-470-14925-6

MACINTOSH

978-0-470-87868-2

978-1118-49823-1

Also available:
- iMac For Dummies 978-0-470-20271-5
- iPod Touch For Dummies 978-1-118-12960-9
- iPod & iTunes For Dummies 978-1-118-50864-0
- MacBook For Dummies 978-1-118-20920-2
- Macs For Seniors For Dummies 978-1-118-19684-7
- Mac OS X Lion All-in-One For Dummies 978-1-118-02206-1

PETS

978-0-470-60029-0

978-0-7645-5267-0

Also available:
- Cats For Dummies 978-0-7645-5275-5
- Ferrets For Dummies 978-0-470-13943-1
- Horses For Dummies 978-0-7645-9797-8
- Kittens For Dummies 978-0-7645-4150-6
- Puppies For Dummies 978-1-118-11755-2

SPORTS & FITNESS

978-0-470-88279-5

978-1-118-01261-1

Also available:
- Exercise Balls For Dummies 978-0-7645-5623-4
- Coaching Volleyball For Dummies 978-0-470-46469-4
- Curling For Dummies 978-0-470-83828-0
- Fitness For Dummies 978-0-7645-7851-9
- Lacrosse For Dummies 978-0-470-73855-9
- Mixed Martial Arts For Dummies 978-0-470-39071-9
- Sports Psychology For Dummies 978-0-470-67659-2
- Ten Minute Tone-Ups For Dummies 978-0-7645-7207-4
- Wilderness Survival For Dummies 978-0-470-45306-3
- Wrestling For Dummies 978-1-118-11797-2
- Yoga with Weights For Dummies 978-0-471-74937-0